Execution ▸

SECOND E

Other titles available from Law Society Publishing

Companies Act 2006: A Guide to the New Law
Gary Scanlan, Andrew Harvey, Terence Prime and Tunde Ogowewo

Company Law Handbook
Stephen Griffin

Data Protection Handbook (2nd edn)
Edited by Peter Carey

Drafting Confidentiality Agreements (2nd edn)
Mark Anderson and Simon Keevey-Kothari

Precedent Library for the General Practitioner
Martin Smith

Titles from Law Society Publishing can be ordered from all good bookshops or direct (telephone 0870 850 1422, email **law.society@prolog.uk.com** or visit our online shop at **www.lawsociety.org.uk/bookshop**).

EXECUTION OF DOCUMENTS

SECOND EDITION

Mark Anderson and Victor Warner

The Law Society

All rights reserved. No part of this publication may be reproduced in any material form, whether by photocopying, scanning, downloading onto computer or otherwise without the written permission of the Law Society and the authors except in accordance with the provisions of the Copyright, Designs and Patents Act 1988. Applications should be addressed in the first instance, in writing, to Law Society Publishing. Any unauthorised or restricted act in relation to this publication may result in civil proceedings and/or criminal prosecution.

The views expressed in this publication should be taken as those of the authors only unless it is specifically indicated that the Law Society has given its endorsement.

The authors have asserted the right, under the Copyright, Designs and Patents Act 1988, to be identified as authors of this work.

Crown Copyright material is reproduced with the permission of the Controller of Her Majesty's Stationery Office.

© Mark Anderson 2008

ISBN 978–1–85328–699–5

First edition published in 2005

This second edition published in 2008 by the Law Society
113 Chancery Lane, London WC2A 1PL

Typeset by J&L Composition Ltd, Filey, North Yorkshire
Printed by CPI Antony Rowe, Chippenham, Wilts

Mixed Sources
Product group from well-managed
forests and other controlled sources
www.fsc.org Cert no. SGS-COC-2953
© 1996 Forest Stewardship Council

The paper used for the text pages of this book is FSC certified. FSC (The Forest Stewardship Council) is an international network to promote responsible management of the world's forests.

Contents

Preface

In the first edition of this guide we set ourselves the goal of providing more than a recitation of the law concerning the execution of documents, in particular by:

- providing a practical outline of the situations when particular methods of execution must or should be used; and
- including some practical guidance on drafting issues.

This continues to be the goal of this second edition.

We are conscious we could have written a much longer book, and gone more deeply into particular areas of law and practice. We hope we have struck the right balance.

This second edition has been updated as follows:

- changes to the law made by the Regulatory Reform (Execution of Deeds and Documents) Order 2005 have been incorporated into the relevant chapters (they were only proposals in the first edition);
- changes made by the Companies Act 2006 in relation to the execution of documents by various forms of companies have been incorporated; and
- a new chapter on the work of notaries has been added (together with a selection of the practical issues that commonly arise from the work of a notary).

We would like to invite users of this book to provide us with examples, tips, practice points or suggestions for the new topics or indeed for existing material in this edition. These can be sent to Mark Anderson (mark@andlaw.eu) or Victor Warner (victor@andlaw.eu).

Where this book makes statements of the law, we have tried to be up to date as of 1 August 2008.

Mark Anderson and Victor Warner
August 2008

Acknowledgements

We are grateful to the following persons and organisations for reading and commenting on various chapters:

George Curran, partner, F. E. Johnson & Co.;
The Darbari Trust UK;
Abdul Hafezi, principal, Hafezis Solicitors;
Smita Jamdar, partner, Martineau;
Andrew Keogh, partner, Keogh Solicitors;
Dayan Litgenstein, The Federation of Synagogues;
Meera Shah, assistant, Covington & Burling;
Tina Williams, member, Fox Williams LLP;
Peter Hardingham, notary public and Paul Sherridan, notary public;
Brendan Biggs.

They have all provided helpful suggestions on how the practicality of this volume could be enhanced. Any errors or inadequacies that remain are, of course, our sole responsibility.

Mark Anderson and Victor Warner
August 2008

Table of cases

Table of statutes

Table of statutory instruments and other secondary legislation

Draft statutory instruments

European legislation

Other enactments

Abbreviations

BEA 1882	Bills of Exchange Act 1882
CA 1985	Companies Act 1985
CA 2006	Companies Act 2006
CBCA 1960	Corporate Bodies' Contracts Act 1960
CCA 1974	Consumer Credit Act 1974
CCA 1984	County Courts Act 1984
CLSA 1990	Courts and Legal Services Act 1990
COA 1889	Commissioners for Oaths Act 1889
COA 1891	Commissioners for Oaths Act 1891
CPR	Civil Procedure Rules
ECA 2000	Electronic Communications Act 2000
ESR 2002	Electronic Signatures Regulations 2002, SI 2002/318
FA 1999	Finance Act 1999
FCA 1981	Forgery and Counterfeiting Act 1981
FC(ED)R 1994	Foreign Companies (Execution of Documents) Regulations 1994, SI 1994/950
FCO	Foreign and Commonwealth Office
FPR 1991	Family Proceedings Rules 1991
GLAA 1999	Greater London Authority Act 1999
IA 1978	Interpretation Act 1978
IA 1986	Insolvency Act 1986
IR 1986	Insolvency Rules 1986
LGA 1972	Local Government Act 1972
LGA 2000	Local Government Act 2000
LLPA 2000	Limited Liability Partnerships Act 2000
LLPR 2001	Limited Liability Partnerships Regulations 2001, SI 2001/1090
LPA 1925	Law of Property Act 1925
LP(MP)A 1989	Law of Property (Miscellaneous Provisions) Act 1989
LRA 2002	Land Registration Act 2002
MFPA 1984	Matrimonial and Family Proceedings Act 1984
NCPR 1987	Non-Contentious Probate Rules 1987
OA 1978	Oaths Act 1978
OCR 2008	Draft Overseas Companies Regulations 2008

PA 1890	Partnership Act 1890
PA 1911	Perjury Act 1911
PAA 1971	Powers of Attorney Act 1971
RR(EDD)O 2005	Regulatory Reform (Execution of Deeds and Documents) Order 2005, SI 2005/1906
SA 1891	Stamp Act 1891
SA 1974	Solicitors Act 1974
SDA 1835	Statutory Declarations Act 1835
SDMA 1891	Stamp Duties Management Act 1891
SGA 1979	Sale of Goods Act 1979

Introduction

The purpose of this guide is to provide a convenient summary of how a wide range of documents may be executed by the various types of persons and organisations commonly found in England and Wales.

In part, this guide updates an earlier book published by the Law Society (Robin Spon Smith, *Oaths and Affirmations*, 2nd edn, 1996). That book focused on oaths (both in litigation and non-litigation), affirmations, affidavits and statutory declarations. It did not cover:

- the execution of other types of documents (such as contracts, deeds and powers of attorney);
- how particular organisational types (such as companies, corporations and partnerships) execute documents.

Since that book was last published, much has changed, both in law and practice. Formalities, methods and requirements as to who can execute many types of documents have changed. For example, with the introduction of the Civil Procedure Rules 1998, the principal method for introducing evidence is now the use of witness statements verified by a statement of truth, not affidavits. Consequently, the use of affidavits has decreased substantially and is reserved for a few particular situations. Another important change regards the execution of deeds by companies, where now only one company director needs to sign a deed (although in the presence of witness).

In preparing *Execution of Documents*, we took a fresh look at this subject area. We set ourselves three objectives for this guide, that it should:

- cover the common types of person and organisations which execute documents;
- cover the types of documents commonly encountered by such persons and organisations; and
- have a practical 'how to' focus.

Most lawyers (and many non-lawyers) will know how the persons and organisations they frequently deal with should sign the common range of documents that they encounter. Uncertainty can occur with less common types of documents or less usual types of parties. Often the execution formalities are considered at the last moment; even familiar situations can lead to some element being overlooked (such as the authority of a person to sign a document or form). We thought (and think) that a practical, step-by-step approach in the guide would be helpful.

Consequently, we decided to split the material into two main sections:

- **Procedural guides.** These provide step-by-step guides for the execution of particular documents, commentary on common legal and practical issues that should be considered before execution, precedent material, and common variations encountered. This section should be all that the user needs to consult when checking how a particular document should be executed.
- **Legal commentaries.** These outline the legal background to the procedural guides.

Some key developments since the first edition of *Execution of Documents*

The previous edition outlined in detail the Government's intention to implement proposals by the Law Commission to reduce differences in terminology between various Acts governing the execution of deeds and to clarify ambiguous areas (such as whether an attorney can execute a deed on behalf of the donor of the power of attorney).

These proposals have been implemented as proposed in the form of the Regulatory Reform (Execution of Deeds and Documents) Order 2005 (RR(EDD)O 2005).

The result has been that the following Acts were amended from 1 October 2005:

- Powers of Act 1971;
- Law of Property Act 1925;
- Companies Act 1985 (CA 1985) although this has been superseded by Companies Act 2006; and
- Law of Property (Miscellaneous Provisions) Act 1989 (LP(MP)A 1989).

RR(EDD)O 2005 dealt with:

- differences in terminology between the Acts mentioned above regarding the execution of documents;
- whether, and the extent to which, an attorney can execute a deed on behalf of a donor;
- how an attorney should execute a deed which the attorney is executing on behalf of the donor;
- when, and whether, delivery of a deed takes place;
- differences in the presumption that delivery takes place on execution;
- differences in wording regarding the face value requirement for a deed between CA 1985 and LP(MP)A 1989 (see p.142 for more on this).

Although the reforms put it beyond doubt that one person can execute a deed on behalf of another (see LP(MP)A 1989, s.1(2)(b)), the reforms did not change the requirements for authorising that person to execute the deed on behalf of another, authorisation continuing to be required by the grant of a power of attorney (see pp.151–2 for more on this).

However, the criticism we made in the first edition still stands:

> It is perhaps unfortunate that the Law Commission did not focus on producing a uniform code for the execution of contracts and deeds fit for the 21st century (especially with the move to electronic commerce). Such an approach would have aided commercial certainty and (one hopes) would have simplified the law in this area.

Companies Act 2006 and companies generally

The other key development since the previous edition has been the passing (and partial bringing into force) of Companies Act 2006 (CA 2006). For such a large piece of legislation, the effect of the changes in relation to the execution of documents by a company is fairly small:

- from April 2008, a new method of execution is permitted in addition to existing ones (that a deed can be executed by one director in the presence of a witness); and
- from October 2009, it is put beyond doubt that an attorney can execute documents (including deeds) on behalf of a company (as long as the attorney is appointed by deed).

Methods of execution found in CA 1985 have been re-enacted into CA 2006 (a summary of the relevant changes made by CA 2006 can be found at p.182 and elsewhere in **Chapter 16**).

One unfortunate aspect of the implementation of CA 2006 has been that the Government delayed implementation of substantial parts from October 2008 to October 2009. The result has been that:

- new companies will not be formed until October 2009;
- such matters as the execution of documents by limited liability partnerships and foreign corporations will not be implemented until October 2009.

For the latter point, at August 2008 when this introduction was prepared, the Government had not prepared draft regulations for limited liability partnerships and therefore it is not possible to indicate with any certainty as to how limited liability partnerships will be permitted to execute documents from October 2009. However, based on the changes made for 'ordinary' companies, existing methods used by limited liability partnerships are likely to continue. As for foreign corporations, the Government has published Draft Regulations, and although there has been more than one round of drafts, the proposals relating to execution have not changed (see **Chapters 17** and **18** for more on the changes to be made or likely to be made by CA 2006).

Regarding companies more generally, in preparing material for this book we have had to be selective, and therefore have not covered all types of companies. For example, we have not dealt with companies formed or regulated by Companies Acts prior to 1985, or unregulated or unregistered companies.

Notaries

In this edition we have added a chapter regarding the work of notaries. Increasingly, individuals and companies are involved in transactions or events taking place in other countries. Consequently, we believe it is useful to have an understanding of the work of, and what it involves to use, a notary. Although knowledge of the existence of notaries may be widespread, what a notaries do (or what they have to do) is, in our experience, limited at best.

The purpose of **Chapter 28** aims to change that by outlining common situations when a notary is needed, together with practical examples of what a notary needs to do when dealing with common types of document (such as powers of attorney or providing copies of a document).

The chapter also includes examples of what common 'notarised' documents look like.

HOW TO USE THIS GUIDE

To find appropriate material relating to a particular type of document, consult the relevant section as outlined below.

Procedural guide
- Checklist of points that should be considered before execution
- Examples of wording to be inserted at important parts of a document (how to commence a document)
- Precedent material for signing
- Common variations to the above
- Points to note
- Professional practice points

Legal commentary
- Legal background in respect of the form and use of a particular type of document
- Legal status of particular types of organisation and individual, and their legal authority to execute that particular type of document
- Any formal requirements for its layout and contents
- When it must be used, should be used and can be used
- Layout of that document and occasionally an example of a complete document

PART I

Procedural guide

CHAPTER 1

Agreements under hand

CHECKLIST

- Should the contract be executed as a deed:
  - is it required to be in the form of a deed? or
  - is it conventional or desirable for it to be in the form of a deed because of the underlying transaction or event?

  See **section 14.15**.

- Should the contract be in writing and/or signed:
  - must some, or all, of the provisions of the contract be in writing?
  - does the contract need to be in, or on, a specified form?
  - do some or all the parties to the contract have to sign?
  - are related transactions or events to the contract required to be in writing and/or signed?

  See **sections 13.7–13.8**.

- Are all:
  - the persons who are placed under an obligation; or
  - the persons who are parties to the contract

  named in the document?

- If the contract is stated to be executed by the company (and not on its behalf), does it clearly state that?[1]

- Has the contract been read by, or fully and accurately explained:
  - to the parties to be bound; and
  - where the contract is to be signed on behalf of the parties, to the persons who are to sign the contract?

- Are the parties properly and fully described or named? In the 'parties' clause (see **section 1.1**), state for each party:
  - the parties' full legal names;

---

1 Where a document is signed by a director in the presence of a witness or by two directors or a director and the company secretary *and* states (in whatever words) that it is executed by the company, then the document has the same effect as if executed under the common seal of the company (Companies Act 2006 (CA 2006), s.44(4)). See **Chapter 4** for more on this point.

- the parties' legal status (if not clear from the name, or for the avoidance of doubt, whether they are a particular type of registered company,[2] individual, partnership, etc.);
- for parties who are incorporated, their place of incorporation, their type of incorporation and, if appropriate, the registration number of incorporation;
- their addresses (for companies incorporated under the Companies Acts 1985 (CA 1985) or 2006 (CA 2006), the registered office; for others, the principal place of business).

In the *signature block*, the full legal name for each party should normally be repeated.

• Is the contract executed by or on behalf of the party or parties undertaking obligations or all the parties where required by law?[3]

• Is a person who is not a party to the agreement but who derives some benefit from it able to enforce any of its provisions?[4]
   - is the person sufficiently identified to be able to enforce its provisions?
   - is that person able to enforce all or only some of the provisions? Is this right of enforcement subject to any conditions? Does the contract state that the parties to the agreement can remove that person's rights, e.g. by amending or terminating the agreement?
   - if no one other than the parties is able to enforce any of the provisions, is there wording to indicate this[5]?

• Is the contract being entered into with a party based, incorporated or regulated in another country? If so:
   - does the contract need to be translated into the language of the other country (or does at least one copy of the contract need to be in that language)?
   - if the contract does need to be translated, must it be translated by an official or properly qualified translator?
   - does the contract need to be registered with any governmental or regulatory authorities in the other country?
   - is the contract of a type which needs to be drawn up and/or signed before a notary?
   - if the contract is being signed in England and Wales, does the contract need to be notarised and/or legalised after it has been signed?

---

2 For example, whether they are a private limited company, a public limited company, a limited liability partnership, a company limited by guarantee, a company incorporated by Royal Charter, etc.

3 For example, contracts for the sale or disposition of interests in land need to be signed by all the parties (Law of Property (Miscellaneous Provisions) Act 1989 (LP(MP)A 1989), s.2).

4 The provisions of the Contracts (Rights of Third Parties) Act 1999 should be consulted.

5 In many contractual documents, the provisions of the Contracts (Rights of Third Parties) Act 1999 are excluded with wording such as 'For the purposes of the Contracts (Rights of Third Parties) Act 1999 [and notwithstanding any other provision of this Agreement] this Agreement is not intended to, and does not, give any person who is not a party to it any right to enforce any of its provisions' (from *Encyclopaedia of Forms and Precedents*, vol. 4(3), Form 72.1 [1582]).

1.1 FORM/STRUCTURE OF A CONTRACT

For most contracts, the contents and structure (and whether a signature is required) are left to the agreement of the parties.[6] By convention, many contracts drafted by lawyers will follow a similar structure.[7]

Date of the agreement

The first line of an agreement might read as follows to indicate clearly that it is intended to be a contract and to provide evidence of when it was executed:

THIS AGREEMENT dated _____ 200[. . .] is made by and between:

THIS AGREEMENT dated _____ 200[. . .] is between:

THIS AGREEMENT is made the _____ day of_____ 200[. . .] **BETWEEN:**

Parties to the contract clauses

This part of the contract should clearly and precisely identify the parties to the contract. By convention, for each party a separate paragraph is used setting out the following details:

A party's full legal name

- for a private limited company, state it is 'limited', e.g. ABC Limited;[8]
- for a public limited company, state it is 'plc', e.g. ABC plc;
- for a company limited by guarantee, state that it is 'limited by guarantee', e.g. ABC Limited, a company limited by guarantee;[9]
- for a company incorporated outside England and Wales, the precise requirements will vary depending in which country the company is incorporated (but see below);

---

6 Examples where the contents and form *are* specified would include contracts for the sale or other disposition of land (requiring all the provisions to be in writing) and agreements covered by the Consumer Credit Act 1974 (CCA 1974) (requiring that the agreement be in a specified form and include specific information).

7 This section is not intended to be an outline on how to draft agreements. Readers interested in books providing guidance should consult Anderson and Warner, *Drafting and Negotiating Commercial Contracts*, 2nd edn, Tottel Publishing, 2007; Christou, *Boilerplate: Practical Clauses*, 4th edn, Sweet & Maxwell, 2005; Butt and Castle, *Modern Legal Drafting: A Guide to Using Clearer Language*, Cambridge University Press, 2001.

8 For companies incorporated under CA 1985 or CA 2006 it is possible to do a free search for the full proper name and registered address at **www.companieshouse.gov.uk**.

9 Some companies who are limited by guarantee have obtained permission not to use the word 'limited'. In such cases it is particularly important to state the company's status. See e.g. CA 2006, ss.60–64.

- for a partnership, follow the name of the partnership with 'a firm', e.g. Smith & Jones (a firm);[10]
- for individuals, the full version of their first name(s) and second (family) name, e.g. Joanne Melanie Smith (not Jo Smith);
- for a corporation incorporated by Royal Charter, indicate that it is incorporated by Royal Charter, e.g. the University of Southland, an institution incorporated by Royal Charter;
- for an unincorporated charity, the names of each trustee or those trustees empowered to execute the contract.

A party's legal status (if not clear from the name), place of incorporation and, if appropriate, the registration number of incorporation, and address

- For a private limited company, public limited company and company incorporated by guarantee:

  - in appropriate circumstances, or for the avoidance of doubt, state its legal status;
  - indicate that it is incorporated in England and Wales;
  - state its company registration number;
  - state its registered office.

  A party clause might read:

  > **ABC LIMITED**, [a company incorporated under the Companies Act 1985 and limited by shares,] incorporated in England and Wales under company registration number [. . .], whose registered office is at [. . .]

  > **ABC PLC**, [a public limited company,] incorporated in England and Wales under company registration number [. . .], whose registered office is at [. . .]

  > **ABC [LIMITED]**, [a company limited by guarantee,] incorporated in England and Wales under company registration number [. . .], whose registered office is at [. . .]

- For a company incorporated outside England and Wales:

  - state the country in which the company is incorporated;
  - for companies incorporated in the United States, describe the state in which the company is incorporated;
  - state the principal place of business (although this may be a company's management headquarters rather than the foreign equivalent of a registered office);
  - in appropriate circumstances, for the avoidance of doubt, indicate that the foreign company has the capacity to enter into contracts.

---

10 The names of all the partners are sometimes also listed.

A party clause might read:

ABC, INC., [a Delaware corporation] [incorporated in the State of Delaware] [and having the capacity to enter into contracts], whose principal place of business is at [*address including country*]

ABC, INC., [a corporation organised under the laws of the State of Delaware, USA] [and having the capacity to enter into contracts], with offices at [*address including country*]

ABC S.A., a company incorporated in [France] whose principal place of business is at [*address including country*]

- For a partnership:
  - state the partnership is a firm;
  - state the name of each of the individual partners;
  - state the home address of each partner who is an individual, or if the partner is a registered company, state its legal status, that it is incorporated in England and Wales, its registration number and registered office.

A party clause might read:

SMITH & JONES, a firm, whose partners are [*name of partner*] of [*home address*] and [*name of partner*] of [*home address*]

- For an individual:
  - in appropriate circumstances, for the avoidance of doubt, state that the person is an individual;
  - state any title s/he might have (such as doctor, professor), the full version of the first name(s) and the second (family) name;
  - state the home address.

A party clause might read:

DR JOANNE SMITH, an individual, whose home address is at [*home address*]

- For a corporation incorporated by Royal Charter:
  - state it is incorporated by Royal Charter;
  - state its main office.

A party clause might read:

THE UNIVERSITY OF SOUTHLAND, an institution incorporated by Royal Charter, whose address is [*address*]

'Executed as a contract' clause[11]

The *executed as a contract* clause is not an essential, or a legal, requirement in a written contract. However, the usual practice for conventionally drafted contracts is to include one. Its purpose is to state explicitly that the parties are consenting to the provisions of the agreement and that they have executed it, and it indicates that the signatures are those of the parties.[12]

It is customarily placed after all the other parts of a contract, and:

- immediately before the *signature block*; or
- if schedules are included before the *signature block*, immediately before the schedules.

Point to note

Sometimes it may be appropriate to use more than one *executed as a contract* clause if there are several parties each of a different legal status. Each *executed as a contract* clause would appear immediately above the relevant party's *signature block*.

Traditional format – where all the parties are bodies corporate and for each body corporate, a person is executing the contract on their behalf[13]

> **AS WITNESS** the hand of [*name of person executing on behalf of company*] for and on behalf of [*name of company*] [this [*day*] day of [*month*] [*year*]] [the day and year first above written]

Alternative traditional format – where all the parties are bodies corporate and for each body corporate, a person is executing the contract on their behalf

> **AS WITNESS** the hands of the parties on the day and year first before written

---

11 Formally known as the 'testimonium' clause.

12 The *executed as a contract* clause 'is not necessary for the validity of the agreement but is added merely to preserve the evidence of its due execution. For this reason it may be of importance and, except in instruments relating to registered land, it should never in practice be omitted': *Encyclopaedia of Forms and Precedents*, vol. 12(2), 'Deeds', para. 18 [3104].

13 This format is suitable for a private limited company, public limited company or company limited by guarantee, limited liability partnership, body incorporated by Royal Charter, etc. These forms of *executed as a contract* clause can also be used by a partnership, where one or more persons are signing on behalf of the partnership.

Modern format – where all the parties are bodies corporate and for each body corporate, a person is executing the contract on their behalf

> **AGREED** by the parties [through their authorised signatories] [on the date set out at the head of this Agreement]

Modern format – where a person is executing the contract on behalf of a body corporate

> **SIGNED** by [*name of person executing on behalf of body corporate*] for and on behalf of [*name of body corporate*]

Traditional format – where one or more persons are executing a contract on behalf of a partnership

> **AS WITNESS** the hand of [*name of person executing on behalf of partnership*] [and] [*name of person executing on behalf of partnership*] for and on behalf of [*name of partnership*] [, a firm] [this [*day*] day of [*month*] [*year*]] [the day and year first above written]

Modern format – where one or more persons is/are executing a contract on behalf of a partnership

> **AGREED** by [*name of partnership*] through its agent[s] [*name of person executing on behalf of partnership*] [and] [*name of person executing on behalf of partnership*] [on the date set out at the head of this Agreement]

Traditional format – individuals executing a contract

> **AS WITNESS** [our hands] [the hands of the parties] [this [*day*] day of [*month*] [*year*]] [the day and year first above written]

Modern format – individuals executing a contract

> **AGREED** by the parties [on the date set out at the head of this Agreement]

Traditional format – where there is a mixture of individuals and corporate parties

> **IN WITNESS WHEREOF**, the Parties hereto have caused their duly authorised representatives to execute this Agreement

9

Modern format – where there is a mixture of individuals and corporate parties

> **SIGNED** by each of the parties (or their authorised representatives) [on the date set out at the head of this Agreement]

Traditional format – where a company is formed or regulated by CA 1985 or CA 2006, and the company itself is executing the contract

> **AS WITNESS** this contract has been duly executed by [*name of company*] [this [*day*] day of [*month and year*]] [the day and year first above written]

Modern format – where a company is formed or regulated by CA 1985 and CA 2006, and the company itself is executing the contract

> **EXECUTED** by the above-named [*name of company*] and signed by [two directors] [a director and the secretary]

Or:

> **EXECUTED** by the above-named [*name of company*] and signed by [a director] (signature, name, address and description of attesting witness)

Traditional format – where a contract is being signed on behalf of the parties

> **AS WITNESS** this Agreement has been signed on behalf of the parties

Modern format – where a contract is being signed on behalf of the parties

> **SIGNED** on behalf of the parties to this Agreement.

1.2   FORM/STRUCTURE OF THE SIGNATURE BLOCK[14]

Traditional format – where a person is executing the contract on behalf of a body corporate

> **SIGNED** by [*name of person signing on behalf of body corporate*] [as director] [duly authorised] for and on behalf of [*name of body corporate*]   } (signature of person signing)

---

14 Formally known as the 'attestation' clause.

Modern format – where a person is executing the contract on behalf of a body corporate

For and on behalf of
[*full name of company*]

_____
Signed

_____
Print name

_____
Title

_____
Date

Traditional format – individual executing a contract

SIGNED by [the above-named]   }
[*name of individual*]   }   (signature of individual)

Modern format – individual executing a contract

By [*full name of individual*]

_____
Signed

_____
Print name

_____
Title

_____
Date

1.3 TYPE OF STATEMENT, AFFIRMATION OR OATH THAT MUST BE MADE WHEN THE DOCUMENT IS SIGNED/EXECUTED

None.

1.4 (PROFESSIONAL) PERSONS WHO MUST BE PRESENT WHEN THE DOCUMENT IS SIGNED/EXECUTED AND THEIR ROLE

None.

1.5 HOW ARE ATTACHMENTS/SCHEDULES TO THE MAIN DOCUMENT DEALT WITH?

By convention, attachments are placed before the *executed as a contract* clause and the *signature block*. Other common terms include 'schedules', 'annexes' or 'appendices' and, if there is more than one, each should be numbered: 'schedule 1', 'schedule 2', etc. References in the other parts of a contract to an attachment or schedule are usually expressed in the following terms, e.g.: 'as set out in schedule [1] [to this agreement]'.

More modern drafting practice (particularly in some commercial contracts) sets out attachments or schedules after the *executed as a contract* clause and the *signature block*.

1.6 FEES CHARGED BY THE PROFESSIONAL PERSON

None. But lawyers involved in providing advice and assistance to a client concerning the contract, e.g. in negotiations, drafting, due diligence work, etc. will normally charge for such work.

Points to note

1. By convention the *executed as a contract* clause and *signature block* are placed at the end of the document (either before or after the schedules).
2. Although the signatures of the parties could be placed anywhere on the agreement, what is important is that the signature of each party:
   (a) indicates that that party has the intention of approving, adopting and/or authenticating the contents of the agreement; and
   (b) can be recognised as representing the name of the party signing.[15] Practically:
      (i) placing a signature elsewhere than in the conventional place at the end of the agreement; or
      (ii) having a *signature block* drafted other than in a conventional way
   may not be acceptable to other parties.[16]
3. Witnessing of signatures is not normally required.[17]

---

15 The meaning and form of a signature are considered in **Chapter 13**.

16 And perhaps more practically, in the event of a dispute, it may not be acceptable to a judge deciding what is or what is not acceptable as a signature, see e.g. *Pereira Fernandes SA* v. *Mehta* [2006] EWHC 813 (Ch), [2006] 1 All ER (Comm) 885.

17 But in particular areas of law, having a signature witnessed may be required by one party of another, e.g. *Cornish* v. *Midland Bank plc* [1985] 3 All ER 513: a bank taking a personal guarantee requires the guarantor's signature to be witnessed by a solicitor, with a statement on the guarantee to indicate that the solicitor has explained its effect to the guarantor before

4. For some types of contract such as bank guarantees, normal practice may require that only the party assuming obligations need sign.

5. Parties do not need to be in each other's presence when a contract is signed.

6. There is no formal stage of 'delivery' for contracts under hand (unlike deeds).

7. When a person is to sign for, and on behalf of, more than one party, she should normally sign separately for each party (CA 2006, s.44).[18]

8. Where the name of a person or party is recorded in an official register or used by a government body, then that name should normally be used in future dealings. If the name changes or is not accurately described, then it may be necessary to bring forward evidence for the reason for the change or inaccuracy. If there is a change of name, then a statutory declaration stating that the name has changed may be required.

9. Where a company is not correctly named in a contract, the validity or effect of the contract may not be affected.[19] In practice it is best to be precise, especially as the names of companies incorporated in England and Wales (and their registered offices) are easily checked at the Registrar of Companies' website (**www.companieshouse.gov.uk**).

10. In some countries (such as in Germany and Switzerland), it is usual practice for there to be two signatories for each party.

11. Where a party or person is required to sign a formal document, and it is permitted that a proxy can sign the name of that party or person, then the proxy should normally add 'pp' (or 'per pro') and the initials of the proxy.[20]

---

the guarantor signed. Also, important commercial agreements are sometimes witnessed. In some civil law countries, the *signature block* is sometimes drafted in such a way that one person is said to be witnessing the signature of another rather than two people signing for one party. Some commercial agreements (particularly from the United States) contain a statement that the agreement is '[legally effective] [legal as to form]' and signed or initialled by a party's lawyer.

18 It is perhaps no longer best practice to sign once and make it clear that the person's signature is intended to be for both parties (or that there is evidence of such intention).

19 'I derive assistance from [*Commins* v. *Scott* (1875) LR 20 Eq 11] to show that it is not essential to the validity of a contract made on behalf of a limited company that the company should be described with precision': *F Goldsmith (Sicklesmere) Ltd* v. *Baxter* [1969] 3 All ER 733 per Stamp J.

20 For example, if a contract allows one party to terminate a contract by written notice and the notice must be signed by the chief executive (Jane Smith) but the chief finance officer (John Doe) is permitted to sign in the name of the chief executive, the chief finance officer should sign 'Jane Smith, pp JD', subject to the chief executive's authorising the chief finance officer's use of the chief executive's signature: see *London County Council* v. *Vitamins Ltd* [1955] 2 QB 218, per Lord Denning.

CHAPTER 2

Execution of a deed by an individual

CHECKLIST

- Should the document be a deed:
  - is it required to be in the form of a deed at all? or
  - is it conventional for it to be in the form of a deed? or
  - is it desirable for it to be in the form of a deed because of the underlying transaction or event?

  See **section 14.15**.

- Are the person(s) making it ('the Maker') or the parties to it correctly described?

- Are all:
  - the persons who are placed under an obligation; or
  - parties to a contract;

  named in the document?

- Is the deed required to be in a particular or specified form? See **section 14.15**.

- The document should state that it is intended to be a deed.

- Has the document been read by, or been fully and accurately explained to, the Maker?

- Is the deed to be delivered immediately on it being signed?
  - if not ('delivered in escrow'), add the necessary conditions to the deed, and check that it is not expressed to be delivered on execution;
  - determine how and by whom the deed is to be delivered on signature.

- Ensure that another person ('the Witness') is present at the moment when the Maker intends to sign the document.

- Note that:
  - the Maker is to sign the document in the presence of the Witness; and
  - the signature of the Maker is attested by the Witness, such act being recorded by the signature of the Witness;

  or:
  - at the Maker's direction and in her presence and in the presence of two Witnesses, another person is to sign the document; and
  - the two Witnesses are each to attest the signature of the other person, such acts being recorded by the signatures of the two Witnesses.

- The deed is then delivered.
- Is the deed intended to be used for a transaction or event taking place in another country or is one or more of the persons named in it or parties to it based, incorporated or regulated in another country? If so:
  - does the deed need to be translated into the language of the other country (or does at least one copy of the deed need to be in that language)?
  - if the deed does need to be translated, must it be translated by an official or properly qualified translator?
  - does the deed need to be registered with any governmental or regulatory authorities in the other country?
  - is the deed of a type which needs to be drawn up and/or signed before a notary?[1]
  - if the deed is being signed in England and Wales, does it need to be notarised and/or legalised after it has been signed?

2.1   FORM/STRUCTURE OF THE DOCUMENT

A document intended to be a deed must either:

- be described as a deed; or
- indicate that it is to be executed as a deed.

Described as a deed

Commencement of the document

A document might commence as follows to indicate at once that it is intended as a deed:

> **THIS DEED** dated _____ 200[. . .] is made by and between:
>
> (1)   [*name and address of the first party*]; and
> (2)   [*name and address of the second party*]

Wording in the body of the document

The text indicating that the document is intended to be a deed can also be located in the body of the document (instead of, or in addition to, at the commencement of the document). Such text often signifies the commencement of the main provisions of the deed:

> Now this deed witnesses as follows

---

1 For example, a power of attorney intended for use in another country often has to be signed before a notary.

'Executed as a deed' clause[2]

As an alternative to (or in addition to) describing the document as a deed, the document can state that it is being executed as a deed.

Traditional format – one person executing the document as a deed

> **IN WITNESS** of which [*name of individual*] has set her hand to this deed in the presence of the attesting witness [this [*day*] day of [*month*] [*year*]] [the day and year first above written]

Traditional format – more than one person executing the document as a deed

> **IN WITNESS** of which [*names of individuals*] have set their hands to this deed in the presence of the attesting witness [this [*day*] day of [*month*] [*year*]] [the day and year first above written]

Modern format – one person executing the document as a deed

> Executed as a deed by the undersigned on the date of this Deed

Modern format – more than one person executing the document as a deed

> **EXECUTED** as a **DEED** by the parties on the date of this deed

Alternative format – one person executing the document as a deed and the deed being delivered on execution

> **EXECUTED** as a **DEED** by the undersigned, and delivered, on the date of this deed

Modern format – more than one person executing the document as a deed and the deed being delivered on execution

> **EXECUTED** as a **DEED** by the parties, and delivered, on the date of this deed

---

2 Formally known as the 'testimonium' clause.

2.2 FORM/STRUCTURE OF THE SIGNATURE BLOCK[3]

Traditional format

SIGNED [and DELIVERED] as a DEED by the
above-named [*name of individual*] in the   (signature of person signing)
presence of:

(signature, name, address and description of attesting witness)

Modern format

SIGNED [and DELIVERED   In the presence of:
upon signature] as a
DEED by [*name of individual*]
upon signature

Signature	Signature
	Description
	Address

Format for transfers for registered land, etc.[4]

Signed as a deed* by
[*full name of individual*]   (signature)

Signature of witness _____

Name (in BLOCK CAPITALS) _____

Address _____

_____

*In the case of an assent, the words 'as a deed' may be omitted

2.3 TYPE OF STATEMENT, AFFIRMATION OR OATH THAT MUST BE MADE WHEN THE DOCUMENT IS SIGNED/EXECUTED

None.

---

3 Formally known as the 'attestation' clause.
4 Land Registration Rules 2003, r.206(3), and Sched. 9, Form A and *Land Registry Practice Guide 8*, 'Execution of Deeds', s.3.1, April 2008. As to when this form of *signature block* must be used, see **section 14.15**.

2.4 (PROFESSIONAL) PERSONS WHO MUST BE PRESENT WHEN THE DOCUMENT IS SIGNED/EXECUTED AND THEIR ROLE

None.

2.5 HOW ARE ATTACHMENTS/SCHEDULES TO THE MAIN DOCUMENT DEALT WITH?

By convention, attachments are placed before the *executed as a deed* clause and the *signature block*. Other common terms used are: 'schedules', 'annexes' or 'appendices' and, if there is more than one, each one is numbered: 'schedule 1', 'schedule 2', etc. References in the deed to an attachment or schedule are usually expressed in the following terms, e.g.: 'as set out in schedule [1] [to this deed]'.

More modern drafting practice (particularly in some commercial contracts) sets out attachments/schedules after the *executed as a deed* clause and the *signature block*.

2.6 FEES THAT ARE CHARGED BY THE PROFESSIONAL PERSON

None.

2.7 MAIN VARIATIONS TO ANY OF THE ABOVE

Listed below are some of the possible variations for the *signature block* where the individual wishing to execute the document as a deed chooses not to, or is not able to, sign.

Document signed at the direction of the individual executing it

Signature block – traditional form

SIGNED [and **DELIVERED**] as a **DEED** by the [*person signing on behalf of the person executing the document*] at the direction of and on behalf of the above-named [*name of individual*] in [his/her] presence and the presence of:

} (signature of person signing)

(signature, name, address and description of first attesting witness)

(signature, name, address and description of second attesting witness)

Signature block – modern format

SIGNED [and **DELIVERED**] as a **DEED** by the [*person signing on behalf of the person executing the document*] at the direction of and on behalf of the above-named [*name of individual*] in [her/his] presence and in the presence of:	Witnessed by:	Witnessed by:
_____	_____	_____
Signature	Signature	Signature
	_____	_____
	Description	Description
	_____	_____
	Address	Address

Format for transfers for registered land, etc.[5]

Signed as a deed by [*full name of person signing*] at the direction and on behalf of [*full name of individual*] in [his] [her] presence and in the presence of:

[*Sign here the name of the individual and your own name,* e.g. John Smith by Jane Brown]

Signature of first witness _____

Name (in BLOCK CAPITALS) _____

Address _____

_____

_____

Signature of second witness _____

Name (in BLOCK CAPITALS) _____

Address _____

_____

_____

---

5 Land Registration Rules 2003, r.206(3), and Sched. 9, Form B and *Land Registry Practice Guide 8*, 'Execution of Deeds', s.3.4, April 2008. As to when this form of *signature block* must be used, see **section 14.15**.

The Land Registry recommends this form where the individual is physically incapable of signing the deed *at all*.

Document signed by a person incapacitated in some way

SIGNED [and **DELIVERED**] as a **DEED** by
the above-named [*name of individual*]
**[being deaf and dumb but capable of
reading and having first read and appearing
perfectly to understand the above deed]**
in the presence of:

(signature of executing party)

(signature, name, address and description of attesting witness)

Words in bold: if person is deaf and dumb but capable of reading and writing. Please see below for possible alternatives:

- **if person is deaf and dumb and incapable of reading**:

    being deaf and dumb and incapable of reading (after the above deed had first been interpreted to him in the deaf and dumb alphabet by the undersigned [*name of interpreting witness*] and the above-named [*name of individual*] appeared perfectly to understand the above deed)

- **if person is blind and capable of writing his name**:

    being a blind person (after the above deed had been read over to her and she had stated that she understood the same)

- **if person is incapable of signing his name through illiteracy, illness, etc., but capable of making his mark** (replacing all the text not only that in bold):

    SIGNED (by making his mark he being incapable through [illness (or) illiteracy (or) [*specify*]] of writing his name) [and DELIVERED] AS A DEED by the above-named [*name of individual*] (after the nature of the above deed had been fully explained to him and he appeared to perfectly understand the same) in the presence of:

Format for transfers for registered land, etc. where the person is unable to read or understand a deed – but is able to sign it[6]

Signed as a deed by [*full name
of individual*] in the presence of
the undersigned, [he/she]
having first confirmed that [he/
she] had familiarised [himself/
herself] with its contents by
[*state method used*]:

[*Sign here the name of the
individual and your own name,
e.g.* John Smith by Jane Brown]

---

6 Although this form of *signature block* is not specified by Land Registration Rules 2003, r.206(3), and Sched. 9, the Land Registry is willing to accept it without the person submitting a deed with this *signature block* seeking specific prior approval: *Land Registry Practice Guide 8*, 'Execution of Deeds', s.3.3, April 2008. As to when this form of *signature block* must be used, see **section 14.15**.

Signature of witness _____

Name (in BLOCK CAPITALS) _____

Address _____

_____

_____

This form of the signature can be used in the following circumstances; and the method by which the contents of the deed should be brought to the attention of the individual signing is as follows:

- **the individual is illiterate**: the contents of the deed should be read over to her and the effect of the deed should be fully explained;
- **the individual is physically ill or disabled**: the contents of the deed should be read out to the person, or if possible, the text of the deed should be printed out in large print or a Braille copy made;
- **the individual does not have a sufficient understanding of the English (or Welsh) language**: the contents of the deed should be read out to the person, or a version of the contents be made in her own language.

The Land Registry suggests that the individual's solicitor or licensed conveyancer witnesses the individual's signature as a way of confirming that the correct procedure has been followed (amending the wording of the *signature block* to reflect the steps taken).[7]

Attorney signing under a power of attorney[8]

Attorney signing in the name of the donor

An example of an *executed as a deed* clause using traditional wording:

> **IN WITNESS** of which [*name of attorney*] of [*address of attorney*] has in exercise of a power of attorney under the hand of [*name of donor of power*] dated the [*day*] day of [*month and year*] set the hand of [*name of donor of power*] to this deed [this [*day*] day of [*month and year*]] [the day and year first above written]

An example of an *executed as a deed* clause using modern wording:

> Executed as a deed by [*name of attorney*] of [*address of attorney*] on the date of this deed under a power of attorney given by [*name of donor of power*] dated [*date*]

---

7 *Land Registry Practice Guide 8*, 'Execution of Deeds', s.3.3, April 2008.
8 Further examples of *signature as a deed* clauses and *signature block* are given in **Chapter 4**.

An example of a *signature block* – traditional form:

| SIGNED [and DELIVERED] as a DEED for and on behalf of the above-named [*name of the donor of the power of attorney*] by [his/her] above-named attorney in the presence of: | } | (attorney's signature of donor's name)
By (attorney's signature of her own name) |

(signature, name, address and description of attesting witness)

An example of a *signature block* – modern form:

| SIGNED [and DELIVERED upon signature] as a DEED by [*name of attorney*] as the attorney and in the name of [*name of donor of power*] in the presence of: | Witnessed by: |

Signature (attorney's signature of name of donor) by [her/his] attorney (signature of attorney)

_____ Signature

_____ Description

_____ Address

An example of a *signature block* for transfers for registered land, etc.[9]

| Signed as a deed by [*full name of individual or corporation*] acting by [his/her/its] attorney [*full name of attorney*] in the presence of: | } | [*Sign here your name and name of the individual/corporation, e.g. John Smith/John Smith Ltd by his/its attorney by Jane Brown*] |

Signature of witness _____

Name (in BLOCK CAPITALS) _____

Address _____

Attorney signing in his own name

An example of an *executed as a deed* clause:

IN WITNESS of which [*name of attorney*] of [*address*] as attorney of [*name of donor of power*] and in exercise of a power of attorney under the hand of [*name of donor of*

---

9 This form is not required by the Land Registry Rules 2003, but is acceptable to the Land Registry; *Land Registry Practice Guide 8*, 'Execution of Deeds', 10.6.1, April 2008.

power] dated the [*day*] day of [*month and year*] has duly executed this deed [this [*day*] day of [*month*] [*year*]] [the day and year first above written]

An example of a *signature block* – traditional form:

SIGNED [and **DELIVERED**] as a **DEED** for
and on behalf of the above-named [*name*
of the donor of the power of attorney] by [his/
her] above-named attorney in the presence of:

By (attorney's signature
of her own name)

(signature, name, address and description of attesting witness)

An example of a *signature block* – modern form:

SIGNED [and **DELIVERED** upon signature]
as a **DEED** by [*name of attorney*] as the
attorney for [*name of donor of power*] in
the presence of:

Witnessed by:

Signature (attorney's signature) as attorney for (signature by attorney of name of donor)

_____ Signature

_____ Description

_____ Address

An example of a *signature block* for transfers for registered land, etc.[10]

Signed as a deed by [*full name*
of attorney] as attorney for [*full*
name of individual or of corporation]
in the presence of:

[*Sign here your own name and*
name of the individual/corporation,
e.g. Jane Brown as attorney for
John Smith/John Smith Ltd]

Signature of witness _____

Name (in BLOCK CAPITALS) _____

Address_____

---

10 This form is not required by the Land Registry Rules 2003, but is acceptable to the Land Registry; *Land Registry Practice Guide 8*, 'Execution of Deeds', 10.6.1, April 2008.

Escrow

SIGNED and **DELIVERED** as a **DEED** and as an escrow by
the above-named [*name of individual*] and placed in
the hands of [*name of person to hold escrow*] of
[*address*] to be delivered up to the above-named
[*other executing party*] [when the above-mentioned
sum of £ [. . .] has been paid by [*other executing
party*] to [*name of person to hold escrow*] as the
agent and on behalf of [*name of individual*] [*or
specify*]] in the presence of:

(signature of
person signing)

(signature, name, address and description of attesting witness)

Where alterations, additions or deletions have been made to the deed (prior to signing)

SIGNED [and **DELIVERED**] as a **DEED** by the above-
named [*name of individual*] and the following words
[*insert the words added*] have been added between
[*insert first phrase to locate place of insert*] and
[*add second phrase to locate place of insert*] in the
presence of:

(signature of
executing party)

(signature, name, address and description of attesting witness)

Points to note

1. The *executed as a deed* clause and the *signature block* should normally be kept together on one page (where possible). In particular the *signature block* should never be split over two pages. But if the *signature block* runs over more than one page (i.e. where there are several parties and the modern format is used), the *signature block* should be separated at a logical place (e.g. all the wording for a particular party being kept together).
2. By convention, witnesses are required to state their address and print their name and their description (occupation) in addition to their signature. Such a practice allows for the witness to be contacted if there is doubt about the document, its method of execution, etc.
3. A 'signature' can mean making no more than a mark (such as an 'X'). It can also include signing with a pencil, or applying a rubber stamp which contains an exact copy of the individual's real signature. (The use of the two last practices may not be acceptable to everyone involved in a transaction or matter.) In particular, the Law Commission recommends for deeds that a handwritten signature is used by the person or parties to a deed.
4. The words 'described as a deed' do not always mean that a document has to contain the word 'deed' in it. Other words which describe the doc-

ument or how it is signed or executed could be used. For example, the document could be described as a type of document which in the circumstances can only be a deed, such as a conveyance, a mortgage or a lease of real property, or a grant of a power of attorney.

5. If a deed is dated at the top of its front page then the date does not have to be repeated in the *executed as a deed* clause or the *signature block*.

6. The date to be inserted in the deed is the date when the deed is delivered, which may be different from the date when the deed was signed, witnessed and attested. The *executed as a deed* clause or the *signature block* should be carefully considered when drafting a deed to allow for situations when a deed is not intended to have effect when it is signed, witnessed and attested.

7. Where a deed is not delivered when it is signed, the deed might commence with the following words:

THIS DEED delivered as a deed on ＿＿＿＿＿＿＿＿＿＿＿＿＿＿＿ 200[. . .]

or add a reference to the date of delivery in the *executed as a deed* clause as evidence of delivery.

8. A deed delivered in escrow is dated on the date it is signed and delivered in escrow and not the date when the condition is fulfilled.[11]

9. At least for transfers of registered land, a signature made using foreign characters (for example, Arabic or Chinese characters) will be considered valid by the Land Registry. The Land Registry will require:

    (a) that the *signature block* be expanded to confirm that the individual signing:

        (i) understands English; or

        (ii) has familiarised herself with the contents of the deed (e.g. by having the contents of the deed read over to her);

    or:

    (b) a separate certificate prepared by the solicitor or licensed conveyancer acting for the individual confirming the points mentioned in (a)(i) or (ii).

---

11 This proposition is not correct for stamp duty purposes: the date of delivery is the date when the condition is fulfilled: Stamp Act 1891 (SA 1891), s.122(1A).

CHAPTER 3

Execution of a deed by a corporation (non-CA 2006 or CA 1985)[1]

CHECKLIST

- Should the document be a deed:
  - is it required to be in the form of a deed at all? or
  - is it conventional for it to be in the form of a deed? or
  - is it desirable for it to be in the form of a deed because of the underlying transaction or event?

  See **section 14.15**.

- Are the person(s) and body/bodies corporate making the deed (the Maker) and/or the parties to it correctly described?

- Are all:
  - the persons and body/bodies corporate who are placed under an obligation; or
  - the parties to the deed

  named in the deed?

- Is the deed required to be in a particular or specified form? See **section 14.15**.

- Does the document state on its face that it is intended to be a deed?

- Has the deed been read by, or been fully and accurately explained to, the person(s) who are to execute the deed (such as the member(s) of the body corporate's governing body, its secretary, or the persons authorised to sign it)?

- Has the constitution[2] of the corporation been checked for the correct method of applying the seal of the corporation, such as:
  - is a meeting of the governing body required?
  - is the governing body required to specifically authorise use of the seal in specified instances?

---

1 This chapter does not cover corporations which are companies registered under, or regulated by, CA 2006.

2 The precise name of the constitution may vary (e.g. charter or articles). The precise method of signing and use of the seal may be found in 'subsidiary' documentation to the constitution, such as regulations or standing orders or even sometimes as specified in decisions of the ruling body of the corporation. Less commonly, if founded by statute, the statute may state the method.

- – is the seal required to be affixed at a meeting of the governing body of the corporation?
  - – is the seal required to be affixed in the presence of the person(s) who will sign?

- Who among the members of the governing body can sign the deed:
  - – one or more members?
  - – one member and the corporation's secretary?
  - – the secretary alone?
  - – some other person authorised by the governing body to sign documents on behalf of the governing body of the corporation? Do they have unlimited authority or have they been given specific authority in a particular instance?[3]

- If the deed is to be executed other than by:
  - – two members of the governing council; or
  - – one member and the body corporate's clerk, secretary or other permanent officer (or deputy),

  will it matter to a purchaser that the deed will not be deemed to have been duly executed by the corporation (see below)?[4]

- Who has custody of the seal (normally the secretary to the corporation)?

- Will the deed be delivered immediately on being signed or at a later date?
  - – if not ('delivered in escrow'), add the necessary conditions to the deed, and ensure that it is not expressed to be delivered on execution;
  - – determine how and by whom it is to be delivered on signature.

- Affix the seal.

- The persons who are required to sign should do so as determined by the constitution or such other document governing execution of deeds.

- The deed is then delivered.

- Is the deed intended to be used for a transaction or event taking place in another country or is one or more of the persons named in it or parties to it based, incorporated or regulated in another country? If so:
  - – does the deed need to be translated into the language of the other country (or does at least one copy of the deed need to be in that language)?
  - – if the deed does need to be translated, must it be translated by an official or properly qualified translator?
  - – does the deed need to be registered with any governmental or regulatory authorities in the other country?
  - – is the deed of a type which needs to be drawn up and/or signed before a notary?[5]
  - – if the deed is being signed in England and Wales, does it need to be notarised and/or legalised after it has been signed?

---

3 For example, a large corporation may allow (some) senior management to sign all documents relating to routine matters or transactions without needing to refer the matter to the governing body, such as completing the formalities on the sale or purchase or leasing of property or entering into certain types of contracts or contracts up to a certain amount.
4 See Law of Property Act 1925 (LPA 1925), s.74(1), under which the seal needs to be affixed to the deed in the presence of and attested by these persons.
5 For example, a power of attorney intended for use in another country often has to be signed before a notary.

3.1   FORM/STRUCTURE OF THE DOCUMENT

A document intended to be a deed must be described as a deed or indicate that it is to be *executed as a deed.*

Described as a deed

Commencement of the document

A document might commence as follows to indicate at once that it is intended as a deed:

> **THIS DEED** dated _____ 200[. . .] is made by and between:
>
> (1)   [*name and address of the first party*]; and
> (2)   [*name and address of the second party*]

Wording in the body of the document

The text indicating that the document is intended to be a deed can also be located in the body of the document (instead of or in addition to at the commencement of the document). Such text often signifies the commencement of the main provisions of the deed:

> Now this deed witnesses as follows

'Executed as a deed' clause[6]

As an alternative to (or in addition to) describing the document as a deed, the document can state that it is being *executed as a deed.*

Traditional format – following a resolution of the governing body

> **IN WITNESS** of which [*name of corporation*] pursuant to a resolution of its [*name of governing body*] duly passed [on this [*day*] day of [*month and year*]] has caused its common seal to be affixed to this deed [and has delivered it upon dating it] [this [*day*] day of [*month and year*]] [the day and year first above written]

Traditional format – where there is no need for a resolution to use the seal of the governing body

> **IN WITNESS** of which [*name of corporation*] has caused its common seal to be affixed to this deed [and has delivered it upon dating it] [this [*day*] day of [*month and year*]] [the day and year first above written]

---

6 Formally known as the 'testimonium' clause.

28

Modern format

> **EXECUTED** as a **DEED** by the parties [and delivered] on the date of this deed

3.2 FORM/STRUCTURE OF THE SIGNATURE BLOCK[7]

Traditional format

SIGNED [and **DELIVERED**] as a **DEED** and **THE COMMON SEAL OF** [*name of the corporation*] affixed [pursuant to a resolution of the [*name of the governing body*]] in the presence of [two members of the [*name of the governing body*]]:	(seal of the corporation)

(signature of a member/two members of the governing body and/or the corporation's secretary)

The precise details of who (and how many) can sign will depends on the corporation's statute, charter, articles, constitution, standing orders, etc.

Words in bold and in brackets: if only one member of the governing body is required to sign, please see below for possible alternatives:

- **if only one member of the governing body is required to sign**:

  one member of the [*name of governing body*]

- **if one member of the governing body and the corporation's secretary are required to sign**:

  one member of the [*name of governing body*] and the secretary of the [*name of governing body*]

- **if only the secretary is required to sign**:

  the secretary of the [*name of governing body*]

- **if a person authorised by the corporation or the governing body is authorised to sign**:

  a person authorised by the [*name of governing body*] to sign for, and on behalf of, the [*name of governing body*] [*name of corporation*]

Note: not all corporations are required to pass a resolution in order to authorise the use of the seal. This will depend on any requirements set out in the corporation's constitution. If not, then the following words can be deleted:

pursuant to a resolution of the [*name of governing body*] dated [*date*]

---

7 Formally known as the 'attestation' clause.

Note: if the corporation's constitution requires signature of a deed other than in accordance with the requirements of Law of Property Act 1925 (LPA 1925), s.74(1), then the presumption of valid execution provided by LPA 1925, s.74(1) (where either two members of the governing body or one member of the governing body and the secretary, clerk, etc. need to sign) may not apply. A purchaser may have to rely on common law provisions only.

Modern format

SIGNED [and **DELIVERED**] as a **DEED** and **THE COMMON SEAL OF** [*name of the corporation*] affixed [pursuant to a resolution of the [*name of the governing body*]] in the presence of [**two members of the [*name of governing body*]**]:

(signature of [*name of governing body*] member)

(seal of the corporation)

Words in bold and in brackets: if two members of the governing body are required to sign. Please see below for possible alternatives:

- **if only one member of the governing body is required to sign**:

  one member of the [*name of governing body*]

- **if one member of the governing body and the corporation's secretary are required to sign**:

  one member of the [*name of governing body*] and the secretary of the [*name of governing body*]

- **if only the secretary is required to sign**:

  the secretary of the [*name of governing body*]

- **if a person authorised by the corporation or the governing body is authorised to sign**:

  a person authorised by the [*name of governing body*] to sign by, and on behalf of, the [*name of governing body*] [*name of corporation*]

Note: not all corporations are required to pass a resolution in order to authorise the use of the seal. This will depend on any requirements set out in the corporation's constitution. If not, then the following words can be deleted:

pursuant to a resolution of the [*name of governing body*]

Note: if the corporation's constitution requires signature of a deed other than in accordance with the requirements of LPA 1925, s.74(1), then the presumption of valid execution provided by LPA 1925, s.74(1) (where two members of the governing body or one member of the governing body and the secretary, clerk, etc. need to sign) may not apply. See p.174. A purchaser may have to rely on common law provisions only.

Format for transfer for registered land, etc.[8]

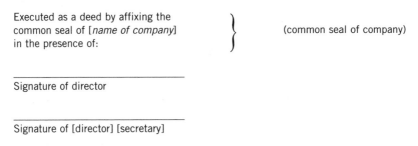

Executed as a deed by affixing the common seal of [name of company] in the presence of:

(common seal of company)

_____

Signature of director

_____

Signature of [director] [secretary]

Note: the points made above about presumed due execution under LPA 1925, s.74(1) apply.

3.3 (PROFESSIONAL) PERSONS WHO MUST BE PRESENT WHEN THE DOCUMENT IS SIGNED/EXECUTED AND THEIR ROLE

None.

3.4 HOW ARE ATTACHMENTS/SCHEDULES TO THE MAIN DOCUMENT DEALT WITH?

By convention, attachments are placed before the *executed as a deed* clause and the *signature block*. Other common terms used are: 'schedules', 'annexes' or 'appendices' and, if there is more than one, each one is numbered: 'schedule 1', 'schedule 2', etc. References in the deed to an attachment or schedule are usually expressed in the following terms, e.g.: 'as set out in schedule [1] [to this deed]'.

More modern drafting practice (particularly in some commercial contracts) sets out attachments/schedules after the *executed as a deed* clause and the *signature block*.

3.5 FEES THAT ARE CHARGED BY THE PROFESSIONAL PERSON

None.

_____

8 This form (which is for companies incorporated under CA 1985) if included in a deed is acceptable to the Land Registry without the corporation providing further evidence (see *Land Registry Practice Guide 8*, 'Execution of Deeds', s.6.1, April 2008).

Points to note

1. The *executed as a deed* clause and the *signature block* should normally be kept together on one page (where possible). In particular, the *signature block* should never be split over two pages. If the *signature block* runs over more than one page (i.e. there are several parties and the modern format is used), then the *signature block* should be separated at a logical place (e.g. all the wording for a particular party being kept together).

2. A 'signature' can mean making no more than a mark (such as an 'X'). It can also include signing with a pencil, or applying a rubber stamp which contains an exact copy of the individual's real signature (although these two last practices should be used with care – and are practices which may not be acceptable to everyone involved in the transaction or matter).

3. The words 'described as a deed' do not always mean that a document has to contain the word 'deed' in it. Other words which describe the document or how it is signed or executed could be used. For example, the document could be described as a type of document which in the circumstances can only be a deed (such as a conveyance, a mortgage or a lease of real property, or a grant of a power of attorney).

4. If a deed is dated at the top of its front page then the date does not have to be repeated in the *executed as a deed* clause or the *signature block*.

5. The date to be inserted in the deed is the date when the deed is delivered, which may be different from the date when the deed was signed, witnessed and attested. The *executed as a deed* clause or the *signature block* should be carefully considered when drafting a deed to allow for situations when a deed is not intended to have effect when it is signed, witnessed and attested.

6. Where a deed is not delivered when it is signed, the deed might commence with the following words:

    THIS DEED delivered as a deed on _____ 200[. . .]

    or add a reference to the date of delivery in the *executed as a deed* clause as evidence of delivery.

7. A deed delivered in escrow is dated on the date it is signed and delivered in escrow and not the date when the condition is fulfilled.[9]

8. For the transfer of registered land, etc., the Land Registry:[10]

    (a) requires that corporations aggregate and sole execute deeds under seal, unless the corporation making an application to the Land Registry is able to show a specific statutory exemption relating to that corporation;

---

9 This proposition is not correct for stamp duty purposes, where the date of delivery is the date when the condition is fulfilled: SA 1891, s.122(1A).

10 *Land Registry Practice Guide 8*, 'Execution of Deeds', s.6.1, April 2008.

(b) will accept a deed from a corporation aggregate which has a *signature block* in the prescribed form for a company regulated under CA 1985 which uses a common seal[11] without calling for further evidence (LPA 1925, s.74(1) will be assumed to apply in favour of a purchaser);

(c) will not accept, without further evidence, a deed executed otherwise than in accordance with LPA 1925, s.74(1). In this case the Land Registry will wish to see the legislation or document of incorporation (such as the Royal Charter).[12]

---

11 This is set out at p.31. This part of the guidance will most probably be revised to reflect the provisions of CA 2006.

12 If the legislation is a public Act, then this is not required to be supplied, just a reference to the appropriate section number(s). Corporations regularly executing deeds can make an arrangement with the Land Registry so that the document of incorporation is lodged with the Land Registry's Commercial Arrangements Section. On subsequent occasions when a deed is executed which needs to be sent to the Land Registry, the document of incorporation will not need to be sent with it.

CHAPTER 4

Execution of a deed by a company formed under, or regulated by, CA 2006 (or CA 1985)[1]

4.1 TYPES OF COMPANIES COVERED BY CA 2006 AND CA 1985

Formed under CA 2006 and CA 1985

These are:

- companies limited by shares;
- companies limited by guarantee (not having a share capital);
- companies limited by guarantee (having a share capital);
- unlimited companies

whether they are private or public companies.

Regulated by CA 2006 and CA 1985[2]

The following corporate bodies are regulated as to their ability to enter into contracts, and execute documents (including deeds) in the same way as UK limited companies:

- limited liability partnerships;
- overseas companies;
- unregistered companies.

---

1 The provisions relating to the execution of documents (including deeds) found in CA 2006 came into force from April 2008 and apply to the type of companies dealt with in this chapter, including those formed or regulated by CA 1985 (see Companies Act 2006 (Commencement No. 5 etc) Order 2007, SI 2007/3495).
2 The requirements for limited liability partnerships and overseas companies to execute documents are dealt with in separate chapters. The requirements are very close to those described in this chapter. The requirements for unregistered companies to execute documents are the same as for companies formed under CA 2006.

CHECKLIST

- Should the document be a deed:
  - is it required to be in the form of a deed at all? or
  - is it conventional for it to be in the form of a deed? or
  - is it desirable for it to be in the form of a deed because of the underlying transaction or event?

  See **section 14.15**.

- Are the person(s) making it or the parties to it correctly described?

- Are all:
  - the persons who are placed under an obligation; or
  - the parties to a contract

  named in the document?

- Is the deed required to be in a particular or specified form? See **section 14.15**.

- Does the document states on its face that it is intended to be a deed?

- Does the deed clearly state that it has been executed by the company?[3]

- Has the deed been read by, or fully and accurately explained to, the person(s) who are to execute the deed (such as the director, two directors or a director and the company secretary)?

- Are there any restrictions on the person(s) who are to sign as to what documents they can sign?[4]

- Is the deed to be delivered immediately on being signed?
  - if not ('delivered in escrow'), add the necessary conditions to the deed, and check that it is not expressed to be delivered on execution;
  - determine how and by whom the deed is to be delivered.

- Consider who the document is executed by:

  if the company does not use, or have, a common seal

  - a director in the presence of a witness (who attests the director's signature); or
  - a director and the company secretary (if the company has, or is required to have, a company secretary);[5] or
  - two directors

  signing the document; or

---

3 See Points to note (3), p.45.

4 For some companies, only certain directors may be permitted to deal with some matters, or there may be policies whereby some matters can routinely be dealt with by a particular director or directors without the need to call a board meeting, while other matters may need a board meeting. For very important transactions, particularly in larger companies, the minute book for directors and/or shareholders may need to be checked for any resolutions/decisions of the directors/shareholders concerning this point.

5 Only public companies will be required to have a company secretary.

if the company does have a common seal and wishes to use it, and the default provision relating to the use of the common seal in the model articles of association under CA 2006 applies,[6] the fixing of the common seal of the company; and then:

- a director in the presence of a witness (who attests the director's signature); or
- a person (previously authorised by the directors) in the presence of a witness (who attests the director's signature)

signing the document;

or:

if the company does have a common seal and wishes to use it, and the default provision relating to the use of the common seal in Table A under CA 1985 applies,[7] the fixing of the common seal of the company; and then:

- a director and the company secretary; or
- two directors; or
- a person (previously authorised by the directors)

signing the document.

- The deed is then delivered.
- Is the deed intended to be used for a transaction or event taking place in another country or is one or more of the persons named in it or parties to it based, incorporated or regulated in another country? If so:
  - does the deed need to be translated into the language of the other country (or does at least one copy of the deed need to be in that language)?
  - if the deed does need to be translated, must it be translated by an official or properly qualified translator?
  - does the deed need to be registered with any governmental or regulatory authorities in the other country?
  - is the deed of the type which needs to be drawn up and/or signed before a notary?[8]
  - if the deed is being signed in England and Wales, does it need to be notarised and/or legalised after it has been signed?

4.2   FORM/STRUCTURE OF THE DOCUMENT

A document intended to be a deed must be described as a deed or indicate that it is to be executed as a deed.

---

6 If the company utilises the unamended provisions relating to seals in the model articles of association. For private companies limited by shares see Sched. 1, art. 50, for private companies limited by guarantee see Sched. 2, art. 36 and for public companies see Sched. 3, art. 81 of the Companies (Model Articles) Regulations 2007 (currently in draft).

7 For companies which utilise the unamended provisions of Table A, CA 1985, these will continue to apply despite the coming into force of CA 2006 and the provisions of the Companies (Model Articles) Regulations 2007 (see the Companies (Model Articles) Regulations 2007, reg. 5 (currently in draft)).

8 For example, a power of attorney intended for use in another country often has to be signed before a notary.

Described as a deed

Commencement of the document

A document might commence as follows to indicate at once that it is intended as a deed:

> **THIS DEED** dated _____ 200[. . .] is made by and between:
>
> (1) [*name and address of the first party*]; and
> (2) [*name and address of the second party*]

Wording in the body of the document

The text indicating that the document is intended to be a deed can also be located in the body of the document (instead of or in addition to at the commencement of the document). Such text often signifies the start of the main provisions of the deed:

> Now this deed witnesses as follows

'Executed as a deed' clause[9]

As an alternative to (or in addition to) describing the document as a deed, the document can state that it is being executed as a deed.

Traditional format – a company executing a deed following a resolution of the board of directors

> **IN WITNESS** of which [*name of company*] has duly executed this deed pursuant to a resolution of its board of directors duly passed [and has delivered it upon dating it] [this [*day*] day of [*month and year*]] [the day and year first above written]

Traditional format – a company executing a deed where there is no need for a resolution of the board of directors

> **IN WITNESS** of which [*name of company*] has duly executed this deed [and has delivered it upon dating it] [this [*day*] day of [*month and year*]] [the day and year first above written]

---

9 Formally known as the 'testimonium' clause.

Traditional format – a company using its common seal following a resolution of the board of directors

> **IN WITNESS** of which [*name of company*] pursuant to a resolution of its board of directors duly passed has caused its common seal to be affixed to this deed [and has delivered it upon dating it] [this [*day*] day of [*month and year*]] [the day and year first above written]

Traditional format – where there is no need for a resolution to use the common seal of the company

> **IN WITNESS** of which [*name of company*] has caused its common seal to be affixed to this deed [and has delivered it upon dating it] [this [*day*] day of [*month and year*]] [the day and year first above written]

Modern format – execution without a resolution of the board of directors

> **EXECUTED** as a **DEED** [and **DELIVERED**] by the above-named [*name of company*] and signed by [a director] [two directors] [a director and the secretary]

Modern format – execution following a resolution of the board of directors

> **EXECUTED** as a **DEED** [and **DELIVERED**] by [*name of company*] pursuant to a resolution of its board of directors duly passed[, a certified copy of which was delivered upon the execution of this deed]

Modern format – further alternatives

> **EXECUTED** as a Deed by the parties [and delivered] on the date of this Agreement.

4.3   FORM/STRUCTURE OF THE SIGNATURE BLOCK[10]

For a company not using, or having, a common seal – modern format

> **SIGNED** [and **DELIVERED**] as a **DEED** by [*name of company*] acting through a director

> (director's signature)   Witnessed by:

> Signature   _____

> Description   _____

> Address   _____

---

10 Formally known as the 'attestation' clause.

Or:

SIGNED [and **DELIVERED**] as a **DEED** by [*name of company*] acting through a director and the company secretary

_____   _____

Director's signature   Company secretary's signature

Or:

SIGNED [and **DELIVERED**] as a **DEED** by [*name of company*] acting through two of its directors

_____   _____

Director's signature   Director's signature

For a company not using, or having, a common seal – traditional format

EXECUTED [and **DELIVERED**] as a **DEED** by [*name of company*] acting through a director in the presence of: }	(signature of director) (signature, name, address and description of attesting witness)

Or:

EXECUTED [and **DELIVERED**] as a **DEED** by [*name of company*] acting through two of its directors }	(signatures of directors)

Or:

EXECUTED [and **DELIVERED**] as a **DEED** by [*name of company*] acting through a director and the company secretary }	(signatures of the director and the company secretary)

If the company uses its common seal – by a director and the company secretary or two directors (for companies using the model articles of association, CA 2006)

EXECUTED [and **DELIVERED**] as a **DEED** and **THE COMMON SEAL OF** [*name of company*] affixed in the presence of: }	(common seal) (signature of a director) (signature, name, address and description of attesting witness)

If the company does have a common seal – by a person authorised by the directors (for companies using model articles of association, CA 2006)[11]

EXECUTED [and **DELIVERED**] as a **DEED** by
[*name of company*] acting through a
person authorised by the directors

(signature of the person
authorised by the
directors)
(signature, name, address and
description of attesting witness)

If the company uses its common seal – by a director and the company secretary or two directors (for companies using Table A, CA 1985)

EXECUTED [and **DELIVERED**] as a **DEED** and
THE COMMON SEAL OF [*name of company*]
affixed in the presence of:

(common seal)
(signatures of two directors
or a director and the
company secretary)

If the company does have a common seal – by a person authorised by the directors (for companies using Table A, CA 1985)[12]

EXECUTED [and **DELIVERED**] as a **DEED** by
[*name of company*] acting through a
person authorised by the directors

(signature of the person
authorised by the
directors)

Note: the following all apply to CA 1985 only. Some of the Land Registry suggested forms concerning the use of a seal are likely to remain unaltered on implementation of CA 2006 (i.e. for companies who use Table A, CA 1985 in its unamended form, which will continue to apply where companies wish to use their seal). For documents signed by the newly permissible method of one director signing a deed in the presence of a witness (who attests the director's signature), new suggested forms will be necessary (whether or not a seal is used). At the time material for this book was prepared the Land Registry had not published such new forms (although it seems likely that they will be close to the versions set out below).

---

11 This is a possibility if the directors authorise a person to sign a deed: e.g. for private companies limited by shares see Sched. 1, art. 50, for private companies limited by guarantee see Sched. 2, art. 36 and for public companies see Sched. 3, art. 81 of the Companies (Model Articles) Regulations 2007 (currently in draft).
12 This is a possibility if the directors authorise a person to sign a deed under art. 101 of unamended Table A, CA 1985.

Format for transfers for registered land, etc. by a company registered under CA 1985 (or CA 2006), or an unregistered company, using its common seal[13]

The common seal of [*name of company*] was affixed in the presence of:	[common seal of company]
_____	_____
Signature of director	Signature of secretary

Where a company permits a person who is not a director or secretary to affix the seal,[14] the Land Registry may ask for evidence that the person attesting the affixing of the seal is duly authorised to do so by the company's articles of association, and where the authority depends on a decision of the directors of the company, a certified copy of the board resolution of the directors may need to be provided.[15]

Format for transfers for registered land, etc. by a company registered under CA 1985 (or CA 2006), or an unregistered company, without using a common seal[16]

Signed as a deed by [*name of company*] acting by a director in the presence of:	Signature of director (signature, name, address and description of attesting witness)

Or:

Signed as a deed by [*name of company*] acting by [a director and its secretary] [two directors]	(signature) Director (signature) [Secretary] [Director]

The Land Registry will require additional evidence that a deed has been duly executed by a company where a document does not have the common seal of the company and purports to be executed on behalf of the company by signatories who are described otherwise than as a director or secretary or two

---

13 Land Registration Rules 2003, r.206(3), and Sched. 9, Form C. As to when this form of *signature block* must be used see **section 14.15**. This form of execution will ensure that the purchaser is protected by LPA 1925, s.74(1).

14 Such as provided in the default articles of association (art. 101, Table A, CA 1985).

15 *Land Registry Practice Guide 8*, 'Execution of Deeds', s.4.1, April 2008 .

16 Land Registration Rules 2003, r.206(3), and Sched. 9, Form D and *Land Registry Practice Guide 8*, 'Execution of Deeds', s.4.2, April 2008. As to when this form of *signature block* must be used see **section 14.15**.

directors. If the evidence is not forthcoming, then the Land Registry will require that the deed is executed following the procedure laid out in CA 2006, s.44(4).[17]

Format for transfers for registered land, etc. by a company registered under CA 1985 (or CA 2006), or an unregistered company, using its common seal and where execution is by a director or a secretary that is also a company[18]

Executed as a deed by affixing the common seal of [*name of company*] in the presence of a director and [*name of individual*] duly authorised by [*name of corporate director/secretary*] to attest the affixing of the seal on its behalf as [director] [secretary] of [*executing company*]	[common seal of company]

_____	_____
Signature of director	Signature of [director] [secretary]

Format for transfers for registered land, etc. by a company registered under CA 1985 (or CA 2006), or an unregistered company, without using a common seal, and where execution is by a director or a secretary that is also a company[19]

Signed as a deed by [*executing company*] acting by a director and [*name of individual*] duly authorised by [*name of corporate director/secretary*] to sign on its behalf as [director] [secretary] of [*executing company*]	(signature) Director (signature) On behalf of [Secretary] [Director]

Or:

---

17 *Land Registry Practice Guide 8*, 'Execution of Deeds', s.4.2, April 2008.
18 This form of execution will ensure that the purchaser is protected by LPA 1925, s.74(1).
19 Although this form of *signature block* is not specified by Land Registration Rules 2003, r.206(3), and Sched. 9, the Land Registry suggests this form of signature should be used (and adapted as is necessary): *Land Registry Practice Guide 8*, 'Execution of Deeds', s.4.4, April 2008. As to when this form of *signature block* must be used, see **section 14.15**.

Signed as a deed by
[*name of company*] duly
authorised by [*name of
corporate director*] to sign
on its behalf as director of
[*executing company*] in
the presence of:

Signature of director
(signature, name, address and
description of attesting witness)

Format for transfers for registered land, etc. by a company registered under CA 1985, or an unregistered company, without using a common seal, and where execution is by a director or a secretary on behalf of two or more companies[20]

Signed as a deed by
[*names of executing
companies*] by [*name of
first individual signing as
director*] being a director
of each of the executing
companies and [*name of
second individual*] being
[a director] [the secretary]
of each of the executing
companies

Signature of director of first
executing company

Signature of [secretary] [director] of first
executing company

Signature of director of second
executing company

Signature of [secretary] [director]
of second executing company

Or:

Signed as a deed by
[*names of executing
companies*] acting by
[*name of director*] being
director of each of the
executing companies in
the presence of:

Signature of director of first
executing company

Signature of director of second
executing company

Signature of witness

Name (in BLOCK CAPITALS)

Address

20 See *Land Registry Practice Guide 8*, 'Execution of Deeds', 4.4, April 2008.

(Applicable from April 2008 to take account of the new method of signing available to companies under CA 2006, s.44(2)(b)) **Format for transfers for registered land, etc. by a company registered under CA 1985 or CA 2006, or an unregistered company, without using its common seal**

Signed as a deed by	Signature of director
[*name of company*] by	
a director in the presence of:	_____
Signature of witness	_____
Name (in BLOCK CAPITALS)	_____
Address	_____

4.4 TYPE OF STATEMENT, AFFIRMATION OR OATH THAT MUST BE MADE WHEN THE DOCUMENT IS SIGNED/EXECUTED

None.

4.5 (PROFESSIONAL) PERSONS WHO MUST BE PRESENT WHEN THE DOCUMENT IS SIGNED/EXECUTED AND THEIR ROLE

None.

4.6 HOW ARE ATTACHMENTS/SCHEDULES TO THE MAIN DOCUMENT DEALT WITH?

By convention, attachments are placed before the *executed as a deed* clause and the *signature block*. Other common terms used are 'schedules', 'annexes' or 'appendices' and, if there is more than one, each one is numbered: 'schedule 1', 'schedule 2', etc. References in the other parts of the deed to an attachment or schedule are usually expressed in the following terms, e.g.: 'as set out in schedule [1] [to this deed]'.

More modern drafting practice (particularly in some commercial contracts) sets out attachments/schedules after the *executed as a deed* clause and the *signature block*.

4.7 FEES CHARGED BY THE PROFESSIONAL PERSON

None.

Points to note

1. With the coming into force of CA 2006 there are now two equally valid alternative methods of signing deeds:
   (a) a director signing the deed in the presence of a witness (who attests the director's signature); or
   (b) two directors or a director and the company secretary signing the deed.

   It appears that irrespective of the number of directors or whether or not the company has a company secretary, a company can choose either method of signing a deed. Note that only public companies need to have a company secretary.

2. Where two directors or a director and the company secretary are signing:
   (a) there appears to be no requirement that they need to be in each other's presence when they sign the deed; and
   (b) one of them is not acting as a witness to the other's signature (as required when one director signs a deed (needing the presence of a witness)).

3. Where a document is signed in accordance with (1) above *and* states (in whatever words) that it is executed by the company then the document has the same effect as if executed under the common seal of the company (CA 2006, s.44(4)).

4. If a person is signing a document in more than one capacity, she needs to sign in each of her capacities for the document to be considered duly signed (CA 2006, s.44(6)).

5. Where:
   (a) a document is being signed by a director and/or secretary; and
   (b) the holder of those offices is another company, then
   any reference to a document being signed by a director or secretary is a reference to the document being signed by a person authorised by the other company for the purposes of CA 2006, s.44.

6. The *executed as a deed* clause and the *signature block* should normally be kept together on one page (where possible). In particular, the *signature block* should not be split over two pages but if the *signature block* will run over more than one page (i.e. where there are several parties and the modern format is used), then the *signature block* should be separated at a logical place (e.g. all the wording for a particular party being kept together).

7. For deeds executed by the company there is a presumption as to delivery: delivery of a deed takes place on execution, unless the contrary intention is proved.

   The normal practice of stating that deeds are delivered upon signature needs to be handled with care in light of this presumption. A deed dated and signed will be considered delivered, which may not be the intention of one or more of the parties to the deed. Commercial parties may not be familiar with the practice of signing a document and agreeing a date for the document which will be added by hand which will be the date when the deed is delivered. Also needing consideration is how delivery takes place, whether in escrow (the deed does not take effect until some condition is fulfilled – and the deed is irrevocable) or the document is given to another person who is authorised to deliver it at the appropriate time (the deed is not delivered – and can be recalled).

8. In favour of a purchaser, a document signed in accordance with the alternative methods in (1) above is deemed to have been duly executed by a company.[21]

9. The words 'described as a deed' do not always mean that a document has to contain the word 'deed' in it. Other words which describe the document or how it is signed or executed could be used. For example, the document could be described as a type of document which in the circumstances can only be a deed, such as a conveyance, a mortgage or a lease of real property, or a grant of a power of attorney.

10. If a deed is dated at the top of its front page then the date does not have to be repeated in the *executed as a deed* clause or the *signature block*.

11. The date inserted in the deed is the date when the deed is delivered, which may be different from the date when the deed was signed, witnessed and attested. The *executed as a deed* clause or the *signature block* should be carefully considered when drafting a deed to allow for situations when a deed is not intended to have effect when it is signed, witnessed and attested.

12. Where a deed is not delivered when it is signed, the deed might commence with the following words:

THIS DEED delivered as a deed on _____ 200[. . .]

or add a reference to the date of delivery in the *executed as a deed* clause as evidence of delivery.

13. A deed delivered in escrow is dated on the date it is signed and delivered in escrow and not the date when the condition is fulfilled.[22]

---

21 'Purchaser' means a purchaser for valuable consideration and includes a lessee, mortgagee or other person who for valuable consideration acquires an interest in property.
22 This statement is not correct for stamp duty purposes, where the date of delivery is the date when the condition is fulfilled: SA 1891, s.122(1A).

CHAPTER 5

Execution of a deed by a limited liability partnership[1]

CHECKLIST

• Should the document be a deed:
   – is it required to be in the form of a deed at all? or
   – is it conventional for it to be in the form of a deed? or
   – is it desirable for it to be in the form of a deed because of the underlying transaction or event?
See **section 14.15**.
 	
• Are the person(s) making it or the parties to it correctly described? Are all:
   – the persons who are placed under an obligation; or
   – the parties to a contract
named in the document?
 	
• Is the deed required to be in a particular or specified form? See **section 14.15**.
 	
• Ensure that the document states on its face that it is intended to be a deed.
 	
• Has the document been read by, or fully and accurately explained to, the one or two members who are to execute the deed?
 	
• Is the deed to be delivered immediately on being signed?:
   – if not ('delivered in escrow'), add the necessary conditions to the deed, and check that it is not expressed to be delivered on execution;
   – determine how and by whom the deed is to be delivered on signature.
 	
• The document is executed by:
 	
(likely to apply until October 2009) if the limited liability partnership does not use, or have, a common seal

---

1 Formed under the Limited Liability Partnerships Act 2000 (LLPA 2000). Note that the provisions governing the signing of documents for limited liability partnerships are closely modelled on or expressly incorporate the provisions of CA 1985, and it is assumed that relevant provisions of CA 2006 will be similarly utilised for limited liability partnerships. At the time material for this book was prepared, the government was still consulting on the extent to which the law concerning limited liability partnerships would be altered other than through a straightforward implementation of the relevant provisions of CA 2006. These proposals are set out in **Chapter 17**. A key effect of this timetable is that the changes to be made to the way that companies sign documents from April 2008 will not apply to limited liability partnerships until October 2009.

- two members signing the document; or

if the limited liability partnership does have a common seal, and wishes to use it, and the provisions in the partnership agreement relating to the use of the common seal are the same as in Table A in their unamended form[2]

the fixing of the common seal of the limited liability partnership; and then:
- two members; or
- a person (previously authorised by the directors)
signing the document.

(likely to apply from October 2009) if the limited liability partnership does not use, or have, a common seal

- a member in the presence of a witness (who attests the member's signature) signing the document; or

if the limited liability partnership does have a common seal, and wishes to use it, and the provisions in the partnership agreement relating to the use of the common seal are the same as in the model articles of association under CA 2006

the fixing of the common seal of the limited liability partnership; and then:
- a member in the presence of a witness (who attests the member's signature); or
- a person (previously authorised by the directors)
signing the document; or

if the limited liability partnership does have a common seal, and wishes to use it, and the provisions in the partnership agreement relating to the use of the common seal are the same as in Table A under CA 1985 in their unamended form

the fixing of the common seal of the limited liability partnership; and then:
- two members; or
- a person (previously authorised by the directors)
signing the document.

- The deed is then delivered.

- Is the deed intended to be used for a transaction or event taking place in another country or is one or more of the persons named in it or parties to it based, incorporated or regulated in another country? If so:
  - does the deed need to be translated into the language of the other country (or does at least one copy of the deed need to be in that language)?
  - if the deed does need to be translated, must it be translated by an official or properly qualified translator?
  - does the deed need to be registered with any governmental or regulatory authorities in the other country?

---

2 If the limited liability partnership has entered into a limited liability partnership agreement which contains a provision the same as e.g. the Companies (Model Articles) Regulations 2007, Sched. 1, art. 50 (currently in draft).

> – is the deed of a type which needs to be drawn up and/or signed before a notary?[3]
> – if the deed is being signed in England and Wales, does it need to be notarised and/or legalised after it has been signed?

5.1 FORM/STRUCTURE OF THE DOCUMENT

A document intended to be a deed must be described as a deed or indicate that it is to be executed as a deed.

Described as a deed

Commencement of the document

A document might commence as follows to indicate at once that it is intended as a deed:

THIS DEED dated _____ 200[. . .] is made by and between:

(1) [*name and address of the first party*]; and
(2) [*name and address of the second party*]

Wording in the body of the document

The text indicating that the document is intended to be a deed can also be located in the body of the document (instead of or in addition to at the commencement of the document). Such text often signifies the start of the main provisions of the deed:

Now this deed witnesses as follows

'Executed as a deed' clause[4]

As an alternative to (or in addition to) describing the document as a deed, the document can state that it is being executed as a deed.

---

3 If the limited liability partnership has entered into a limited liability partnership agreement which contains a provision the same as art. 101 of the Table A articles of association for a company.
4 Formally known as the 'testimonium' clause.

Traditional format – a limited liability partnership executing a deed following a resolution of its members

IN WITNESS of which [*name of limited liability partnership*] has duly executed this deed pursuant to a resolution of its members duly passed [and has delivered it upon dating it] [this [*day*] day of [*month and year*]] [the day and year first above written]

Traditional format – a limited liability partnership executing a deed – where there is no need for a resolution of its members

IN WITNESS of which [*name of limited liability partnership*] has duly executed this deed [and has delivered it upon dating it] [this [*day*] day of [*month and year*]] [the day and year first above written]

Traditional format – a limited liability partnership using its common seal following a resolution of its members

IN WITNESS of which [*name of limited liability partnership*] pursuant to a resolution of its members duly passed has caused its common seal to be affixed to this deed [and has delivered it upon dating it] [this [*day*] day of [*month and year*]] [the day and year first above written]

Traditional format – where there is no need for a resolution to use the common seal of the limited liability partnership

IN WITNESS of which [*name of limited liability partnership*] has caused its common seal to be affixed to this deed [and has delivered it upon dating it] [this [*day*] day of [*month and year*]] [the day and year first above written]

Modern format – execution without a resolution of the members

EXECUTED as a **DEED** [and **DELIVERED**] by the above-named [*name of limited liability partnership*] and signed by [one member][5] [two members]

Modern format – execution following a resolution of the members

EXECUTED as a **DEED** [and **DELIVERED**] by [*name of limited liability partnership*] pursuant to a resolution of its members duly passed[, a certified copy of which was delivered upon the execution of this deed]

---

5 This option is likely to apply from October 2009.

Modern format – further alternative

    EXECUTED as a **DEED** by the parties [and delivered] on the date first above written

5.2   FORM/STRUCTURE OF THE SIGNATURE BLOCK[6]

Likely to apply until October 2009

Modern format – for a limited liability partnership not using, or having, a common seal

    SIGNED [and **DELIVERED**] as a Deed by [*name of limited liability partnership*] acting through two members

_____	_____
Member's signature	Member's signature

Traditional format – for a limited liability partnership not using, or having, a common seal

    EXECUTED [and **DELIVERED**] as a **DEED** by [*name of limited liability partnership*] acting through two of its members: } (signatures of members)

Traditional format – if the limited liability partnership uses its common seal

    EXECUTED [and **DELIVERED**] as a **DEED** and **THE COMMON SEAL OF** [*name of limited liability partnership*] was affixed in the presence of: } (common seal) (signatures of two members)

Traditional format – if the limited liability partnership does have a common seal – by a person authorised by the members[7]

    EXECUTED [and **DELIVERED**] as a **DEED** by [*name of limited liability partnership*] acting through a person authorised by the members } (signature of the person authorised by the members)

---

6 Formally known as the 'attestation' clause.
7 This is a possibility if the members authorise a person to sign a deed and the limited liability partnership has a provision in a limited liability partnership agreement similar to art. 101 of the unamended Table A articles of association.

Format for transfers of registered land, etc. by a limited liability partnership[8]

Signed as a deed by [*name*	(signature)
of limited liability	
partnership] acting by two	Member
members	(signature)
	Member

Likely to apply from October 2009

Modern format – for a limited liability partnership not using, or having, a common seal

SIGNED [and **DELIVERED**] as a **DEED** by [*name*	}	Witnessed by:
of limited liability partnership] acting through		
one member		
Member's signature	Signature	
	Description	
	Address	

Or:

SIGNED [and **DELIVERED**] as a **DEED** by [*name of limited liability partnership*] acting through two members

_____   _____
Member's signature   Member's signature

Traditional format – for a limited liability partnership not using, or having, a common seal

EXECUTED [and **DELIVERED**] as a **DEED** by [*name*	}	(signature of member)
of limited liability partnership] acting through		
one of its members:		

(signature, name, address and description of attesting witness)

Traditional format – if the limited liability partnership uses its common seal (using model articles of association, CA 2006)

EXECUTED [and **DELIVERED**] as a **DEED** and	}	(common seal)
THE COMMON SEAL of [*name of limited liability*		(signature of
partnership] affixed in the presence of:		member)

(signature, name, address and description of attesting witness)

---

8 Land Registration Rules 2003, r.206(3), and Sched. 9, Form F. As to when this form of *signature block* must be used, see **section 14.15**.

Traditional format – if the limited liability partnership does have a common seal – by a person authorised by the members

> **EXECUTED** [and **DELIVERED**] as a **DEED** by [*name of limited liability partnership*] acting through a person authorised by the members }
> (signature of the person authorised by its members)
>
> (signature, name, address and description of attesting witness)

Traditional format – if the limited liability partnership uses its common seal (and uses Table A, CA 1985)

> **EXECUTED** [and **DELIVERED**] as a **DEED** and **THE COMMON SEAL OF** [*name of limited liability partnership*] affixed in the presence of: }
> (common seal)
> (signatures of two members)

Traditional format – if the limited liability partnership does have a common seal – by a person authorised by the members (using Table A, CA 1985)

> **EXECUTED** [and **DELIVERED**] as a Deed by [*name of limited liability partnership*] acting through a person authorised by the members }
> (signature of the person authorised by the members)
>
> (signature, name, address and description of attesting witness)

5.3 TYPE OF STATEMENT, AFFIRMATION OR OATH THAT MUST BE MADE WHEN THE DOCUMENT IS SIGNED/EXECUTED

None.

5.4 (PROFESSIONAL) PERSONS WHO MUST BE PRESENT WHEN THE DOCUMENT IS SIGNED/EXECUTED AND THEIR ROLE

None.

5.5 HOW ARE ATTACHMENTS/SCHEDULES TO THE MAIN DOCUMENT DEALT WITH?

By convention, attachments are placed before the *executed as a deed* clause and the *signature block*. Other common terms used are 'schedules', 'annexes' or 'appendices' and, if there is more than one, each one is numbered: 'schedule 1', 'schedule 2', etc. References in the other parts of the deed to an attachment or schedule are usually expressed in the following terms, e.g.: 'as set out in schedule [1] [to this deed]'.

More modern drafting practice (particularly in some commercial contracts) sets out attachments/schedules after the *executed as a deed* clause and the *signature block*.

5.6   FEES CHARGED BY THE PROFESSIONAL PERSON

None.

Points to note

1. When the provisions of CA 2006 are applied to limited liability partnerships (likely from October 2009) there will be two equally valid alternative methods of signing deeds:
    (a)   a member signing the deed in the presence of a witness; or
    (b)   two members signing the deed.
    It appears that irrespective of the number of members, the limited liability partnership may adopt either method of signing a deed.
2. When two members sign a deed:
    (a)   there appears to be no requirement that they need to be in each other's presence when they sign the deed; and
    (b)   one of them is not acting as a witness to the other's signature (as required when one member signs a deed).
3. The *executed as a deed* clause and the *signature block* should normally be kept together on one page (where possible). In particular, the *signature block* should not be split over two pages, but if the *signature block* will run over more than one page (i.e. there are several parties and the modern format is used) then the *signature block* should be separated at a logical place (e.g. all the wording for a particular party being kept together).
4. For deeds executed by limited liability partnerships, there are presumptions as to delivery: delivery of a deed takes place on execution, unless the contrary intention is proved.[9]

    The normal practice of stating that deeds are delivered upon signature needs to be handled with care because of this presumption. A deed dated and signed will be considered delivered, which may not be the intention of one or more of the parties to the deed. Commercial parties may not be familiar with the practice of signing a document and agreeing a date for the document which will be added by hand which will be the date when the deed is delivered. Also needing consideration is how delivery takes place, whether in escrow (the deed does not take effect until some condition is fulfilled – and the deed is irrevocable) or the

---

9 'Purchaser' means a purchaser for valuable consideration and includes a lessee, mortgagee or other person who for valuable consideration acquires an interest in property.

document is given to another person who is authorised to deliver it at the appropriate time (the deed is not delivered – and can be recalled).

5.   The words 'described as a deed' do not always mean that a document has to contain the word 'deed' in it. Other words which describe the document or how it is signed or executed could be used. For example, the document could be described as a type of document which in the circumstances can only be a deed, such as a conveyance, a mortgage or a lease of real property, or a grant of a power of attorney.

6.   If a deed is dated at the top of its front page then the date does not have to be repeated in the *executed as a deed* clause or the *signature block*.

7.   The date inserted in the deed is the date when the deed is delivered, which may be different from the date when the deed was signed, witnessed and attested. The *executed as a deed* clause or the *signature block* should be carefully considered when drafting a deed to allow for situations when a deed is not intended to have effect when it is signed, witnessed and attested.

8.   Where a deed is not delivered when it is signed, the deed might commence with the following words:

THIS DEED delivered as a deed on _____ 200[. . .]

or add a reference to the date of delivery in the *executed as a deed* clause as evidence of delivery.

9.   A deed delivered in escrow is dated on the date it is signed and delivered in escrow and not the date when the condition is fulfilled.[10]

---

10 This proposition is not correct for stamp duty purposes, where the date of delivery is the date when the condition is fulfilled: SA 1891, s.122(1A).

CHAPTER 6

Execution of a deed by a company incorporated outside Great Britain[1]

CHECKLIST

- Should the document be a deed:
    - is it required to be in the form of a deed at all? or
    - is it conventional for it to be in the form of a deed? or
    - is it desirable for it to be in the form of a deed because of the underlying transaction or event?
  See **section 14.15**.

- Are the person(s) making it or the parties to it correctly described?

- Are all:
    - the persons who are placed under an obligation; or
    - the parties to a contract
  named in the document?

- Is the deed required to be in a particular or specified form? See **section 14.15**.

- Does the document state on its face that it is intended to be a deed?

- Has the deed been read by, or fully and accurately explained to, the person(s), the director(s) and/or the secretary who are to execute it?

- Is the deed to be delivered immediately on it being signed?
    - if not ('delivered in escrow'), add the necessary conditions to the deed, and check that it is not expressed to be delivered on execution;
    - determine how and by whom the deed is to be delivered.

  The document is executed as follows:

  (likely to apply when the relevant provisions of CA 2006 are implemented to overseas companies) in a manner permitted for the execution of documents

---

1 The material in this chapter is prepared on the basis that the draft regulations concerning overseas companies (Overseas Companies Regulations 2008) are passed in the same form as the December 2007 draft available at the time material for this book was prepared (a new draft was promised in 'Spring 2008'). CA 2006, s.44 governs the way companies can sign documents (including deeds) from 6 April 2008, but this does not apply to overseas companies. The new regime for overseas companies (which will apply CA 2006, s.44 and other relevant provisions to overseas companies) will come into force in October 2009 (see draft Overseas Companies Regulations 2008, reg. 1). It must therefore be assumed that the provisions of CA 1985, s.36A will continue to apply until October 2009.

by the laws of the territory in which the foreign company is incorporated, for example, by:

- one or more directors of the foreign company; or
- one or more officers or employees of the foreign company

signing the document;

or:

(likely to apply until October 2009) if the usual provisions of CA 1985 are to apply and if the company does not use, or have, a common seal

- a director and the company secretary; or
- two directors

signing the document;

or:

if the usual provisions of CA 1985 are to apply and if the company does have a common seal and wishes to use it, and the default provision relating to use of the common seal in Table A applies (or its equivalent)[2]

the fixing of the common seal of the company; and then:

- a director and the company secretary; or
- two directors; or
- a person (previously authorised by the directors)

signing the document;

or:

(likely to apply from October 2009, on implementation of the relevant provisions of CA 2006), if the usual provisions of CA 2006 are to apply and if the company does not use, or have, a common seal

- a director in the presence of a witness (who attests the director's signature); or
- a director and the company secretary (if the company has, or is required to have, a company secretary); or
- two directors

signing the document;

or:

if the usual provisions of CA 1985 are to apply and the company does have a common seal and wishes to use it, and the default provision relating to the use of the common seal in the model articles of association under CA 2006 applies

the fixing of the common seal of the company; and then signature of the document by:

- a director in the presence of a witness (who attests the director's signature); or
- a person (previously authorised by the directors) in the presence of a witness.

● The deed is then delivered.

---

2 If the company utilises the unamended provision relating to seals in the Table A articles of association (art. 101).

- Is the deed intended to be used for a transaction or event taking place in another country or is one or more of the persons named in it or parties to it based, incorporated or regulated in another country? If so:
  - does the deed need to be translated into the language of the other country (or does at least one copy of the deed need to be in that language)?
  - if the deed does need to be translated, must it be translated by an official or properly qualified translator?
  - does the deed need to be registered with any governmental or regulatory authorities in the other country?
  - is the deed of a type which needs to be drawn up and/or signed before a notary?
  - if the deed is being signed in England and Wales, does it need to be notarised and/or legalised after it has been signed?

6.1   FORM/STRUCTURE OF THE DOCUMENT

A document intended to be a deed must be described as a deed or indicate that it is to be executed as a deed.

Described as a deed

Commencement of the document

A document might commence as follows to indicate at once that it is intended as a deed:

THIS DEED dated _____ 200[. . .] is made by and between:

(1)   [*name and address of the first party*]; and
(2)   [*name and address of the second party*]

Wording in the body of the document

The text indicating that the document is intended to be a deed can also be located in the body of the document (instead of or in addition to at the commencement of the document). Such text often signifies the start of the main provisions of the deed:

Now this deed witnesses as follows

'Executed as a deed' clause[3]

As an alternative to (or in addition to) describing the document as a deed, the document can state that it is being executed as a deed.

---

3 Formally known as the 'testimonium' clause.

Traditional format – a company executing a deed in a manner permitted by the laws of the territory in which it is incorporated

IN WITNESS of which [*name of company*] has duly executed this deed in a manner permitted by the laws of [*name of country in which foreign company is incorporated*] [and has delivered it upon dating it] [this [*day*] day of [*month and year*]] [the day and year first above written]

Traditional format – a company executing a deed following a resolution of the board of directors

IN WITNESS of which [*name of company*] has duly executed this deed pursuant to a resolution of its board of directors duly passed [and has delivered it upon dating it] [this [*day*] day of [*month and year*]] [the day and year first above written]

Traditional format – a company executing a deed where there is no need for a resolution of the board of directors

IN WITNESS of which [*name of company*] has duly executed this deed [and has delivered it upon dating it] [this [*day*] day of [*month and year*]] [the day and year first above written]

Traditional format – a company using its common seal following a resolution of the board of directors

IN WITNESS of which [*name of company*] pursuant to a resolution of its board of directors duly passed has caused its common seal to be affixed to this deed [and has delivered it upon dating it] [this [*day*] day of [*month and year*]] [the day and year first above written]

Traditional format – where there is no need for a resolution to use the common seal of the company

IN WITNESS of which [*name of company*] has caused its common seal to be affixed to this deed [and has delivered it upon dating it] [this [*day*] day of [*month and year*]] [the day and year first above written]

Modern format – signature block stating it is executed in a manner permitted by the laws of the territory in which the foreign company is incorporated

EXECUTED as a **DEED** [and delivered] by [*name of company*] and signed by [*status of peson(s) who are signing the document*] as permitted by the laws of [*name of the country in which the foreign company is incorporated*]

Modern format – execution without a resolution of the board of directors

> **EXECUTED** as a **DEED** [and delivered] by the above-named [*name of company*] and signed by [director][4] [two directors] [a director and the secretary]

Modern format – execution following a resolution of the board of directors

> **EXECUTED** as a **DEED** [and delivered] by [*name of company*] pursuant to a resolution of its board of directors duly passed, a certified copy of which was delivered upon the execution of this deed

Modern format – further alternative

> **EXECUTED** as a **DEED** by the parties [and delivered] on the date first above written

6.2 FORM/STRUCTURE OF THE SIGNATURE BLOCK[5]

In a manner permitted for the execution of documents by the laws of the territory in which the foreign company is incorporated

> **SIGNED** [and **DELIVERED**] as a **DEED** by [*name of company*] through [*status of person(s) signing*] [who is] [who are] permitted to sign in accordance with the laws of [*name of the country in which the foreign company is incorporated*]

_____   _____

[*status of person*]'s signature   [if a second person is signing – *status of person*]'s signature

For a company not using, or having, a common seal – modern format

> **SIGNED** [and **DELIVERED**] as a **DEED** by [*name of company*] acting through a director and the company secretary

_____   _____

Director's signature   Company secretary's signature

Or:

> **SIGNED** [and **DELIVERED**] as a **DEED** by [*name of company*] acting through two of its directors

_____   _____

Director's signature   Director's signature

---

4 This choice is available from October 2009.
5 Formally known as the 'attestation' clause.

Or *(from October 2009 on application of CA 2006, s.44 to overseas companies):*

SIGNED [and **DELIVERED**] as a **DEED** by   Director's signature
[*name of company*] acting through a director

(signature, name, address and description of attesting witness)

For a company not using, or having, a common seal – traditional format

EXECUTED [and **DELIVERED**] as a **DEED** by [*name*   }
of company] acting through two of its directors   }   (signatures of directors)

Or:

EXECUTED [and **DELIVERED**] as a **DEED** by   }
[*name of company*] acting through a   }   (signatures of the director
director and the company secretary   }   and the company secretary)

Or *(from October 2009 on implementation of CA 2006, s.44 to overseas companies):*

EXECUTED [and **DELIVERED**] as a **DEED** by   }
[*name of company*] acting through a   }   (signature of the director)
director in the presence of: }

(signature, name, address and description of attesting witness)

If the company uses its common seal – by a director and the company secretary or two directors (until October 2009)

EXECUTED [and **DELIVERED**] as a **DEED**   }   (common seal)
and **THE COMMON SEAL OF** [*name of*   }   (signatures of two directors or
company*] was affixed in the presence of: }   a director and the company
                                                      secretary)

If the company does have a common seal – by a person authorised by the directors (until October 2009)[6]

EXECUTED [and **DELIVERED**] as a **DEED**   }
[and **THE COMMMON SEAL OF** [*name of*   }   (common seal)
company*] affixed in the presence of a   }   (signature of the person authorised
person authorised by the directors   }   by the directors)

6 This is a possibility if the directors authorise a person to sign a deed under art. 101 of unamended Table A.

If the company uses its common seal – by a director and the company secretary or two directors (for overseas companies using the model articles of association, CA 2006)

EXECUTED [and **DELIVERED**] as a **DEED** and **THE COMMON SEAL OF** [*name of company*] affixed in the presence of:

}

(common seal)

(signature, name, address and description of attesting witness)

(signature of a director)

If the company does have a common seal – by a person authorised by the directors (for overseas companies using model articles of association, CA 2006)

EXECUTED [and **DELIVERED**] as a **DEED** by [*name of company*] acting through a person authorised by the directors

}

(common seal)
(signature of the person authorised by the directors)

(signature, name, address and description of attesting witness)

6.3 TYPE OF STATEMENT, AFFIRMATION OR OATH THAT MUST BE MADE WHEN THE DOCUMENT IS SIGNED/EXECUTED

None.

6.4 (PROFESSIONAL) PERSONS WHO MUST BE PRESENT WHEN THE DOCUMENT IS SIGNED/EXECUTED AND THEIR ROLE

None.

6.5 HOW ARE ATTACHMENTS/SCHEDULES TO THE MAIN DOCUMENT DEALT WITH?

By convention, attachments are placed before the *executed as a deed* clause and the *signature block*. Other common terms used are 'schedules', 'annexes' or 'appendices' and, if there is more than one, each one is numbered: 'schedule 1', 'schedule 2', etc. References in the other parts of the deed to an attachment or schedule are usually expressed in the following terms, e.g.: 'as set out in schedule [1] [to this deed]'.

More modern drafting practice (particularly in some commercial contracts) sets out attachments/schedules after the *executed as a deed* clause and the *signature block*.

6.6 FEES CHARGED BY THE PROFESSIONAL PERSON

None.

Points to note

1. With the coming into force of CA 2006 (for overseas companies likely to be from October 2009) there will be two equally valid alternative methods of signing deeds:
    (a) a director signing the deed in the presence of a witness; or
    (b) two directors or a director and the company secretary signing the deed.
    It appears that irrespective of the number of directors or whether or not the company has a company secretary, a company can choose either method of signing a deed. Note that only public companies need to have a company secretary.
2. Where two directors or a director and the secretary sign a deed:
    (a) there appears to be no requirement that they need to be in each other's presence when they sign the deed; and
    (b) one of them is not acting as a witness to the other's signature (as required when one director signs a deed (needing the presence of a witness)).
3. The *executed as a deed* clause and the *signature block* should normally be kept together on one page (where possible). In particular, the *signature block* should not be split over two pages but if the *signature block* will run over more than one page (i.e. there are several parties and the modern format is used), then the *signature block* should be separated at a logical place (e.g. all the wording for a particular party being kept together).
4. For deeds executed by a company there is a presumption that delivery takes place on execution, unless the contrary intention is proved.[7]
    The normal practice of stating that deeds are delivered upon signature needs to be handled with care in light of this presumption. A deed dated and signed will be considered delivered, which may not be the intention of one or more of the parties to the deed. Commercial parties may not be familiar with the practice of signing a document and agreeing a date for the document which will be added by hand which will be

---

7 This proposition is not correct for stamp duty purposes, where the date of delivery is the date when the condition is fulfilled: SA 1891, s.122(1A).

the date when the deed is delivered. Also needing consideration is how delivery takes place, whether in escrow (the deed does not take effect until some condition is fulfilled – and the deed is irrevocable) or the document is given to another person who is authorised to deliver it at the appropriate time (the deed is not delivered – and can be recalled).

5. The words 'described as a deed' do not always mean that a document has to contain the word 'deed' in it. Other words which describe the document or how it is signed or executed could be used. For example, the document could be described as a type of document which in the circumstances can only be a deed, such as a conveyance, a mortgage or a lease of real property, or a grant of a power of attorney.

6. If a deed is dated at the top of its front page then the date does not have to be repeated in the *executed as a deed* clause or the *signature block*.

7. The date inserted in the deed is the date when the deed is delivered, which may be different from the date when the deed was signed, witnessed and attested. The *executed as a deed* clause or the *signature block* should be carefully considered when drafting a deed to allow for situations when a deed is not intended to have effect when it is signed, witnessed and attested.

8. Where a deed is not delivered when it is signed, the deed might commence with the following words:

THIS DEED delivered as a deed on _____ 200[. . .]

or add a reference to the date of delivery in the *executed as a deed* clause as evidence of delivery.

9. A deed delivered in escrow is dated on the date it is signed and delivered in escrow and not the date when the condition is fulfilled.[8]

---

8 'Purchaser' means a purchaser for valuable consideration and includes a lessee, mortgagee or other person who for valuable consideration acquires an interest in property.

CHAPTER 7

Execution of a deed by a local authority[1]

CHECKLIST

- Should the document be a deed:
    - is it required to be in the form of a deed at all? or
    - is it conventional for it to be in the form of a deed? or
    - is it desirable for it to be in the form of a deed because of the underlying transaction or event?

    See **section 14.15**.

- Are the person(s) and/or body/bodies corporate making it or the parties to it correctly described?

- Are all:
    - the persons and body/bodies corporate who are placed under an obligation; or
    - the parties to a contract

    named in the document?

- Is the deed required to be in a particular or specified form? See **section 14.15**.

- Does the document state on its face that it is intended to be a deed?

- Has the document been read by, or fully and accurately explained to, the member(s), officer or member of staff who is or who are to execute the deed?

- Have standing orders, etc.[2] of the local authority been checked as to who can sign the deed and for the correct method of applying the seal of the local authority, such as:
    - is a meeting of the local authority council or governing body[3] required?
    - is the local authority council or governing body required to specifically authorise use of the seal in specific instances?
    - is the seal required to be affixed at a meeting of the local authority council or governing body?

---

1 See **section 19.3** for the meaning of a local authority.

2 The local authority's or corporation's charter, articles, regulations, or standing orders or rules; or, if found in an Act of Parliament, the statute forming the corporation.

3 Often called the council, directors, body (of trustees), committee, etc. or simply a meeting of the members of the local authority.

- – is the seal required to be affixed in the presence of an appropriate official to whom the task of executing the deed has been delegated by a standing order?
- Is the seal required to be affixed in the presence of the person(s) who will sign?
- Are there rules or standing orders which state which officer(s) or member of staff can sign a deed when it concerns a particular type of transaction or event (classified by value, importance, circumstance, etc.)?
- Who among the members of the governing body can sign the deed:
  - – one or more members?
  - – one member and the local authority's secretary?
  - – the secretary alone?
  - – some other person authorised by the local authority council or governing body to sign documents on behalf of the governing body of the local authority? Do they have unlimited authority or have they been given specific authority in a particular instance?
- If the deed is to be executed other than by either:
  - – two members of the local authority council or governing body; or
  - – one member and the body corporate's clerk, secretary or other permanent officer (or deputy),
  will it matter to a purchaser that it will not have the benefit of the statutory assumption that the document is duly executed by the body corporate?
- Who has custody of the seal (normally the secretary to the local authority)?
- Decide whether the deed is to be delivered immediately on it being signed:
  - – if not ('delivered in escrow'), add the necessary conditions to the deed, and check that it is not expressed to be delivered on execution;
  - – determine how and by whom it is to be delivered.
- Affix the seal.
- Does the fact that the seal has been used need to be recorded in a minute or seals book?
- The persons who are required to sign should sign as determined by the constitution.
- The deed is then delivered.
- Is the deed intended to be used for a transaction or event taking place in another country or is one or more of the persons named in it or parties to it based, incorporated or regulated in another country? If so:
  - – does the deed need to be translated into the language of the other country (or does at least one copy of the deed need to be in that language)?
  - – if the deed does need to be translated, must it be translated by an official or properly qualified translator?
  - – does the deed need to be registered with any governmental or regulatory authorities in the other country?
  - – is the deed of a type which needs to be drawn up and/or signed before a notary?[4]

4 For example, a power of attorney intended for use in another country often has to be signed before a notary.

> – if the deed is being signed in England and Wales, does it need to be notarised and/or legalised after it has been signed?

7.1 FORM/STRUCTURE OF THE DOCUMENT

A document intended to be a deed must be described as a deed or indicate that it is to be executed as a deed.

Described as a deed

Commencement of the document

A document might commence as follows to indicate at once that it is intended as a deed:

THIS DEED dated _____ 200[. . .] is made by and between:

(1) [*name and address of first party*]; and
(2) [*name and address of second party*]

Wording in the body of the document

The text indicating that the document is intended to be a deed can also be located in the body of the document (instead of or in addition to at the commencement of the document). Such text often signifies the commencement of the main provisions of the deed:

Now this deed witnesses as follows

'Executed as a deed' clause[5]

As an alternative to (or in addition to) describing the document as a deed, the document can state that it is being executed as a deed.

Traditional format – following a resolution of the governing body

IN WITNESS of which [*name of corporation*] pursuant to a resolution of its [*name of governing body*] duly passed has caused its common seal to be affixed to this deed [and has delivered it upon dating it] [this [*day*] day of [*month and year*]] [the day and year first above written]

---

5 Formally known as the 'testimonium' clause.

Traditional format – where there is no need for a resolution to use the seal of the governing body

> **IN WITNESS** of which [*name of corporation*] has caused its common seal to be affixed to this deed [and has delivered it upon dating it] [this [*day*] day of [*month and year*]] [the day and year first above written]

Modern format

> **EXECUTED** as a **DEED** by the parties [and delivered] on the date first above written

7.2   FORM/STRUCTURE OF THE SIGNATURE BLOCK[6]

Traditional format

> **THE [COMMON] SEAL OF** [*name of local authority*] affixed [pursuant to a resolution of the [*name of local authority council or governing body*]] [in the presence of] [and signed by] [**two members** of the [*name of local authority council or governing body*]]
>
> (seal of the corporation)
> (signature of authorised person(s))

The precise details of who can sign will depend on the local authority's statute, charter, articles, constitution, standing orders, rules, etc.

Words in bold and in brackets: Please see below for possible alternatives to those who might sign:

- **if only one member of the governing body is required to sign**:

  one member of the [*name of local authority council or governing body*]

- **if one member of the governing body and the corporation's secretary are required to sign**:

  one member of the [*name of local authority council or governing body*] and the secretary of the [*name of local authority council or governing body*]

- **if only the secretary is required to sign**:

  the secretary of the [*name of local authority council or governing body*]

- **if a person authorised by the corporation or the governing body is authorised to sign**:

  a person authorised by the [*name of local authority council or governing body*] [*specify specific authority to sign, e.g. name of standing order and date passed*] [to sign by, and on behalf of, the [*name of local authority council or governing body*] [local authority]]

---

6 Formally known as the 'attestation' clause.

Notes:

1. Not all local authorities are required to pass a resolution in order to authorise use of the seal. If not, then the following words can be deleted:

   pursuant to a resolution of the [*name of local authority council or governing body*].

2. Not all constitutions or Acts state that the seal must be affixed in the presence of the person(s) who is or who are to sign. If this is the case, then the words 'in the presence of' could be replaced by 'and signed by'.

3. If the local authority's constitution requires signature of a deed other than under the requirements of LPA 1925, s.74(1), then the presumption of valid execution provided by LPA 1925, s.74(1) may not apply (where either two members of the governing body or one member of the governing body and the secretary, clerk, etc. need to sign). Any purchaser may have to rely on common law provisions only.

Modern format

SIGNED [and **DELIVERED**] as a **DEED** and **THE [COMMON] SEAL OF** [*name of local authority*] affixed [pursuant to a resolution of the [*name of local authority council or governing body*]] [in the presence of] [and signed by] [**two members of the [*name of local authority council or governing body*]**]:

_____

Signature of [*name of **local authority council or** governing body*] member

(seal of the
corporation)

_____

[Signature of [*name of **local authority council or** governing body*] member]

_____

[Signature of [*name of local authority council or governing body*]'s secretary]

The precise details of who can sign will depend on the local authority's statute, charter, articles, constitution, standing orders, rules, etc.

Words in bold and in brackets: Please see below for possible alternatives to those who might sign:

- **if one member of the governing body is required to sign**:

  one member of the [*name of local authority council or governing body*]

- **if one member of the governing body and the corporation's secretary are required to sign**:

  one member of the [*name of local authority council or governing body*] and the secretary of the [*name of local authority council or governing body*]

- **if only the secretary is required to sign**:

  the secretary of the [*name of local authority council or governing body*]

- **if a person authorised by the local authority council or the governing body is authorised to sign**:

  a person authorised by the [*name of local authority council or governing body*] to sign on, and on behalf of, the [local authority]

Notes:

1. Not all local authorities are required to pass a resolution in order to authorise use of the seal. If not, then the following words can be deleted:

    pursuant to a resolution of the [*name of governing body*]

2. Not all constitutions or Acts state that the seal must be affixed in the presence of the person(s) who is or who are to sign. If this is the case, then the words 'in the presence of' could be replaced by 'and signed by'.

3. If the local authority's constitution requires signature of a deed other than under the requirements of LPA 1925, s.74(1), then the presumption of valid execution provided by LPA 1925, s.74(1) may not apply (where either two members of the governing body or one member of the governing body and the secretary, clerk, etc. need to sign). Any purchaser may have to rely on common law provisions only.

7.3   (PROFESSIONAL) PERSONS WHO MUST BE PRESENT WHEN THE DOCUMENT IS SIGNED/EXECUTED AND THEIR ROLE

None.

7.4   HOW ARE ATTACHMENTS/SCHEDULES TO THE MAIN DOCUMENT DEALT WITH?

By convention attachments are placed before the *executed as a deed* clause and the *signature block*. Other common terms used are 'schedules', 'annexes' or 'appendices' and, if there is more than one, each one is numbered: 'schedule 1', 'schedule 2', etc. References in the other parts of the deed to an attachment or schedule are usually expressed in the following terms, e.g.: 'as set out in schedule [1] [to this deed]'.

More modern drafting practice (particularly in some commercial contracts) sets out attachments/schedules after the *executed as a deed* clause and the *signature block*.

7.5   FEES CHARGED BY THE PROFESSIONAL PERSON

None.

Points to note

1. The *executed as a deed* clause and the *signature block* should normally be kept together on one page (where possible). In particular, the *signature block* should never be split over two pages. If the *signature block* runs over more than one page (i.e. there are several parties and the modern format is used), then the *signature block* should be separated at a logical place (e.g. all the wording for a particular party being kept together).

2. A 'signature' can mean making no more than a mark (such as an 'X'). It can also include signing with a pencil, or applying a rubber stamp which contains an exact copy of the individual's real signature (although these last two practices should be used with care – and are practices which may not be acceptable to everyone).

3. The words 'described as a deed' do not always mean that a document has to contain the word 'deed' in it. Other words which describe the document or how it is signed or executed could be used. For example, the document could be described as a type of document which in the circumstances can only be a deed (such as a conveyance, mortgage or lease of real property, etc.).

4. If a deed is dated at the top of its front page then the date does not have to be repeated in the *executed as a deed* clause or the *signature block*.

5. The date inserted in the deed is the date when the deed is delivered, which may be different from the date when the deed was signed, witnessed and attested. The *executed as a deed* clause or the *signature block* should be carefully considered when drafting a deed to allow for situations when a deed is not intended to have effect when it is signed, witnessed and attested.

6. Where a deed is not delivered when it is signed, the deed might commence with the following words:

   THIS DEED delivered as a deed on _____ 200[. . .]

   or add a reference to the date of delivery in the *executed as a deed* clause as evidence of delivery.

7. A deed delivered in escrow is dated on the date it is signed and delivered in escrow and not the date when the condition is fulfilled.[7]

8. For the transfer of registered land, etc., the Land Registry:[8]
   (a) requires that corporations aggregate and sole execute deeds under seal, unless the corporation making an application to the Land

---

7 This statement is not correct for stamp duty purposes, where the date of delivery is the date when the condition is fulfilled: SA 1891, s.122(1A).
8 *Land Registry Practice Guide 8*, 'Execution of Deeds', s.6.1, April 2008.

Registry is able to show a specific statutory exemption relating to that corporation;

(b) will accept a deed from a corporation aggregate which has a *signature block* in the prescribed form for a company regulated under CA 1985 which uses a common seal without calling for further evidence (LPA 1925, s.74(1) will be assumed to apply in favour of a purchaser);

(c) will not accept, without further evidence, a deed executed otherwise than in accordance with LPA 1925, s.74(1). In this case the Land Registry will wish to see the legislation or document of incorporation (such as the Royal Charter).[9]

---

9 If the legislation is a public Act, then this is not required to be supplied, just a reference to the appropriate section number(s). Corporations regularly executing deeds can make an arrangement with the Land Registry so that the document of incorporation is lodged with the Land Registry's Commercial Arrangements Section. On subsequent occasions when a deed is executed which needs to be sent to the Land Registry, the document of incorporation will not need to be sent with it.

CHAPTER 8

Execution of a deed by a partnership[1]

CHECKLIST

- Should the document be a deed:
  - is it required to be in the form of a deed at all? or
  - is it conventional for it to be in the form of a deed? or
  - is it desirable for it to be in the form of a deed because of the underlying transaction or event?

  See **section 14.15**.

- Are the person(s) making it or the parties to it correctly described?

- If not all the partners are to execute the deed, then:
  - have the partners who are to execute the deed been given *explicit* authority to execute the deed?
  - has the authority to be given by deed?
  - is the deed correctly worded so that it cannot be interpreted as binding only those partners who have executed it?

- Is the receiver of the deed prepared to accept it if all the partners have not executed it?

- Are all:
  - the persons who are placed under an obligation; or
  - the parties to a contract

  named in the document?

- Is the deed required to be in a particular or specified form? See **section 14.15**.

- Ensure that the document states on its face that it is intended to be a deed.

- Has the document been read by, or fully and accurately explained to, the partner(s) who are to execute the deed?

- Is the deed to be delivered immediately on it being signed?
  - if not ('delivered in escrow'), add the necessary conditions to the deed, and check that it is not expressed to be delivered on execution;
  - determine how and by whom the deed is to be delivered.

---

1 This chapter only provides a summary of the methods of execution for individuals, corporations and companies. For more detail the relevant chapters should be consulted.

Execution by each partner who is an individual

- The partner:
    - is to sign the document in the presence of a witness;
    - and is to have her signature attested by the witness, such act being recorded by the signature of the witness.

Or:

- At the partner's direction and in her presence and in the presence of two witnesses:
    - another person is to sign the document;
    - and the two witnesses are each to attest the signature of the other person, such acts being recorded by the signatures of the two witnesses.

Execution by a partner who is a company formed under or regulated by CA 2006 (or CA 1985)

- If the company does not use, or have, a common seal:
    - a director in the presence of a witness (who attests the director's signature); or
    - a director and the company secretary; or
    - two directors

    sign the document.

Or:

- If the company does have a common seal and wishes to use it, and the default provision relating to the use of the common seal in the model articles of association under CA 2006 applies:

    the common seal of the company is affixed; and then:
    - a director in the presence of a witness (who attests the director's signature); or
    - a person (previously authorised by the directors) in the presence of a witness (who attests the person's signature)

    sign(s) the document.

Or:

- If the company does have a common seal and wishes to use it, and the default provision relating to the use of the common seal in Table A under CA 1985 applies:

    the common seal of the company is affixed; and then:
    - a director and the company secretary; or
    - two directors; or
    - a person (previously authorised by the directors)

    sign(s) the document.

Execution by a partner who is a corporation (but not a company formed or regulated by CA 2006 or CA 1985)

- The constitutional documents of the corporation should be checked for the correct method of applying the seal of the corporation:
    - is a meeting of the governing body required?
    - is the governing body required to specifically authorise use of the seal in specific instances?

- – is the seal required to be affixed at a meeting of the governing body of the corporation?
- – is the seal required to be affixed in the presence of the person(s) who will sign?

- Who among the members of the governing body can sign the deed:
  - – one or more members?
  - – one member and the corporation's secretary?
  - – the secretary alone?
  - – some other person authorised by the governing body to sign documents on behalf of the governing body of the corporation? Do they have unlimited authority or have they been given specific authority in a particular instance?

- If the deed is to be executed other than by either:
  - – two members of the governing body; or
  - – one member and the body corporate's clerk, secretary or other permanent officer (or deputy),

  will it matter to a purchaser that it will not have the benefit of the statutory assumption that the document is duly executed by the body corporate?

- Who has custody of the seal (normally the secretary to the corporation)?

- Affix the seal.

- The persons who are required to sign should sign as determined by checking the constitutional document (as documented in standing orders, for example).

- The deed is then delivered.

- Is the deed intended to be used for a transaction or event taking place in another country or is one or more of the persons named in it or parties to it based, incorporated or regulated in another country? If so:
  - – does the deed need to be translated into the language of the other country (or does at least one copy of the deed need to be in that language)?
  - – if the deed does need to be translated, must it be translated by an official or properly qualified translator?
  - – does the deed need to be registered with any governmental or regulatory authorities in the other country?
  - – is the deed of a type which needs to be drawn up and/or signed before a notary?
  - – if the deed is being signed in England and Wales, does it need to be notarised and/or legalised after it has been signed?

8.1   FORM/STRUCTURE OF THE DOCUMENT

A document intended to be a deed must be described as a deed or indicate that it is to be executed as a deed.

Described as a deed

Commencement of the document

A document might commence as follows to indicate at once that it is intended as a deed:

THIS DEED dated _____ 200[. . .] is made by and between:

(1)   [*name and address of the first party*]; and
(2)   [*name and address of the second party*]

Wording in the body of the document

The text indicating that the document is intended to be a deed can also be located in the body of the document (instead of or in addition to at the commencement of the document). Such text often signifies the start of the main provisions of the deed:

Now this Deed witnesses as follows

'Executed as a deed' clause[2]

As an alternative to (or in addition to) describing the document as a deed, the document can state that it is being executed as a deed.

Traditional format – all the partners executing a deed following a meeting of the partnership

IN WITNESS of which [*name of partnership*] has duly executed this deed pursuant to a meeting of [*name of partnership*] [and has delivered it upon dating it] [this [*day*] day of [*month and year*]] [the day and year first above written]

Traditional format – all the partners executing a deed where there is no meeting of the partnership

IN WITNESS of which [*name of partnership*] has duly executed this deed [and has delivered it upon dating it] [this [*day*] day of [*month and year*]] [the day and year first above written]

---

2 Formally known as the 'testimonium' clause.

Traditional format – all the partners executing a deed and some required to use their common seal or companies who choose to use their common seal

> **IN WITNESS** of which this deed has been duly executed by [*name of partnership*] and those partners using a common seal have caused their common seal to be affixed to this deed [and have delivered it upon dating it] [this [*day*] day of [*month and year*]] [the day and year first above written]

Or:

> **IN WITNESS** of which this deed has been duly executed by [*name of partnership*] and a partner using a common seal has caused its common seal to be affixed to this deed [and has delivered it upon dating it] [this [*day*] day of [*month and year*]] [the day and year first above written]

Modern format – execution by all the partners where there is no meeting of the partners

> **EXECUTED** as a **DEED** [and delivered] by the above-named [*name of partnership*] and signed by all the partners of [*name of partnership*]

Modern format – execution by all the partners following a partnership meeting

> **EXECUTED** as a **DEED** [and delivered] by [*name of partnership*] pursuant to a meeting of the [*name of partnership*] [a certified copy of the minute of which was delivered upon the execution of this deed] and signed by all the partners of [*name of partnership*]

Modern format – further alternative

> **EXECUTED** as a **DEED** by [*name of partnership*] [and delivered] on the date first above written

Because of the particular issues raised when one partner is to execute a deed (and the wording to be used), it is suggested that the wording of the *executed as a deed* clause should either:

- state that the deed is executed by the partnership (as in the two examples above) and then elsewhere in the deed indicate that the firm has given *explicit* authority to one or more partners to execute the deed on their behalf, and that the deed is binding on the firm; or
- incorporate into the *executed as a deed* clause a statement that explicit authority has been given, perhaps as follows:

> **IN WITNESS** of which this **DEED** has been duly executed by [*name of partnership*], through its agent[s] [*name of partner(s) executing*], [*name of partnership*], having given authority to [*name of partner executing*] to execute this deed on its behalf

[following a meeting of the [*name of partnership*] on [*day*] day of [*month and year*]] [and [*name of partner executing*] has delivered it upon dating it] [this [*day*] day of [*month and year*]] [the day and year first above written]

8.2   FORM/STRUCTURE OF THE SIGNATURE BLOCK[3]

Where one partner is to sign on behalf of the firm

Where all the partners are to sign, the *signature block* will be as for those found in the chapters on individuals, corporations and companies (with the number of *signature block* elements depending on the number of partners in the firm). The examples below cover the situation where one partner is to sign the deed on behalf of the firm.

Where the partner who is executing the deed is an individual

SIGNED [and DELIVERED] as a DEED
by [*name of the partnership*] through
its agent [*name of partner signing*]
in the presence of:

}

(partner's signature of
firm's name)
by (partner's signature of
her own name)

(signature, name, address and description of attesting witness)

Where the partner who is executing the deed is a company formed under or regulated by CA 1985 or CA 2006

SIGNED [and DELIVERED] as a DEED by [*name of partnership*] acting through its agent [*name of partner which is a company*] by [a director and the company secretary of [*name of partner which is a company*]] [by two directors of [*name of partner which is a company*]]

_____

Director's signature

_____

[Director] [Company secretary]'s
signature

Or:

SIGNED [and DELIVERED] as a DEED by [*name of partnership*] acting through its agent [*name of partner which is a company*] by [a director of [*name of partner which is a company*]]

Director's signature

(signature, name and address of attesting witness)

_____

3 Formally known as the 'attestation' clause.

Where the partner who is executing the deed is a corporation

SIGNED [and **DELIVERED**] as a **DEED** by [*name of partnership*] acting through its agent [*name of partner which is a corporation*] by [*name of partner which is a corporation*] affixing its **COMMON SEAL** in the presence of [**two members of the [*name of governing body*]**]:

(signatures of two members of the governing body)

The precise details of who can sign will depend on the corporation's statute, charter, articles, constitution, standing orders, etc.

Words in bold and in brackets: if only one member of the governing body is required to sign, please see below for possible alternatives:

- **if one member of the governing body is required to sign**:

  one member of the [*name of governing body*]

- **if one member of the governing body and the corporation's secretary are required to sign**:

  one member of the [*name of governing body*] and the secretary of the [*name of governing body*]

- **if only the secretary is required to sign**:

  the secretary of the [*name of governing body*]

- **if a person authorised by the corporation or the governing body is authorised to sign**:

  a person authorised by the [*name of governing body*] to sign for, and on behalf of, the [governing body] [corporation]

Notes:

1. Not all corporations are required to pass a resolution in order to authorise the use of the seal. This will depend on any requirements set out in the corporation's constitution. If not, then the following words can be deleted:

    pursuant to a resolution of the [*name of governing body*].

2. If a corporation's constitution requires signature of a deed other than under the requirements of LPA 1925, s.74(1), then the presumption provided by LPA 1925, s.74(1) (where two members or one member of the governing body and the secretary, clerk, etc. need to sign) may not apply. See **section 15.10**.

Format for transfers for registered land

Here, the *signature block* which is appropriate for a particular partner is the one which relates to that partner's status, as an individual or a company.[4]

8.3 TYPE OF STATEMENT, AFFIRMATION OR OATH THAT MUST BE MADE WHEN THE DOCUMENT IS SIGNED/EXECUTED

None.

8.4 (PROFESSIONAL) PERSONS WHO MUST BE PRESENT WHEN THE DOCUMENT IS SIGNED/EXECUTED AND THEIR ROLE

None.

8.5 HOW ARE ATTACHMENTS/SCHEDULES TO THE MAIN DOCUMENT DEALT WITH?

By convention attachments are placed before the *executed as a deed* clause and the *signature block*. Other common terms used are 'schedules', 'annexes' or 'appendices' and, if there is more than one, each one is numbered: 'schedule 1', 'schedule 2', etc. References in the other parts of the deed to an attachment or schedule are usually expressed in the following terms, e.g.: 'as set out in schedule [1] [to this deed]'.

More modern drafting practice (particularly in some commercial contracts) sets out attachments/schedules after the *executed as a deed* clause and the *signature block*.

8.6 FEES CHARGED BY THE PROFESSIONAL PERSON

None.

Points to note

1. If more than one partner is to sign the deed, there appears to be no requirement for the partners to be in each other's presence when they sign the deed.

---

4 For an individual, see **section 2.2**. For companies, see **section 4.3**.

2.   Where more than one partner is signing the deed, one partner is not acting as a witness to another's signature. Each partner is signing on her own account.

3.   Good practice would suggest that where the signing partner is an individual, another partner should not attest and witness her signature.[5]

4.   The *executed as a deed* clause and the *signature block* should normally be kept together on one page (where possible). In particular, the *signature block* should never be split over two pages, but if the *signature block* will run over more than one page (i.e. there are several parties and the modern format is used), then the *signature block* should be separated at a logical place (e.g. all the wording for a particular party being kept together).

5.   The words 'described as a deed' do not always mean that a document has to contain the word 'deed' in it. Other words which describe the document or how it is signed or executed could also be used. For example, the document could be described as a type of document which in the circumstances can only be a deed (such as a conveyance, a mortgage or a lease of real property, or a grant of a power of attorney).

6.   If a deed is dated at the top of its front page then the date does not have to be repeated in the *executed as a deed* clause or the *signature block*.

7.   The date inserted in the deed is the date when the deed is delivered, which may be different from the date when the deed was signed, witnessed and attested. The *executed as a deed* clause or the *signature block* should be carefully considered when drafting a deed to allow for situations when a deed is not intended to have effect when it is signed, witnessed and attested. For companies (where CA 1985, s.36A, has effect) there are presumptions that delivery takes place on execution, and these presumptions may need to be rebutted.

8.   Where a deed is not delivered when it is signed, the deed might commence with the following words:

   THIS DEED delivered as a deed on _____ 200[. . .]

   or add a reference to the date of delivery in the *executed as a deed* clause as evidence of delivery.

9.   A deed delivered in escrow is dated on the date it is signed and delivered in escrow and not the date when the condition is fulfilled.[6]

---

5 Who can act as a witness is considered further at **section 14.5**.
6 This statement is not correct for stamp duty purposes, where the date of delivery is the date when the condition is fulfilled: SA 1891, s.122(1A).

CHAPTER 9

Statutory declarations

<table>
<tr><td>

CHECKLIST

- For a person ('the Declarant') wishing to execute a statutory declaration, the following need to occur.

- The Declarant should:
  - ensure that the facts and evidence or records of events or actions are true and accurate;
  - use the form of words specified by statute to commence and end the statutory declaration and add the signature block;
  - sign the statutory declaration;
  - appear before a person authorised to take a statutory declaration ('the Commissioner').

- The Commissioner should:
  - confirm that the person before her is the person named in the statutory declaration;
  - if the statutory declaration is already signed when presented to the Commissioner, ask whether the signature is that of the Declarant, or if it is not signed see the Declarant sign the statutory declaration;
  - ask the Declarant whether she understands why she is making the statutory declaration;
  - asks the Declarant whether she understands what the purpose of making the statutory declaration is: to confirm that its contents (and any attachments) are true;
  - check that any attachments are correct;
  - hear the Declarant read a set form of words provided in writing by the Commissioner (for example, on a card) or repeat the words said by the Commissioner;
  - sign the declaration;
  - in writing (by hand) or by means of a rubber stamp impress her name, qualification and address; and
  - state the place where, and the date on which, the declaration of the Declarant is taken.

</td></tr>
</table>

9.1   FORM OF COMMENCEMENT OF THE STATUTORY DECLARATION

Every statutory declaration must commence with the following words:

I [*name of Declarant*] of [*their address*] do solemnly and sincerely declare that

9.2   FORM OF CONCLUSION OF THE STATUTORY DECLARATION

Every statutory declaration must conclude with the following words:

AND I make this solemn declaration conscientiously believing the same to be true and by virtue of the Statutory Declarations Act 1835

9.3   FORM/STRUCTURE OF THE SIGNATURE BLOCK

Traditional form

DECLARED at [*place where the Commissioner is taking the declaration of the Declarant*] this [*day*] of [*month and year*]   (signature of Declarant)

before me

(signature of Commissioner)

a [Commissioner for Oaths] [solicitor empowered to administer oaths]

Modern form

DECLARED at [*place where Commissioner is taking declaration of Declarant*] on _____ 200[. . .]

_____
(signature of Declarant)

before me _____
(signature of Commissioner)

a [Commissioner for Oaths] [solicitor empowered to administer oaths]

9.4   TYPE OF STATEMENT, AFFIRMATION OR OATH THAT MUST BE MADE WHEN THE DOCUMENT IS SIGNED/EXECUTED

Alternative methods can be used for the Declarant to state the required form of words.

Declarant stating set form of words

When the Declarant appears before the Commissioner, the procedure is as follows.

- The document containing the statutory declaration is placed on a desk/table or held in front of the Declarant.
- The Commissioner either:
  - shows the Declarant the set form of words printed on a card or other document; or
  - asks the Declarant to repeat the set form of words after the Commissioner states them.

- The Declarant states or repeats the following words:

  I solemnly and sincerely declare that this is my name and handwriting and that the contents of this my declaration are true [*if there are exhibits add* and that [this is/these are] the exhibit[s] referred to]

- At the moment when the Declarant states or repeats the words 'this is my name and handwriting' the Commissioner points to the Declarant's signature on the document.

Commissioner stating set form of words[1]

When the Declarant appears before the Commissioner, the procedure is as follows.

- The Commissioner asks (as well as pointing to the Declarant's signature):

  Is this your name and handwriting?

- The Declarant replies, stating:

  It is.

- The Commissioner then asks:

  Do you solemnly and sincerely declare that the contents of this your declaration are true?

- The Declarant replies, stating:

  I do.

- *If there are exhibits*: the Commissioner then asks:

  [Is this/Are these] the exhibit[s] referred to in this your declaration?

- The Declarant replies, stating:

  [It is/They are].

---

1 Derived from *Encyclopaedia of Forms and Precedents*, vol. 12(2), 'Deeds', Form 153.

9.5 (PROFESSIONAL) PERSONS WHO MUST BE PRESENT WHEN THE DOCUMENT IS SIGNED/EXECUTED AND THEIR ROLE

The following people can take statutory declarations:

- Commissioners for Oaths, comprising:
  - solicitors (holding a current practising certificate);
  - barristers;
  - notaries public (but not ecclesiastical notaries);
  - licensed conveyancers;
  - Fellows of the Institute of Legal Executives (if they pay a full subscription to the Institute; but not retired Fellows);
  - a justice of the peace.[2]

9.6 HOW ARE ATTACHMENTS/EXHIBITS TO THE MAIN DOCUMENT DEALT WITH?

In the statutory declaration the reference to the attachment/exhibit should be noted with an identifying initial and number (for example, the third exhibit of a statutory declaration by Ms Jane Smith might be numbered 'JS3'). The attachment/exhibit which is referred to in the statutory declaration should be kept separate from the statutory declaration and should be produced at the same time as the statutory declaration before the Commissioner. Such attachments/exhibits should be marked with an identifying initial and number matching that found at the relevant place in the statutory declaration.
Each attachment/exhibit can be marked as follows:[3]

> This is the [*specify attachment/exhibit*] marked [*initials/number referred to in statutory declaration*] referred to in the annexed declaration of [*name of Declarant*] declared before me this [*day*] day of [*month*] [*year*]
>
> (signature of Commissioner)
>
> a [Commissioner for Oaths] [solicitor empowered to administer oaths]

The use of such marking is not required but is suggested as best practice.

---

2 But apparently only for the purposes of the Stamp Duties Management Act 1891 (SDMA 1891).
3 In practice, this form of words might be written by hand on the attachment/exhibit.

9.7   MAKING AMENDMENTS

There appears to be no commonly accepted method of making amendments (unlike the position for affidavits or witness statements). It is not clear whether the method used for making amendments for affidavits and/or witness statements would be suitable or effective in the case of a statutory declaration. Perhaps the best way is to draft a further statutory declaration noting the changes over the earlier one and have this latter document taken before a Commissioner.

9.8   FEES CHARGED BY THE PROFESSIONAL PERSON

For taking a statutory declaration, a Commissioner for Oaths shall charge £5 for each person making the statutory declaration and £2 for each exhibit referred to in the statutory declaration.[4]

9.9   MAIN VARIATIONS TO ANY OF THE ABOVE

In the authors' experience, professional practice when taking statutory declarations can vary quite considerably. They have encountered the following requirements:

- the declaration to be made by the Declarant is made in the same manner as the swearing of an oath for an affidavit (see **section 12.1**);
- the Declarant is required to sign the statutory declaration in the presence of the Commissioner;
- the Declarant is required to provide proof of their signature (e.g. provide something bearing their signature, such as a bank/credit card or driving licence);
- the Declarant is required to provide proof of their identity;
- the Commissioner requires the Declarant to state a longer form of words (than those stated above);
- the Commissioner does not require the Declarant to state or repeat any form of words as noted above, but the Commissioner simply signs and dates the statutory declaration.

Points to note

1.   There appears to be no set procedure for taking a statutory declaration, and the procedure and form of words set out under **section 9.4** is that of

---

4 The Commissioners for Oaths (Fees) Order 1993, SI 1993/2297 and the Commissioner for Oaths (Authorised Persons) (Fees) Order 1993, SI 1993/2298.

established custom only based on the procedure for administering an oath. But note the particular requirements on solicitors below.

2.   There are no specific provisions relating to a Declarant who cannot, or is unable to, read or sign a statutory declaration. It is suggested that the procedure, and form of *signature block*, used for affidavits should be adopted (see **section 12.6**).

3.   A Commissioner will not normally be responsible for the contents of the statutory declaration. For solicitors, guidance in the Solicitors' Code of Conduct 2007 puts this point beyond doubt, unless the solicitor has good reason to believe that the contents are false. In such cases the solicitor should not proceed with taking the declaration.[5]

4.   There are specific matters which a solicitor must ensure when taking a statutory declaration:[6]

   (a)   that the Declarant is present;

   (b)   that the statutory declaration is signed in the presence of the solicitor or, if it is already signed, that the Declarant confirms that the signature is that of the Declarant;

   (c)   that any attachments are correct;

   (d)   that:

      (i)   the Declarant understands what they are doing; and

      (ii) the Declarant understands that the purpose of making the statutory declaration is to confirm that its contents and any attachments are true.

5.   Only an individual can make a statutory declaration. Therefore a statutory declaration could not be drafted in the name of a company, with a director, for example, signing it. However, the statutory declaration could be drafted in the name of the director.

6.   More than one person can be named in the same statutory declaration, with each person making a separate declaration (and the Commissioner being able to charge a separate fee).

7.   There is no requirement for the statutory declaration to be signed in the presence of the Commissioner. In particular, guidance in the Solicitors' Code of Conduct 2007 indicates that there is no requirement to see the statutory declaration signed, and that a solicitor can accept the Declarant's word that the signature on the statutory declaration is that of the Declarant, unless there is clear evidence to the contrary.[7]

---

5 Solicitors' Code of Conduct 2007, guidance to rule 10.03, para. 11.

6 See Solicitors' Code of Conduct 2007, guidance to rule 10.03, para. 10; see **Appendix 3**.

7 Solicitors' Code of Conduct 2007, guidance to rule 10.03, para. 13. This is not further explained, but relevant situations could include, for example, where the solicitor sees a signed declaration and recognises that the signature does not match the signature on documents the solicitor has previously seen, or where the signature is in a different name from that of the Declarant (e.g. the statutory declaration is in the name of Jane Brown, but the signature appears to state 'Rachel Smith').

8. Commissioners must not take a statutory declaration in any matter in which they are interested.[8]

9. A solicitor cannot take a declaration where that solicitor or the solicitor's firm is acting for any of the parties in a matter.[9]

10. As can be judged from the points above, the Commissioner must be a person independent of the parties and the parties' representatives. The following points were given as examples of when a solicitor should not take a statutory declartaion under the (now superseded) *Guide to the Professional Conduct of Solicitors 1999*:

    (a) in relation to a local authority's business where the solicitor is a member or employee of that local authority;

    (b) regarding proofs in bankruptcy when acting for that proving creditor or regarding the winding-up of an estate when acting for the personal representatives;

    (c) when employed part-time by another solicitor for a client of that employer;

    (d) when in the full or part-time employment of a company in matters in which the company is concerned.

These still seem circumstances where it would be sensible for a solicitor or other professional able to act as Commissioner not to deal with a statutory declaration.

---

8 Commissioners for Oaths Act 1889 (COA 1889), s.1(3).

9 Solicitors' Code of Conduct 2007, rule 10.03; see **Appendix 3**. See also guidance to rule 10.03, para. 12, where reference is made to Solicitors Act 1974 (SA 1974), s.81(2), which prohibits a solicitor taking a declaration where the solicitor or the solicitor's firm is acting for any party in a matter. The guidance to rule 10.03 indicates that the effect of such a prohibition would mean, for example, that a solicitor cannot take the declaration of the solicitor's spouse where it arises out of a personal matter. Under the (now superseded) *Guide to the Professional Conduct of Solicitors 1999*, the restriction here related to 'proceedings'. The 2007 Code is wider in this respect, as it refers to any 'matter', which would cover both litigation and non-litigation matters.

CHAPTER 10

Powers of attorney[1]

10.1 HOW MUST THE DOCUMENT BE SIGNED/EXECUTED?

A grant of a power of attorney must be executed as a deed. The person who grants or gives the power of attorney is called the 'donor' and the person who is authorised by the power of attorney to act on behalf of the donor is called the 'attorney' or 'donee'. A document which is to be executed as a deed and which is entered into by an attorney on behalf of the donor of the power must also be executed as a deed.

The descriptions of the formalities for executing deeds found in the chapters for individuals, corporations and companies equally apply here and are not repeated. Only particular aspects relevant to powers of attorney are considered in this chapter.

By the person granting a power of attorney

- If the power of attorney is drafted as a general power of attorney, does it follow the form set out in the Powers of Attorney Act 1971 (PAA 1971), Sched.1; or is it in a form of like effect and which is expressed to be under PAA 1971, s.10?[2]
- If the power of attorney is for a specific purpose, does it give sufficient authority for the transaction(s) that the donee is to enter into or for the activities that the donee is to carry out?
- State in the document creating the power of attorney:

  - that the power of attorney is being granted in accordance with PAA 1971, s.10; or
  - *for a company formed or regulated by CA 1985* (until October 2009), where the power of attorney is being granted to an attorney on behalf

---

1 This book does not deal with lasting powers of attorney (under the Mental Capacity Act 2005) which have their own particular rules.
2 If so, then the power of attorney shall operate to confer on the donee of the power (or if there is more than one donee, on the donees acting jointly or acting jointly or severally, as the case may be) authority to do on behalf of the donor anything which she can lawfully do by an attorney (PAA 1971, s.10(1)).

of the company for use outside the United Kingdom, that the power of attorney is being granted in accordance with CA 1985, s.38(1). The document must have the common seal of the company; or

– *for a company formed or regulated by CA 1985 or CA 2006 (from October 2009)*, where the power of attorney is being granted to an attorney who is to act on behalf of the company for use inside or outside the United Kingdom, that the power of attorney is being granted in accordance with CA 2006, s.47(1). The document must be executed as a deed by the company.

• If the power of attorney is being granted in a document whose main purpose is not the grant of the power, ensure that the document is correctly described as a deed, with the correct types of *executed as a deed* clause and *signature block*.

10.2 FORM/STRUCTURE OF THE DOCUMENT

Execution of a power of attorney by a donor

The normal type of *executed as a deed* clause described in the other chapters (the form depending on the status of the donor) can be used for granting a power of attorney.

Execution of deeds by an attorney on behalf of the donor

However, for the execution of a deed by an attorney on behalf of a donor, the *executed as a deed* clause normally indicates that the attorney is executing a deed on behalf of the donor.

Creation of a power of attorney (as a stand-alone document) – described as a deed

Commencement of the document

A document might commence as follows to indicate at once that it is intended as a power of attorney:

THIS POWER OF ATTORNEY dated _____ 200[. . .] is made by and between:

(1) [*name and address of the first party*]; and
(2) [*name and address of the second party*].

Or using the wording in the PAA 1971:

THIS GENERAL POWER OF ATTORNEY is made this [*day*] day of [*month and year*] by [*name of donor*] of [*address of donor*]

I appoint [*name of attorney*] of [*address of attorney*] [*add other attorneys as necessary*] [jointly or jointly and severally] to be my attorney[s] in accordance with section 10 of the Powers of Attorney Act 1971

In witness, etc.

There is no requirement to use the words 'power of attorney'; the word 'deed' is equally appropriate, as mention of the granting of the power will be in the body of the document (see below).

Wording in the body of the document to indicate that a power of attorney is being granted

It is usual to state expressly that a person or corporation is appointing a power of attorney.

For an individual:

[I/We] [*name of person(s)*] appoint [*name of attorney(ies)*] of [*address of attorney(ies)*] to [*describe nature of appointment*]

For a corporation or company:

[*name of company*] [The Company] appoints [*name of attorney(ies)*] of [*address of attorney(ies)*] to [*describe nature of appointment*]

'Executed as a deed' clause where an attorney is executing a deed on behalf of a donor[3]

Traditional format – where the deed is executed by an attorney (as an individual) under an ordinary power of attorney

IN WITNESS of which this deed has been executed on behalf of [*name of donor*] by his attorney [*name of attorney*] of [*address of attorney*] [dated the [*day*] day of [*month and year*]] [the day and year first above written]

Modern format – where the deed is executed by an attorney (as an individual) under an ordinary power of attorney

EXECUTED as a **DEED** by [*name of attorney*] on behalf of the [*name of donor*] on the date of this Agreement

---

3 Formally known as the 'testimonium' clause.

91

10.3   FORM/STRUCTURE OF THE SIGNATURE BLOCK[4]

Traditional format – by the attorney (as an individual) executing a deed on behalf of the donor[5]

SIGNED [and DELIVERED] as a DEED on behalf of the
above-named [*name of donor*] by his above-named   }   (signature of attorney)
attorney [*name of attorney*] in the presence of:

(signature, name, address and description of attesting witness)

Traditional format – by the attorney (as an individual) executing a deed on behalf of the donor (alternative format)

SIGNED [and DELIVERED] as a DEED for and on   (attorney's signature of
behalf of the above-named [*name of donor*] by   }   name of donor)
his above-named attorney [*name of attorney*] in   by his attorney
the presence of: (signature of attorney)

(signature, name, address and description of attesting witness)

Alternative wording

SIGNED [and DELIVERED] as a DEED by the above-named [*name of attorney*] as the
attorney and in the name of the above-named [*name of donor*] in the presence of:

Modern format – by the attorney (as an individual) executing a deed on behalf of the donor (alternative format)

SIGNED [and DELIVERED] as a DEED by the
above-named [*name of attorney*] as the attorney   }   (attorney's signature of name
and in the name of the above named [*name of*   of donor)
donor] in the presence of: (signature of attorney)

Witnessed by: Signature ——————————————————

                                 Description ——————————————————

                                 Address ——————————————————

---

4 Formally known as the 'attestation' clause.

5 The *signature block* which follows for an attorney as an individual is perhaps the safest from the attorney's point of view (to protect the attorney from being held liable under the deed). This *signature block* would be in accordance with PAA 1971, s.7(1). Some of the issues and problems concerning powers of attorney are discussed in **Chapter 22**.

Traditional format – by the attorney (as a company formed or regulated by CA 1985 or CA 2006) executing a deed on behalf of the donor

SIGNED [and DELIVERED] as a DEED by [*name of attorney company*] acting by [*name of director*], in the presence of: }	(signature of one director)

(signature, name, address and description of attesting witness)

Or:

SIGNED [and DELIVERED] as a DEED by [*name of attorney company*] acting by [*name of director*], director and [*name of director/secretary*], [director] [secretary] as attorney for [*name of donor*] }	(signatures of two directors or a director and a secretary)

Traditional format – by the attorney (as a corporation) executing a deed on behalf of the donor

SIGNED [and DELIVERED] and THE COMMON SEAL OF [*name of attorney corporation*] acting as attorney for [*name of donor*] affixed in the presence of **[two members of the board of directors, council or other governing body of [name of attorney corporation]]** }	(signatures of two members of the board, etc. or a member and the secretary)

The precise details of who can sign will depend on the corporation's statute, charter, articles, constitution, standing orders, rules, etc.

Words in bold and in brackets: if only one member of the governing body is required to sign, please see below for possible alternatives:

- **if only one member of the governing body is required to sign**:

  one member of the [*name of governing body*]

- **if one member of the governing body and the corporation's secretary are required to sign**:

  one member of the [*name of governing body*] and the secretary of the [*name of governing body*]

- **if only the secretary is required to sign**:

  the secretary of the [*name of governing body*]

- **if a person authorised by the corporation or the governing body is authorised to sign**:

  a person authorised by the [*name of governing body*] to sign for, and on behalf of, the [governing body] [corporation].

If the corporation's constitution requires signature of a deed other than in accordance with the requirements of LPA 1925, s. 74(1), then the presumption of valid execution provided by LPA 1925, s.74(1) (where either two members of the governing body or one member of the governing body and the secretary, clerk, etc. need to sign) may not apply. It may have to rely on common law provisions only.

Format suggested by the Land Registry for transfers for registered land, etc. by an attorney who is an individual (whether the donor is an individual or a corporation)

Signed in name of attorney

Signed as a deed by [*full name of attorney*] as attorney for [*full name of individual or corporation*] in the presence of:

[*Sign here your own name and the name of the individual/corporation, e.g. Jane Brown as attorney for John Smith/John Smith Ltd*]

Signature of witness _____

Name (in BLOCK CAPITALS) _____

Address _____

Signed in name of donor

Signed as a deed by [*full name of individual or corporation*] acting by his/her/its attorney [*full name of attorney*] in the presence of:

[*Sign here your own name and the name of the individual/corporation, e.g. John Smith/John Smith Ltd by his/its attorney Jane Brown*]

Signature of witness _____

Name (in BLOCK CAPITALS) _____

Address _____

Format suggested by the Land Registry for transfers of registered land, etc. by an attorney who is a corporate body (whether the donor is an individual or a corporation)

Corporate body using its own seal

Executed as a deed by affixing the common seal of [*name of corporate attorney*] as attorney for [*full name of individual or corporation*] in the presence of:

(common seal of company)
_____
Signature of director

_____
Signature of [director] [secretary]

Corporate attorney having no seal or not using its seal

Signed as a deed by [*name of corporate
attorney*] acting by [a director] [and its
secretary] [two directors] as attorney for
[*name of individual or corporation*]

_____
Signature of director

_____
Signature of [director] [secretary]

The board of directors, council or other governing body of a corporate attorney appointing an officer to execute the deed in the name of the donor (LPA 1925, s.74(4))

Signed as a deed in the name of and
on behalf of [*full name of individual or
corporation*] by [*full name of officer*], an officer
appointed for the purpose by the board of
directors [*name of corporate attorney*],
[his/her/its] attorney, in the presence of:

[*Sign here the name of the donor
individual or corporation, the
name of the corporate attorney and
your own name, e.g. John Smith/
John Smith Ltd by his/its attorney
Jane Brown Limited acting by
James Green*]

Signature of witness _____

Name (in BLOCK CAPITALS) _____

Address _____

10.4 TYPE OF STATEMENT, AFFIRMATION OR OATH THAT MUST BE MADE WHEN THE DOCUMENT IS SIGNED/EXECUTED

None.

10.5 (PROFESSIONAL) PERSONS WHO MUST BE PRESENT WHEN THE DOCUMENT IS SIGNED/EXECUTED AND THEIR ROLE

None.

10.6 HOW ARE ATTACHMENTS/SCHEDULES TO THE MAIN DOCUMENT DEALT WITH?

By convention attachments are placed before the *executed as a deed* clause and
the *signature block*. Other common terms used are 'schedules', 'annexes' or
'appendices' and, if there is more than one, each one is numbered: 'schedule 1',
'schedule 2', etc. References in the other parts of the deed to an attachment

or schedule are usually expressed in the following terms, e.g.: 'as set out in schedule [1] [to this deed]'.

More modern drafting practice (particularly in some commercial contracts) sets out attachments/schedules after the *executed as a deed* clause and the *signature block*.

10.7   FEES CHARGED BY THE PROFESSIONAL PERSON

None.

10.8   MAIN VARIATIONS TO ANY OF THE ABOVE

Companies granting a power of attorney

Company granting a power of attorney following a resolution of the board of directors

An example of an *executed as a deed* clause:

> **IN WITNESS** whereof the Company has, in accordance with its constitution and a resolution of its directors duly passed on [*date of resolution*], executed this Power of Attorney as a deed on the day first before written.

Where an attorney (who is a corporation) is authorised under a power of attorney[6] to execute a deed on behalf of a donor concerning the conveyance of any interest in property under LPA 1925, s.74(4)[7]

SIGNED [and **DELIVERED**] as a **DEED** by [*name of donor*] acting by [*name of officer appointed by attorney corporation*] appointed to execute as an officer of its attorney [*name of attorney corporation*] in the presence of:

(Officer to sign name of donor) by [*name of officer*] duly appointed officer of its attorney [*name of attorney corporation*]

(signature, name, address and description of attesting witness)

---

6 LPA 1925, s.74(4) also applies where the corporation is authorised under any statutory or other power.

7 Its provisions are described at **section 22.4**. It is not required to use this form of *signature block* where the conveyance of any interest in property is concerned.

Where an attorney (who is an individual) is authorised under a power of attorney to execute a deed on behalf of a donor corporation concerning the conveyance of any interest in property under LPA 1925, s.74(3)[8]

SIGNED [and **DELIVERED**] as a **DEED** for and on behalf of the above-named [*name of donor corporation*] by its attorney [*name of attorney*] in the presence of: } (Attorney to sign name of donor corporation)

by [*name of attorney*]

(signature, name, address and description of attesting witness)

Points to note

1. Where a deed is to be executed by an attorney on behalf of a donor, then the following is suggested as good practice:
    (a) the donor should be mentioned in the deed; and
    (b) it should be stated that the attorney is executing the deed on behalf of the donor; and
    (c) in addition it should be stated that the attorney is executing the deed as an attorney.
2. The *executed as a deed* clause and the *signature block* should normally be kept together on one page (where possible). In particular, the *signature block* should never be split over two pages, but if the *signature block* will run over more than one page (i.e. there are several parties and the modern format is used), then the *signature block* should be separated at a logical place (e.g. all the wording for a particular party being kept together).
3. By convention, a witness is required to state their address and print their name and their description in addition to their signature. Such a practice allows for the witness to be contacted if there is doubt about the document, its method of execution, etc.
4. A 'signature' can mean making no more than a mark (such as an 'X'). It can also include signing with a pencil, or applying a rubber stamp which contains an exact copy of the individual's real signature (although these two last practices should be used with care – and are practices which may not be acceptable to everyone).[9]
5. If a deed is dated at the top of its front page then the date does not have to be repeated in the *executed as a deed* clause or the *signature block*.

---

8 Its provisions are described at **section 22.4**. It is not required to use this form of *signature block* where the conveyance of any interest in property is concerned.

9 In particular, the Law Commission recommends for deeds that a handwritten signature is given by the person or parties to a deed.

6.   The date inserted in the deed is the date when the deed is delivered, which may be different from the date when the deed was signed, witnessed and attested. The *executed as a deed* clause or the *signature block* should be carefully considered when drafting a deed to allow for situations when a deed is not intended to have effect when it is signed, witnessed and attested.

7.   Where a deed is not delivered when it is signed, the deed might commence with the following words:

THIS DEED delivered as a deed on _____ 200[. . .]

or add a reference to the date of delivery in the *executed as a deed* clause as evidence of delivery.

8.   A deed delivered in escrow is dated on the date it is signed and delivered in escrow and not the date when the condition is fulfilled.[10]

---

10 This statement is not correct for stamp duty purposes, where the date of delivery is the date when the condition is fulfilled: SA 1891, s.122(1A).

CHAPTER 11

Statements of truth

CHECKLIST

The party or witness wishing to execute a document verified by a statement of truth should do the following:

- use the appropriate form or, if the document is a witness statement or expert report, comply with the appropriate formatting and content requirements (see **section 23.10**);
- ensure that the facts stated in the document are true and accurate;
- have an honest belief in the truth of the document;
- use one of the specified forms of words (see below);
- use the appropriate form of words to indicate the status of the person signing;
- sign;[1]
- print her full name clearly beneath her signature;
- add the date when the signature is made; and
- where the party or witness cannot read or sign, ensure that the document contains a certificate by an authorised person (see **section 23.9**).

11.1 FORM/STRUCTURE OF THE SIGNATURE BLOCK

General form of signature block as used on most court forms

Statement of Truth

*[I believe] [The [1] believes] that the facts stated in [2] are true

*I am duly authorised by the [1] to sign this statement

---

1 For starting certain types of claims and for submitting certain documents electronically, the statement of truth is not signed conventionally but the name of the person is typed or some other specified method is used, see p.239.

Full name _____

Name of [1]'s solicitor's firm _____

Signed _____ Position or office held _____

*[1] Litigation friend   (if signing on behalf of firm or company)
*[1]'s solicitor

*delete as appropriate

Notes: 1. For **1**, this will be: 'claimant', 'defendant', 'applicant', 'judgment creditor', or similar.
2. For **2**, this will be: 'these particulars of claim', or 'this claim form', or 'this form', or 'this defence form', or 'this application form', or 'this witness statement'.

On most court forms the statement of truth will be in the above form (or variations thereof). To complete each element of the above statement of truth where the party to the litigation is an individual or a company/corporation:

[I believe] [The [1] believes] that the facts stated in [2] are true	*Individual – not legally represented (or legal representative is not signing):* '[The [1] believes]' should be struck out
	Individual – legally represented: '[I believe]' should be struck out
	Company/corporation – not legally represented (or legal representative is not signing): '[I believe]' should be struck out
I am duly authorised by the [1] to sign this statement	*Individual – not legally represented (or legal representative is not signing):* 'I am duly authorised by the [1] to sign this statement' should be struck out
	Individual – legally represented: 'I am duly authorised by the [1] to sign this statement' should **not** be struck out
	Company/corporation – not legally represented (or legal representative is not signing): 'I am duly authorised by the [1] to sign this statement' should **not** be struck out
Full name	*Individual – not legally represented (or legal representative is not signing):* The individual's full name should be inserted in block capitals

	Individual – legally represented: The name of the legal representative should be inserted in block capitals – the name of the legal representative signing and not the name of the legal representative's firm (if a firm of solicitors)
	Company/corporation – not legally represented: The name of the director, manager, etc. who is signing on behalf of the company/corporation should be inserted in block capitals
	Company/corporation – legally represented: The name of the legal representative should be inserted in block capitals – the name of the legal representative signing and not the name of the legal representative's firm (if a firm of solicitors)
Name of [1]'s solicitor's firm	Should only be completed if the individual's or company/corporation's legal representative is a solicitor or legal executive at a firm of solicitors
Signed	The signature of the name of the person who entered their name in 'Full name' should be inserted here
[1] Litigation friend [1]'s solicitor	*Individual – not legally represented (or legal representative is not signing):* '[1]'s solicitor' should be struck out
	Individual – legally represented: '[1] Litigation friend' should be struck out
	Individual – acting on behalf of a child or a patient (and legal representative is not signing): '[1]' and '[1]'s solicitor' should be struck out
	Company/corporation – not legally represented: '[1]'s solicitor' should be struck out
	Company/corporation – legally represented: '[1] Litigation friend' should be struck out
Position or office held (if signing on behalf of firm or company)	The position held by the person who is signing on behalf of a company/corporation to be inserted here (e.g. director, manager, etc.)

General form of signature block as used in documents not originating from the court

For an individual

> I believe that the facts stated in [this witness statement] [these particulars of claim] are true
>
> Signed _____
>
> Full name _____
>
> Date _____

On behalf of a company or corporation

> I believe that the facts stated in [this witness statement] [these particulars of claim] are true. I am duly authorised by the defendant to sign this statement.
>
> Signed _____
>
> Full name _____
>
> Position or office held _____
>
> Date _____

General forms of signature block and method of signing a statement of truth for a money claim commenced electronically

The *signature block* is specified to be in the following forms:

> [I believe] [The claimant believes] that the facts stated in this claim form are true

or

> [I believe] [The defendant believes] that the facts stated in this defence are true

The claimant on the online claim form or the defendant on the defence form signs the statement of truth by typing their name.

11.2 TYPE OF STATEMENT, AFFIRMATION OR OATH THAT MUST BE MADE WHEN THE DOCUMENT IS SIGNED/EXECUTED

None.

11.3 (PROFESSIONAL) PERSONS WHO MUST BE PRESENT WHEN THE DOCUMENT IS SIGNED/EXECUTED AND THEIR ROLE

None, except in the following specific situations:

- where a legal representative is signing the document to be verified by a statement of truth on behalf of their client;
- where a person is unable to read or sign a document required to be verified by a statement of truth (see **section 11.7**).

11.4 HOW ARE ATTACHMENTS/EXHIBITS TO THE MAIN DOCUMENT DEALT WITH?

Witness statements are the main type of document to be verified by a statement of truth. They may include documents or things (such as objects) ('exhibits') (see CPR PD 22.18.3) which are referred to in the witness statement.

Exhibits need to be marked with an identifying number matching that found at the relevant place in the witness statement (see CPR PD 32.18.4). The conventional way of doing this is, for example, that the third exhibit attached to a witness statement made by Jane Smith would be given the number 'JS3'.

11.5 MAKING AMENDMENTS

For *witness statements*, any alterations and amendments made need to be initialled by the person signing the witness statement.

11.6 FEES CHARGED BY THE PROFESSIONAL PERSON

None. But a legal representative, if asked to sign on behalf of her client, may charge for the time taken to do so in the normal way for legal work undertaken.

11.7 MAIN VARIATIONS TO ANY OF THE ABOVE

If a person is unable to read or sign a document required to be verified by a statement of truth[2]

If a document contains a statement of truth which is to be signed by a person who is unable to read or sign the document ('Signer'), then the document

---

2 There is no specific CPR rule which states that the authorised person is required to sign, in addition to the witness, the statement of truth, but it appears that it is the practice among some lawyers for the authorised person to sign as well.

must contain a statement made by an authorised person (CPR PD 22.3A.1). An authorised person is a person who can administer oaths or take affidavits. An authorised person does not need to be independent of the parties or the parties' representatives (CPR PD 22.3A.2):

- the authorised person must certify that:
  - she has read the document to the Signer;
  - the Signer appears to understand the document;
  - the Signer has approved the contents of the document;
  - the declaration of truth has been read to the Signer;
  - the Signer appears to understand the declaration and the consequences of making a false declaration; and
  - the Signer signed or made her mark in the presence of the authorised person.

The approved form of the certificate to be used (CPR PD 22.3A.4, CPR PD 22 Annex) is:

> I certify that I [*name and address of authorised person*] have read over the contents of this document and the declaration of truth to the person signing the document [*if there are exhibits, add* 'and explained the nature and effect of the exhibits referred to in it'] who appeared to understand (a) the document and approved its content as accurate and (b) the declaration of truth and the consequences of making a false declaration, and made his mark in my presence

Points to note for legal representatives

The following points should be considered where a legal representative is representing a client who is a party to litigation.

1. Is the legal representative prepared to sign a statement of truth on behalf of her client at all? Some solicitors, as a matter of policy, always require their client (or the client's representative, such as a person in a senior position for a company) to sign.
2. Legal representatives should advise their clients that in signing a statement of truth that contains a false statement the client could face contempt proceedings. Such advice should indicate what such proceedings might mean: a fine, paying some or all of the costs of the person bringing the contempt proceedings, and, in the worst cases, possibly jail (see *Kabushiki Kaisha Sony Computer Entertainment (also trading as Sony Computer Entertainment Inc) and others* v. *Ball and others* [2004] EWHC 1984 (Ch)).[3]

---

3 The court did not explicitly state that a legal representative must explain to a client the consequences of making a false statement verified by a statement of truth, i.e. that proceedings for contempt could follow. But this is the inference to be drawn. The first defendant

3. If the legal representative signs the statement of truth, she is verifying the belief of the client, not the belief of the legal representative, as it relates to the truth of the facts stated in the document which is signed.

4. Nevertheless, in signing the statement of truth, the legal representative is verifying that, as the representative of the client, the legal representative has complied with the requirements of CPR PD 22.3.8. The point is that the legal representative would not be guilty of contempt of court because she has signed the statement of truth on behalf of the client who has acted dishonestly, but the legal representative might be guilty of contempt if she has not complied with the requirements of CPR PD 22.3.8. CPR PD 22.3.8 is set out in full in **Appendix 2**. The main requirements of CPR PD 22.3.8 are:

    (a) the legal representative is authorised by the client to sign on the client's behalf; and

    (b) before the legal representative signs the statement of truth, the legal representative has explained to the client that in signing the statement of truth the legal representative is confirming the client's belief that the facts in the document are true; and

    (c) before signing the statement of truth, the legal representative has explained the possible consequences to the client if subsequently it is found that the client did not have an honest belief in the truth of those facts.

5. Best practice would be for the legal representative to obtain the client's written authorisation to sign the statement of truth on behalf of the client and for the client also to indicate that they acknowledge that the legal representative has explained the consequences of a false statement. Second best would be for the legal representative to make a sufficiently detailed file note to indicate she has received the client's verbal authorisation and that she has explained fully the consequences of a client making a false statement.[4]

6. For a corporate client who is engaged in numerous claims or defences, a single letter of authority may be sufficient for all documents signed by the legal representative on behalf of that client. For an individual client

---

was legally unrepresented when he made several statements verified by statements of truth, which were false. The claimants' lawyers wrote several times to him pointing out that he could face contempt proceedings if his statements verified by statement of truth were untrue, and if they were made without an honest belief in their truth. The lawyers also asked the first defendant to confirm that he understood the meaning of a statement of truth and that he believed that all statements in his defence were true. After obtaining legal representation, the first defendant repeated some of the false statements and expanded on them. The judge found that the consequences of making a false statement had been 'fully brought home to [the first defendant]'. He was found guilty of contempt, fined and ordered to pay at least part of the costs of the claimants, but not jailed (see also **section 30.4**).

4 For more specific guidance on continuing obligations as to whether the statement remains true, consult specialist litigation material.

it may be necessary to obtain their signed authorisation on each occasion and fully explain the consequences of making a false statement
(whether or not the client in fact signs the document) – in which case it
could be argued that it might be easier and less time-consuming to get
the client to sign each statement of truth.[5]

---

5 See O'Hare and Browne, *Civil Litigation*, 13th edn, Sweet & Maxwell, 2007, para. 12.004
for discussion of the practicalities of getting the statement of truth signed.

CHAPTER 12

Affidavits

CHECKLIST
<ul><li>The affidavit must be verified by an oath or solemn affirmation made by the maker ('the Deponent')[1] of the affidavit. The oath or solemn affirmation must be made by the Deponent before a person authorised to administer the oath or take the solemn affirmation (known as 'the Commissioner' in this chapter; see **section 12.2**); and<ul><li>it must be signed by the Deponent (or all the Deponents, if more than one); and</li><li>it must be signed by the Commissioner.</li></ul></li><li>Prior to taking the oath or solemn affirmation the Commissioner should:<ul><li>confirm that the person before her is the person named in the affidavit;</li><li>if the affidavit is already signed when presented to the Commissioner, ask whether the signature is that of the Deponent, or if not signed see the Deponent sign the affidavit;</li><li>asks the Deponent whether she understands what the purpose of making the affidavit is: to confirm that its contents (and any attachments) are true;</li><li>check that any attachments are correct.</li></ul></li><li>The Commissioner must state in writing (by hand) (or by means of a rubber stamp impress) her name, qualification and address in full beneath the Commisioner's signature.</li><li>The Commissioner must state at what place and on what date the oath is administered or the solemn affirmation is taken.</li></ul>

---

1 CPR PD 32.2: 'A deponent is a person who gives evidence by affidavit or affirmation'.

Form/structure of signature block[2]

[SWORN] [AFFIRMED] at [*address where the affidavit is sworn*] the [*day*] of [*month*] [*year*] }

(signature of Deponent)

Before me   (signature of person before whom affidavit is sworn)

[*name of person before whom affidavit is sworn*]
[*qualification of person before whom affidavit is sworn – e.g. Solicitor/Commissioner for Oaths, etc.*]
[*address of person before whom affidavit is sworn*]

12.1   TYPE OF STATEMENT, AFFIRMATION OR OATH THAT MUST BE MADE WHEN THE DOCUMENT IS SIGNED/EXECUTED

Oath

If the Deponent is to swear an oath, then the procedure and the statement required are:

- the Deponent must be in the presence of the Commissioner;
- the Deponent is to hold:
  - the New Testament; or
  - if a Jew, the Old Testament
- in their uplifted hand;
- the Deponent is to say (or repeat after the Commissioner) the following words:

I swear by Almighty God that this is my name and handwriting and that the contents of this my affidavit are true [and that these are the exhibits referred to therein]

Affirmation

If the Deponent wishes to make an affirmation, then the procedure and the statement required are:

- the Deponent must be in the presence of the Commissioner;
- the Deponent is to say (or repeat after the Commissioner) the following words:

I, [*name of Deponent*], do solemnly, sincerely and truly declare and affirm that this is my name and handwriting and that the contents of this my affirmation are true [and that these are the exhibits referred to therein]

---

2 Formally known as the 'jurat': CPR PD 32.5.1.

Manner of administering the words of the oath or affirmation

The normal practice is for the words of the oath to be dictated phrase by phrase to the Deponent by the Commissioner. This enables the Commissioner, on saying the words 'this is my name and handwriting', to point to the Deponent's signature.

Alternatively, the Commissioner may have a card showing the words of the oath or affirmation, which would be shown or handed to the Deponent. The Deponent would then be asked to read them in the Commissioner's presence.

12.2 (PROFESSIONAL) PERSONS WHO MUST BE PRESENT WHEN THE DOCUMENT IS SIGNED/EXECUTED AND THEIR ROLE

The following people can administer the oath or take the affirmation (CPR PD 32.9.1):

- Commissioners for Oaths, comprising:

    - solicitors (holding a current practising certificate);
    - barristers;
    - notaries public (but not ecclesiastical notaries);
    - licensed conveyancers;
    - Fellows of the Institute of Legal Executives (if they pay a full subscription to the Institute; but not retired Fellows);

- certain officials of the Supreme Court;
- circuit judges or district judges;
- justices of the peace;
- certain officials of any county court appointed by the judge of that court for the purpose; and
- official receivers and deputy official receivers.

12.3 HOW ARE ANY ATTACHMENTS/EXHIBITS TO THE MAIN DOCUMENT DEALT WITH?

Documents or things (such as physical objects) (known formally as 'exhibits': CPR PD 32.11) which are referred to in the affidavit are to be kept separate from the affidavit but must be produced at the same time as the affidavit before the Commissioner. Such exhibits need to be marked with the identifying initials and number matching that found in the relevant place in the affidavit.

Each of the exhibits can be marked as follows:

This is the [*specify attachment/exhibit*] marked [*initials and number referred to in affidavit*] referred to in the annexed affidavit of [*name of Deponent*] sworn/affirmed before me this [*day*] day of [*month*] [*year*]

(signature of Commissioner)

a [Commissioner for Oaths] [solicitor empowered to administer oaths]

In practice, this form of words might be written by hand on the attachment/exhibit.

12.4   MAKING AMENDMENTS

Any alterations and amendments after the affidavit has been sworn or affirmed must be initialled by the maker of the affidavit and Commissioner before whom the affidavit was sworn or affirmed (CPR PD 32.8.1).

12.5   FEES CHARGED BY THE PROFESSIONAL PERSON

For taking an affidavit, a Commissioner for Oaths shall charge £5 for each person making the affidavit and £2 for each exhibit referred to in the affidavit.[3]

12.6   MAIN VARIATIONS TO ANY OF THE ABOVE

If the Deponent cannot or is unable to read or sign the affidavit

The *signature block* is altered so that the Commissioner certifies (CPR PD 32.7.1):

- he has read the affidavit to the Deponent;
- the Deponent appeared to understand it; and
- the Deponent signed or made his mark, in the Commissioner's presence.

---

3 The Commissioners for Oaths (Fees) Order 1993, SI 1993/2297 and the Commissioners for Oaths (Authorised Persons) (Fees) Order 1993, SI 1993/2298.

If the Commissioner reads the affidavit to the Deponent

A certificate should be added to the *signature block* in the following terms:[4]

[SWORN] [AFFIRMED] at [*address where the*   (mark or signature of
affidavit is sworn] the [*day*] of [*month*] [*year*]   Deponent)

*Before me, I having first read over the contents of this [affidavit *if sworn*] [affirmation *if affirmed*] to the deponent [*if there are exhibits, add* and explained the nature and effect of the exhibits referred to in it] who appeared to understand it and approved its content as accurate, and made his mark on the [affidavit *if sworn*] [affirmation *if affirmed*] in my presence.

(signature of person before whom affidavit is sworn)

[*name of person before whom affidavit is sworn*]

[*qualification of person before whom affidavit is sworn – e.g. Solicitor/Commissioner for Oaths, etc.*]
[*address of person before whom affidavit is sworn*]

* Wording after 'Before me' can be replaced by the following wording: 'the witness to the mark of the deponent having been first sworn that he had read over [etc. as above] and that he saw him make his mark on the affidavit'. (Witness must sign.)

If the Deponent does not wish to use the standard oath but wishes to be sworn

The oath can be administered in any other lawful manner, and if the Deponent is religious then the oath should be sworn in some manner binding on the Deponent's conscience.

Particular religious requirements

Persons from different religious faiths may wish to use a different version of the oath indicated above together with, in some other instances, other requirements. Alternatively, instead of using an oath, an affirmation can be used if it is not practical or convenient to accommodate the formalities required by a particular religious faith.

Jews

Orthodox Jews are likely to be reluctant to swear an oath for religious reasons. They will normally prefer to affirm, and should be made aware of the

---

4 If one of these certificates is not included then the affidavit may not be used in evidence, unless the court is satisfied that it was read to the Deponent and that the Deponent appeared to understand it (CPR PD 32.7.2).

possibility of affirmation. Even those Jews willing to swear an oath may feel uncomfortable mentioning the name of God and would probably prefer words such as 'I swear by the Holy Torah'.

Many Jews (especially Orthodox Jews) will find it difficult to hold a non-Jewish version of the Old Testament while swearing the oath. They would prefer to hold an orthodox Jewish version of the Old Testament (such as those commonly used in synagogues in the United Kingdom).[5]

In addition to taking the oath on the Old Testament in the form specified above, some Jewish men may wish to cover their heads (as a solemn occasion).

Muslims

A Muslim will normally take the oath on the Koran (or Qur'an), commencing the oath by:

> I swear by almighty Allah that . . .

The Koran, whether in English or in Arabic, should be kept in a cover.

A strict Muslim may require a copy of the Koran in Arabic, rather than a translation. A Muslim may wish to wash his hands or some other part of his body before taking the oath.

Liberal and strict Muslims recognise the Old Testament or the Torah. However, strict Muslims are unlikely to take the oath on the Old Testament or the Torah. Liberal Muslims, on the other hand, would have no problem in taking the oath on the Old Testament or the Torah (if the Koran was not available).

Parsees

A Parsee takes the oath upon the Zendavesta.

Sikhs

A Sikh will normally take the oath on the Guru Granth Sahib (or any part of it, which can be the Japji Shahib). However, the Guru Granth Sahib is a very large volume which is considered extremely sacred by Sikhs, and for oath purposes the Japji Sahib should suffice, as it is small in size.[6] A Sikh will begin the oath by saying:

> I swear by Sat Guru Nanak Dev ji that . . .

---

5 For example, the Hertz Chumash or the Artscroll Stone edition of the Tanach (the Torah/Prophets/Writings). The reason for this is that there are significant differences between the non-Jewish and the Jewish version of the Old Testament.
6 The Japji Sahib is the first part of the the Guru Granth Sahib. It describes God, his creation and what a Sikh should do to be emancipated.

The Guru Granth Sahib (or any part of it, such as the Japji Sahib) must always be covered with expensive and good-quality cloth, as the Guru Granth Sahib (or any part of it) is considered by Sikhs as the physical body of their Gurus, and the body of their Gurus must always be dressed in the most expensive 'attire'.

A Sikh may wish to wash his hands or some other part of his body before taking the oath. He may also wish to remove his shoes or cover his head.

Hindus

A Hindu will normally take the oath on the Bhagavad Gita, commencing the oath by:

> I swear by the Bhagavad Gita that . . .

A Hindu may wish to remove his shoes before taking the oath. It is advisable that the Bhagavad Gita is kept in a wrapper of orange or red cotton cloth.

Rastafarians

A Rastafarian may wish to commence the oath by:

> I swear by Jah that . . .

Buddhists

Buddhists will normally affirm.

Taking oaths of clients or persons of different religious beliefs

A Commissioner who has before her a person from a different religious or ethnic background may be sometimes uncertain how that person should be addressed, what religious text they use to take an oath with, or the ceremonies involved in taking an oath. What is set out above will provide some guidance, but the points as set out in Table 12.1 below will provide some context.[7]

Children

There appears to be no special form of oath or affirmation as regards children. Nor is there any special duty on a Commissioner to make enquiries

---

7 These points are taken from the Judicial Studies Board publication 'Fairness in Courts and Tribunals' (**www.jsboard.co.uk**). They were written for taking oaths in court but equally apply to taking oaths outside of courts. Also of interest are acceptable and non-acceptable ways of describing or naming persons from different racial minorities and outlines of different religious faiths, their holy books and major religious festivals.

about the age of the child, her capacity or her understanding. Perhaps best practice is for the Commissioner to satisfy herself that the Deponent child understands the contents of the proposed affidavit and that she understands she is to be sworn to the truth of those contents.[8]

Table 12.1   Oath taking in relation to different religious beliefs

Oath taking	Naming and naming systems
• Religious practices in relation to oath taking should be handled sensitively – not as though they are a nuisance. • Not everyone from miniority communities is religious: some may prefer to affirm. • Muslim, Hindu and Sikh women may prefer to affirm if having to give evidence during menstruation or shortly after childbirth. • Requests to wash hands, feet or other body parts before taking the oath should be treated with respect. • Some witnesses may want to remove shoes or cover their heads or bow with folded hands. • Holy books should be covered in cloth or velvet bags at all times when not in use. When uncovered, they should only be touched by the person taking the oath, not by the Commissioner. They should not be marked inside or out. • In many faith traditions the holy scripture is believed to contain the actual presence of that faith's divinity and is accordingly revered.	• It is more important to treat people with courtesy and address them properly than to try to learn all the different naming systems. • Ask individuals how they would like to be addressed, how to pronounce their name and how to spell it. • Ask for full name: first, middle and last. Do not ask for 'Christian' name or 'surname'. • Do not record or address a male Muslim or Sikh by his religious name only; e.g. Mohammed or Allah, or Singh – check in case these are last names. • Do not record or address a female Muslim or Sikh by her religious name only: e.g. Begum, Bibi or Kaur.

Persons unable to speak or understand the English language

If the Deponent is unable to speak or understand the English language, an interpreter must be employed. The interpreter will interpret the text of the

8 See Solicitors' Code of Conduct 2007, guidance to rule 10.03, para. 10; see **Appendix 3**.

affidavit (or swear or affirm that she has already done so) and the words of the oath or the affirmation to the Deponent, after having been herself duly sworn.

Points to note

The following points should be considered.

1. The *signature block* should follow on immediately from the main text of the affidavit, and should not be put on a separate page.
2. The Commissioner must be a person independent of the parties and the parties' representatives. The following were given as examples of when a solicitor should not act under the (now superseded) *Guide to the Professional Conduct of Solicitors 1999*:
   (a) in relation to a local authority's business where the solicitor is a member or employee of that local authority;
   (b) regarding proofs in bankruptcy when acting for that proving creditor or regarding the winding-up of an estate when acting for the personal representatives;
   (c) when employed part-time by another solicitor for a client of that employer;
   (d) when in the full or part-time employment of a company in matters in which the company is concerned.
   These still seem circumstances where it would be sensible for a person not to deal with an affidavit as a Commissioner.
3. Only an individual can make an affidavit.
4. There appears to be nothing in either the court rules governing the use of affidavits or other legislation that requires the Deponent to make her signature or mark in the presence of the Commissioner.
5. There are specific matters which a solicitor must ensure when administrating an oath or affirmation:
   (a) that the Deponent is present;
   (b) that either the affidavit is signed in the presence of the solicitor, or if already signed, that the Deponent confirms that the signature is that of the Deponent;
   (c) that any attachments are correct;
   (d) that the Deponent understands what they are doing and that the purpose of making the affidavit is to confirm that its contents and any attachments are true.

PART II
Legal commentary

CHAPTER 13

Agreements under hand

13.1 INTRODUCTION

This chapter is concerned mainly with contracts that are signed but do not have to be signed as deeds.[1]

A general principle under English law is that contracts do not need to be recorded in writing and/or signed. A distinguishing feature of English law is the relative informality accorded the recording of many transactions, events and contracts.

The requirements to use writing and/or signatures are now found mainly in statute and are usually confined to particular situations. This chapter considers the following topics:

1. Formalities to enter into a contract and some terminology.
2. The execution of contracts.
3. What makes up, and the significance of, a signature.[2]
4. The main contractual and contract-related situations that need to be recorded in writing and/or signed.
5. The meaning of 'writing'.

The meaning of a signature is considered in some depth because of the consequences for the signatory who signs a document (she is generally bound by the signature) and because the form and function of a signature can take many different forms. The aim of this chapter is to provide a convenient summary

---

1 It is not possible to document even a small number of instances when there is a statutory requirement for a document to be in writing and/or signed because of the sheer numbers involved. For example, according to research, there are more than 6,000 references to the use of signatures in legislation: C. Reed, 'What is a Signature', *Journal of Information, Law and Technology*, issue 3, 2000 (available from **http://www2.warwick.ac.uk/fac/soc/law/elj/jilt/2000_3/reed/**). For an up-to-date summary of the meaning, uses and form of a signature see Stephen Mason, *Electronic Signatures in Law*, 2nd edn, Tottel Publishing, 2007, Chs 1 and 2.
2 This section will also focus on the meaning of a 'signature' in two areas of importance to many solicitors: contracts for the sale or other disposition of interests in land, and invoices.

of the law in this area when faced with particular instances of a signature that is not 'normal' or used in an 'acceptable' manner or form.

13.2   CONTRACTS

Methods for entering into a contract

Contracts can be entered into:

- by word of mouth; or
- in writing (either made as a deed or not); or
- partly in writing and partly by word of mouth; or
- by implication from the conduct of the parties.

Except in particular cases, the parties to a contract are free to construct the form of the contract as they wish (i.e. whether it is made by word, in writing, the form of the writing, whether it needs to be signed, etc.).[3]

It is possible to enter into a written contract without signing it. By convention, where a contract is completely or partially in writing, the parties to it will sign the document containing the provisions of the contract which are in writing (or at least the party under an obligation will sign).[4] In many cases, one or more parties have no choice but to sign; it is a term of the contract (sometimes by implication) that one or more parties have to sign, or simply one party will demand that the parties each sign or that the other party signs.[5] This is not normally a requirement of law but arises from the (presumed) agreement of the parties.

Usually, therefore, the important issue for agreements under hand is what the signature is intended to mean (when or if it is required to be used), rather than the requirement that it take place.[6]

---

3 There is also statutory provision for this freedom, in principle, as to the form of a contract; for example: Sale of Goods Act 1979 (SGA 1979), s.4(1) which provides that a contract of sale may be made in writing (either with or without a seal), or by word of mouth, or partly in writing and partly by word of mouth, or may be implied from the conduct of the parties. Although this provision is stated not to apply to corporations, there are provisions in relevant legislation concerning corporations which allow them to enter into contracts with the same amount of formality as an individual: Corporate Bodies' Contracts Act 1960 (CBCA 1960), s.1; CA 1985, s.36.
4 Although the available methods of making a signature have changed, particularly with the use of electronic and digital signatures (see **Chapter 25**).
5 For example, in many consumer contracts, where the consumer is entering into a contract with a large organisation, the consumer will often be presented with a standard form of terms, and she will be asked to sign if she wishes to enter into the contract in question. The organisation will simply refuse to enter into the contract without the signature of the consumer.
6 For example, for a deed made by an individual, it is a requirement that the individual has to sign the deed. She has no choice but to sign if she wishes to produce a valid and legally

The binding nature of a contract will depend on the general requirements of contract law (offer and acceptance, the presence of adequate consideration, the intention to create legal relations, etc.).[7]

Some terminology

Conventionally, a contract:

(a)   in writing (but not required to be in the form of a deed) is called an agreement 'under hand', and in 'simple form';

(b)   entered into by word of mouth is sometimes known as an oral contract or a parol agreement;

(c)   made in the form of a deed is in 'solemn form'.

13.3   EXECUTION OF CONTRACTS

Usually, where an individual or body corporate[8] wishes to execute a contract with a signature, all that is required is that the individual or body corporate (normally by a person on its behalf) simply signs in the appropriate place in the agreement – a signature being no more than the writing with a pen of the name of the person actually signing. This is a simple example. The meaning and form of a signature is considered further at **section 13.4**.

Because of the lack of formality as to the form that characterises the entering into contracts under English law, the way individuals and bodies corporate sign and the wording used in agreements have developed mainly by practice with particular developments arising from case law. CA 2006 and CBCA 1960, which govern most bodies corporate in England and Wales, enable contracts to be made on behalf of bodies corporate. These Acts do not specify any particular requirements when the contracts are made in writing (for example, no requirement that a written contract needs to be signed or expressed in a particular way if there is no general or particular legal requirement for so doing).

By convention, at the end of a written agreement there is a formal statement indicating that the parties to the contract have agreed to its terms and

---

effective deed (as well as fulfilling the other requirements for creating a valid and legally effective deed). A signature when used in a contract can have a number of meanings, which are considered below.

7 For the formation of binding contracts, consult standard contract textbooks such as *Chitty on Contracts, Treitel on the Law of Contract*, etc.

8 The term 'corporation' or 'body corporate' used in this chapter includes most forms of organisation in England which have a separate legal identity and will include companies formed under or regulated by CA 2006. The meaning of a 'corporation' is covered in **Chapter 15**.

conditions,[9] and a statement with places for the parties to sign to indicate their consent to the contract's terms and conditions.[10]

'Executed as a contract' clause

The *executed as a contract* clause is not required for the contract to be legally valid or for the valid execution of the contract. It

> is added merely to preserve the evidence of its due execution. For this reason it may be of importance and, except in instruments relating to registered land, it should never in practice be omitted.[11]

Traditionally drafted *executed as a contract* clauses commence with the words 'AS WITNESS' (rather than 'IN WITNESS' if the agreement is executed as a deed). Modern precedents often commence with other wording such as 'Agreed by' or 'Signed by' or 'Executed by'. Examples are given in **Chapter 1**. Other forms, perhaps in letter agreements, or on pre-printed forms, might state 'I agree to be bound by the terms and conditions', or 'Agreed'.

In other types of document executed as a deed (e.g. a power of attorney), the authors' recommendation would be to use the traditional language to avoid any risk that the document would be misinterpreted – the relatively relaxed attitude of the courts to the format and language of commercial contracts may not apply to formal types of instrument such as powers of attorney and trust deeds.

Signature block

There are no mandated forms or contents for a *signature block*. By convention, there is usually wording to indicate that, for an individual, the agreement is being signed by that individual, and for a body corporate, the agreement is being signed either by the body corporate, or for and on behalf of the body corporate. It is usual to provide in the *signature block* that the person who is signing should print their name, and where appropriate indicate their job title; and sometimes (particularly if parties may sign on different dates) the *signature block* may also state the date their signature was made. These latter points can be useful pointers as to which individual actually signed an agreement, in case of subsequent disagreement between the parties. Examples are given in **Chapter 1**.

---

9 Formally known as the testimonium, or as the *executed as a contract* clause.
10 Formally known as the attestation clause, or as the *signature block*.
11 *Encyclopaedia of Forms and Precedents*, vol.12(2), 'Deeds', para.18 [3104].

Points to note

Signing *by* a company

CA 2006 permits a company *itself* to execute a contract. This is achieved by the contract being signed by:

- a director in the presence of a witness (who attests the director's signature); or
- two directors; or
- a director and a secretary of the company;

and there being some words in the contract or document that state that the contract is executed by the company (CA 2006, s.42(2), (3), (4)). The company can, also, use its seal (if it has one).

Signing on behalf of another person or organisation

Bodies corporate usually cannot execute documents themselves; the documents need to be executed on their behalf. An exception is indicated above. Individuals, partnerships and other types of person will often have documents executed on their behalf. For example, a sole trader may have routine contracts signed by a member of her staff. The usual expressions that are found in a *signature block* to indicate that the document is being executed on behalf of another include:

- for;
- on behalf of;
- for, and on behalf of;
- on account of.

These expressions are normally to indicate that another person will be liable for an obligation entered into as described in the document and not the person who is signing the document.[12] This will, at least, imply a form of agency relationship between the signatory and her principal. Also, the signatory will be giving at least an implied warranty or undertaking that she can sign and bind the principal.[13] The wording used (such as 'for and on behalf of'), the placement of the wording and any external evidence called if a case

---

12 See *Stroud's Judicial Dictionary*, 2nd edn, Sweet & Maxwell, under heading 'For'.
13 *Aggs* v. *Nicholson* (1856) 25 LJ Ex 348: where solicitors wrote in a letter to the plaintiffs solicitors: '"in consideration of" plaintiff "consenting to the sale [of goods]" "we hereby, on behalf of the assignees, consent that the net proceeds" shall be paid to the plaintiff'. This offer was accepted, the goods were sold, but the net proceeds were not paid over. It was held that the solicitors did not contract for themselves. It was also held that in such cases there is an implied undertaking by the professed agent that he has the authority he professes to have and, if an agent did not have authority to bind the principal, the agent would not stand in place of the principal and be liable for the contract, but could be sued for deceit (if there was fraud) or be liable for damages (Lord Campbell, CJ).

results because of a dispute, may make the signatory personally liable.[14] In practice:

- wording such 'on behalf of', etc. should always be positioned next to the place where the signatory is to sign;
- if there is any doubt that she is acting as agent for the principal, clear wording should be used in the body of the document, the *executed as a contract* clause, or in the *signature block*;
- the role of the signatory should be stated (in the *signature block*); or
- an employee or officer of a body corporate should state their job title and print their name for ease of identification.

13.4 SIGNATURES

Introductory points

There appears to be no substantive definition of what makes up a signature in English legislation. Many legislative measures require use of a signature but none, it appears, provides an authoritative definition or description of what makes up a signature or specifies a particular form.[15]

Case law has been the main source of the meaning of different forms and functions of a signature. Much of this case law has concerned the interpretation of the Statute of Frauds 1677 (virtually all of it is now repealed, except for the section concerning guarantees), LPA 1925, s.40 (now repealed), and the Wills Act 1837. The requirements of the Statute of Frauds 1677, are considered briefly at the end of this chapter (**section 13.11**). What follows can be no more than a *brief* summary of the law in this area.

Perhaps the most obvious view of a signature is a person writing her own name with her own hand on a piece of paper.

---

14 See *H O Brandt & Co.* v. *H N Morris & Co.* [1917] 2 KB 784: the plaintiff gave to the defendant a bought note, which stated at the beginning 'For and on behalf of' a foreign third party and stated 'we have bought from you 60 tons pure aniline oil' and was signed by the plaintiff in the name of plaintiff. The plaintiff was sued for non-delivery of the oil. Held that the plaintiff was the contracting party and was entitled to sue upon the contract. Read CJ relied on the judgment of Mellish LJ in *Gadd* v. *Houghton* (1876) 1 Ex D 357:

> The language used must be interpreted according to its plain and natural meaning. As is said in the note to Thomson v. Davenport 2 Sm. L. C., 12th edn, 379, when a man signs a contract in his own name he is prima facie a contracting party and liable, and there must be something very strong on the face of the instrument to shew that the liability does not attach to him. But if there are plain words to show that he is contracting on behalf of somebody else, why are we not to give effect to them?

15 In his research, Reed did not find any legislation which '*expressly* limits valid signatures to a particular form' (original emphasis), but some legislation which did more than merely state that a signature was required indicated that the meaning of a signature included the use of facsimiles and that a signature had to be made in a writing (the actual signing of a physical object). The Interpretation Act 1978 (IA 1978) does not deal with signatures at all.

Different meanings of 'signature'

A valid signature can be defined according to whether it comes within an acceptable category of methods of expression, or performs some function. A valid signature:

- can be the signature of a full name, the signature of just a surname, or the use of initials, a mark, a facsimile, and so on; and
- can have the purpose:
  - to authenticate the contents of the document to which the signature is appended; or
  - to indicate that the person who has signed the document has assented, approved or agreed to all the provisions contained in the document; or
  - to indicate and confirm the identity of the person signing.

One definition of a 'signature' which has received judicial approval is:

Signed; signature. (1) Generally, a signature is the writing, or otherwise affixing of, a person's name, or a mark to represent his name, by himself or by his authority ... with the intention of authenticating a document as being of, or as binding on, the person whose name or mark is so written or affixed.[16]

13.5 COURT DECISIONS ON WHAT MAKES UP A 'SIGNATURE'

The following points have been decided concerning signatures in specific situations.

What can amount to a valid signature

Valid signatures include the following:

- a signature placed on any part of a document, as long as it relates to every part of a document, and the purpose of the signature is to authenticate all of the document;[17]

---

16 *Stroud's Judicial Dictionary*, 2nd edn, Sweet & Maxwell, vol. 4, p. 2783, cited with approval by Romer LJ, *Goodman* v. *J Eban Ltd* [1954] 1 All ER 763 at 770.

17 *Caton* v. *Caton* (1867) LR 2 HL 127: per Lord Westbury: 'the signature must be so placed as to shew that it was intended to relate and refer to, and that in fact it does relate and refer to, every part of the instrument'; *Evans* v. *Hoare* [1892] 1 QB 593; *Brooks* v. *Billingham* (1912) 56 Sol Jo 503, where a signature written in the body of a memorandum of a purchase transaction by some person lawfully authorised to write it by the purchaser was sufficient to satisfy the Statute of Frauds, s.4. In this case, when the agreement was entered into the vendor's son-in-law was present and wrote a memorandum at the direction of the purchaser. The memorandum recorded details of the transaction, acknowledged receipt of a deposit and was signed in the name of the vendor by her son-in-law; *Leeman* v. *Stocks* [1951] Ch 941, 1 All ER 1043, concerned a sale of land by public auction where the agreement was signed only by the purchaser. The vendor's name and initials had been inserted at the head of the agreement by the auctioneer before the auction. The court

- a signature in pencil;[18]
- a signature consisting of initials;[19]
- a partial signature;[20]
- a signature consisting of a mark,[21] and the name of the person does not need to appear in the document;[22]
- a signature made by means of a stamp;[23]

---

held that in procuring through his agent (the auctioneer) the purchaser's signature to the document so as to bind the purchaser, the vendor was, by his agent, recognising his name which was written at the beginning of the document. Since the purchaser signed on the understanding that the document contained the terms of his contract with the vendor (whose name was in the document) and as it was the intention of both the purchaser and the vendor's agent that the document should be the final written record of the contract which had already been made between the parties, then the document was a sufficient memorandum to satisfy LPA 1925, s.40(1).

18 *Lucas* v. *James* (1849) 7 Hare 410 at 419; *Geary* v *Physic* (1826) 5 B & C 234: 'There is no authority for saying that where the law requires a contract to be in writing, that writing must be in ink' (Abbot CJ), where there was a signature on a promissory note in pencil, and per Bayley J:

> I think that a writing in pencil is a writing within the meaning of that term at common law, and that it is a writing within the custom of merchants. I cannot see any reason why, when the law requires a contract to be in writing, that contract should be void if it be written in pencil ... I think, therefore, that this is a valid writing at common law, and also that it is an indorsement according to the usage and custom of merchants; for that usage only requires that the indorsement should be in writing, and not that the writing should be made with any specific materials.

19 *Phillimore* v. *Barry* (1808) 1 Camp 513, 170 ER 1040: a case concerning a contract, where a signature (in the form of initials, together with certain documentation, was a sufficient memorandum in writing to satisfy the Statute of Frauds 1677; *Chichester* v. *Cobb* (1866) 14 LT 433; *Caton* v. *Caton* (1867) LR HL 127 at 143 per Lord Westbury; *Re Blewitt's Goods* (1880) 5 PD 116; *Re Savory's Goods* (1851) 15 Jur 1042. *Hill* v. *Hill* [1947] Ch 231, [1947] 1 All ER 54, concerning the renewal of a lease, where initials inserted in a rent book which referred to and authenticated the words 'renewed lease' constituted a memorandum or note of the contract, signed by the party to be charged within (the now repealed) LPA 1925, s.40; *Re Schultz* (1984) 8 DLR (4th) 147.

20 *Re Chalcraft* [1948] P 222: where the testatrix signed 'E. Chal' but did not finish signing the name. She was in bad health and signed when it was clear that she was near death. Held that the partial signature amounted to a valid signature, but the court took the surrounding issues into account, that she knew and approved the contents of the will and that what she signed was intended to be her signature.

21 *Morton* v. *Copeland* (1855) 16 CB 517 at 535: 'Signature does not necessarily mean writing a person's Christian and surname, but any mark which identifies as the act of the party.' per Maule J at 535; *Re Field's Goods* (1843) 2 Curt 752, 163 ER 890; *Baker* v. *Dening* (1838) 8 Ad & El 94, 112 ER 771, where under the Statute of Frauds 1677, the making of a mark by the devisor, to a will of real estate, is a sufficient signing, and it is not necessary to prove that he could not write his name at the time, although external evidence may be called to indicate that the will was correctly attested; *Harrison* v. *Harrison* (1803) 8 Ves 185, 32 ER 234, where signing a will with a cross did not make the will void.

22 *Re Bryce's Goods* (1839) 2 Curt 325, 163 ER 427: a will signed with a mark but the testatrix's name did not appear in the will.

23 *Bennett* v. *Brumfitt* (1867) LR 3 CP 28; *Jenkins* v. *Gaisford and Thring* (1863) 3 Sw & Tr 93; *McDonald* v. *John Twiname Ltd* [1953] 2 QB 304, [1953] 2 All ER 589, CA; *Goodman* v. *J Eban Ltd* [1954] 1 QB 550, [1954] 1 All ER 763, where a bill of costs sent to a client by

- the answerback of the sender of a telex would constitute a signature;[24]
- a signature contained in a facsimile;[25]
- a signature made by means of printing;[26]

---

a solicitor, which concluded with 'Yours faithfully, Goodman, Monroe & Co' and beneath these typed words was applied a stamp of the name of the solicitors, being a facsimile of their handwritten signature; *British Estate Investment Society Ltd* v. *Jackson (HM Inspector of Taxes)* (1956) 37 TC 79, 35 ATC 413, where an Additional Commissioner signed documents in volumes of evidence with a rubber stamp, and the applicants contended that the documents were not signed in accordance with the relevant tax Act. The court held them to be properly signed and that there was a 'presumption in law ... the document has been properly signed until the contrary has been shown by a person who desires to upset that conclusion' (Danckwerts J).

24 *Clipper Maritime Ltd* v. *Shirlstar Container Transport Ltd, The Anemone* [1987] 1 Lloyd's Rep 546: *obiter* view of Staughton J, concerning whether a valid contract of guarantee had been created, that exchange of telexes constituted part of the evidence for the formation of the contract. Also *obiter* was Staughton's view that the answerback of the *receiver* of a telex would not constitute a signature as it only authenticates the document and does not convey approval of the contents.

25 *Re a debtor (No. 2021 of 1995), ex p. Inland Revenue Commissioners* v. *The Debtor* [1996] 2 All ER 345: concerning a proxy form sent by the Commissioners by post and then by facsimile, and whether the proxy form sent by facsimile was signed for the purposes of the Insolvency Rules 1986, r.8.2(3), the judge (Laddie J) held that the proxy form was signed for the purposes of the Insolvency Rules; he went on to state (at 351–2):

> When a creditor faxes a proxy form to the chairman of a creditors' meeting he transmits two things at the same time, the contents of the form and the signature applied to it. The receiving fax is in effect instructed by the transmitting creditor to reproduce his signature on the proxy form which is itself being created at the receiving station. It follows that, in my view, the received fax is a proxy form signed by the principal or by someone authorised by him. The view which I have reached appears to me to be consistent with the realities of modern technology. If it is legitimate to send by post a proxy form signed with a rubber stamp, why should it not be at least as authentic to send the form by fax?

> The facts of the present case illustrates (*sic*) the point well. Here the proxy form was sent both by post and by fax. Such being the nature of postal delivery, the creditor could not be certain whether his proxy was received at all or on time. On the other hand, when the fax is transmitted he knows that it has been received because, first, he obtains an answerback code and, second, an activity report is normally printed out. From the chairman's point of view, there is nothing about a received fax which puts him in a worse position to detect forgeries than when he receives through the post or by hand delivery a document signed by hand by a person whose signature he has never seen before or one signed by stamping. The reality is that fax transmission is likely to be a more reliable and certainly is a more speedy method of communication than post. It would be a pity if r.8.3(3) required creditors to convey their views to the chairman by the older, slower and less reliable form of communication.

26 *Brydges* v. *Dix* (1891) 7 TLR 215: where a printed signature, of the clerk to the local health authority, to notices under the Public Health Act 1875 is sufficient within the meaning of s.266 of that Act. This case raised a question as to the mode of affixing signatures to legal documents or documents required by way of notice or otherwise under any statute. The court concluded that if a signature was required (and they thought it was not) a manual signature was not necessary and the printed signature was sufficient. All that was necessary was that the notice should be authenticated as coming from the town clerk. The court also took note of *Bennett* v. *Brumfitt* (1867) LR 3 CP 28 where it was

- a signature made by means of typewriting (*Newborne* v. *Sensolid (Great Britain) Ltd* [1954] 1 QB 45);
- where an illiterate person holds the top of a pen, and another person writes the name of the illiterate person with the pen (*Helsham* v. *Langley* (1841) 11 LJ Ch 17);
- where a person makes a mark, her hand being guided by another person;[27]
- a signature can consist of a trade name;[28]
- a third party can write the signature at the request of a party (*Brooks* v. *Billingham* (1912) 56 Sol Jo 503);
- the signature of a person engraved on to a stamp and then applied by a third party in the presence of the person;[29]
- the name of a person can be applied by an agent even where the agent is not in the presence of the person, provided that the agent has specific[30] or general authority (*France* v. *Dutton* [1891] 2 QB 208);

---

held that a notice of objection, to which the objector's signature was only stamped, was sufficient.

27 *Wilson* v. *Beddard* (1841) 12 Sim 28, 59 ER 1041: where a person was too ill to sign, his making the mark on the last page of the will and faint strokes on the other pages of the will was evidence that he intended to sign the will.

28 *Cohen* v. *Roche* [1927] 1 KB 169: where the defendant was an auctioneer and the plaintiff traded under the name of 'Fredericks'. The defendant auctioned goods to the plaintiff, and then wrote the amount and the name 'Fredericks' in the sale catalogue. The defendant refused to deliver the goods to the plaintiff. Held that the printed name of the defendant in the catalogue constituted a signature and together with the note of the amount and 'Fredericks' constituted a signed memorandum of the sale of the goods as required by the Sale of Goods Act 1893, s.4.

29 *Jenkins* v. *Gaisford & Thring, in the Goods of Jenkins* (1863) 3 Sw & Tr 93: in this case a testator had his signature engraved onto a stamp while he was well. When he became ill he made a codicil to his will, and had his servant apply the stamp to the codicil in his presence. Held that the will was validly signed under the Statute of Wills 1540: 'the word "signed" in [s.9] must have the same meaning whether the signature is made by the testator himself, or by some other person in his presence or by his direction . . . The mark by the instrument or stamp was intended to stand for and represent the signature of the testator' (Sir C. Cresswell). In *Bennett* v. *Brumfitt* (1867) LR 3 CP 28, the signature of the defendant was engraved on a stamp. The stamp was used to sign a notice of objection under the now repealed Parliamentary Voters Registration Act 1843, s.17: 'The ordinary mode of affixing a signature to a document is not by the hand alone, but by the hand coupled with some instrument, such as a pen or pencil. I see no distinction between using a pen or a pencil and using a stamp, where the impression is put upon the paper by the proper hand of the party signing' (Bovill CJ). See also *Blades* v. *Lawrence* (1874) LR 9 QB 374, (1874) 43 LJQB 133, where the signature of a judge was engraved on a stamp, and stamp applied by the judge's clerk; *McDonald* v. *John Twiname Ltd* [1953] 2 QB 304, CA, where an apprenticeship agreement was signed by the company by application of a stamp containing the name of the company.

30 *R* v. *Kent JJ* (1873) LR 8 QB 305; *London County Council* v. *Vitamins Ltd* [1955] 2 QB 218, where tenancy agreements contained a clause whereby should the landlords desire to terminate the tenancy, 'it must be by a written notice signed by the valuer to the council'. The LCC served notices to quit on the tenants on which the name of the valuer to the council appeared as signatory, but his name was written by an assistant valuer, with nothing on the document to indicate that the signature was by proxy. At first instance the tenants contended that, as the tenancy agreements required that the notices should be signed by the

- an agent can sign on behalf of one of the contracting parties;
- a signature can be 'I, Jane Smith have agreed' or 'Ms Jane Smith has agreed' where either is written at the beginning of a handwritten contract (that is, there is no 'conventional' signature written on the document);[31]
- a signature can be just a surname;[32]
- a signature can be the contraction of the name of a firm;[33]
- a signature does not need to include the first name or the second name, but can be a mark that identifies the person signing (*Morton* v. *Copeland* (1855) 16 CB 517 at 535);
- a signature can consist of an expression where the expression is intended to represent the name of the person using the expression;
- the expression used 'your loving mother' (and where that mother's name also appeared in the document – but see below, p.130);[34]
- when signing on behalf of an organisation, signing the name of the organisation;[35]
- the use of a rubber stamp;[36]

---

valuer to the council and they were not so signed, the notices were bad. The county court judge accepted this view and gave judgment for the defendants. On appeal the court (Denning, Romer and Parker LJJ) held that since in general a person sufficiently 'signs' a document if it is signed in his name and with his authority by somebody else, and there was nothing in the tenancy agreements to displace that common law rule, the notices were valid provided that the valuer authorised the signatures. (It was also held that since the court had decided that an authorised signature would suffice, LCC should be given an opportunity of proving due authority. The appeals were allowed and a new trial (to prove due authority) was ordered in each case.)

31 *Knight* v. *Crockford* (1794) 1 Esp 190; *Wood* v. *Smith* [1993] Ch 90, [1992] 3 All ER 556, CA.

32 *Lobb and Knight* v. *Stanley* (1844) 5 QB 574: a case concerning a written promise signed by a person after his bankruptcy, and the name of the bankrupt was stated only by his surname ('Mr Stanley'). It appears that the defendant did not actually make a signature but wrote his name several times in the body of the letter, but because of the way the promise was written that writing of 'Mr Stanley' constituted a signature which made it 'a signature of the party when he authenticates the instrument by writing his name in the body. Here it is true, the whole name is not written, but only "Mr Stanley". I think more is not necessary' (Lord Denham CJ).

33 *Bartletts de Reya* v. *Byrne* (1983) 127 Sol Jo 69, CA: where a firm of solicitors signed a bill of costs with just the name 'Bartletts' (where the bill of costs had printed the full name of the partnership on it at the top of the letter and underneath the signature). The defendant refused to pay because the signature of 'Bartletts' did not comply with SA 1974, s.69(2). Held by the Court of Appeal to be properly signed.

34 *In the Estate of Cook (deceased), Murison* v. *Cook and another* [1960] 1 All ER 689: a will 'signed' by a testator using the expression 'your loving mother' (but commencing with the words 'I, Emmie Cook of . . .'). The will was properly attested in accordance with the Wills Act 1837, held to be properly executed and admitted to probate, the judge relying on the following words from *Hindmarsh* v. *Charlton* (1861) 8 HL Cas 160: 'there must be either the name or some mark which is intended to represent the name'.

35 *Goodman* v. *J Eban Ltd* [1954] 1 QB 550 at 563; *Bartletts de Reya* v. *Byrne* (1983) 127 Sol Jo 69, CA.

36 *Bennett* v. *Brumfitt* (1867) LR 3 CP 28; *British Estate Investment Society Ltd* v. *Jackson (HM Inspector of Taxes)* [1956] TR 397, 37 Tax Cas 79; *Lazarus Estates Ltd* v. *Beasley* [1956] 1 QB 702; *London County Council* v. *Vitamins Ltd* [1955] 2 QB 218.

- can be in pen, pencil or *otherwise* if the purpose of applying one of them is to authenticate the document (*Goodman* v. *J Eban Ltd* [1954] 1 QB 550 at 557);
- a mark or symbol (which is not identifiable as that of the person who made or placed it on the document) if there is evidence that can indicate that it is the mark or symbol of the person and she intended it to be her signature (*Baker* v. *Dening* (1838) 8 A & E 94);
- the use of words that are not the name of the person signing if there is external evidence that the person intended the words used to identify herself and that she wished to adopt the document signed (*Re Redding's Goods* (1850) 14 Jur 1052, 2 Rob Eccl 339);
- a typed name on an email, where the email is printed out on to paper.[37]

What would not amount to a signature (and which would not bind one or more parties or make a transaction or event legally effective)

The following have been decided:

- a signature on a letter does not cover a postscript sent with the letter, but which is not referred to in the letter (*Kronheim* v. *Johnson* (1877) 7 Ch D 60);
- a name inserted into a letter in the body of the letter, and inserted for a particular purpose, is not sufficient to be a signature;[38]
- a name entered by typewriter for a purchaser does not amount to a signature (although the vendor provided a handwritten signature);[39]
- the tracing over a signature with a dry pen is not a signature;[40]
- the names of the parties to a contract need to appear in the document or in the signatures, so a contract only signed with 'your affectionate mother' was not sufficiently signed;[41]

---

37 *Hall* v. *Cognos Ltd* (1997) Hull Industrial Tribunal Case No 1803325/97, where the applicant made various travel expense claims later than allowed by his employer. There was an exchange of emails between him and the relevant representatives of the employer regarding this. The employer's representatives 'signed' the emails by typing their first names in each email. Agreement was reached for payment of the expenses but the employer subsequently refused to pay. The Industrial Tribunal held that the printed-out versions of the emails were in writing and signed.

38 *Stokes* v. *Moore* (1786) 1 Cox Eq Cas 219; *Caton* v. *Caton* (1867) LR 2 HL 127.

39 *Firstpost Homes Ltd* v. *Johnson* [1995] 4 All ER 355, [1995] 1 WLR 1567, CA. This case is discussed below.

40 *Re Maddock's Goods* (1874) LR 3 P&D 169; *Re Cunningham* (1860) 4 Sw & Tr 194.

41 *Selby* v. *Selby* (1817) 3 Mer 2: where a mother promised to provide an annuity to her son, documented in various letters. A letter started 'Dear Robert' and concluded 'Do me the justice to believe me the most affectionate of mothers', but did not contain the name of the mother. Held not to be sufficiently signed for the purposes of the Statute of Frauds 1677.

- a document which contained the names of the parties, and which concluded with the words: 'As witness our hands', but contained no signatures, was not sufficiently signed;[42]
- a document which is altered by one of the parties in her handwriting but is not signed by her is not sufficiently signed (*Hawkins* v. *Holmes* (1721) 1 P Wms 770);
- a document containing a handwritten signature of a seller and the typed name and address of a purchaser is not signed by the purchaser;[43]
- where a signature is added by a party (or her agent) as the witness of the other party, the first party is not bound by the signature.[44]

Signatures and contracts or other dispositions of an interest in land

Following the implementation of LP(MP)A 1989, s.2, a decision of the Court of Appeal (*Firstpost Homes Ltd* v. *Johnson* [1995] 4 All ER 355) has cast doubt on whether much of the case law stated above applies to, at least, contracts or other dispositions of an interest in land. Because of the comments made regarding previous decisions relating to signatures, and the importance of contracts relating to land, the case is outlined in some detail.

To start with, LP(MP)A 1989, s.2 (see **Appendix 1**) contains significant differences from the now repealed LPA 1925, s.40.[45] The principal ones are:

LP(MP)A 1989, s.2	LPA 1925, s.40
• Contract must be in writing	• Contract does not need to be in writing, a memorandum or note of the contract is sufficient
• Oral contracts not allowed	• Oral contracts allowed, subject to a memorandum or note of the contract being made
• All the terms of the contract must be incorporated in writing	• Only some of the terms needed to be documented in the memorandum or note of the contract being made
• The contract must be signed by all the parties (or on behalf of the parties) to the contract	• The contract did not need to be signed at all, only the memorandum or note to it, and then only by the person charged (or someone lawfully authorised by him)

---

42 *Hubert* v. *Treherne* (1842) 4 Scott NR 486. Distinguished in *Leeman* v. *Stocks* [1951] Ch 941, [1951] 1 All ER 1043.
43 *Firstpost Homes Ltd* v. *Johnson* [1995] 4 All ER 355, but this decision may be limited to cases concerning LP(MP)A 1989, s.2. This case is considered further below.
44 *Gosbell* v. *Archer* (1835) 2 Ad & El 500, where Williams J stated: 'It appears to me a great strain to say that the signature by another person's clerk is a signature by an authorised agent of the defendant, and that when he signs, not as agent, but as witness. Unless there be something to shew that he is termed a witness merely by a mistake, it cannot be said that he signed as agent'; *Kerns* v. *Manning* [1935] IR 869.
45 This is set out in n. 54 below, p. 135.

• The terms of the contract must be incorporated only in one document (or where contracts are exchanged, in each)	• The note or memorandum could be incorporated in more than one document
• A contract which does not comply with LP(MP)A 1989, s.2 is ineffective	• Contracts which do not comply with LPA 1925, s.40 are unenforceable in the courts

1.   Key facts in the case:

    (a)   the purchaser entered into an oral agreement with the seller whereby the seller would sell some land to the purchaser;

    (b)   the purchaser prepared a letter for the seller to sign. The letter was typed so that it was addressed to the purchaser, and stated that the seller agreed to sell the land to the purchaser, indicating the acreage and the price per acre and stating that the land to be sold was indicated on an enclosed plan. There was a space for the seller to sign. The plan was signed by the purchaser. The purchaser did not sign the letter. The name and address of the purchaser were typed on the letter;

    (c)   the letter and the plan were delivered to the seller. The seller signed the letter and the plan;

    (d)   the purchaser claimed there was a concluded contract, but the seller stated there was no contract satisfying the requirements of LP(MP)A 1989.

2.   Key points from the judgment:

    (a)   that what constituted a sufficient signature for the purposes of the Statute of Frauds 1677 and LPA 1925, s.40 should not govern the interpretation of the word 'signed' in LP(MP)A 1989, s.2;[46]

---

46 *Firstpost Homes Ltd* v. *Johnson* [1995] 4 All ER 355 per Balcombe LJ at 363:

I am not prepared to construe the word 'signed' in s.2(3) of the Law of Property (Miscellaneous Provisions) Act 1989 by reference to the old learning on what amounted to a signature of a note or memorandum sufficient for the purposes of the Statute of Frauds (1677) or s.40 of the Law of Property Act 1925. To do so would . . . defeat the obvious intention of s.2 of the 1989 Act, which is to ensure that a contract for the sale of land must be made in writing, in one document (leaving aside the position where contracts are exchanged), and with the document being signed by or on behalf of each party obviously so as to authenticate the document . . . The clear policy of the section is to avoid the possibility that one or other party may be able to go behind the document and introduce extrinsic evidence to establish a contract, which was undoubtedly a problem under the old law.

(b) to state that the typing or printing of the name of the addressee (in this case the purchaser) was a signature would be an 'artificial use of language';[47]

(c) that to sign a document requires that a person must write his name with his own hand;[48]

(d) that the letter and the plan did not constitute one document but two, with the letter incorporating the plan by reference, and that the letter was a document which is required by LP(MP)A 1989, s.2(3) to be signed, and had not been, by the purchaser. Therefore, the signature on the plan did not suffice;[49]

(e) the decision in this case is limited to where the party 'whose signature is said to appear on a contract is only named as the addressee of a letter prepared by him. No doubt other considerations will apply in other circumstances'.[50]

Although this case appears to be limited to particular facts, it appears to be the only case so far reported that deals substantively with signatures under LP(MP)A 1989. Perhaps its importance rests with highlighting the more restrictive regime concerning the form of a signature under LP(MP)A 1989.

---

47 Ibid. per Peter Gibson LJ at 362:

In my judgment, it is an artificial use of language to describe the printing or the typing of the name of an addressee in the letter as the signature by the addressee when he has printed or typed that document. Ordinary language does not, it seems to me, extend so far; and for this there appears to be the powerful support of Evershed MR and Denning LJ in *Goodman* v. *J Eban Ltd* [1954] 1 All ER 763 at 765, 768, [1954] 1 QB 550 at 555, 561, Denning LJ saying: 'In modern English usage, when a document is required to be "signed" by someone, that means that he must write his name with his own hand on it.' In any event, I do not accept that authorities on what was a sufficient signature for the purposes of the Statute of Frauds and s.40 of the 1925 Act should continue to govern the interpretation of the word 'signed' in s.2 of the 1989 Act. Prior to the 1989 Act the courts viewed with some disfavour those who made oral contracts but did not abide by them. The courts were prepared to interpret the statutory requirements generously to enable contracts to be enforced and in relation to the question whether there was a sufficient memorandum evidencing an agreement extrinsic evidence was admissible.

48 Ibid. Peter Gibson LJ at 362, quoting with approval statements of Evershed MR and Denning LJ in *Goodman* v. *J Eban Ltd* [1954] 1 All ER 763, [1954] 1 QB 550.
49 Ibid. per Peter Gibson LJ at 359.
50 Ibid. per Peter Gibson LJ at 362. In the later case of *Bircham & Co., Nominees (2) Ltd and another* v. *Worrell Holdings Ltd* [2001] EWCA Civ 775, [2001] All ER (D) 269 (May), at first instance the Vice Chancellor held that a facsimile of a document which had been signed by or on behalf of the offeror would, if signed by or on behalf of the offeree, be sufficient for the purposes of LP(MP)A 1989, s.2(3).

13.6 SIGNING BILLS OF COSTS WITH THE USE OF A RUBBER STAMP OR OTHER MECHANICAL MEANS BY A SOLICITOR

As noted above a facsimile of a signature engraved on a rubber stamp can be applied to a bill of costs, but it is perhaps useful to outline some of the points from the leading judgment in the case *Goodman* v. *J Eban Ltd* [1954] 1 All ER 763 as to why it may not always be desirable to do so.

- As a matter of good practice the 'signature' of a bill of costs, or of a letter enclosing such a bill, by means of a rubber stamp, generally, is undesirable.
- The purpose of s.65[51] is to impose on the solicitor (or on one of the members of a partnership firm of solicitors) personal responsibility for any bill of costs delivered.
- The client is intended to have the assurance by means of the personal authentication of the solicitor (or of a partner in a firm) that the bill delivered was proper (although there are other provisions in SA 1974 for the protection of the client, including under s.66(1) a right to have the bill taxed).
- If there was not (extensive prior) authority regarding what can constitute a signature:

  I should be disposed to think, as a matter of a common sense and of the ordinary use of language, that when Parliament required that the bill or letter should be 'signed' by the solicitor, it was intended that the solicitor should personally 'sign' the bill or letter in the ordinary way by writing his name (or, where appropriate, the name of his firm) in his own hand with a pen or pencil.[52]

Concluding point on signatures

From the reported cases, it appears that the courts are prepared to accept a wide variety of forms of signature where there is evidence:

- '[of] the identity of the signatory;
- that the signatory intended the "signature" to be her signature; and
- that the signatory approves of and adopts the contents of the document'.[53]

13.7 REQUIREMENT FOR WRITING

There are a number of documents, contracts, transactions or events:

- that are required to be in writing; or

---

51 Solicitors Act 1932, s.65 (now SA 1974, s.69 which is expressed in almost identical terms).
52 *Goodman* v. *J Eban Ltd* [1954] 1 All ER 763, per Evershed MR at 765; [1954] 1 QB 550.
53 Reed, section 3.1.1: he suggests that the courts in the last 150 years have concentrated on the function, rather than the form, of a signature in reaching the quoted conclusion.

- that are required to be evidenced in writing; or
- where certain provisions are required to be documented in writing; and/or
- that must be signed by one or more parties to the document, contract, transaction or event.

These requirements are separate from those for the execution of deeds.

13.8 SITUATIONS OR EVENTS NEEDING TO BE DOCUMENTED IN WRITING

The list that follows aims to cover no more than the main situations where writing is required for documents under hand which have a contract or contract-related connection.

- Contracts for the sale or disposition of interests in land can only be made in writing. The contract must be signed by or on behalf of each party to the contract (LP(MP)A 1989, s.2).[54]
- A will is not valid unless:
  - it is in writing;
  - it is signed by the testator (or some other person who signs in the testator's presence and by the testator's direction); and
  - it appears that the testator's signature is intended by the testator to give effect to her will; and
  - the testator's signature is made or acknowledged by the testator in the presence of two or more witnesses present at the same time; and
  - each witness either:
    - attests and signs the will; or
    - acknowledges her signature

    in the presence of the testator (but a witness does not need to be in the presence of another witness) (Wills Act 1837, s.9).[55]
- No interest in land can be created or disposed of except in writing and signed by the person (or her agent) creating or conveying the same (or by will or by operation of law) (LPA 1925, s.53(1)(a)).

---

54 This applies to contracts entered into after 27 September 1989. For sales or other dispositions made before that date LPA 1925, s.40 continues to apply. LP(MP)A 1989, s.2 is set out in **Appendix 1**. LP(MP)A 1989, s.2 provisions do not apply to a contract to grant a lease not in writing for a term less than three years, as mentioned in LPA 1925, s.54(2) or a contract made in the course of a public auction; or a contract regulated under the Financial Services and Markets Act 2000 (other than a regulated mortgage contract): LP(MP)A 1989, s.2(5). LPA 1925, s.40 provided:

No action may be brought upon any contract for the sale or other disposition of land or any interest in land, unless the agreement upon which such action is brought, or some memorandum or note thereof, is in writing, and signed by the party to be charged or some other person by him lawfully authorised.

55 The section also provides that no particular form of attestation is required.

- Upon written request of a tenant, the landlord is required to provide the tenant with a written statement of the landlord's name and address within the period of 21 days (Landlord and Tenant Act 1985, s.2).[56]
- A landlord is required to provide a rent book, the contents of which are prescribed (Landlord and Tenant Act 1985, s.4).[57]
- A declaration of trust regarding any land or any interest in land must be in writing, signed by the person who is able to declare such trust (or by her will) (LPA 1925, s.53(1)(b)).
- A disposition of an equitable interest or trust subsisting at the time of the disposition must be in writing and signed by the person (or agent) disposing of the same (or by will) (LPA 1925, s.53(1)(c)).
- An absolute assignment by writing of a debt or other legal thing in action is where express notice in writing is given to the debtor, trustee or other person from whom the assignor would have been entitled to claim such debt or thing in action (LPA 1925, s.136).
- A contract is required to be in writing and signed by or on behalf of all the parties, where money is advanced by way of loan to a person engaged or about to engage in any business on a contract with that person that the lender shall receive a rate of interest varying with the profits, or shall receive a share of the profits arising from carrying on the business. Without a contract the loan does not make the lender a partner with the person or persons carrying on the business or liable as such (Partnership Act 1890, s.2(3)(d)).
- Contracts of guarantees or liabilities must be in writing or some note or memorandum be made concerning it, and the contract or note or memorandum signed by the person to be charged or someone authorised by him (Statute of Frauds 1677, s.4).[58]
- A solicitor's remuneration agreement concerning non-contentious business shall be in writing and be signed by the person to be bound (SA 1974, s.57(3)). Remuneration agreements concerning contentious business can also be made in writing (SA 1974, s.59).[59]

---

56 Failure to comply with this provision is a criminal offence.
57 Failure to comply with this provision is a criminal offence.
58 This section has now a highly restricted meaning, i.e. this section does not apply to indemnities, e.g. *Yeoman Credit Ltd* v. *Latter* [1961] 2 All ER 294 at 296, [1961] 1 WLR 828: 'An indemnity is a contract by one party to keep the other harmless against loss, but a contract of guarantee is a contract to answer for the debt, default or miscarriage of another who is to be primarily liable to the promisee'. Readers who wish to gain an understanding of when the Statute of Frauds 1677, s.4, applies should consult Furmston, *The Law of Contract*, 2nd edn, Butterworths, 2003, paras. 2.290–2.296 (citation in Chitty). Section 4 provides:

> No action shall be brought ... whereby to charge the defendant upon any speciall promise to answere for the debt default or miscarriages of another person ... unlesse the agreement upon which such action shall be brought or some memorandum or note thereof shall be in writeing and signed by the partie to be charged therewith or some other person thereunto by him lawfully authorized.

59 But there appears to be no wording in SA 1974 which requires that they must be in writing and signed by the person to be bound by the agreement.

- Under a contract of commercial agency, the principal and the agent are each entitled to receive from the other a written document setting out the terms of the contract of agency between them (including any terms subsequently agreed). The party providing the document must sign it (Commercial Agents (Council Directive) Regulations 1993, SI 1993/3053, reg. 13).
- If the provisions of the Arbitration Act 1996 are to apply, an arbitration agreement must be in writing. The form of the writing is satisfied in a number of ways:
  - if the agreement is made in writing (whether or not it is signed by the parties);
  - if the agreement is made by exchange of communications in writing;
  - if the agreement is evidenced in writing;
  - if the parties agree otherwise than in writing (e.g. orally) by reference to terms which are in writing; or
  - in an exchange of written submissions in arbitral or legal proceedings in which the existence of an agreement otherwise than in writing is alleged by one party against another party and not denied by the other party (Arbitration Act 1996, s.5).

  'Writing' includes recording by any means (Arbitration Act 1996, s.5(5)).
- Any transfer of a registered ship, or a share in such a ship, shall be effected by a bill of sale in a prescribed form (Merchant Shipping Act 1995, Sched. 1, para. 2(1)).
- A written statement must be provided to all employees within two months of their commencement of employment. The statement must contain certain details (Employment Rights Act 1996, s.1).
- Certain negotiable instruments must be in writing, sent by one person to another, and signed by the person giving it:
  - bills of exchange (Bills of Exchange Act 1882 (BEA 1882), s.3);[60]
  - cheques (BEA 1882, s.73);[61]
  - promissory notes (BEA 1882, s.83).[62]

---

60 A bill of exchange is:

> an unconditional order in writing addressed by one person to another, signed by the person giving it, requiring the person to whom it is addressed to pay on demand or at a fixed or determinable future time a sum certain in money to or to the order of a specified person or to bearer.

The person does not need to sign himself, the person's signature can be made by some other person by or under his authority: BEA 1882, s.91(1); a corporation can use a seal: BEA 1882, s.91(2). A 'person' for the purposes of BEA 1882 is 'a body of persons whether incorporated or not': BEA 1882, s.2.

61 A cheque being 'a bill of exchange drawn on a banker payable on demand'.
62 A promissory note: 'is an unconditional promise in writing made by one person to another signed by the maker, engaging to pay, on demand or at a fixed or determinable future time, a sum certain in money, to, or to the order of, a specified person or to bearer'.

The meaning of 'writing' includes printing (BEA 1882, s.2).

- The appointment of a new trustee is required in writing (Trustee Act 1925, s.36(1), (6)).
- A memorandum declaring a trustee of property held for the purposes of a charity to have been appointed or discharged by resolution of a meeting of the charity's trustees, members or other persons. Such a memorandum shall be sufficient evidence of that fact if the memorandum is signed either at the meeting by the person presiding or in some other manner directed by the meeting and is attested by two persons present at the meeting (Charities Act 1993, s.83(1)).[63]
- An assignment or mortgage of, or right in, a patent or a patent application is required to be signed by the assignor (or on their behalf). An assent is to be signed by, or on behalf of, the personal representatives. Bodies corporate can use their seal instead of signing. Failure to comply with these provisions makes the assignment, etc. void (Patents Act 1977, s.30(6)).
- An assignment of copyright or of a database right is to be signed by, or on behalf of, the assignor. Failure to comply with this provision makes the assignment 'ineffective' (Copyright, Designs and Patents Act 1988, s.90(3) and Copyright and Rights in Databases Regulations 1997, SI 1997/3032, reg. 23).
- An assignment of, or an assent relating to, a registered trademark are to be signed by or on behalf of the assignor or personal representative, as the case may be. Failure to do so will make the assignment or assent not 'effective'. For a body corporate, its seal can be used (Trade Marks Act 1994, s.24(3)).
- Regulated consumer credit or hire agreements must be in a prescribed form, and contain prescribed information and all the expressly agreed terms. All the terms must be legible. Such documents must be signed by the debtor or hirer and by, or on behalf of, the creditor or owner. There are also detailed provisions relating to the provision of a copy of the agreement (depending on when the debtor or hirer signs). Failure to comply with any of these provisions means that the agreement cannot be enforced against the debtor or hirer except where the court makes an enforcement order or where the debtor or hirer consents to enforcement (Consumer Credit Act 1974, s.61).
- Where the sale, recommendation or arranging of certain financial products takes place, an authorised person is required to provide certain information to a private customer (Financial Services and Markets Act 2000, regulations made under the Act and requirements of the Financial Services Authority).
- Estate agents are required to give prospective clients a statement in writing stating the amount of remuneration payable to the agent, circumstances

---

63 If the memorandum is to be considered to have a vesting declaration, then it would need to be executed as a deed: Charities Act 1993, s.83(2).

when payment is due, etc. (Estate Agents Act 1979, s.18 and Estate Agents (Provision of Information) Regulations 1991, reg. 4).

13.9 MEANING OF 'WRITING'

For the above instances 'writing' requires expression in some visible form, which practically will mean reproduction on to some form of paper. Where there is a reference to writing in an Act or statutory instrument, the meaning of writing (under the Interpretation Act 1978 (IA 1978), s.5, Sched. 1) includes:

> typing, printing, lithography, photography and other modes of representing or reproducing words in a visible form, and expressions referring to writing are construed accordingly.

Writing can cover the following forms:

- writing in pen, pencil or otherwise;[64]
- a photocopy;[65]
- writing partly by one method and partly by another.[66]

Other concepts sometimes seen are 'instrument' and 'document'. An 'instrument' does not appear to have a statutory definition, but according to *Halsbury's Laws*, 'Deeds and other Instruments', para. 139:

> An instrument under hand only is a document in writing which either creates or affects legal or equitable rights or liabilities, and which is authenticated by the signature of the author, but is not executed by him as a deed.

A document is defined by the Civil Evidence Act 1995, s.13 as:

> anything in which information of any description is recorded, and 'copy' in relation to a document, means anything onto which information recorded in the document has been copied, by whatever means and whether directly or indirectly.

This is a wider definition (not limited to reproducing writing) than under IA 1978 and could include non-visible forms of recording. Readers interested in the meaning of a document should consult Mason, *Electronic Signatures in Law*, Butterworths, 2003, section 2.6, and the references given there. A document does not have to be in visible form but can include computer systems and computer data.[67]

---

64 *Geary* v. *Physic* (1826) 5 B & C 234. Also *Co-operative Bank plc* v. *Tipper* [1996] 4 All ER 366.
65 *Lockheed-Arabia Corpn* v. *Owen* [1993] 3 All ER 641, CA. The case concerned whether a photocopy was admissible in evidence. Held that a handwriting expert could form an opinion using a photocopy for the purposes of Criminal Procedure Act 1865, s.8.
66 *Dench* v. *Dench* (1877) 2 PD 60: where a will was partly lithographed and partly written in pen.
67 For example, in *Victor Chandler International* v. *Customs and Excise Commissioners* [2000] 1 WLR 1296 it was held that a computer system and a computer database were documents for the purposes of the Betting and Gaming Duties Act 1981.

13.10   EFFECT OF A SIGNATURE

The effect of a person signing a document will normally be:

- a written agreement will be enforced against a person who has signed it on proof of the signature being hers (*Parker v. South Eastern Railway Company* (1877) 2 CPD 416 at 422, CA);
- it does not matter whether the person has read the contents of the agreement or knows what the contents are;[68]
- a signature is usually very strong evidence that the person who has signed the agreement has assented to all the provisions of the agreement, including any exemption clauses;[69]
- it is for the person relying on a signed document to show that document has been signed by the signing person and/or she has approved or authorised its contents.[70]

The above only apply where the agreement is wholly in writing, and may not apply to those parts not made in writing. The above may not apply where there has been fraud, mistake or misrepresentation or where a particular clause has no legal effect.

13.11   STATUTE OF FRAUDS 1677

Scope covered

The Statute of Frauds 1677 sets out formal requirements for a number of instruments, including those listed below:

1.   a number of different types of contracts including:

    (a)   contracts of guarantee;
    (b)   contracts for the sale or creation of interests in land;
    (c)   contracts for the sale of goods for a price of £10 or more;

2.   conveyances of land;

---

68 *Parker* v. *South Eastern Railway Co.* (1877) 2 CPD 416 at 422, CA; *L'Estrange* v. *Graucob* [1934] 2 KB 394 at 404, CA: 'the plaintiff having put her signature to the document and not having been induced to do so by any fraud or misrepresentation, cannot be heard to say that she is not bound by the terms of the document because she has not read them'.

69 *Curtis* v. *Chemical Cleaning & Dyeing Co. Ltd* [1951] 1 KB 805 at 808, CA: 'If the party affected signs a written document, knowing it to be a contract which governs the relationship between him and the other party, his signature is irrefragable evidence of his assent to the whole contract, including the exempting clauses, unless the signature is shown to be obtained by fraud or misrepresentation'.

70 *British Estate Investment Society Ltd* v. *Jackson* (1956) 37 TC 79 at 87: 'It seems to me that the presumption in law is that the document has been properly signed until the contrary has been shown by a person who desires to upset that conclusion'.

3.   the creation of leases;
4.   wills; and
5.   declarations of trust.

Formality required

No action could be taken on these instruments unless:

1.   the contract, lease, etc. was in writing; or
2.   there was some written memorandum of the contract, lease, etc. which was signed by the party or parties to be charged or signed by some person lawfully authorised by the party/parties.

If the formalities were not complied with, the underlying contract, lease, etc. was not invalid but was unenforceable in the courts.[71]

Carrying forward of the Statute of Frauds 1677

The Statute of Frauds 1677 has been the subject of a considerable body of case law and legislative reform, but now only applies to guarantees. It continued to apply, for example, to contracts for goods over £10 into the twentieth century (Sale of Goods Act 1893, s.4), and to the contracts for the creation or disposition of interests in land until 27 September 1989, when it was repealed by LP(MP)A 1989 (but not retrospectively).[72]

---

71 *Leroux* v. *Brown* (1852) 12 CB 801; *Maddison* v. *Alderson* (1883) 8 App 467; *Steadman* v. *Steadman* [1976] AC 536, [1974] 2 All ER 977; *Elias* v. *George Sahely & Co (Barbados) Ltd* [1982] 3 All ER 801.
72 As LPA 1925, s.40 provided: 'No action may be brought under any contract for the sale or other disposition of land or any interest in land, unless the agreement upon which such action is brought, or some memorandum or note thereof, is in writing, and signed by the party to be charged or by some other person by him lawfully'.

CHAPTER 14

Execution of a deed by an individual

14.1 INTRODUCTION

This chapter focuses on the requirements for the execution of a deed by an individual. Some points are of general application and will apply whether the person executing is an individual or a corporation. In other chapters, the points of general application are not repeated.

The requirements for the valid execution of a deed by an individual are a mixture of common law and statute law. The major legal reform in recent years has been LP(MP)A 1989, as amended by Regulatory Reform (Execution of Deeds and Documents) Order 2005, SI 2005/1906 (RR(EDD)O 2005), which made substantial changes to the common law provisions for deeds as regards individuals. But LP(MP)A 1989 did not abolish the common law provisions which are not expressly dealt with by the Act.

The main changes introduced by LP(MP)A 1989 (as amended) are:

- to abolish any restrictions on the substance on which a deed can be written;
- to abolish the requirement that deeds, to be validly executed, had to be sealed;
- to put on a statutory basis the requirement that to execute a deed validly an individual must sign the deed in the presence of a witness, who must signify that she has witnessed the individual's signature by adding her own signature;
- a document will not be a deed unless it makes it clear on its face that it is intended to be a deed by the person making, or the parties to, the deed;[1]
- a document will not be a deed merely because it is executed under seal;
- a document can be validly executed on behalf of a person by an individual who is authorised to do so;
- where an individual signs on behalf of another person, she signs in her status as an individual, whether or not the other person is an individual.

---

1 The 'face-value' requirement, as described by the Law Commission in its Consultation Paper 143.

14.2   WHAT IS A 'DEED'?

Two main elements can be identified which are essential for the creation of a deed:

- certain formalities must be complied with concerning the description and signing of a document (see **section 14.4**); and
- that:

  – an interest, right or property passes or is confirmed; or
  – an obligation binding on some person is created or confirmed.[2]

For example, a share certificate of a company incorporated under CA 1985 or CA 2006, if sealed, would not be a deed, as it is only prima facie evidence of a person's title to the shares (CA 2006, s.786; also, *South London Greyhound Racecourses Ltd* v. *Wake* [1931] 1 Ch 496 at 503).

In addition, a deed can also be defined by:

- distinguishing it from other types of documents (those 'under hand' (see **Chapters 1** and **13**)) by the formality that has to be used when it is executed. A deed requires more formality in order to be executed ('in solemn form'). This definition would mean that a transaction or event could be recorded in writing and the written document either, simply, be signed by the parties to it or be executed as a deed (with the extra formalities required for a deed); or
- relation to the underlying transaction it documents. Certain transactions are only effective if they are made by a deed;[3]
- the effect of a deed compared to a document 'under hand':

  – *consideration*: a gratuitous promise made without or in return for valuable consideration is not enforceable unless it is made in a deed;[4]

---

2 Law Commission Report, LC 253, para. 2.4. An alternative, longer definition from *Halsbury's Laws*, 'Deeds', para. 1 is:

> [an instrument] must be executed in the manner specified below by some person or corporation named in the instrument. Thirdly, as to subject matter, it must express that the person or corporation so named makes, confirms, concurs in or consents to some assurance (otherwise than by way of testamentary disposition) of some interest in property or of some legal or equitable right, title, or claim, or undertakes or enters into some obligation, duty or agreement enforceable at law or in equity, or does or concurs in some other act affecting the legal relations or position of a party to the instrument or of some other person or corporation.

3 Most transactions concerning real property, such as conveyances, mortgages, etc. A list of the most important instances when a deed must be used is given at **section 14.15**. If a deed is not used, the underlying transaction or event may still be enforceable in equity.
4 *Sharrington* v. *Strotton*, 1 Plowd 308, 75 ER 469; *Morley* v. *Boothby* (1825) 3 Bing 107 at 112; *Cannon* v. *Hartley* [1949] Ch 213 at 217. Also see *Halsbury's Laws*, 'Deeds', para. 58 for some of the implications of this proposition; e.g. a gratuitous promise is enforceable by an order for specific performance: *Jeffreys* v. *Jeffreys* (1841) Cr & Ph 138 at 141, 41 ER 443 at 444; *Re Ellenborough, Towry Law* v. *Burne* [1903] 1 Ch 697 (on the basis that equity will not assist a volunteer).

- *limitation period*: the limitation period for a breach of a contract is 12 years when the contract is made by deed, compared to six years when made 'under hand' (Limitation Act 1980, ss.5 and 8);
- *estoppel*: a person making a deed, as a general rule, is estopped from claiming that the contents of the deed did not correctly express that person's intentions or that there are reasons why the deed should not take effect.[5]

14.3 TYPES OF DEEDS

Deeds are classified into two types, a deed poll and an indenture. This classification is of less importance and use today, but some consequences flow from the distinction.

Deed poll

A deed poll is a deed made by one person (or more than one person and those persons are expressing a common intention). The person(s) are binding themselves to an obligation.

By a deed poll a person can enforce any obligation undertaken in her favour, although she has not executed the deed.[6] She can be named or sufficiently identified in the deed. She does not have to be identified by name (*Sunderland Marine Insurance Co* v. *Kearney* (1851) 16 QB 925 at 938).

An indenture (a deed *inter partes*)[7]

An indenture is a deed where two or more persons are named as parties, and which describes or indicates an agreement between them (other than a common intention as for a deed poll).Unless a person is a party to the deed *inter partes* she cannot take an immediate benefit under the deed or sue upon any covenant contained in the deed (*Harmer* v. *Armstrong* [1934] Ch 65 at 86, CA, per Lawrence LJ). There are exceptions to this principle,[8] the most important being that a person may take an immediate or other interest in land or other (real) property, or the benefit of any condition, right of entry, covenant or

---

5 *Whelpdale's Case* (1604) 5 Co Rep 119; *Goodtitle* d. *Edwards* v. *Bailey* (1777) 2 Cowp 597; *Xenos* v. *Wickham* (1866) LR 2 HL 296: *First National Bank plc* v. *Thompson* [1996] 2 WLR 293 at 298 per Millett LJ.
6 *Scudamore* v. *Vanderstene* (1587) 2 Co Inst 673; *Green* v. *Horne* (1694) 1 Salk 197; *Lowther* v. *Kelly* (1723) 8 Mod Rep 115 at 118.
7 There is also a distinction between indentures *inter partes* and indentures which are not *inter partes*: see *Halsbury's Laws*, 'Deeds', para. 3.
8 The provisions of the Contracts (Rights of Third Parties) Act 1999, which may be said to provide another exception in some circumstances, are not covered in this book.

agreement over or respecting land or other (real) property, although she may not be named as a party to the conveyance or other instrument.[9]

Although the distinction between the two different types of deed remains, the courts have interpreted a deed in appropriate circumstances as being 'analogous to a deed poll' when a person not a party to the deed clearly benefits (*Chelsea & Walham Green Building Society* v. *Armstrong* [1951] Ch 853, [1951] 2 All ER 250). A recent case[10] is an illustration of this point. A company was sold by the claimants to the second defendant, a company simply set up as vehicle to acquire the claimant's company. The purchase price was made up of an immediate payment plus further payments made in instalments. In the event of default by the second defendant in making the further payments, the outstanding balance would be met by guarantee payable by the first defendant whose business was granting corporate risk guarantees. The guarantee was entered into only by the first and second defendants as a deed. The claimants were not a party to the guarantee but the guarantee was clearly drafted so that the claimants were intended to benefit in just these circumstances. The second defendant defaulted and the claimants sought payment under the guarantee. The first defendant argued that because the guarantee was a deed *inter partes*, the claimants were not able to benefit from the provisions of the deed as they were not parties to it. The judge rejected this argument. The judge draw attention to the need to examine the true intention of the document and not its form.[11]

There is a possible further distinction between a deed poll and a deed *inter partes*. A deed poll is in the nature of a quasi-public document which is addressed to all the world, and a deed *inter partes* is normally a contract (or a document which carries out one or more of the provisions of a contract) which is done in private (*Chelsea & Waltham Green Building Society* v. *Armstrong* [1951] Ch 853, [1951] 2 All ER 250 at 252).

---

9 LPA 1925, s.56(1). This section does not extend to personal property (other than chattels real): *Beswick* v. *Beswick* [1968] AC 58. *Halsbury's Laws*, 'Deeds', para. 61 discusses the implications of this proposition.

10 *Moody and another* v. *Condor Insurance Ltd and another* [2006] EWHC 100 (Ch), [2006] 1 All ER (Comm) 419.

11 See para. 18 of the judgment: 'In my judgment it is necessary to consider, not just whether one or two persons executed the documents, and not just whether the word "between" appears. It is necessary to examine what the parties who execute a document, saying that they are executing it "as a deed" . . . set out to do by it. Does one or more of them in fact make promises to the other or others (as one would expect of a deed *inter partes*), or do they rather seek to use the document as a means for each of them to make unilateral promises to a person who is not a party to it (or to persons who are not parties to it)? When the conventional word "between" appears, is it an appropriate word given the content of what appears in the document that follows? When those questions are asked in this case it becomes, in my judgment, clear that the loan note and guarantee instrument and the guarantee were the types of deeds which not merely were intended to create rights enforceable by non-parties [the claimants], but which in law achieved the intention.'

145

14.4 REQUIREMENTS TO EXECUTE A DOCUMENT VALIDLY AS A DEED BY AN INDIVIDUAL

The following are the requirements for an individual to execute a document validly as a deed:

- it must be in writing;[12] and
- the writing can be placed on any type of material (LP(MP)A 1989, s.1(1)(a));[13] and
- the document will not be a deed unless the document makes it clear that it is intended to be a deed by the person making it or the parties to it. This intention can be expressed by the document:

  - describing itself as a deed; or
  - expressing itself to be executed or signed as a deed; or
  - describing itself in some other way (LP(MP)A 1989, s.1(2)(a));[14] and

- the document will not be a deed unless it is validly executed as a deed by the individual, and will be validly executed in the following two ways:

  - the individual signs the deed in the presence of a witness who attests the individual's signature (LP(MP)A 1989, s.1(3)(a)(i)); or
  - the individual directs that another person signs the deed in her presence and in the presence of two witnesses who each attest the signature (LP(MP)A 1989, s.1(3)(a)(ii));

- the deed is delivered (LP(MP)A 1989, s.1(3)(b));
- where the deed is being signed by an individual on behalf of another person (whether that other person is an individual or a body corporate):

  - the individual is authorised to do so and can sign in the name of the other person or on behalf of that person (LP(MP)A 1989, s.1(2)(b));
  - the individual signs in her status as an individual (i.e. in accordance with the methods provided in LP(MP)A 1989, s.1(3)) (LP(MP)A 1989, s.1(4A)).

---

12 *Goddard's Case* (1584) 2 Co Rep 4b at 5a, 76 ER 396 at 398–399. 'Writing' under common law did not require the use of pen or ink, but could include pencil or with paint: *Geary* v. *Physic* (1826) 5 B & C 234 at 237. The meaning of the word 'writing' in any Act includes: 'typing, printing, lithography, photography and other modes of representing or reproducing words in a visible form': IA 1978, s.5, Sched. 1.
13 Abolishing the common law rule that a deed had to be written on paper, parchment or vellum (*Goddard's Case* (1584) 2 Co Rep 4b at 5a, 76 ER 396 at 398–399).
14 'In some other way' can mean that the document does not state that it is a deed at all but the document is stated to be a type of document which, in the circumstances, can only be a deed. For example, a document might be described, or stated to be executed as, a 'conveyance': LPA 1925, s.52.

14.5 STRUCTURE OF A DEED

Some examples of deeds are given at the end of this chapter. There is normally no requirement that a deed should have a specific layout or use particular terminology. By convention, however, deeds do follow a certain layout and terminology. This is particularly true for conveyancing and other property-related transactions. In most circumstances, the failure to follow a conventional layout and terminology will not prevent the deed taking effect in law (*R* v. *Wooldale (Inhabitants)* (1844) 6 QB 549) as long as the language used to express the parties' intentions is reasonably clear (*Re Arden, Short* v. *Camm* [1935] Ch 326 at 333 per Clauson J).

Starting from the top of the document to be executed as a deed, the following fall to be considered.

Title

Words describing the document, such as 'Deed', 'Deed of Assignment', 'Conveyance', 'Settlement', 'Mortgage' or 'Power of Attorney'.[15]

Date

Conventionally the date is inserted at the beginning of the document. The date should be the date of delivery and not the date it is signed (and witnessed). The wording could be as follows:

THIS LEGAL CHARGE is made the [*day*] day of [*month and year*] BETWEEN

Or:

THIS DEED dated _____ 200[. . .] is made by and between

If the deed is not to take effect on delivery, then this can be reflected here as well as in the *executed as a deed* clause and in the *signature block*, for example:

THIS LEGAL CHARGE delivered as a deed on [*day*] day of [*month and year*] between

The date to be inserted for deeds delivered in escrow should be the date when the deed was originally signed and delivered, not the date when the condition is fulfilled (*Alan Estates Ltd* v. *WG Stores Ltd* [1982] Ch 511, [1981] 3 All ER 481, CA).

---

15 See LPA 1925, s.57, where 'any deed . . . may be described (at the commencement thereof or otherwise) as a deed simply . . . or otherwise according to the nature of the transaction intended to be effected'.

Parties

The names, addresses (and descriptions where appropriate) of the person(s) making or the parties to the deed should be inserted. Some documents used by organisations (such as pre-printed forms) refer to the parties by a title (e.g. the 'mortgagor'), and list the actual names and addresses of the parties in a schedule.

Care needs to be taken about who is made a party or is named in a deed, especially with transactions concerning real property.[16]

Practically, anybody who is to take any immediate estate, interest, right or benefit (whether proprietary or otherwise) under an instrument, as well as the persons who are to grant rights or assume obligations, should be not merely identified in the instrument, but made a party to it, if possible.

Recitals

Recitals are normally statements of facts on which the transaction or event which is to be recorded in the operative part of the deed is based. For example:

- a description of the nature of the transaction or event; or
- a description of how the parties to the deed came to make the deed or contract.

There should not normally be any binding obligations placed in this part of the deed. Recitals are usually helpful but unnecessary parts of the deed.

Body of the deed (the testatum or witnessing part)

This part sets out the operative intentions of the parties under the deed.

Deeds drafted using traditional language usually have the following phrase after the recitals clause:

NOW THIS DEED WITNESSES as follows

followed by the operative intentions of the parties.

'Executed as a deed' clause (testimonium)

There is no statutory requirement for a testimonium clause. Its absence does not affect the validity of the deed. It is added as evidence of the deed's execution.[17]

---

16 See e.g. *Encyclopaedia of Forms and Precedents*, vol. 12(2), 'Deeds', paras. 5, 6, and in particular the possible implications of naming a person as a party in a deed under LPA 1925.

17 *Burdett* v. *Spilsbury* (1843) 10 Cl & Fin 340, HL. The inclusion of a testimonium clause may be of importance (*Lawrie* v. *Lees* (1881) 7 App Cas 19, HL).

The clause is, however, rarely omitted in practice. Examples are shown in **Chapter 2**.

In practice, any particular conditions concerning the parties or the execution of the deed should be noted in this clause (for example, that the document is being executed in escrow or that one or more of the parties is suffering under a disability).

Schedules

Conventionally, the schedules (if any) appear before the *signature block* in English legal practice. The traditional reasoning is that such a practice hinders any addition to the deed. If the schedules are added after the *signature block*, then, to comply with this conventional reasoning, just the signatures of the parties can be added at the end of the schedules (to indicate the schedules are complete).

More modern practice (particularly in the case of some commercial contracts) sometimes places the schedules after the *signature block*.

Signature block (attestation)

The basic elements of the *signature block* are now specified by LP(MP)A 1989, which specifies that a deed must be signed by the person or persons making it (either by her/themselves or by someone at the direction of the person(s) making it), and such signature(s) must be made in the presence of another person, who attests that the signature(s) has been witnessed (LP(MP)A 1989, s.1(2)(b), (3)).[18]

Normally, witnesses should sign their name, then add their name in print, together with their address and description (e.g., doctor/neighbour) (*Halsbury Laws*, 2007 reissue, vol. 13, para. 36).

Where an individual is authorised to execute a deed for a person or party making the deed, the individual can do so in the name of the person or party

---

18 A deed still may be valid if signed in the absence of a witness: *Shah* v. *Shah* [2001] EWCA Civ 527, [2001] 3 All ER 138. In this case it was held that LP(MP)A 1989 did not exclude the operation of an estoppel. Pill LJ held that a document could not be a deed unless it was signed but he could detect there was

> no social policy which requires the person attesting the signature to be present when the document is signed. The attestation is at one stage removed from the imperative out of which the need for formality arises. It is not fundamental to the public interest, which is in the requirement for a signature. Failure to comply with the additional formality of attestation should not in itself prevent a party into whose possession an apparently valid deed has come from alleging that the signatory should not be permitted to rely on the absence of attestation in his presence. It should not permit a person to escape the consequences of an apparently valid deed he has signed, representing that he has done so in the presence of an attesting witness, merely by claiming that in fact the attesting witness was not present at the time of signature (at para. 30).

making the deed or on behalf of the person or party making the deed (LP(MP)A 1989, s.1(2)(b)). Presumably the latter means that the individual can sign in her own name. The individual is signing in her status as an individual, irrespective of the status of the person or party making the deed (LP(MP)A 1989, s.1(4A)). Therefore, if the deed were being made by a body corporate, and the body corporate had authorised an individual to sign the deed on its behalf, the individual would sign in the presence of a witness (in compliance with LP(MP)A 1989, s.1(3)).

Who can be a witness? Generally, there appear to be few or no restrictions on who can be a witness. Therefore husbands and wives can witness each other's signatures (*Halsbury Laws*, 2007 reissue, vol. 13, para. 36); however, the practice appears to be to discourage relatives from witnessing signatures of other relatives, 'in case the veracity of the evidence of such a witness is called into question' (*Encyclopaedia of Forms and Precedents*, vol. 12(2), 'Deeds', para. 25). But one party to a deed cannot also be a witness for another party.[19]

What constitutes a signature?

The word 'signed' is not expressly defined by LP(MP)A 1989 other than to state that a signature can constitute the making of a mark (LP(MP)A 1989, s.1(4)(b)). Therefore, it seems a 'signature' could be made without signing the name of the person at all.

Where an individual is signing a deed for a person or party making a deed, the individual's signature can include signing the name of the person or party making the deed (LP(MP)A 1989, s.1(4)(a)).

What can constitute a signature (including using facsimile methods such as rubbers stamps or a laser printer) is discussed in more detail at **section 13.5**, but for deeds it seems that the best practice requires that the person signing should physically sign the deed with a pen (whether with a full signature or by making a mark).[20]

Who must execute the deed?

A person who is not undertaking an obligation should not normally need to execute the deed at all or only sign it under hand.[21] The person could enforce

---

19 *Coles* v. *Trecothick* (1804) 9 Ves 234 at 251; *Freshfield* v. *Reed* (1842) 9 M & W 404; *Wickham* v. *Marquis of Bath* (1865) LR 1 Eq 17 at 25; *Seal* v. *Claridge* (1881) 7 QBD 516 at 519; *Re Parrott ex p. Cullen* [1891] 2 QB 151.
20 Law Commission Report LC 253, paras. 3.58–3.63, recommends that there be no relaxation in the requirement for a personal signature. It argues that a signature is required by the person to, or the parties to, a deed: e.g. LP(MP)A 1989, s.1(3).
21 For example, a person who purchases registered property would not normally execute the transfer of registered land if there were no covenants which are entered into between

the obligation if the deed is a deed poll or 'analogous to a deed poll' (see **section 14.3**).

Although a person may not need to sign a deed where she is not undertaking an obligation, sometimes that person will sign the deed (but not as a deed).

If a contract is executed as a deed, then all the parties to the contract need to execute the deed if they wish to enforce the contract unless they are able to enforce it as third parties under the Contracts (Rights of Third Parties) Act 1999.

14.6   REQUIREMENT TO READ A DEED BEFORE EXECUTION

The general principle is that a deed is binding on a person who executes it even though that person has not read the contents of the deed, or believes its contents are different from what the deed states (even if she is blind or illiterate).[22]

Normally, it will be difficult for an individual to avoid obligations contained in a deed that they have validly executed (especially if they are of normal or full capacity). Most persons should take such precautions as they reasonably can as to the effect and nature of the document they are to sign. Relying on the advice of a legal adviser or another person (for example, a company director relying on the advice or explanation of a more junior employee) will not normally be enough to avoid the deed.[23]

14.7   EXECUTION ON BEHALF OF THE PERSON OR PARTY WHO IS TO BE BOUND BY THE DEED

In the name of, or on behalf of, the person or party making the deed

LP(MP)A 1989 (as amended by RR(EDD)O 2005) specifically enables an individual to sign a deed in the name of or on behalf of the person or party making the deed (LP(MP)A 1989, s.1(4)(a)). The manner in which the individual will sign the deed is governed by their status as an individual and not that of the person or party making the deed (i.e. if the party making the deed is a corporate body then the individual will still sign based on their status as an individual and in compliance with LP(MP)A 1989, s.1(3)) (LP(MP)A 1989, s.1(4A)).

---

her and the seller. See Land Registration Rules 2003, SI 2003/1417, rr. 58 and 206, Scheds. 1 and 9. Form TR1 makes this clear at box 13.

22 *Thoroughgood's Case* (1584) 2 Co Rep 9a at 9b; *Maunxel's Case* (1583) Moore KB 182 at 184.

23 That is, to establish the plea of *non est factum*. See the comments of Lord Reid in *Saunders* v. *Anglia Building Society* [1971] 3 All ER 961 at 963–964.

At the direction of the person making the deed

An individual ('the Maker') can have a deed signed on his behalf as long as the other person:

- is signing the deed at the direction of the Maker;
- is signing in the presence of the Maker; and

two witnesses are also present, who each attest the other person's signature (LP(MP)A 1989, s.1(3)(a)(ii)).

This is useful where the Maker is unable to sign herself, for example, because of physical disability. The *executed as a deed* clause and *signature block* are often amended to explain why the Maker cannot sign the deed (see **section 2.7**).

Power of attorney

A power of attorney allows one person to execute a deed on behalf of another individual,[24] without both persons being present (as required by LP(MP)A 1989 (see above)).

The formalities for creating a power of attorney, as a form of deed, would be the same as those covered in this chapter for creating a deed. This topic is covered in **Chapter 10**.

14.8   MEANING OF DELIVERY AND ESCROW [25]

A deed must be delivered. Although LP(MP)A 1989 indicates that delivery is essential for a document to be validly executed as a deed, it does not provide a definition of delivery. It appears that the meaning of, and the activities constituting, delivery are to be found in the common law.

---

24 As to whether an attorney can execute a deed on behalf of a corporation, see **section 22.4**.

25 Delivery is a complex topic, covering such issues as when delivery takes place, the distinction between delivery and delivery in escrow, the consequences that flow therefrom, etc. It involves a detailed consideration of extensive case law in the field, dating back over several centuries, as well as the particular practices in individual areas of law (e.g. domestic conveyancing, commercial property law, tax). A proper outline of the law in this area is outside the remit of this book. (Indeed, a proper discussion would require a book of the size of this one.) This section in this chapter provides no more than an outline of some of the relevant issues. See further Law Commission Consultation Paper 143 and Report LC 253 which provide further summaries of the law in this area.

Meaning of 'delivery'

Delivery is the final stage in the execution process indicating that the party signing the document intends to be bound by the provisions of the deed; see *Xenos* v. *Wickham* (1866) LR 2 HL 296 at 312, per Blackburn J:

> as soon as there are acts or words sufficient to [show] that it is intended by the party to be executed as his deed presently binding on him,

the deed is delivered, although the party may retain physical possession of the deed.

How is delivery effected?

Originally delivery occurred by the actual physical delivery of the deed into the possession or custody of the person intended to take the benefit of the deed,[26] or by a specific form of words; these are no longer necessary.

Delivery can now occur by words or conduct, expressly or by implication. However delivery is effected, the person executing the deed is acknowledging his intention to be immediately and unconditionally bound by the provisions contained in the deed.[27]

No particular form of words or act needs to be used to effect delivery, but the fact of delivery is often recorded in the deed itself (see *Encyclopaedia of Forms and Precedents*, vol. 12(2), 'Deeds', paras. 27–28).

Delivery at time of execution

A deed can be expressed to be delivered at the time of signing (with such words as 'Signed and Delivered as a Deed' in the *signature block*), or after signing (with such words as 'Signed as a Deed but not delivered until [*day and month*] 200[. . .]' in the *signature block*), but delivery cannot take place until the deed is signed.[28] LP(MP)A 1989 does not state that signing the deed means or implies that it is delivered (s.1(3)(b)).[29]

---

26 *Doe* d. *Garnons* v. *Knight* (1826) 5 B & C 671 at 689–692; *Exton* v. *Scott* (1833) 6 Sim 31; *Grugeon* v. *Gerrard* (1840) 4 Y & C Ex 119 at 130; *Fletcher* v. *Fletcher* (1844) 4 Hare 67 at 79; *Xenos* v. *Wickham* (1866) LR 2 HL 296; *Macedo* v. *Stroud* [1922] 2 AC 330, PC.

27 *Chamberlain* v. *Stanton* (1588) Cro Eliz 122; *Thoroughgood's Case* (1612) 9 Co Rep 136b; Co Litt 36a, 49b; Shep Touch 57–58; *Hall* v. *Bainbridge* (1848) 12 QB 699; *Tupper* v. *Foulkes* (1861) 9 CBNS 797; *Xenos* v. *Wickham* (1866) LR 2 HL 296; *Vincent* v. *Premo Enterprises (Voucher Sales) Ltd* [1969] 2 QB 609, [1969] 2 All ER 941, CA; *Taw* v. *Bury* (1559) 2 Dyer 167a; *Parker* v. *Tenant* (1560) 2 Dyer 192 b; *Shelton's Case* (1582) Cro Eliz 7; *Hollingworth* v. *Ascue* (1594) Cro Eliz 356; *R* v. *Longnor (Inhabitants)* (1833) 4 B & Ad 647 at 649; *London Freehold & Leasehold Property Co* v. *Baron Suffield* [1897] 2 Ch 608, CA.

28 *Perryman's Case* (1599) 5 Co Rep 84; *Xenos* v. *Wickham* (1866) LR 2 HL 296 at 323, per Lord Cranworth; *Alan Estates Ltd* v. *WG Stores Ltd* [1982] Ch 511.

29 This provision makes delivery a separate step. Note the different position for companies executing deeds under the provisions of CA 1985, s.36AA, where a deed is presumed to be delivered upon its being so executed.

A deed can be expressed to be delivered (unconditionally) or in escrow whether expressly or impliedly (where certain conditions need to be fulfilled).

Once a deed is delivered it cannot be withdrawn (*Venetian Glass Gallery Ltd* v. *Next Properties Ltd* [1989] 2 EGLR 42).

Delivery subject to conditions (escrow)

A deed can be made subject to conditions before it becomes fully binding on the individual who is to be bound by the deed. Such conditions might include that a party needs to carry out some act or pay some money, or some document must be executed.

A document subject to a condition is known as an escrow, which does not become the deed of the party expressed to be bound by it until the condition has been performed.[30]

Delivery of a deed subject to conditions can be either express or implied, either in words or by conduct. The condition(s) on which the escrow is delivered can be inferred from the circumstances (*Kingston* v. *Ambrian Investment Co. Ltd* [1975] 1 All ER 120, [1975] 1 WLR 161, CA). No particular form or use of words is necessary other than indicating that the party is willing to be bound (whether expressly or by implication) on fulfilment of the condition on which the deed is delivered as an escrow.

To whom may the escrow be delivered?

The following persons can receive the deed delivered as an escrow:

- the person who has signed and is to be bound by the deed can retain the deed;[31]
- an attorney acting for all the parties to the deed (*Millership* v. *Brookes* (1860) 5 H & N 797);
- the solicitor of a client who is a party who is to benefit under the deed, provided the deed is delivered to the solicitor as agent for all the parties to the deed (*Watkins* v. *Nash* (1875) LR 20 Eq 262).

A deed delivered as an escrow cannot be delivered to the party intended to benefit under the deed because delivery to that party would constitute delivery as a deed. Any condition needing to be performed would not be effective.[32]

---

30 *Halsbury's Laws*, 'Deeds', para. 37, and a deed is delivered in escrow where one party executes a deed on the condition that another party is to execute the deed; such a deed will not take effect until executed by all the parties: *Halsbury's Laws*, 'Deeds', para. 52.

31 *Gudgen* v. *Besset* (1856) 6 E & B 986; *Phillips* v. *Edwards* (1864) 33 Beav 440; *Walker* v. *Ware, etc. Rly Co* (1865) 35 Beav 52; *Xenos* v. *Wickham* (1866) LR 2 HL 296.

32 *Whyddon's Case* (1596) Cro Eliz 520; *Williams* v. *Green* (1602) Cro Eliz 884; *Thoroughgood's Case* (1612) 9 Co Rep 136b at 137b; *Holford* v. *Parker* (1618) Hob 246; *Bushell* v. *Pasmore* (1704) 6 Mod Rep 217 at 218; *Coare* v. *Giblett* (1803) 4 East 85 at 95,

Effect of delivery as escrow

A deed delivered as an escrow cannot take effect as a deed until the condition is fulfilled.

It cannot be recalled before the condition is fulfilled.[33] The conditions cannot be wholly in the control of the maker of the deed (*Governors and Guardians of the Foundling Hospital* v. *Crane* [1911] 2 KB 367 at 379).

Once the condition is fulfilled, the deed immediately becomes effective.

Dating of a deed and delivery

A deed takes effect from the date on which the execution of the deed is completed by delivery[34] and not the date of execution. Therefore the deed should be dated when delivery takes place. Where several parties need to execute the deed for the deed to be valid, the deed is delivered on the execution of the last party.[35]

For a deed delivered in escrow, the deed takes effect from the date of delivery in escrow and not the fulfilment of the condition.[36]

If no date is added to a deed, the validity of the deed is not usually affected, and external evidence can be called to indicate the correct date (*Morrell* v. *Studd and Millington* [1913] 2 Ch 648 at 658). There is a rebuttable presumption that the date stated in a deed is the date when it took effect (*Browne* v. *Burton* (1847) 17 LJQB 49, 5 Dow & L 289).

Distinction between execution of a deed and delivery, delivery in escrow and a deed executed but not delivered

As indicated above, a deed which is executed and is delivered unconditionally takes effect immediately. A deed which is executed and delivered in escrow takes effect on the condition being fulfilled, but cannot be recalled before the condition is fulfilled.

There is a third possibility, where a deed is signed and handed to the Maker's agent (such as her solicitor) with instructions to deliver it when a

---

per Lord Ellenborough CJ. The position in equity may be different, i.e. that a deed may be delivered to the person to benefit under the deed but subject to a condition.

33 *Beesly* v. *Hallwood Estates Ltd* [1961] Ch 105; *Kingston* v. *Ambrian Investment Co. Ltd* [1975] 1 WLR 161 at 166.

34 *Universal Permanent Building Society* v. *Cooke* [1952] 1 Ch 95 at 101; *Abbey National Building Society* v. *Cann* [1991] 1 AC 56.

35 *Bishop of Crediton* v. *Bishop of Exeter* [1905] 2 Ch 455; *Lady Naas* v. *Westminster Bank Ltd* [1940] AC 366; *Sinclair* v. *IRC* (1942) 24 TC 432.

36 *Jennings* v. *Bragg* (1595) Cro Eliz 447; *Butler & Baker's Case* (1591) 3 Co Rep 25 at 35; *Perryman's Case* (1599) 5 Co Rep 84; *Graham* v. *Graham* (1791) 1 Ves Jun 272; *Coare* v. *Giblett* (1803) 4 East 85; *Copeland* v. *Stephens* (1818) 1 B & Ald 593; *Edmunds* v. *Edmunds* [1904] P 362; *Alan Estates Ltd* v. *WG Stores Ltd* [1982] Ch 511. This proposition is not correct for stamp duty purposes, where the date of delivery is the date when the condition is fulfilled: SA 1891, s.122(1A).

certain event occurs. Instructions of this kind would generally be revocable and accordingly the deed would have no effect unless and until delivered by the agent.[37] The deed is not delivered in escrow, but goes straight from non-delivery to complete delivery.[38]

The Court of Appeal stated that this was common conveyancing practice.[39]

14.9 DELIVERY ON BEHALF OF THE PERSON MAKING THE DEED

Under LP(MP)A 1989, any rule of law which requires the authority given by one person to another to deliver an instrument itself to be given as a deed on her behalf is abolished (LP(MP)A 1989, s.1(1)(c)). Such a deed should have a *signature block* which states that it is 'Signed as a deed' (*Encyclopaedia of Forms and Precedents*, vol. 12(2), 'Deeds', para. 28.3).

Where a solicitor, public notary or licensed conveyancer (or their agent or employee) in the course of or in connection with a transaction, purports to deliver an instrument as a deed on behalf of a party to the instrument, it shall be conclusively presumed in favour of a purchaser that he is authorised to deliver the instrument (LP(MP)A 1989, s.1(5)).[40]

14.10 DEEDS EXECUTED BEFORE LP(MP)A 1989 CAME INTO FORCE

The method of execution of documents as deeds described above applies to documents executed as deeds on or after 31 July 1990.[41] The above provisions of LP(MP)A 1989 are explicitly indicated not to apply to documents delivered as deeds before it came into force (LP(MP)A 1989, s.1(11)).

Before that date, the requirements to execute a deed included the following:

- that it must be written on parchment or paper;
- that it must be executed by some person named in the deed;
- that the document must be sealed with the individual's seal (or with what is taken to be their seal);

---

37 *Longman* v. *Viscount Chelsea* (1989) 58 P & CR 189 at 195. The case was decided before LP(MP)A 1989, which meant that in order for a person to deliver an instrument as a deed on behalf of another person, the delivering person had to be given authority by a deed. This is no longer required.

38 The deed, being held to the order of the party who executed the deed by the primary party's lawyer is thus undelivered and recallable.

39 Although the court cited common conveyancing practice as a primary reason for its decision, the decision has been controversial and an opposite decision was reached in the same year (and on different facts) in *Venetian Glass Gallery Ltd* v. *Next Properties* [1989] 2 EGLR 42. There is an analysis of delivery and these decisions in the Law Commission Consultation Paper 143.

40 'Purchaser' has the same meaning as in LPA 1925 (LP(MP)A 1989, s.1(6)).

41 LP(MP)A 1989, s.5(1) and (2) and Law of Property (Miscellaneous Provisions) (Commencement) Order 1990, SI 1990/1175.

- that the individual must sign the deed; and
- delivery of the deed (words or conduct expressly or impliedly acknowledging that the individual intends to be bound immediately and unconditionally by the provisions of the deed).

14.11   ALTERATIONS AND AMENDMENTS TO DEEDS

Before execution

The writing on a deed can be added to or deleted before execution. The validity of the deed is not affected.[42] There is a rebuttable presumption that alterations, deletions or interlineations are made before execution.[43]

When the deed has been altered, the changes made should be noted in the attestation clause.

After execution

Changes made by or with the consent of a party to or a person entitled under the deed – deed void

A deed is void if alterations (additions, deletions or interlineations) are made to a *material* part of the deed and are made without the consent of a person liable under the deed, and the change is made by, or with the consent of, a party to or a person who benefits under the deed.[44]

A person wishing to rely on this proposition has to show that the alteration is *potentially* prejudicial to that person's legal rights or obligations under the deed.[45]

The alteration made has to be a material alteration, which varies the legal position of the parties as expressed in the deed as originally executed (*Gardner* v. *Walsh* (1855) 5 E & B 83 at 89). A material alteration can be where a provision in the deed which was certain becomes uncertain[46] or one

---

42 *Cole* v. *Parkin* (1810) 12 East 471; *Matson* v. *Booth* (1816) 5 M & S 223 at 226; *Doe* d. *Lewis* v. *Bingham* (1821) 4 B & Ald 672; *Hall* v. *Chandless* (1827) 4 Bing 123; *Jones* v. *Jones* (1833) 1 Cr & M 721.
43 *Trowel* v. *Castle* (1661) 1 Keb 21 at 22; *Fitzgerald* v. *Lord Fauconberge* (1729) Fitz-G 207 at 214; *Doe* d. *Tatum* v. *Catomore* (1851) 16 QB 745; *Simmons* v. *Rudall* (1851) 1 Sim NS 115; *Williams* v. *Ashton* (1860) 1 John & H 115 at 118.
44 The rule in *Pigot's Case* (1614) 11 Co Rep 26b. This proposition extends to where a deed is altered by a person not a party to, nor entitled under, a deed and the deed is in the custody of the person entitled under it.
45 On the assumption that the parties acted in accordance with the other terms of the contract. No actual prejudice has to be shown: *Raiffeisen Zentralbank Österreich AG* v. *Crossseas Shipping Ltd* [2000] 1 All ER (Comm) 76, CA.
46 *Markham* v. *Gonaston* (1598) Cro Eliz 626 at 627; *Eagleton* v. *Gutteridge* (1843) 11 M & W 465 at 468–469; *Re Barned's Banking Co., ex p. Contract Corpn* (1867) 3 Ch App 105 at 115.

which may vary the position of a party to the deed as originally executed (*Halsbury's Laws*, 'Deeds', para. 85).

The avoidance of a deed materially altered operates from the time of the alteration and does not nullify any transaction which has taken place and will prevent the person who has made the alteration (or allowed it to be made) from using the document to enforce an obligation, covenant, etc. against a person bound by it.[47] The effect of an alteration is the same as if the deed had been cancelled.

Changes made need to be material

An immaterial alteration made after execution will not affect the validity of a deed, whether the immaterial alteration is made by a party[48] or a stranger[49] to the deed. The following appear to be examples which are not material alterations made after execution:

- filling in the date of a deed;[50]
- filling in the name of occupiers where the property that was to be assured could be properly identified without their names being written in the deed (*Adsetts* v. *Hives* (1863) 33 Beav 52);
- altering the first name of one of the parties;[51]
- deleting the word 'Company' which had been wrongly inserted in a company name (*Lombard Finance Ltd* v. *Brookplain Trading Ltd and others* [1991] 2 All ER 762);
- changing the name of a bank's customer in a guarantee, where the name written in before execution was the name of the guarantors not the name of the customer, and the change was made in pencil;[52]

---

47 *Gilford* v. *Mills* (1511) Keil 164; *Markham* v. *Gonaston* (1598) Cro Eliz 626 at 627; *Pigot's Case* (1614) 11 Co Rep 26b; *Master* v. *Miller* (1791) 4 Term Rep 320 at 329–332, 345 (on appeal (1793) 2 Hy Bl 141 at 142–143, Ex Ch); 1 Smith LC (13th edn) 789; *Weeks* v. *Maillardet* (1811) 14 East 568; *Langhorn* v. *Cologan* (1812) 4 Taunt 330; *Fairlie* v. *Christie* (1817) 7 Taunt 416; *Forshaw* v. *Chabert* (1821) 3 Brod & Bing 158; *Davidson* v. *Cooper* (1844) 13 M & W 343 at 352, Ex Ch; *Fazakerly* v. *McKnight* (1856) 6 E & B 795; *Sellin* v. *Price* (1867) LR 2 Exch 189; *Suffell* v. *Bank of England* (1882) 9 QBD 555 at 559–560, 571, CA; *Lowe* v. *Fox* (1887) 12 App Cas 206 at 214, 216, HL; *Ellesmere Brewery Co.* v. *Cooper* [1896] 1 QB 75; and see also *Bank of Hindustan, China and Japan* v. *Smith* (1867) 36 LJCP 241; *Pattinson* v. *Luckley* (1875) LR 10 Exch 330 at 333–334.
48 *Aldous* v. *Cornwell* (1868) LR 3 QB 573 at 579; *Bishop of Crediton* v. *Bishop of Exeter* [1905] 2 Ch 455 at 459.
49 *Pigot's Case* (1614) 11 Co Rep 26b at 27a. See *Raiffeisen Zentralbank Österreich AG* v. *Crossseas Shipping Ltd* [2000] 1 All ER (Comm) 76, CA.
50 *Keane* v. *Smallbone* (1855) 17 CB 179; *Adsetts* v. *Hives* (1863) 33 Beav 52; *Bishop of Crediton* v. *Bishop of Exeter* [1905] 2 Ch 455.
51 *Re Howgate & Osborn's Contract* [1902] 1 Ch 451; *Eagleton* v. *Gutteridge* (1843) 11 M & W 465.
52 *Co-operative Bank plc* v. *Tipper* [1996] 4 All ER 366. The natural inference to be drawn from an amendment made in pencil to a document in print, type or ink is that the amendment is not intended to be an operative and final alteration.

- adding the name and contact details for an agent of the guarantor who is to accept service of legal documents on behalf of the guarantor made without the consent or knowledge of the guarantor (*Raiffeisen Zentralbank Österreich AG* v. *Crossseas Shipping Ltd and others* [2000] 1 All ER (Comm) 76, CA);
- a change which does not alter or vary the legal effect of the deed in its original state, but expresses what is implied by law as the deed was originally written[53] as long as the alteration does not otherwise prejudice the party liable under it (*Adsetts* v. *Hives* (1863) 33 Beav 52);
- if the change made is immaterial against a particular party, and any agreement in the deed may be enforced against that party (if liable under the deed) as if the deed had not been altered (*Hall* v. *Chandless* (1827) 4 Bing 123).

Other than specific instances as to what is not an immaterial alteration, the onus is on the party who wishes to avoid a deed to show that the alteration was potentially prejudicial to her legal rights or obligations (*Raiffeisen Zentralbank Österreich AG* v. *Crossseas Shipping Ltd and others*).

Change made by or at the direction of a person liable under a deed

If a person liable under a deed alters or defaces the deed, the party entitled under the deed can still enforce the liability against that person (*Brown* v. *Savage* (1674) Cas *temp* Finch 184).

Alteration by consent

If a deed is altered in a material part with the consent of the person(s) liable, the deed is not necessarily avoided, and the party entitled is not estopped from enforcing any agreement it contains against that person or those persons.[54]

If it is altered in such a way as to make it a new instrument, it needs to be stamped again,[55] but re-execution does not appear to be necessary.

---

53 *Waugh* v. *Bussell* (1814) 5 Taunt 707 at 711; *Aldous* v. *Cornwell* (1868) LR 3 QB 573.
54 *Markham* v. *Gonaston* (1598) Cro Eliz 626, 9 East 354n; *Zouch* v. *Clay* (1671) 2 Lev 35; *Paget* v. *Paget* (1688) 2 Rep Ch 410; *Bates* v. *Grabham* (1703) 3 Salk 444; *French* v. *Patton* (1808) 9 East 351 at 355–357; *Matson* v. *Booth* (1816) 5 M & S 223 at 227; *Eagleton* v. *Gutteridge* (1843) 11 M & W 465; *Adsetts* v. *Hives* (1863) 33 Beav 52; *Rudd* v. *Bowles* [1912] 2 Ch 60; *Re Danish Bacon Co. Ltd Staff Pension Fund, Christensen* v. *Arnett* [1971] 1 All ER 486, [1971] 1 WLR 248.
55 SA 1891, s.14(4). With regard to those instruments requiring stamping, if they are not restamped, there may be issues regarding their being received in evidence. Not all instruments need to be stamped (e.g. a deed which assigns intellectual property).

Accidental alteration

If a deed is obliterated or defaced (including, where a seal is required or used, by the seal becoming detached) by accident (e.g. fire, by a child), a responsible human is not involved, then the deed is not avoided, nor is it stopped from being used in evidence. If the damage done is so severe as to make the deed totally or partially illegible, then secondary evidence of its contents is admissible.

Furthermore, accidental, unintentional or inadvertent damage done by a human may not allow avoidance of the deed or stop it being used in evidence. This extends to where the damage was performed by the person entitled.

Forgery

If a deed or document is altered in an immaterial way and the change is made in good faith, it does not amount to forgery for the purposes of the Forgery and Counterfeiting Act 1981, s.1 (*Lombard Finance Ltd* v. *Brookplain Trading Ltd and others* [1991] 2 All ER 762).

14.12   CANCELLATION

Cancellation of a deed is effected by defacing it, or altering it, so that it becomes void.

A deed can be cancelled by the following:

- the person who has it in her possession as being solely entitled under it (*Harrison* v. *Owen* (1738) 1 Atk 520);
- mutual consent (*Lord Ward* v. *Lumley* (1860) 5 H & N 87);
- under the terms of an agreement between the parties (*Bamberger* v. *Commercial Credit Mutual Assurance Society* (1855) 15 CB 676 at 693–694);
- an order of the court.

A deed which is provided in a cancelled state is, on first impression, evidence that it is void.[56] A deed made void by cancellation does not have a retrospective effect or make it void from execution. For example, property conveyed under a subsequently cancelled deed will not be reconveyed.[57]

---

56 *Knight* v. *Clements* (1838) 8 Ad & El 215 at 220; *Earl of Falmouth* v. *Roberts* (1842) 9 M & W 469 at 471; *Alsager* v. *Close* (1842) 10 M & W 576 at 583; *Meiklejohn* v. *Campbell* (1940) 56 TLR 663 at 665 (affd 56 TLR 704, CA).
57 *Knight* v. *Clements* (1838) 8 Ad & El 215 at 220; *Earl of Falmouth* v. *Roberts* (1842) 9 M & W 469 at 471; *Alsager* v. *Close* (1842) 10 M & W 576 at 583; *Meiklejohn* v. *Campbell* (1940) 56 TLR 663 at 665 (affd 56 TLR 704, CA).

14.13   DISCHARGE OF CONTRACTS MADE BY DEED

A contract made by deed can be discharged in the same manner as one made under hand (before or after breach) (*Steeds* v. *Steeds* (1889) 22 QBD 537). It is possible to vary an obligation created by a deed by a contract made under hand (*Berry* v. *Berry* [1929] 2 KB 316).

14.14   VARYING A DEED

A deed can be amended or varied by an agreement which is not a deed (*Plymouth Corporation* v. *Harvey* [1971] 1 All ER 623, [1971 1 WLR 549; *Mitas* v. *Hyams* [1951] 2 TLR 1215, CA). Case law is not entirely clear whether the amending or varying agreement has to be supported by consideration in order for it not to be made by deed.[58]

14.15   REQUIREMENT TO USE A DEED

In some situations the use of a deed is mandatory. Failure to use a deed may make the transaction or event recorded in the deed not effective in law. In some cases, a particular form for the deed is also required. Such requirements are now mostly found in statute. There are other categories where it is conventional to use a deed or where one or more party to a transaction may wish to use a deed. Common examples of each type follow.

---

58 For example, in the *Plymouth* case, the dispute involved a lease (executed as a deed). One of the terms was that the defendant would remove some caravans by a set date. He failed to do so. The parties agreed that the date for removal would be extended, the defendant would make a payment and he would also execute a deed of surrender of the lease which was delivered in escrow and would only take effect if he failed to remove the caravans by the new date. These new terms were contained in a letter from the claimant to the defendant. The defendant executed the deed of surrender and made the payment. The judge held that the agreement varied the lease so the date contained in the lease for the removal of the caravans was varied to the new date in the letter of the claimant. And such variation did not need to be executed as a deed in order to vary by an agreement, citing *Mitas* v. *Hyams* [1951] 2 TLR 1215, CA as support for this proposition. It seems clear from these facts there was consideration to support the varying of the date for the removal of the caravans (although not explicitly stated in the case report).

When must a deed be used – statutory requirements

LPA 1925

A deed is required in the following circumstances:

- a conveyance of land, or of any interest in land, for the purpose of conveying or creating a legal estate (s.52(1));[59]
- a mortgage, if the mortgagee is to have the following powers:

  - to sell when the mortgage money has become due on the mortgaged property or any part of it;
  - to insure, after the mortgage deed is entered into, against loss or damage by fire, any building or any effects or property of an insurable nature;
  - to appoint a receiver when the mortgage money has become due;
  - to cut and sell timber, etc. while the mortgagee is in possession (LPA 1925, s.101(1));

- conveyances of a property sold by a mortgagee exercising the power of sale conferred by LPA 1925, s.104(1);
- a mortgage in a statutory form of freehold or leasehold land (LPA 1925, s.117(1));[60]
- enlargement of a term of years into fee simple estates (LPA 1925, s.153);
- a release of, or a contract not to exercise, the power given to a person (whether coupled with an interest or not) (LPA 1925, s.155);
- a power given to a person can be disclaimed by that person by deed (whether coupled with an interest or not) (LPA 1925, s.156).[61]

Land Registration Act 2002 and Land Registration Rules 2003

Particular instruments to be registered under the Land Registration Act 2002 are required to be made as a deed, and to be made on specified forms, including:[62]

---

59 If not, then the conveyance is void. The meaning of a 'conveyance' 'includes a mortgage, charge, lease, assent, vesting declaration, vesting instrument, disclaimer, release and every other assurance of property or of an interest therein by any instrument, except a will; "convey" has a corresponding meaning; and "disposition" includes a conveyance and also a devise, bequest, or an appointment of property contained in a will; and "dispose of" has a corresponding meaning': LPA 1925, s.205(1). 'Land' 'includes land of any tenure, and mines and minerals, whether or not held apart from the surface, buildings or parts of buildings (whether the division is horizontal, vertical or made in any other way) . . . and an easement, right, privilege, or benefit in, over, or derived from land'.
60 LPA 1925, Sched. 4 sets out the statutory forms referred to in s.117(1).
61 After the disclaimer, that person shall not be capable of exercising or joining in the exercise of the power.
62 Land Registration Act 2002, ss.18, 21 and 25(1). Land Registration Rules 2003, SI 2003/1417, rr.98 and 206–209. These are required to be in a specified manner on specified forms.

- assent of whole of registered title (Form AS1);
- assent of charge (Form AS2);
- assent of part of registered title(s) by a personal representative (Form AS3);
- legal charge of a registered estate (Form CH1);
- transfer of part of registered title(s) (Form TP1);
- transfer of part of registered title(s) under power of sale (Form TP2);
- transfer of a portfolio of titles (Form TP3);
- transfer of whole of registered title(s) (Form TR1);
- transfer of whole of registered title(s) under power of sale (Form TR2);
- transfer of charge (Form TR3);
- transfer of a portfolio of charges (Form TR4);
- transfer of portfolio of whole titles (Form TR5).

Normally, these specified forms must be used where required by the Rules,[63] and there are also specified forms of *signature block* (Land Registration Rules 2003, Sched. 9). Although they are close to the examples given in the Procedural Guide sections of this book (see **Chapters 1–12**), there are some minor differences in wording and layout and in the normal course of events they must be used. In each chapter the specified form of signature is set out.[64]

Trustee Act 1925

The following must be done as a deed and contain the appropriate declaration:

- a declaration by a trustee of his desire to be discharged under the Trustee Act 1925, s.39(1);
- a memorandum evidencing the appointment or discharge of a trustee of charity property by a resolution if the trust is to operate under the Charities Act 1993, s.83(1)–(4) as if it contained a vesting declaration.

Other statutory examples

These include:

- bills of sale made or given by way of security for the payment of money by the grantor (Bills of Sale Act (1878) Amendment Act 1882, s.9).[65] The form of words to be used is specified (Bills of Sale Act (1878) Amendment Act 1882, Sched.);

---

63 Land Registration Rules 2003, r.206(1). Land Registration Rules 2003, r.209, provides a limited exception.
64 Land Registration Rules 2003, r.206(3). This rule also provides that the Registrar of the Land Registry may allow alterations and additions: *Land Registry Practice Guide 8*, 'Execution of Deeds', s.3.3, April 2008.
65 They are made in a statutory form. If not made as a deed, then they are void.

- transfer of a ship (or part of a ship) (Merchant Shipping Act 1995, s.10);[66]
- mortgage of a registered ship (or part of a registered ship);
- leases authorised by the Settled Land Act 1925, s.42 to be made by tenants for life and others of any settled land.[67]

Powers of attorney

A deed is required for creation of a power of attorney (PAA 1971, s.1(1)).

When a deed is preferred

There are several situations when a document is executed as a deed because the person making it or the parties to it find some benefit from the document being a deed. In some cases, by convention in a particular legal area, a transaction or event is recorded through the use of a deed.

Contract

The following are the more common situations where deeds are preferred:

- where there is doubt about the consideration:
  - because it is past consideration (*Re McArdle* [1951] Ch 669); or
  - it is not clear whether consideration has moved from the promisee, i.e. whether a person has provided consideration in return for a promise (*Tweddle* v. *Atkinson* (1861) 1 B & S 393);
- where the parties to a contract wish to take advantage of the extended period to bring an action for breach of contract where a contract is executed as a deed – 12 years (Limitation Act 1980, s.8)[68] instead of six (Limitation Act 1980, s.5);
- where a contract is amended and it is not clear that all the parties are providing consideration, e.g. the amendments are all to the advantage of only one party. There may be doubt whether the amended contract would be legally binding, so it is made as a deed.

---

66 Must be made by a bill of sale and must satisfy prescribed regulations. This is not required if the transfer will no longer have a British connection: Merchant Shipping Act 1995, Sched. 1, para. 2(1).

67 It is no longer possible to create new settlements under the Settled Land Act 1925: Trusts of Land and Appointments of Trustees Act 1996, s.2(1). Subject to certain conditions, leases for less than three years are made by writing not deed: Settled Land Act 1925, s.42(5)(ii).

68 The Act uses the term 'speciality', which is thought to mean the same as a 'deed' or 'agreement under seal': *Aiken* v. *Stewart Wrightson Members' Agency Ltd* [1995] 1 WLR 1281 at 1292.

Situations when it is conventional to use a deed

These include the following:

- a purchaser of a company will require the vendors to execute a deed in which they covenant with the company to indemnify it against certain tax liabilities;
- the assignment of intellectual property (patents, copyright, design right, trademarks);
- for the release of a security;
- banks often require a guarantee to be by deed where the guarantee is for amounts previously advanced (unless it is clear that the bank is providing consideration, such as not enforcing one of its rights – e.g. calling in the loan).

CHAPTER 15

Execution of a deed by a corporation (non-CA 2006 or CA 1985)

15.1 INTRODUCTION

This chapter does not cover corporations which are companies formed under or regulated by CA 2006 or CA 1985 (see **Chapter 16**). The requirements for the valid execution of a deed by corporations are a mixture of common law and the particular Act of Parliament or Royal Charter forming them, together with some generally applicable statutes.[1] The major reform regarding the execution of deeds in recent years has been in LP(MP)A 1989 and LPA 1925, s.74 (both as amended by RR(EDD)O 2005). As regards most corporations, some changes have been made to the common law position regarding the execution of deeds. LP(MP)A 1989 did not change those common law provisions which were not expressly dealt with by it. The amendment to LPA 1925 has altered the number of persons who need to sign a document in order for the presumption of due execution to apply (LPA 1925, s.74(1)).

The main changes introduced by LP(MP)A 1989 (as amended) were:

- a document will not be a deed unless it makes it clear on its face that it is intended to be a deed by the person making the deed (or, if more than one party to it, the parties to it);[2]
- abolishing any restrictions regarding the substances on which a deed may be written;
- a document will not be a deed merely because it is executed under seal;
- a document can be validly executed on behalf of a person by an individual who is authorised to do so;
- where an individual signs on behalf of another person, she signs in her status as an individual, whether or not the other person is an individual.

---

1 This statement does not apply to companies formed under, or regulated by, CA 1985 (see **Chapter 16**) and a few other corporations.
2 The 'face value' requirement, as described by the Law Commission in its Consultation Paper 143.

LP(MP)A 1989 also abolished the requirement for an individual to apply a seal to a deed (LP(MP)A 1989, s.1(1)(b). However, the requirement to use a seal to execute a deed still applies to many corporations in England and Wales. The most significant and wide-ranging exceptions to this are companies formed under, or regulated by, CA 2006 or CA 1985; see **Chapter 16**.

The principal changes to LPA 1925, s.74(1) concern:

- the number of persons who need to execute an instrument for the statutory presumption of execution by the corporation to operate; and
- what happens when an instrument is executed by a corporation in the name of or on behalf of another person.

15.2   WHAT IS A 'CORPORATION'?

Corporations (or bodies corporate) in England and Wales are most types of organisations that have a legal identity separate from their owners or members. The meaning of a corporation extends from a minister of the Crown, through to local authorities, many types of charities, public bodies (such as the National Health Service, the Post Office) and companies formed under, or regulated by, CA 2006 or CA 1985.

Method of formation

Most corporations are now formed:

- by an Act of Parliament (private or public – such as the Post Office, the National Trust, the Information Commissioner);
- under an Act of Parliament (public – such as companies formed under CA 1985, CA 2006 or LLPA 2000); or
- by Royal Charter (such as many universities).

Classification of corporations

There are a number of methods of classifying corporations. One of the common methods is to distinguish between:

- *a corporation aggregate*: a body of persons;[3] or

---

3 *Halsbury's Laws*, 2006 reissue, vol. 9(2), 'Corporations', para. 1109:

A collection of individuals united into one body under a special denomination, having perpetual succession under an artificial form, and vested by the policy of the law with the capacity of acting in several respects as an individual, particularly of taking and granting property, of contracting obligations and of suing, of enjoying privilege and immunities in common and exercising a variety of political rights, more or less extensive, according to the design of the institution, or the powers conferred on it, either at the time of its creation of at any subsequent period of its existence.

- *a corporation sole*: an office occupied by one person[4,5]

which have a separate legal existence that is different from the body of persons or the holder of an office.[6]

Not all associations and bodies of persons are corporations, but some are regarded as quasi-corporations,[7] having key features of a corporation such as the ability to sue and be sued in its own name and to hold property (including entering into contracts) in its own name.

The general principle, under common law, was that all corporations required a seal which needed to be fixed to deeds, and such use was to be authenticated by the signature of one or more members of the corporation's governing body and/or its clerk or secretary or as otherwise provided by the corporation's governing document. For many corporations, the requirement to use a seal and how it is authenticated is governed by the Act of Parliament or the Royal Charter incorporating the corporation.

This general principle has been modified in recent years. Some corporations are no longer required to have a seal.[8]

15.3 REQUIREMENTS TO EXECUTE A DOCUMENT VALIDLY AS A DEED BY A CORPORATION

The following are the requirements for a corporation to validly execute a document as a deed:

- it must be in writing;[9] and

---

4 *Halsbury's Laws*, 2006 reissue, vol. 9(2), 'Corporations', para. 1111:

> A corporation sole is a body politic having perpetual succession, constituted in a single person, who, in right of some office or function, has a capacity to take, purchase, hold and demise (and in some particular instances, under qualifications and restrictions introduced by statute, power to alienate) real property, and now, it would seem, also to take and hold personal property, to him and his successors in such office for ever, the succession being perpetual, but not always uninterruptedly continuous, that is, there may be and often are, periods in the duration of a corporation sole, occurring irregularly, in which there is a vacancy, or no one in existence in whom the corporation resides and is visibly represented.

5 *Sutton's Hospital Case* (1612) 10 Co Rep 1a at 23a, 29b, Ex Ch; 1 Roll Abr 512. Grant, *Law of Corporations* 1, 626.
6 *Halsbury's Laws*, 2006 reissue, vol. 9(2), 'Corporations', para. 1111.
7 Examples are registered friendly societies (registered under the Friendly Societies Act 1974), trustee savings banks, former volunteer corps, the former War Damage Commission (now dissolved: War Damage Act 1964, s.2(1)), Inns of Court, trade unions: *Halsbury's Laws*, 'Corporations', para. 1111.
8 The most notable modification has been for companies regulated by CA 1985. Other examples are given below.
9 *Goddard's Case* (1584) 2 Co Rep 4b at 5a, 76 ER 396 at 398–399. 'Writing' under common law did not require the use of pen or ink, but could include pencil or with paint: *Geary* v. *Physic* (1826) 5 B & C 234 at 237. The meaning of the word 'writing' in any Act

- the writing can be placed on any type of material (LP(MP)A 1989, s.1(1)(a));[10] and
- the document shall not be a deed unless the document makes it clear that it is intended to be a deed by the person making it or the parties to it. This intention can be expressed by the document:

  - describing itself as a deed; or
  - expressing itself to be executed or signed as a deed; or
  - describing itself in some other way (LP(MP)A 1989, s.1(2)(a));[11] and

- affixing the seal of the corporation to the document; and
- the undertaking of certain formalities in order for the seal of the corporation to be used (who is to sign, the procedure to be used in order for the person to sign, etc.);[12] and
- delivery of the deed.

The formalities are normally detailed in the corporation's constitution, charter, articles, regulations or standing orders. Some corporations are set up by statute, and the statute may specify the formalities.

Formalities

Such formalities will normally cover some or all of the following:

- which person or official of the corporation has custody of the seal (usually the secretary or clerk to the corporation or its governing body);
- who on the governing body can execute documents (on some governing bodies only certain members can execute documents or can only execute documents in certain circumstances);
- how many members of the governing body are required to execute documents (for example, two members, one member and the secretary/clerk or the secretary/clerk alone);
- the circumstances in which documents can be executed by the governing body (following a resolution or decision by the governing body, or what happens in cases of emergency (and how these are defined and who can act in these circumstances));
- whether the use of the seal can be delegated to a person or persons who are not members of the governing body and such person(s) can execute documents in the name of, and on behalf of, the governing body.

---

includes: 'typing, printing, lithography, photography and other modes of representing or reproducing words in a visible form' (IA 1978, s.5, Sched. 1).

10 Abolishing the common law rule that a deed had to be written on paper, parchment or vellum (*Goddard's Case* (1584) 2 Co Rep 4b at 5a, 76 ER 396 at 398–399).

11 'In some other way' can mean that the document does not state that it is a deed at all but the document is stated to be a type of document which, in the circumstances, can only be a deed.

12 *Clarke* v. *Imperial Gas Light and Coke Co.* (1832) 4 B & Ad 315 at 324–326.

Formalities for most modern corporations

The particular requirements for each corporation will be found in the Act of Parliament or Royal Charter creating it or in its articles, regulations or standing orders. However, a general approach appears among corporations set up in recent years as to the formalities required to execute a document with the corporation's seal (see Law Commission Consultation Paper 143, paras. 4.20–4.21). The relevant constitutional documents of such corporations tend to provide:

- that the corporation is a body corporate;
- that the corporation is to have a seal; and
- the affixing of the seal is to be authenticated by the signature of:
  - a member of the governing body of the corporation; or
  - the secretary of the corporation or the governing body; or
  - a person authorised by the governing body; and

there is a presumption (normally rebuttable) that a document purported to be sealed and authenticated as detailed immediately above is a document of the corporation.

15.4   CORPORATE BODIES GENERALLY REQUIRED TO USE A SEAL: CORPORATIONS AGGREGATE

Deeds

Corporations aggregate need to use seals for the execution of deeds.[13]

Some statutes forming public corporations have provisions concerning the requirement to have a seal and how they should be used.[14]

Certain corporations are required to use a seal, but are not required to have their own seal. They can use the seal(s) of their members: parish councils (Local Government Act 1972 (LGA 1972)), s.14(3)); community councils in Wales (LGA 1972, s.33(3) and (4)), and parochial church councils (Parochial Church Councils (Powers) Measure 1956, s.3).

The use of a seal alone will not make an instrument a deed merely because it is executed under seal (LP(MP)A 1989, s.1(2A)). Clear wording will need to be used indicating that the instrument is intended to be a deed (as well as having it properly executed by the persons or the parties to it) (LP(MP)A 1989, s.1(2)).

---

13 For example, Law Commission Consultation Paper 143; *Halsbury's Laws*, 'Corporations', para. 1122, and 'Deeds', para. 32. But see **section 15.6**.
14 Some examples are provided below.

Contracts

Seals are not required in order for a corporation aggregate to enter into a contract (CBCA 1960, s.1(1)) although if the corporation wishes to use a seal it can do so (CBCA 1960, s.1(4)).

15.5 CORPORATE BODIES GENERALLY REQUIRED TO USE A SEAL: CORPORATIONS SOLE

Deeds

A person wishing to execute a deed in their capacity as a corporation sole is required to use a wafer seal (*Halsbury's Laws*, 'Corporations', para. 1122). Statutory provision is made for the having of, and use of, seals by government ministers and officers who are corporations sole.

The abolition by LP(MP)A 1989 of the requirement for an individual to use a seal does not apply to corporations sole (s.1(10)).

15.6 CORPORATE BODIES NOT REQUIRED TO HAVE A SEAL

The principal examples of corporations not required to have or use a seal are:

- companies formed under, or regulated by CA 2006 or CA 1985 (provisions concerning a company not needing a seal: (until October 2009) CA 1985, s.36A(5); (from October 2009) CA 2006, s.45(1));
- friendly societies (Friendly Societies Act 1992, s.7(6), Sched. 6);
- charity trustees incorporated under the Charities Act 1993, Part VII (Charities Act 1993, s.60);[15]
- open-ended investment companies.[16]

---

15 The trustees of a charity become an incorporated body, not the charity itself. If the charity itself wishes to incorporate, it can do so as a company limited by guarantee.

16 Open-Ended Investment Companies Regulations 2001, SI 2001/1228, reg. 57(3). Note that in favour of a purchaser, a document is deemed to have been duly executed by a company if it purports to be signed by at least one director or, in the case of a director which is a body corporate, it purports to be executed by that director; and, where it makes it clear on its face that it is intended by the person or persons making it to be a deed, it is deemed to have been delivered upon its being executed. And a document that is signed by at least one director and expressed (in whatever form of words) to be executed by the company has the same effect as if executed under the common seal of the company (see reg. 57 for further details as to the execution of documents and deeds).

15.7 USE OF SEALS

If a corporation has, in its constitution, a specified way of executing its deeds (including any formalities for the placement of the seal), the specified way and the formalities required must be carried out if a deed is to be binding.[17] Such formalities can be found in the corporation's constitution, regulations, articles, or standing orders, or the Royal Charter or Act of Parliament creating them.

The 'default' articles of association of companies regulated by the Companies Acts (CA 2006 or CA 1985) specify how a seal is to be used (although a seal (if it exists) does not have to be used).[18]

15.8 FORM OF THE SEAL

Generally, the seal of a corporation does not appear to need any special wording or engraving to be a corporate seal.

What constitutes a seal

In particular cases, the courts have decided the following in relation to seals:

- a seal does not require wax, wafer, a piece of paper, or the making of an impression (*Re Sandilands* (1871) LR 6 CP 411 at 413);
- a seal can constitute a piece of green ribbon;[19]
- a seal can constitute a circle printed on a document, which contains the letters 'L.S.';[20]
- a document does not need to contain a seal at all,[21] if there is evidence (for example, attestation) indicating that the document in question was intended to be executed as a deed;[22]
- the seal used can be the seal of another person. What is required is that the seal used at a particular time on a document is the seal of the corporation;[23]

---

17 *Clarke* v. *Imperial Gas Light and Coke Co.* (1832) 4 B & Ad 315 at 324–326; *Ernest* v. *Nicholls* (1857) 6 HL Cas 401 at 418–422, per Lord Wensleydale; *D'Arcy* v. *Tamar, Kit Hill & Callington Rly Co.* (1866) LR 2 Exch 158.
18 See **Chapter 16** for the default methods provided by CA 2006 and CA 1985.
19 *Ex p. Sandilands* (1871) LR 6 CP 411 at 413; *Stromdale & Ball Ltd* v. *Burden* [1952] Ch. 233 at 230.
20 *First National Securities Ltd* v. *Jones* [1978] Ch 109; 'L.S.' means *locus sigilli* (Latin: the place of the seal).
21 *First National Securities Ltd* v. *Jones* [1978] Ch 109; *Commercial Credit Services* v. *Knowles* [1978] CL 6.
22 *National Provincial Bank of England* v. *Jackson* (1886) 33 Ch D 1; *Re Balkis Consolidated Co. Ltd* (1888) 58 LT 300; *Re Smith* (1892) 67 LT 64.
23 *Halsbury's Laws*, 'Corporations', para. 123. Law Commission Consultation Paper 143.

- a deed which is stated to be 'signed, sealed and delivered' may be validly executed. If another relies on such a document to her detriment then the person who executed the deed is estopped from stating that it has not been sealed.[24]

Corporations where the content of the seal is specified

For some types of corporations what appears on their seal is specified. The main examples are:

- where a company is formed under CA 2006 or CA 1985 and has a common seal, the name of the company is to be engraved in legible characters ((until October 2009) CA 1985, s.350; (from October 2009) CA 2006, s.45(2));
- where a limited liability partnership is formed under the LLPA 2000, the name of the limited liability partnership is to be engraved in legible characters ((likely until October 2009) CA 1985, s.350 (after that date, likely to be the equivalent of CA 2006, s.45(2)));[25]
- the common seal of a building society shall bear the registered name of the building society (Building Societies Act 1986, Sched. 2, para. 9(1)).

15.9 FIXING OF SEAL FOR NON-STATUTORY CORPORATIONS

Seals for non-statutory corporations must be fixed at a duly constituted meeting of the corporation and following a resolution passed by a majority of the members present at the meeting (*Mayor etc & Co. of Merchants of the Staple of England* v. *Governor & Co. of Bank of England* (1887) 21 QBD 160 at 165, 166, CA). Such a corporation can appoint an attorney to execute a deed on its behalf, provided it uses the procedure described in the previous sentence to appoint her.[26]

---

24 *TCB Ltd* v. *Gray* [1986] 1 All ER 587 at 595: a person executing a document drafted as a deed and which states that she has signed, sealed and delivered it in the presence of a witness is making a representation of fact that it was in fact sealed. The document was executed with the intention that the document should be relied on and was in fact relied on. The claimant relied on it and suffered a detriment (the claimant lent money in reliance of the document executed as a deed). The judge stated that the case 'had all the necessary elements of a classic estoppel'.

25 CA 1985 is applied to limited liability partnerships by the Limited Liability Partnerships Regulations 2001, SI 2001/1090, reg. 4, Sched. 2.

26 *Kidderminster Corpn* v. *Hardwick* (1873) LR 9 Exch 13 at 18, 24; *Oxford Corpn* v. *Crow* [1893] 3 Ch 535 at 539.

15.10   PRESUMPTION OF DUE EXECUTION

It appears that generally, whether at common law or by the Acts of Parliament forming corporations or under which corporations are formed, there is a presumption that a deed (whether with or without a seal) is correctly executed, if the formalities required by the particular corporation are reflected in the document in question. The following points illustrate the extent and requirements of such a presumption.

At common law

There is a presumption of due execution where the seal of the corporation has been affixed by those with legal custody of the seal, and the onus of proving that it has not been affixed with the necessary authority lies with the other party.[27] This may reflect the general principle that if a deed appears to be valid, there will be a presumption of due execution, and that if a person challenges the validity of the deed, it is for that person to prove their case (*Campbell* v. *Campbell* [1996] NPC 27).

Statutory presumption

LPA 1925

By LPA 1925, s.74(1),[28] in favour of a purchaser, an instrument will be deemed to have been duly executed by a corporation aggregate if its seal

---

27 *Clarke* v. *Imperial Gas Light and Coke Co.* (1832) 4 B & Ad 315, 110 ER 473; *Hill* v. *Manchester and Salford Water Works Co.* (1833) 5 B & Ad 866 at 872–874, 110 ER 1011 at 1014; and *Re Barned's Banking Co., ex p. The Contract Corporation* (1867) LR 3 Ch App 105: seal affixed by directors. Under the statute of incorporation, the directors were given custody of the seal and the power to use it for the affairs of the company. Authority of the members in general meeting required for the contract in question, but no evidence before the court to show that the forms prescribed by the statute had not been complied with. Contract held to be valid. See also *Hill* v. *Manchester & Salford Water Works Co.* (1833) 5 B & Ad 866 at 872–874, 110 ER 1011 at 1014; and *Re Barned's Banking Co., ex p. The Contract Corporation* (1867) LR 3 Ch App 105 (no provisions in the constitutional documents governing sealing: directors of trading company held to have authority to affix seal: no need to enquire further into the practices of the company). These cases may reflect a wider principle that where a deed is regular on its face, the court will start from a presumption of due execution, and it is for the person disputing its validity to prove their case: e.g. *Campbell* v. *Campbell* [1996] NPC 27 (deed of gift by individual; plaintiff failed to prove that maker did not sign in the presence of the attesting witness).

28 A 'purchaser' means 'a purchaser in good faith for valuable consideration and includes a lessee, mortgagee or other person who for valuable consideration acquires an interest in property, except that in Part I of [LPA 1925] and elsewhere where so expressly provided "purchaser" only means a person who acquires an interest in or charge on property for money or money's worth; and in reference to a legal estate includes a chargee by way of legal mortgage; and where the context so requires "purchaser" includes an intending purchaser; "purchase" has a meaning corresponding with that of "purchaser"; and "valuable

174

(purporting to be the corporation's seal) purports to be affixed to the deed in the presence of and attested by:

- two members of the board of directors, council or other governing body of the corporation; or
- one member and the clerk, secretary or other permanent officer of the corporation or his deputy.

For an instrument to be validly executed by a corporation as a deed for the purposes of LP(MP)A 1989, s.1(2)(b), the instrument needs to be validly executed by the corporation and be delivered as a deed (LPA 1925, s.74A(1)). An instrument is presumed delivered upon it being executed, unless a contrary intention is proved (LPA 1925, s.74A(2)).

Note that this presumption of due execution does not apply to matters relating only to real property.

However, this provision of LPA 1925 does not override any mode of execution or attestation authorised by law or by practice or by the statute, charter, or constitutional document constituting or regulating the corporation (LPA 1925, s.74(6)).

CA 2006 and CA 1985

In favour of a purchaser a document is deemed to have been duly executed by a company if it purports to be signed by:

- one director in the presence of a witness (who attests the signature of the director); or
- two directors or a director and the company secretary (CA 2006, s.44(2), (5)).[29]

A document executed in this way and expressed, in whatever words, to be executed by the company has the same effect as if executed under the common seal of the company (CA 2006, s.44(4)).

For a document to be validly executed by a company as a deed for the purposes of LP(MP)A 1989, s.1(2)(b), the document needs to be validly executed by the company (as set out immediately above) and be delivered as a deed

---

consideration" includes marriage [and formation of a civil partnership] but does not include a nominal consideration in money': LPA 1925, s.205(1)(xxi). This provision would also cover companies formed or regulated by CA 2006 or CA 1985.

Where a seal is being affixed in the presence of and attested by an officer of the corporation, and that officer is not an individual but another corporation, the following will apply: the seal will be affixed in the presence of and attested by an individual authorised by the other corporation (LPA 1925, s.74(1B)).

29 A 'purchaser' means a purchaser in good faith for valuable consideration and includes a lessee, mortgagee or other person who for valuable consideration acquires an interest in property.

(CA 2006, s.46(1)). A document is presumed delivered upon it being executed, unless a contrary intention is proved (CA 2006, s.46(2)).

Other sources

Many other Acts contain provisions concerning the status of documents executed by a corporation, for example, for Transport for London under the Greater London Authority Act 1999, Sched. 10, para. 12(2):

> Every document purporting to be an instrument or issued by or on behalf of Transport for London and to be duly executed under the seal of Transport for London, or to be signed or executed by a person authorised by Transport for London for the purpose, shall be received and be treated, without further proof, as being so made or so issued unless the contrary is shown.

And for the Health and Safety Executive under Health and Safety at Work etc. Act 1974, Sched. 2, para. 12:

> A document purporting to be duly executed under the seal of the Executive shall be received in evicdence and shall, unless the contrary is provided, be deemed to be so executed.

15.11 EXECUTION BY A CORPORATION ON BEHALF OF ANOTHER PERSON

The method of execution of an instrument set out under **section 15.10** under LPA 1925 applies where a corporation is executing an instrument on behalf of another person, whether or not that other person is a corporation (LPA 1925, s.74(1A)). For example, if a corporation is executing a deed on behalf of an individual, then it would sign the deed (after applying the seal) with the signatures of two directors.

15.12 AUTHENTICATION NOT ATTESTATION

Witnessing and attestation are not normally required when a seal is used by a corporation. The signature of one or more officers or representatives of a corporation is known as *authentication*[30] – the officers or representatives are indicating that the document and the seal that is applied are the document and the seal of the corporation.

---

30 *Encyclopaedia of Forms and Precedents*, vol. 12(2), 'Deeds', para. 35. It is suggested that if attestation is needed then some person(s) other than other officers or representatives of the corporation act as witnesses. The signature by the officer(s) or representative(s) of the corporation when the seal is affixed is considered to be part of the process of sealing: *Deffell* v. *White* (1866) LR 2 CP 144; *Shears* v. *Jacob* (1866) LR 1 CP 513.

15.13   EXAMPLES OF CORPORATIONS

The following are examples of corporations aggregate or corporations sole.

Corporations aggregate

- Central government: Parliament.[31]
- Local government authorities: created by charter or order of the appropriate minister for London boroughs (Local Government Act 1963, s.1) and local government outside central London (county and district councils, parish councils, and community councils (LGA 1972, ss.2, 14, 21, 33)).
- Other local government bodies: e.g. Local Government Boundary Commission for Wales (LGA 1972, s.53, Sched. 8).
- Health-related bodies: e.g. NHS Trusts (National Health Service Act 2006, Sched. 4, Part 1, para. 1); Strategic Health Authorities (National Health Service Act 2006, s.13).
- Health-related regulatory bodies: General Medical Council (Medical Act 1983, s.1); General Dental Council (Dentists Act 1984, s.1); General Optical Council (Opticians Act 1989, s.1); Council for the Regulation of Health Care Professionals (National Health Service Reform and Health Care Professions Act 2002, s.25); Commission for Healthcare Audit and Inspection (Health and Social Care (Community Health and Standards) Act 2003, s.41, Sched. 6).
- Pensions Regulator (Pensions Act 2004, s.1).
- Financial Services Authority (FSMA 2000, s.1(1)).
- Health and Safety Executive and Commission (Health and Safety at Work etc. Act 1974, s.10).
- Royal Society (incorporated by Charles II in 1665).
- Board of the British Library (British Library Act 1972, Sched.1).
- Law Society (incorporated by Royal Charter in 1845).
- An incorporated body of trustees of a charity (Charities Act 1993, s.50).

Corporations sole

- The Sovereign (see *Halsbury's Laws*, vol. 9(2), 'Corporations', para. 1111).
- Certain ministers are treated or created as corporations sole (Ministers of the Crown Act 1975, ss.2, 6, Sched.1).[32]
- Official custodian for charities (Charities Act 1993, s.2).
- The Public Trustee (Public Trustee Act 1906, s.1(2)).

---

31 Consisting of the Sovereign, the Lords Spiritual and Temporal and the Commons: *River Tone Conservators* v. *Ash* (1829) 10 B & C 349 at 383, per Littledale J.

32 Not all ministers are corporations sole and in some cases the position is not entirely clear: *Halsbury's Laws*, vol. 9(2), 'Corporations', para. 1112, note 4.

- The Information Commissioner (Data Protection Act 1998, Sched. 5).
- A number of ecclesiastical persons (such as an archbishop, a bishop, a canon, etc.) (see *Halsbury's Laws*, vol. 9(2), 'Corporations', para. 1112).

Corporations aggregate incorporated by Royal Charter

- Arts Council of England.
- Crafts Council.
- Engineering Council.
- Royal Pharmaceutical Society of Great Britain.[33]

15.14   REQUIREMENTS FOR SEALING IN PARTICULAR CASES

The following are examples of the methods used by various corporations (aggregate and sole) to affix their seal.

Ministers of the Crown[34]

Sealing

Certain ministers of the Crown:

- shall have an official seal;
- which will be authenticated by the signature of:

    - the minister; or
    - a secretary to the ministry; or
    - any person authorised by the minister to act in that behalf.

A minister of the Crown is to be a corporation sole for all purposes.

Every document purporting to be an instrument made or issued by the minister and to be sealed with the seal of the minister authenticated in the manner provided above shall be received in evidence and be deemed to be so made or issued without further proof, unless the contrary is shown.

By hand

A certificate signed by the minister that any instrument purporting to be made or issued by him was so made or issued shall be conclusive evidence of that fact.

---

33 From the Society's 2004 Supplemental Charter: 'The Society shall in accordance with the remaining effect of the Charter of 1843 continue to be a body corporate with a common seal, and the right to renew the said seal from time to time, and to sue and be sued in all Our Courts'.
34 Ministers of the Crown Act 1975, Sched. 1, paras. 5–7.

Pensions Regulator[35]

The Pensions Regulator is a body corporate. The fixing of the common seal of the Regulator shall be authenticated by the signature of a person authorised by the Regulator to act for that purpose. A document purporting to be duly executed under the seal of the Authority or purporting to be signed on its behalf shall be received in evidence and shall, unless the contrary is proved, be deemed to be so executed or signed.

Parish council[36]

A parish council is a body corporate. A parish council is not required to have a common seal. But where a parish council is required to execute a document (such as a deed) with a seal, and the parish council does not have a seal, the document can be executed by the signature and seal of two members of the parish council.

Board of the British Library[37]

The Board of the British Library is a body corporate, with a common seal. Deeds are to be executed with the seal and authenticated by the signature of the secretary to the board. The Board can also authorise a person, whether generally or specially, to sign.

A document purporting to be a document duly executed under the seal of the Board, or to be signed on behalf of the Board, shall be received in evidence and shall, unless the contrary is proved, be deemed to be so executed or, as the case may be, signed.

The Information Commissioner[38]

The Information Commission is a corporation sole. The use of the seal of the Information Commissioner is authenticated by the Information Commissioner's signature, or by the signature of another person authorised for the purpose.

Any document purporting to be an instrument issued by the Commissioner and to be duly executed under the Information Commissioner's seal or to be signed by, or on behalf of, the Information Commissioner shall be received in evidence and shall be deemed to be such an instrument unless the contrary is shown.

---

35 Pensions Act 2004, ss. 1, 22.
36 Local Government Act 1972, s.14(3).
37 British Library Act 1972, Sched. 1, paras. 1, 9 and 10.
38 Data Protection Act 1998, Sched. 5, paras. 1, 6 and 7.

National Trust[39]

The National Trust is a body corporate and shall have a common seal. An instrument required to be under seal if made by an individual will be under the seal of the National Trust.

Any notice, consent, approval or other document issued by, or on behalf of, the National Trust shall be deemed to be duly executed if signed by the chairman, the deputy chairman or the secretary of the National Trust. But any appointment made by the National Trust and any contract, order or other document made by or proceeding from the National Trust shall be deemed to be duly executed either if sealed with the seal of the National Trust or if signed by two or more members of the council authorised to sign by a resolution of the council or the executive committee.

It will not be necessary in any legal proceedings to prove that the members signing any such contract, order or other document were authorised to sign and such authority shall be presumed until the contrary is proved.

NHS Trust[40]

An NHS Trust is a body corporate.

The fixing of the seal of an NHS Trust must be authenticated by the signature of the chairman or of some other person authorised (whether generally or specifically) by the NHS Trust for that purpose, and of one other director.

A document purporting to be duly executed under the seal of an NHS Trust must be received in evidence and must, unless the contrary is proved, be taken to be so executed. A document purporting to be signed on behalf of an NHS Trust must be received in evidence and must, unless the contrary is proved, be taken to be so signed.

---

39 National Trust Act 1907, s.3; National Trust Act 1971, s.15.
40 National Health Service Act 2006, Sched. 4.

CHAPTER 16

Execution of a deed by a company formed under, or regulated by, CA 2006 (or CA 1985)

16.1 INTRODUCTION[1]

The requirements for the valid execution of a deed by a company are a mixture of common law and statute law. In recent years, various statutory provisions have enacted major reforms to the law on execution of deeds, including provisions of CA 2006, amendments to CA 1985, and amendments to LP(MP)A 1989. These reforms have made substantial changes to the way a deed can be executed by a company. But none of these statutory provisions has abolished the common law provisions in areas which are not expressly dealt with by the Acts.

The main changes introduced by CA 2006 and the amendments to CA 1985 were:

- a company is no longer required to have a common seal;
- a document (whether or not a deed) executed by one director (in the presence of a witness who attests the signature of the director) or two directors or a director and a company secretary, and expressed to be executed by the company, has the same effect as if executed under the common seal of a company;
- a deed can be executed by applying the common seal or by one director (in the presence of a witness who attests the signature of the director) or by two directors or a director and the company secretary signing it. The use of the seal will be governed by the articles of association of the company and the default provisions are different for companies formed under CA 1985 or under CA 2006.

The main changes introduced by LP(MP)A 1989 (as amended) as they applied to a company, were:

---

1 This chapter only deals with the parts particularly relevant for the execution of deeds by companies. More general points relating to deeds, such as the structure and form of a deed, when its use is required, conventional, or desirable, delivery, etc. are considered at **Chapter 14**. Issues relating to powers of attorney are dealt with in **Chapters 10** and **22**.

- to abolish any restrictions on the substance on which a deed can be written;
- to abolish the requirement that deeds, to be validly executed, had to be sealed;
- to make it clear that a document will not be a deed unless it is clear on its face that the person(s) making it intend(s) it to be a deed;
- to state that a document can be executed by or on behalf of the parties to the deed.

16.2 SUMMARY OF CHANGES MADE BY CA 2006

In relation to the execution of deeds and other types of documents by, or on behalf of, a company, the changes made by CA 2006 can be summarised as follows:

- the abolition of the requirement to have a company secretary for a private limited company (from April 2008);
- an additional method of execution (whether for deeds or for other forms of documents) is now permitted, namely the signing of a document by one director in the presence of a witness, as an alternative to the equally valid method of signing of a document by two directors, or one director and the company secretary (from April 2008). This method is presumably to allow for the fact that private limited companies can legally exist and operate with one director and no company secretary (public companies will continue, however, to need a company secretary);
- new forms of articles of association are provided, which govern, *inter alia*, the use of seals (from October 2009 and for companies incorporated under CA 2006);
- a company will be expressly permitted to use an attorney to execute documents (including deeds), subject to the attorney's being appointed under deed (from October 2009);
- existing articles of associations (i.e. for companies formed under CA 1985) which use the unamended version of the provisions relating to seals in Table A will continue to apply to the use of company seals.[2]

16.3 WHAT IS A 'COMPANY'?

A company incorporated or regulated by CA 2006 or CA 1985 is a form of corporation or body corporate (CA 2006, s.16(2), (3); CA 1985, s.13(3)). For more on corporations see **Chapter 15**.

---

2 For companies which utilise the unamended provisions of Table A, CA 1985, these will continue to apply despite the coming into force of CA 2006 and the provisions of the Companies (Model Articles) Regulations 2007 (see r.5).

16.4   TYPES OF COMPANIES TO WHICH CA 2006 AND CA 1985 APPLY

The following table indicates the main types of companies covered by CA 2006 and CA 1985.

Type of companies	Public or private
A company limited by shares[3]	Both
A company limited by guarantee (not having a share capital)[4]	Private only
A company limited by guarantee (having a share capital)[5]	Both
An unlimited company[6]	Private only
An unregistered company[7]	n/a
An oversea company[8]	n/a
A limited liability partnership[9]	n/a

16.5   REQUIREMENTS TO EXECUTE A DOCUMENT VALIDLY AS A DEED BY A COMPANY

- For a company to execute a document validly as a deed:

    - it must be in writing;[10]
    - the writing can be placed on any type of material (LP(MP)A 1989, s.1(1)(a));[11]

---

3 CA 2006, s.3(1), (2).
4 CA 2006, s.3(1), (3). The definition of a public company does not include a company limited by guarantee and not having a share capital: CA 2006, s.4(2).
5 Such companies cannot be formed after 22 December 1980: CA 2006, s.5.
6 CA 2006, s.3(4).
7 CA 2006, s.1043.
8 CA 1985, s.744; Foreign Companies (Execution of Documents) Regulations 1994, SI 1994/950.
9 Limited Liability Partnerships Act 2000, s.1; Limited Liability Partnerships Regulations 2001, SI 2001/1090, reg. 4, Sched. 2, Part I.
10 *Goddard's Case* (1584) 2 Co Rep 4b at 5a, 76 ER 396 at 398–399. 'Writing' under common law did not require the use of pen or ink, but could include pencil or with paint: *Geary* v. *Physic* (1826) 5 B & C 234 at 237. The meaning of the word 'writing' in any Act includes: 'typing, printing, lithography, photography and other modes of representing or reproducing words in a visible form': IA 1978, s.1, Sched. 1.
11 Abolishing the common law rule that a deed had to be written on paper, parchment or vellum (*Goddard's Case* (1584) 2 Co Rep 4b at 5a, 76 ER 396 at 398–399).

- the document must indicate clearly on its face that it is intended to be a deed by the person(s) making it or the parties to it;[12] and
- it must be executed by the company and delivered (as set out immediately below).

- Execution:

CA 2006

- If the company has a common seal (and the provisions relating to use of the common seal in model articles of association apply in their unamended form) by affixing the common seal (CA 2006, s.44(1));[13] and
- a director signing the document in the presence of a witness who attests the signature of the director; or
- if the directors have authorised a person to sign, that person signing (in the presence of a witness who attests the person's signature).

There is now no need for a company to have a common seal (CA 2006, s.45).

Or:

CA 1985

- If the company has a common seal (and the provisions relating to use of the common seal in Table A under CA 1985 apply in their unamended form) by affixing the common seal (CA 1985, s.36A(2)); and
- a director and the company secretary signing the document; or
- two directors signing; or
- if the directors have authorised a person to sign (and the articles of the company permit them to do so), that person signing the document.

- Whether or not it has a common seal, documents can be executed as follows, by:

- a director signing the document in the presence of a witness and the witness attesting the signature; or
- two directors (if the company has more than one director) signing the document; or
- one director and the company secretary (if the company has a company secretary) signing the document;

---

12 LP(MP)A 1989, s.1(2)(a).
13 But for most companies using the seal, just affixing the seal may not be enough if they use Table A. See Table A and other articles of association.

and the document must be expressed (in whatever form of words) to be executed by the company. This has the same effect as if executed under the common seal of the company (CA 2006, s.44(4)).

- *Delivery*: the document is delivered as a deed, and it is presumed that the document is delivered upon execution (unless a contrary intention is provided) ((from October 2009) CA 2006, s.46; (until October 2009) CA 1985 s.36AA).
- *Presumption in favour of a purchaser*: in favour of a purchaser, a document is deemed to have been duly executed by a company if it purports to be signed by any of the methods mentioned above (CA 2006, s.44(5)).[14]

Points to note

1. Where a company has, and wishes to use, its common seal and the provision in the model articles of association[15] relating to the use of a company's common seal applies in its unamended form, the company will have greater flexibility as to who can sign a deed than is available under CA 2006, s.44(2). The directors can authorise someone other than a director or the secretary to sign for companies formed under CA 2006, under the model articles (Sched. 1, art. 50); for private companies limited by guarantee, see Sched. 2, art. 36; and for public companies, see Sched. 3, art. 81; for companies formed under CA 1985, see Table A, art. 101. However, in practice, persons who are purchasers and wish to rely on a deed executed by a company may wish for the deed to be executed by one director in the presence of a witness (who attests the director's signature), two directors or a director and the company secretary, in order to have the benefit of the statutory presumptions found in CA 2006, s.44(5) or in LPA 1925, s.74(1).

2. The wording used in CA 2006 and in the model articles of association does not appear to require that, where two directors or both the director and the company secretary are to sign a document, they have to be physically present at the same time when signing. But this issue is not entirely clear, and perhaps best practice suggests that they should be. Where one director or a person authorised by the directors is signing the document, CA 2006 and the model articles of association clearly state that they have to sign in the presence of a witness.

---

14 A 'purchaser' means a purchaser in good faith for valuable consideration and includes a lessee, mortgagee or other person who for valuable consideration acquires an interest in property.

15 For private companies limited by shares, see Sched. 1, art. 50, for private companies limited by guarantee, see Sched. 2, art. 36, and for public companies, see Sched. 3, art. 81. See Companies (Model Articles) Regulations 2007 (currently in draft).

Alternative method for a company to execute a deed

It is possible for a company ('corporation aggregate') also to execute a deed in accordance with the provisions of LPA 1925, s.74(1), which require that the seal is affixed in the presence of (and attested by):

- two members of the board of directors; or
- one member of the board of directors and the secretary.

Execution by this method means, in favour of a purchaser, that the document will be deemed to be duly executed by the company. A document is validly executed by a corporation aggregate if it is duly executed by the corporation and delivered as a deed (and it is presumed delivered upon execution, unless the contrary is proved).[16]

Execution of deeds by Scottish companies

The majority of the provisions in CA 1985 equally apply to Scottish companies, including those concerning the execution of documents, except as described as follows:

- a document is signed by a company if it is signed on its behalf by a director, or by the company secretary, or by a person authorised to sign the document on its behalf (Requirements of Writing (Scotland) Act 1995, Sched. 2, para. 3);
- a company need not have a seal (CA 2006, s.48(2);
- where any enactment provides for a document to be executed under the common seal (or refers to a document so executed), a document signed by or on behalf of the company in accordance with the provisions of the Requirements of Writing (Scotland) Act 1995 has effect as if executed under the common seal of the company (CA 1985, s.36B(2), as inserted by the Requirements of Writing (Scotland) Act 1995, Sched. 4, para. 51);
- the provision for a company to appoint an attorney to execute a deed elsewhere than the United Kingdom does not extend to Scotland (CA 1985, s.38(3), as inserted by the Requirements of Writing (Scotland) Act 1995 Sched. 4, para. 52);[17]
- the provision that an official seal when affixed as provided by CA 1985, s.39 has the same effect as a company's common seal, does not extend to Scotland (CA 1985, s.39(2A), as inserted by the Requirements of Writing (Scotland) Act 1995, Sched. 4, para. 53(a)).

---

16 LPA 1925, s.74A.
17 This provision and the one described in the next bullet are detailed in **Chapters 4** and **10**.

16.6 HOW A COMPANY CAN ENTER INTO A CONTRACT

A company can enter into a contract in two ways:

- by the company itself in writing using its common seal; or
- by a person acting on behalf of the company, under the company's authority (express or implied) ((from October 2009) CA 2006, s.43; (until October 2009) CA 1985, s.36).

Since a company is no longer required to have a seal ((from October 2009) CA 2006, s.45(1); (until October 2009) CA 1985, s.36A(3)), a contract can be entered into *by the company* if it is signed by one director in the presence of a witness (who attests the signature) or two directors or one director and the company secretary (CA 2006, s.44(2)).

The formalities required for an individual to enter into a contract equally apply to a contract made by or on behalf of a company ((from October 2009) CA 2006, s.43(2);) (until October 2009) CA 1985, s.36).

16.7 MEANING OF A 'DOCUMENT'

The meaning of a 'document' (for the purposes of CA 2006) includes, but does not appear to be confined to, 'summons, notice, order, and other legal process, and registers' ((from October 2009) CA 2006, s.1148(1); (until October 2009) CA 1985, s.744).

16.8 ARTICLES OF ASSOCIATION

Although a company does not need to have (or if it has one, use) a common seal, its use will be governed by any provisions found in the model articles of association for that company in addition to the provisions found in CA 2006, s.44 or, for companies formed under CA 1985, the various Tables of articles of association in addition to the provisions found in CA 2006.

Many companies limited by shares (public or private) formed under CA 1985 use the default provisions in the articles of association imposed by CA 1985, s.8, and it has to be assumed that the same will be true for companies formed under CA 2006. Because of the large number of companies formed under CA 1985, the articles of association made under CA 1985 will continue to be of relevance.

The articles of association of formed under CA 1985 or CA 2006 companies are set out in separate statutory instruments under CA 2006 and CA 1985. They both contain provisions concerning the procedure for the sealing of documents:

- the directors of a company can determine who signs an instrument to which the seal is affixed; and
- if the directors do not make such a determination, then the instrument should be signed:

  - *CA 2006*: by a director in the presence of a witness who attests the signature of the director;[18]
  - *CA 1985*: by a director and the company secretary, or two directors.[19]

The default articles provided under CA 2006 and CA 1985 both provide for a further form for the use of the seal of a company. It can be utilised by a person other than those mentioned immediately above signing the document to which the seal is affixed. For example, a deed could be signed by one non-director, if authorised by the directors. However, under CA 2006 such a person would need to sign the document in the presence of a witness who attests the signature of the person.

Under CA 2006, several complete sets of default articles of association are provided for the main types of companies formed under the Act by default (CA 2006, s.20).[20] The wording for the use of the company seal is the same in all of them. Under CA 1985, Table A provides a complete set of articles, with art. 101 covering the use of seals. The other types of company have different Tables of articles imposed by default (CA 1985, s.8(4)).[21] All incorporate by default art. 101. The default tables for the different types of companies under CA 2006 and CA 1985 are set out in the following table:

Types of companies	CA 2006	CA 1985
A company limited by shares	Sched. 1	Table A
A company limited by guarantee (not having a share capital)	Sched. 2	Table C

18 For private companies limited by shares, see Sched. 1, art. 50, for private companies limited by guarantee, see Sched 2, art. 36, and for public companies, see Sched. 3, art. 81. See Companies (Model Articles) Regulations 2007 (currently in draft).
19 Table A, art. 101, Companies (Tables A–F) Regulations 1985, SI 1985/805.
20 See Companies (Model Articles) Regulations 2007 (currently in draft).
21 Companies (Tables A–F) Regulations 1985, SI 1985/805, set out the text of the various Tables, and for Tables C–E, set out which of the articles of Table A do not apply.

A public company limited by guarantee (having a share capital)		Table D Part I
A private company limited by guarantee (having a share capital)		Table D Part II
A company (public or private) limited by guarantee (having a share capital		Table D Part III
An unlimited company (having a share capital)		Table E
A public company limited by shares	Sched. 3	(Table A)

16.9 REQUIREMENT TO HAVE A COMMON SEAL

A company formed or regulated by CA 2006 or CA 1985 can choose whether or not to have a seal and if it does have one whether or not it needs to use it when executing a deed ((from October 2009) CA 2006, s.45(1); (until October 2009) CA 1985, s.36A(3)).

Use of the seal to execute a deed

For a company to execute a deed using its seal, the following need to occur:

- the common seal of the company is used;
- the person or persons making the deed must make it clear on the face of the document that it is a deed (LP(MP)A 1989, s.1(2)(a));
- the company affixes the common seal (CA 2006, s.44(1));
- if CA 2006 model form of articles or CA 1985 Table A applies then in addition to the above three requirements the following also need to occur:

  - the use of the seal has to be authorised by the directors (or by a committee of the directors who in turn have been authorised by the directors);
  - then

    CA 2006: a director signs the deed in the presence of a witness (who attests the signature of the director);
    CA 1985: a director and a secretary or two directors sign the deed.

The directors can also authorise who shall sign the deed other than as set out above, but under CA 2006, the person so authorised needs to do so in the presence of a witness (who attests the signature of the person).

- The document is delivered as a deed. It is presumed, unless a contrary intention is proved, that delivery takes place on execution ((from October 2009) CA 2006, s.46(2); (until October 2009) CA 1985, s.36AA).

Points to note

None of the articles under CA 2006 or CA 1985 requires that the seal has to be used in the presence of the person(s) signing the document to which the seal is affixed. The seal could be affixed at one time and the persons signing could do so at another (see ICSA, Company Secretarial Practice, para. 91.6).

Form of the seal

If a company has a common seal, its name is required to be engraved in legible characters on the seal ((from October 2009) CA 2006, s.45(2); (until October 2009) CA 1985, s.350).[22]

But use of a seal which does not conform to this requirement may still make the deed binding on the company which has sealed the deed.[23] If the seal does not contain the registered name of the company, but has, for example, the trading name of the company, the deed may still be effective.[24]

16.10 USE OF A SEAL BY COMPANY REGULATED BY CA 1985 IN OTHER JURISDICTIONS[25]

Meaning of an 'unregistered company'

An unregistered company is a body corporate which:

- is incorporated; and
- has its principal place of business

in the United Kingdom (CA 2006, s.1043), but which is not:

- any body incorporated by, or registered under, any public general Act of Parliament;

---

22 Failure to have the name in legible characters renders the company liable to a fine. If a director or company secretary or a person acting on behalf of them uses or authorises the use of a seal which does not contain the name of the company in a legible form, they will also be liable to a fine (see CA 2006, s.45(3)–(5)).

23 *Halsbury's Laws*, 'Corporations', para. 1123, note 2, citing *OTV Birwelco Ltd* v. *Technical and General Guarantee Co. Ltd* [2002] EWHC 2240 (TCC), [2002] 4 All ER 668.

24 *OTV Birwelco Ltd* v. *Technical & General Guarantee Co. Ltd* [2002] EWHC 2240 (TCC), [2002] 2 All ER (Comm) 1116.

25 This is covered at **section 18.3**.

- any body not formed for the purpose of carrying on a business which has for its objects the acquisition of gain by the body or its individual members;
- any body exempted by statutory instrument; or
- an open-ended investment company (CA 2006, s.1043(1)).

CHAPTER 17

Execution of a deed by a limited liability partnership

17.1 INTRODUCTION[1]

At the time material for this book was prepared, there were no definite proposals regarding the implementation of the relevant CA 2006 provisions so as to apply to limited liability partnerships. The government was in the process of consultation[2] and had made the following proposals (subject to a further round of discussions):

- any changes concerning the law relating to limited liability partnerships are likely to be implemented at the same time that the bulk of CA 2006 comes into force in October 2009;
- rather than applying large parts of CA 2006 to limited liability partnerships (with necessary amendments), which would mean that there would not be one unified set of regulations containing in one document all the provisions applying to limited liability partnerships, the aim is to set out all the provisions derived from CA 2006 in full in one set of regulations; and
- although not stated precisely, it appears that the government aims to implement the relevant provisions concerning the execution of documents and deeds found in CA 2006 (i.e. ss.43, 44, 46) for limited liability partnerships 'to ensure clarity and equality with company law as currently applied to companies'.

Therefore, it seems that the requirements for the valid execution of a document, including deeds, by a limited liability partnership will continue to be virtually identical to those for a company formed under CA 1985 or CA

---

1 This chapter only deals with the parts particularly relevant for the execution of deeds by limited liability partnerships. More general points relating to deeds, such as the structure and form of a deed, when its use is required, conventional or desirable, delivery, etc. are considered in **Chapter 14**. Issues relating to powers of attorney are dealt with in **Chapters 10** and **22**.

2 Department for Business, Enterprise and Regulatory Reform, *Proposals for the Application of the Companies Act 2006 to Limited Liability Partnerships: A Consultative Document*, November 2007. The closing date for representations was 6 February 2008. This document indicates that further consultation will take place on draft regulations.

2006. In summary, the main differences concern the differences in terminology between a limited liability partnership and a company. This chapter notes the relevant differences only, as for most purposes the user will wish to consult the relevant provisions as set out in **Chapter 16**.

A limited liability partnership is a body corporate (LLPA 2000, s.1(2)); like other corporations it has a legal personality separate from that of its members, and it is incorporated by the Registrar of Companies.

The law is set out below as it is likely to apply until October 2009, with a brief summary of the likely changes.

Note: the key provision in CA 2006 affecting the execution of documents and deeds, s.44,[3] which contains an important change as to how deeds are executed, is likely not to apply to limited liability partnerships from April 2008 (the date from which it does apply to most private and public limited companies). It appears that this change is likely only to happen for limited liability partnerships from October 2009.

17.2 APPLICATION OF CA 1985 TO A LIMITED LIABILITY PARTNERSHIP

The relevant provisions of CA 1985 regarding:

- a company entering a contract (s.36);
- the methods for executing documents and requirement to have a common seal (s.36A) (except that references to a director and the secretary or two directors executing a document are replaced with two members of the limited liability partnership executing the document);
- the execution of deeds abroad (CA 1985, s.38);
- use of an official seal abroad (CA 1985, s.39) (but with the deletion of wording referring to the articles authorising transaction of business in foreign countries);
- manner in which the common seal is made (CA 1985, s.350)

equally apply to a limited liability partnership (Limited Liability Partnerships Regulations 2001, SI 2001/1090 (LLPR 2001), reg. 4, Sched. 2).

A limited liability partnership has an incorporation document rather than a memorandum of association document on its incorporation (LLPA 2000, s.2). By default, there is no equivalent to a limited liability partnership having articles of association. There are only very basic provisions found in the subordinate legislation concerning limited liability partnerships, LLPR 2001, regs. 7 and 8. It is open to the members of the limited liability partnership to

---

3 Providing that documents (including deeds) can be signed by one director in the presence of a witness (who attests the signature of the director) or two directors or a director and the company secretary.

enter into a limited liability partnership agreement[4] between themselves or between the limited liability partnership and the members (LLPA 2000, s.5).

17.3 RELEVANT DIFFERENCES BETWEEN LLPA 2000 AND CA 1985

The following are the main changes in terminology:

- a reference to a company would be a reference to a limited liability partnership (LLPR 2001, reg. 4(1)(a));
- a reference to a director of a company or to an officer of a company would be a reference to a member of a limited liability partnership (LLPR 2001, reg. 4(1)(g));
- a reference to the memorandum of association of a company would be a reference to the incorporation document of a limited liability partnership (LLPR 2001, reg. 4(1)(e)).

17.4 LIMITED LIABILITY PARTNERSHIPS AND CA 2006 (ASSUMED CHANGES FROM OCTOBER 2009)

Application of CA 2006 to a limited liability partnership

The relevant provisions of CA 2006 regarding:

- a company entering a contract (s.43);
- the methods for executing documents and requirement to have a common seal (ss.44 and 46) (except that references to a director and the secretary or two directors executing a document are replaced by two members of the limited liability partnership executing the document);
- the form of a seal (s.45);
- the execution of documents by an attorney (s.47);
- provision of an official seal for use abroad (s.49)

are likely equally to apply to a limited liability partnership, based on the government's current proposals at the time material for this book was prepared.

A limited liability partnership has an incorporation document rather than a memorandum of association on its incorporation (LLPA 2000, s.2).There is no equivalent to default articles of association for a limited liability partnership. There are only very basic provisions found in LLPR 2001, regs. 7 and

---

4 Means 'any agreement express or implied between the members of the limited liability partnership or between the limited liability partnership and the members of the limited liability partnership which determines the mutual rights and duties of the members, and their rights and duties in relation to the limited liability partnership': LLPR 2001, reg. 2.

8. It is open to the members of the limited liability partnership to enter into a limited liability partnership agreement between themselves or between the limited liability partnership and the members (LLPA 2000, s.5).

17.5   RELEVANT DIFFERENCES BETWEEN LLPA 2000 AND CA 2006

The main changes in terminology noted at **section 17.3** are likely equally to apply under CA 2006 from October 2009.

CHAPTER 18

Execution of a deed by a company incorporated outside Great Britain or United Kingdom[1]

18.1 INTRODUCTION[2]

The requirements for the valid execution of a deed (or other document) by a company not incorporated in Great Britain or the United Kingdom can be:

- the same as for companies incorporated under CA 2006 or CA 1985;[3] or
- in any manner permitted by the laws of the territory in which the company is incorporated.

The distinction between Great Britain and the United Kingdom is of importance here because CA 2006 will be implemented in October 2009 (as far as overseas companies are concerned), to the effect that:

- until October 2009, CA 1985 will continue apply, and the regulations made under it will apply to companies incorporated outside Great Britain; and
- from October 2009, CA 2006 will apply, and the regulations intended to be made under it will apply to companies incorporated outside the United Kingdom.

Thus, CA 1985 applies to companies formed in Great Britain (i.e. England, Wales and Scotland), while CA 2006 covers companies formed in the United Kingdom (i.e. Great Britain and Northern Ireland).

---

1 At the time material for this book was prepared, the Overseas Companies Regulations 2008 were still in draft form only. Although the government's consultation regarding these draft regulations raised no comments, it is possible that there may be changes made to the regulations when finally enacted. (A further draft was promised in 'Spring 2008'.)

2 This chapter only deals with the points particularly relevant for the execution of deeds by companies incorporated outside the UK. More general points relating to deeds, such as the structure and form of a deed, when its use is required, conventional or desirable, delivery, etc. are considered in **Chapter 14**. Issues relating to powers of attorney are dealt with in **Chapters 10** and **22**.

3 Great Britain means England, Wales and Scotland. England includes the Isles of Scilly: IA 1978, s.5, Sched. 1.

However, the effect of the introduction of CA 2006, in substance, makes little change to the position under CA 1985.

Whether under CA 2006 or CA 1985, a company incorporated outside Great Britain or the United Kingdom can enter into contracts or execute documents and deeds in any manner permitted by the laws of the territory in which the company is incorporated.

A company incorporated outside Great Britain is a body corporate (CA 1985, s.740; CA 2006, s.1173(1)).

The material below is divided into two sections setting out the position under CA 1985 and that under CA 2006.

Note: the key provision in CA 2006 affecting the execution of documents and deeds, s.44, which contains an important change as to how deeds are executed, is likely not to apply to overseas companies from April 2008 (the date from which it does apply to most private and public limited companies). It appears that this change is likely only to happen for overseas companies from October 2009.

18.2 COMPANY INCORPORATED OUTSIDE GREAT BRITAIN, CA 1985 (UNTIL OCTOBER 2009)

What type of company is covered?

The Foreign Companies (Execution of Documents) Regulations 1994, SI 1994/950 (FC(ED)R 1994) govern the execution of documents by companies incorporated outside Great Britain. FC(ED)R 1994 provide no definition or explanation of the meaning of a 'company' or 'incorporated' or 'incorporated outside Great Britain' (FC(ED)R 1994, reg. 2).

CA 1985 does contain some provisions relating to companies incorporated outside Great Britain including:

- an oversea company (CA 1985, s.744);[4]

  - companies incorporated elsewhere than in Great Britain, and which have established a place of business in Great Britain after the commencement of the 1985 Act; and
  - companies incorporated elsewhere than in Great Britain, and which had before the commencement of the 1985 Act a place of business in Great Britain and continued to have an established place of business in Great Britain at that commencement;

- a company incorporated outside the United Kingdom and Gibraltar and which has a branch in Great Britain (CA 1985, s.690A).[5]

---

4 An overseas company means a company incorporated elsewhere than in Great Britain, and which has established a place of business in Great Britain.

5 Applying the Eleventh Council Directive (89/666/EEC).

The provisions of FC(ED)R 1994 would appear to go much wider than an overseas company or a company incorporated outside the United Kingdom and Gibraltar, and would cover companies that have no connection or presence in Great Britain at all.

18.3 APPLICATION OF CA 1985 TO COMPANIES OUTSIDE GREAT BRITAIN

The relevant provisions of CA 1985 regarding:

- a company entering a contract (s.36);
- the methods for executing documents and the requirement to have a common seal (s.36A);

equally apply to a company incorporated outside Great Britain, subject to the modifications described below (FC(ED)R 1994, reg. 2).

But the provisions relating to:

- the execution of deeds abroad (s.38);
- the use of an official seal abroad (s.39);
- authentication of documents (s.41);
- the manner in which the common seal is made (s.350)

do not apply to a company incorporated outside Great Britain.

Issues with particular countries or places

The following countries or places are commonly thought to be part of Great Britain, but in fact they are not. Therefore, they would be covered by FC(ED)R 1994 and companies incorporated therein would thus be able to execute documents and deeds in ways other than provided by CA 1985, s.36A:

- Northern Ireland;
- the Channel Islands;
- Isle of Man;
- Gibraltar.

18.4 MODIFICATIONS MADE BY FC(ED)R 1994 TO CA 1985[6]

How a company incorporated outside Great Britain can enter into a contract

A company incorporated outside Great Britain can enter into a contract in two ways:

---

6 The full text of CA 1985, ss.36 and 36A as applied by FC(ED)R 1994 is set out in **Appendix 1**.

- in writing using its common seal or in any manner permitted by the laws of the territory in which the company is incorporated for the execution of documents by such a company; or
- on behalf of the company, by any person who, in accordance with the laws of the territory in which the company is incorporated, is acting under the company's authority (express or implied) (CA 1985, s.36 as applied by FC(ED)R 1994, reg. 4).

Execution of documents

Concerning the execution of documents (including deeds), references to:

- use of the common seal are to include an alternative method or any manner permitted by the laws of the territory in which the company is incorporated for the execution of documents by such a company (CA 1985, s.36A(2), as applied by FC(ED)R 1994, reg. 5(a));
- a director and the secretary or two directors signing a document are replaced by a reference to a person or persons signing the document, who, in accordance with the laws of the territory in which the company is incorporated, is or are acting under the authority (express or implied) of that company (CA 1985, s.36A(4) and (6), as applied by FC(ED)R 1994, reg. 5(b) and (c)).

18.5   COMPANY INCORPORATED OUTSIDE UNITED KINGDOM, CA 2006 (FROM OCTOBER 2009)

What type of company is covered?

The Overseas Companies Regulations 2008 (currently in draft) (OCR 2008) govern the execution of documents by companies incorporated outside the United Kingdom. Neither CA 2006 nor OCR 2008 provide a definition or explanation of the meaning of a 'company' or 'incorporated' or 'incorporated outside the United Kingdom'.

CA 2006 contains some provisions relating to such overseas companies, but the meaning of an 'overseas company' is limited to indicating that it is incorporated outside the United Kingdom (CA 2006, s.1044). Most of the provisions in CA 2006 relating to overseas companies concern requirements on, and duties of, such companies when operating in the United Kingdom (see CA 2006, ss.1046–1059 and OCR 2008).

CA 2006, s.1045(1) enables the Secretary of State to make regulations applying the provisions in CA 2006 (ss.43 to 52) concerning companies entering into contracts and the execution of documents to overseas companies, subject to necessary modifications (much in the same way as FC(ED)R 1994). Such provision is made in OCR 2008 at reg. 77. As in FC(ED)R 1994, these provisions do not only apply to those overseas companies having a branch or being established in the United Kingdom, and would cover companies that have no connection or presence in the United Kingdom at all.

18.6   APPLICATION OF CA 2006 TO COMPANIES OUTSIDE UNITED KINGDOM

The relevant provisions of Part 4 of CA 2006 regarding:

- a company entering into a contract (s.43);
- the methods for executing documents (s.44);
- the requirement to have, and content of, etc., a common seal (s.45);
- how a deed is validly executed by a company (s.46);
- execution of documents and deeds by an attorney (s.47);
- execution of documents (under the law of Scotland) (s.48);
- pre-incorporation contracts, deeds and obligations (s.51);
- making, acceptance and endorsement of bills of exchange and promissory notes (s.52)

apply equally to a company incorporated outside the United Kingdom, subject to the modifications described below (OCR 2008, reg. 77).

But the provisions relating to:

- provision of the official seal for use abroad (s.49);
- use of the official seal for share certificates, etc. (s.50)

do not apply to a company incorporated outside the United Kingdom.

Issues with particular countries or places

The following countries or places are commonly thought to be part of the United Kingdom, but in fact they are not. Therefore, they would be covered by OCR 2008 and companies incorporated therein would thus be able to execute documents and deeds in ways other than provided by CA 2006, s.44:

- the Channel Islands;
- Isle of Man;
- Gibraltar.

18.7   MODIFICATIONS MADE BY OCR 2008 TO CA 2006[7]

Generally, references in CA 2006, ss.43, 44, 46, 47, 48, 51, 52 to a 'company' include a reference to an overseas company (OCR 2008, reg. 77).

---

7 The full text of CA 2006, ss.43, 44, 45 and 46, as amended by OCR 2008 is set out in **Appendix 1**.

How a company incorporated outside United Kingdom can enter into a contract

A company incorporated outside the United Kingdom can enter into a contract in two ways:

- in writing using its common seal or in any manner permitted by the laws of the territory in which the company is incorporated for the execution of documents by such a company (CA 2006, s.43(1), as amended by OCR 2008, reg. 77(3)(a); or
- on behalf of the company, by any person who, in accordance with the laws of the territory in which the company is incorporated, is acting under the company's authority (express or implied) (CA 2006, s.43(1), as amended by OCR 2008, reg. 77(3)(b)).

Execution of documents

The provisions concerning the execution of documents (including deeds) are modified:

- to include in addition to the use of a common seal to execute a document (CA 2006, s.44(1)), any manner permitted by the laws of the territory in which the company is incorporated for the execution of documents by such a company (CA 2006, s.44(1)(b), as amended by OCR 2008, reg. 77(4)(a));
- the reference to the document being validly signed by a company if it is signed on its behalf by two authorised persons or a director in the presence of a witness (who attests the director's signature), is replaced by a reference to a person signing the document who, in accordance with the laws of the territory in which the company is incorporated, is acting under the authority (express or implied) of that company and is expressed (in whatever form of words) to be executed by the company (CA 2006, s.44(2), (3) and (4), as amended by OCR 2008, reg. 77(4)(b));
- s.44(7) deals with the issue where a director or secretary of a company is in fact another company. In such a case, references in s.44 to a document being signed by such director or secretary mean that the document can be signed by a person authorised by the other company. In the case of overseas companies, the section is amended to read: 'References in this section to a document being (or purporting to be) signed by a person who, in accordance with the laws of the territory in which the company is incorporated, is acting under the authority (express or implied) of that company are to be read, in a case where that person is a firm, as references to its being (or purporting to be) signed by an individual authorised by the firm to sign on its behalf' (CA 2006, s.44(7), as amended by OCR 2008, reg. 77(4)(c)).

CHAPTER 19

Execution of a deed by a local authority

19.1 INTRODUCTION[1]

The ways in which a deed can be executed by a local authority are in the main the same as described in **Chapter 15** (concerning corporations). This chapter sets out in summary the types of organisation which might fall within the category of a local authority, and outlines some key points to be considered when a document is executed by a local authority. For most purposes the reader should consult **Chapter 15**.

19.2 REQUIREMENTS FOR EXECUTION

Chapter 15 indicates that the formalities for the execution of a deed are governed by the constitution of the corporation. Most local authorities are formed by or under, or are regulated closely by, an Act. Following the introduction of the Local Government Act 2000 (LGA 2000), local authorities have adopted new arrangements[2] for their organisation which include the adoption of constitutions. These constitutions contain rules of procedures (standing orders) which will normally make provision as to the procedure for the execution of documents, who has custody of the seal of the local authority and how it may be used. These rules of procedures are normally found in Part 4 of a local authority's constitution. Local authorities are now required to make their constitutions publicly available at their offices (and many local authorities also make the constitutions available on their websites).[3]

---

1 This chapter only deals with points particularly relevant for the execution of deeds by a local authority. A local authority in this chapter includes corporations such as district and county councils, etc. (an illustrative list is provided at **section 19.3**). More general points relating to corporations are dealt with in **Chapter 15**. More general points relating to deeds, such as the structure and form of a deed, when its use is required, conventional or desirable, delivery, etc. are considered in **Chapter 14**. Issues relating to powers of attorney are dealt with in **Chapters 10** and **22**.
2 These are 'executive arrangements' or 'alternative arrangements'.
3 LGA 2000, s.37(2).

LGA 2000 has provided a level of standardisation as to the use of a seal and the execution of deeds and contracts by a local authority. However, the precise requirements for the use of the seal, who can use it and who can sign documents on behalf of the local authority is still subject to variation. Unless a person is dealing with the execution of deeds and/or use of the seal by a particular local authority on a regular basis, the rules of procedure in the local authority's constitution should be consulted for the precise requirements).[4] There are presumptions of due execution (see **section 15.10**), but their extent and the degree to which they can be relied on will vary. Unfortunately, even in modern Acts (and the rules made under them) there is little consistency of approach in the provisions concerning who can execute a deed, and in some cases there is a failure to address this point at all. It is also important to be aware that LPA 1925, s.74(1) only provides a presumption of due execution where the document is signed by two members of the local authority governing body, or a member plus the secretary or other such official.

For example, the Greater London Authority Act 1999 sets up a number of corporations, including the Greater London Authority, Transport for London and the Cultural Strategy Group for London. All are bodies corporate, but for the first, the Act is silent as to requirements on the use of the seal, and for the latter two there are provisions which are almost identically drafted relating to who can sign a deed and the presumption of due execution: ss.1, 154, 375 and Scheds. 10, 30.

The following are some general points concerning local authorities.

1. Like other corporations, all local authorities are required to use a seal when a deed is executed. As local authorities are corporations, they are not required to use a seal for a contract (except where that contract is required to be executed as a deed or the rules of procedure of the local authority require it).[5]

2. The principal Acts governing local authorities (district and county councils (England), counties and county boroughs (Wales), Greater London councils and the Greater London Authority) appear to have no

---

4 To take two examples: (a) for the London Borough of Richmond, contracts above the value of £50,000 have to be sealed; the seal is to be held in the custody of the head of legal services; only the head of legal services may attest its use (or some other person authorised by him) and it is for the head of legal services to decide which documents need to be sealed; (b) Crewe and Nantwich Council, while having similar provisions, only permits the executive director of legal services or other principal services to attest the use of the seal (i.e. there is no provision allowing these officials to authorise someone else to attest its use).

5 The provisions of CBCA 1960 apply. Notwithstanding this Act, many local authorities insist on sealing contracts for works, services, etc. as a matter of course. This may be influenced by Limitation Act 1980, s.8. The rules of procedure of the London Borough of Richmond, referred to above, are given as an example where a seal is required for some contracts.

wording relating to the execution of deeds or the presumption of due execution.[6]

3. Some local authorities are required to prepare, keep up to date, and allow anyone who wishes to see, certain constitutional documents, including standing orders (LGA 2000, s.37).[7]

4. The local authorities mentioned in **section 19.3** will normally deal with the execution of deeds through rules of procedure which will:

(a) allow the affixing of the seal which is authenticated by an authorised person or persons. These are commonly an official (such as the head of legal services, principal solicitor, etc.) or sometimes a particular council member (such as the chairperson or vice-chairperson); and/or

(b) authorise appropriate (often senior) officers (such as the head of legal services) to sign certain documents (or sometimes several officers for more valuable or important transactions).

5. There appears to be no statutory presumption of due execution of deeds for these types of local authorities. However, for district and county councils, the provision that a document which is purported to be signed by a proper officer, shall be deemed to be duly given, made or issued by the authority of the district or county council (unless the contrary is proved) applies to deeds as well (LGA 1972, s.234(2)).[8]

6. For many bodies with a local authority remit (most of which will be formed by Acts) the following appears to be the position for the execution of a deed:

(a) that the application of the seal of the local authority will be authenticated:

(i) by a member of the local authority or its governing council; or

(ii) (normally but not always) by an officer or employee of the local authority who has been authorised for the purpose (in some cases, the authority can be given generally or for a specific purpose);

(b) that a document purporting to be an instrument made or issued by, or on behalf of, the local authority and sealed with the seal

---

6 See Local Government Acts 1963, 1972 and 1999; e.g. LGA 1972, s.99, Sched. 12, which deal with meetings and proceedings of local authorities, although the constitutions of local authorities will set out to a lesser or greater extent information on this point.

7 The following are governed by this section: a county council, a district council, a London borough council, the Common Council of the City of London in its capacity as a local authority, the Council of the Isles of Scilly and, in relation to Wales, a county council or a county borough council: LGA 2000, s.1. Section 37 applies where a local authority (as defined by the Act) is operating 'executive arrangements' (i.e. a cabinet) or 'alternative arrangements'.

8 This provision also extends to joint authorities, police authorities and others.

of the local authority and/or signed by a person authorised by the local authority is to be received in evidence (and treated without further proof, as being so made or issued, unless a contrary intention is shown);

(c) that the local authority can make its own internal rules to regulate its procedure;

(d) most local authorities keep a sealing register. This records the nature of the document, names of the parties, date of sealing, authorisation for sealing, etc. It is fairly common for each line in this register to be numbered, and the number to be written underneath the seal on the document itself, so that if a question as to the authenticity of the document arises it can be referred back to the register.

It is stressed that these points cover the general position in regard to local authorities. However, each local authority will be governed by its own rules, standing orders and procedures. Lawyers and others who prepare deeds will be familiar with valid signatures and procedures. Others dealing with local authorities will not and may need to check in particular cases (even if they can rely on the presumption of due execution).[9]

19.3 WHAT IS A 'LOCAL AUTHORITY'?

Local authorities

The following are the main types of local authorities in England and Wales:

- district councils (England) (LGA 1972, s.1(1));[10]
- county councils (England) (LGA 1972, s.1(1));[11]
- counties (Wales) (LGA 1972, s.20);[12]
- county boroughs (Wales) (LGA 1972, s.20);[13]

---

9 If they are not prepared to rely on such a presumption of due execution, they may wish to have provisions (such as warranties) as to authority to enter into the transaction recorded in the deed.

10 A district council is a body corporate by the name of 'District Council' with the addition of the name of the particular district: LGA 1972, s.2(3).

11 A county council is a body corporate by the name of 'County Council' with the addition of the name of the particular county: LGA 1972, s.2(3).

12 Such a council to be a body corporate: LGA 1972, s.21(2). Each council for a county in Wales is to have the name of the county with the addition in the case of their English name the words 'County Council' or the word 'Council' and in the case of their Welsh name, of the word 'Cyngor': s.21(3).

13 Such a council to be a body corporate: s.21(2). Each council for a county borough in Wales is to have the name of the county borough with the addition in the case of their English name, the words 'County Borough Council' or the word 'Council' and in the case of their Welsh name, of the words 'Cyngor Bwrdeistref Sirol' or the word 'Cyngor': s.21(4).

- parish councils (England) (LGA 1972, ss.9–16);[14]
- community councils (Wales) (LGA 1972, ss.27–35);[15]
- London Boroughs (LGA 1963, ss.1–2),[16] the City of London[17] and the Temples;[18]
- Greater London Authority (Greater London Authority Act 1999 (GLAA 1999);[19]
- the Council of the Isles of Scilly.

Bodies which have a local authority remit

The following is a list of bodies which have a local authority remit within England and Wales:

- a fire authority constituted by a combination scheme (Fire Services Act 1947, ss.5 and 6);
- a port health authority (Public Health (Control of Disease) Act 1984, s.2);
- an internal drainage board (Land Drainage Act 1991, s.1);
- a local probation board (Criminal Justice and Court Services Act 2000, s.4);
- a joint authority (fire services, civil defence and transport) (LGA 1985, Part IV);
- a body corporate established concerning the transfer of functions to successors of residuary bodies (pursuant to an order under LGA 1985, s.67);
- the Broads authority (Norfolk and Suffolk Broads Act 1988, s.1);
- a joint committee, board or authority established under various provisions (LGA 1992, ss.21 and 22; LGA 1972, ss.102(1)(b) and 263(1));
- a passenger transport executive for a passenger transport area (Transport Act 1968, Part II);

---

14 A parish council is a body corporate: s.14(2), using the name 'Parish Council' with the addition of the name of the particular parish. The title for such a body corporate in a town is 'town council'.
15 A community council is a body corporate consisting of the chairman and community councillors and is to have the functions given to them by LGA 1972 or otherwise (s.33(1)), using the name of the community together with, in English the words 'Community Council' and in Welsh, the words 'Cyngor Cymuned'.
16 Greater London (other than the City of London) boroughs created by Royal Charter or by an incorporation order made by the minister. The Inner Temple and the Middle Temple are separate local administrative areas.
17 The City of London is a corporation by prescription (see *Halsbury's Laws*, 'Corporations', para. 1231). The Common Council of the City of London in its capacity as a local authority or port health authority.
18 The Sub-Treasurer of the Inner Temple or the Under-Treasurer of the Middle Temple, each in his capacity as a local authority. The Inner Temple and the Middle Temple are separate local administrative areas.
19 The Greater London Authority is a body corporate under GLAA 1999, s.1(2).

- the London Development Agency (Regional Development Agencies Act 1998, s.1);
- a regional development agency (Regional Development Agencies Act 1998, s.1);
- a National Park (Environment Act 1995, s.63);
- a joint planning board constituted for an area in Wales outside a National Park (order made under the Town and Country Planning Act 1990, s.2(1B));
- a magistrates' courts committee (Justices of the Peace Act 1997, s.27);
- for each metropolitan county, a fire and civil defence authority (LGA 1985, s.26(1));[20]
- for each metropolitan county, a passenger transport authority (LGA 1985, s.28(1));[21]
- covering Greater London a number of organisations (all bodies corporate):

  - Transport for London (GLAA 1999, s.154);
  - London Transport Users' Committee (GLAA 1999, s.247);
  - Metropolitan Police Authority (GLAA 1999, s.310, inserting s.5B into the Police Act 1996);
  - London Fire and Emergency Planning Authority (GLAA 1999, s.328);
  - Cultural Strategy Group for London (GLAA 1999, s.375);

- Local Government Boundary Commission for Wales (LGA 1972, s.53);[22]
- Electoral Commission (Political Parties, Elections and Referendums Act 2000, s.1);[23]
- Standards Board for England (Local Government Act 2000, s.57(2));
- Audit Commission (Audit Commission Act 1998, s.1(5), Sched.1, para. 1).

19.4 REQUIREMENTS FOR EXECUTION IN PARTICULAR CASES WHERE SPECIFIED BY STATUTE

Parish council[24]

A parish council is a body corporate. A parish council is not required to have a common seal. But where a parish council is required to execute a document (such as a deed) with a seal, and the parish council does not have a seal, the document can be executed by the signature and seal of two members of the parish council.

---

20 It is a body corporate, using the name of the county with the addition of the words 'Fire and Civil Defence Authority'.
21 It is a body corporate, using the name of the county with the addition of the words 'Passenger Transport Authority'.
22 The Commission is a body corporate: LGA 1972, Sched. 8, para. 1(1). The schedule also governs the use of the seal and contains a presumption of due execution.
23 The Commission is a body corporate.
24 LGA 1972, s.14(3).

Community council[25]

A community council is a body corporate. A community council is not required to have a common seal. But where a community council is required to execute a document (such as a deed) with a seal, and the community council does not have a seal, the document can be executed by the signature and seal of two members of the community council.

---

25 LGA 1972, s.33.

CHAPTER 20

Execution of a deed by a partnership

20.1 INTRODUCTION[1]

There are no explicit provisions in the Partnership Act 1890 (PA 1890) which govern the execution of deeds by, or on behalf of, a partnership.

It should be noted that a partnership does not have a separate legal identity (unlike a corporation). Acts carried out by one or more partners for the purpose of the partnership business are carried out as agents for and bind the partnership and the other partners (PA 1890, s.5). As agent(s) for the partnership and the other partners the ability of a partner or partners to execute documents on behalf of the partnership will depend on the provisions found in PA 1890, agency and contract law and in particular the case law which has developed the law relating to partnerships in particular instances.

How a particular partner will execute a deed depends on the status of that partner (whether they are an individual, a corporation or a company). Therefore, the requirements and formalities required for each partner to execute a deed will be as those described in the chapters for individuals, corporations and companies. The status of a partner raises no particular issues as to the form of execution. But there are issues as to:

- whether one partner can execute a deed on behalf of a partnership;
- the way in which the deed should be executed if one partner can execute a deed on behalf of the partnership; and
- whether a deed executed in this way is acceptable to persons receiving such a deed.

What follows is an outline summary of the main provisions found in PA 1890 relevant to the authority of partners and an outline of the law dealing with the three issues outlined above.

---

1 This chapter only deals with the law which is particularly relevant for the execution of deeds by partnerships. More general points relating to deeds, such as the structure and form of a deed, when its use is required, conventional or desirable, delivery, etc. are considered in **Chapter 14**. Issues relating to powers of attorney are dealt with in **Chapters 10** and **22**.

20.2 RELEVANT PROVISIONS OF PA 1890

The following provisions of PA 1890 are relevant to a partner executing a document on behalf of a partnership:

- persons who have entered into a partnership are called collectively a firm (s.4(1));
- the name under which the partnership business is carried out is called the firm-name (s.4(1));
- every partner is an agent of the firm and her other partners for the purpose of the business of the partnership; and

  - the acts of every partner will bind the firm and her partners, if she does any act for carrying on in the usual way business of the kind carried on by the firm;
  - but not if the partner had no authority to act for the firm in the particular matter; *and*

    (a) the person with whom she is dealing either knows that she has no authority; or

    (b) does not know or believe her to be a partner (s.5);[2]

- a partnership (the firm and all the partners) will be bound by an act or instrument which relates to the business of the partnership if the act is done or the instrument is executed in the firm-name or in any other manner showing an intention to bind the firm, by any person authorised, whether a partner or not (s.6);
- the previous provision is subject to its not affecting any general rule of law relating to the execution of deeds or negotiable instruments (s.6) (this provision is not further explained in the PA 1890);
- there is little in the 1890 Act as to which acts would be described as 'carrying on in the usual way business of the kind carried on by the firm'. Case law has established the following.

Actions where partner has authority to bind firm	Actions where partner does not have authority to bind firm
Sell the firm's goods[3]	Execute a deed, save where the partner has a power of attorney or where he has explicit authority to sign in the firm's name[4]

---

2 The power of one or more partners can be restricted if agreed between the partners, and any act done in contravention of that agreement is not binding on the firm with respect to persons who have notice of that agreement: PA 1890, s.8.
3 *Lambert's Case* (1614) Godb 244.
4 *Marchant* v. *Morton Down & Co* [1901] 2 KB 829.

Buy goods of a sort normally used by the firm[5]

Grant a legal mortgage by deed[6]

Hire and fire staff[7]

Compromise a deed by accepting assets *in specie* in satisfaction[8]

Appoint agents on the firm's behalf[9]

Give a guarantee on behalf of the firm (unless there is custom to the contrary)[10]

Receive and provide a valid release for debts owed to the firm[11]

Commit fellow partners to enter into another partnership[12]

Draw cheques or other negotiable instruments (as long as they are in the name of the firm)[13]

Authorise any third-party use of the firm-name[14]

Grant an equitable mortgage by deposit of deeds[15]

Bind the firm to submit a dispute to arbitration[16]

Borrow money for the purposes of the firm's business[17]

Pledge partnership goods as security[18]

20.3 WHAT IS NECESSARY FOR ONE PARTNER TO EXECUTE A DEED ON BEHALF OF A PARTNERSHIP?

The general position is that one or more partners do not have implied authority to execute a deed which will bind the firm (*Harrison* v. *Jackson* (1797) 7 Term Rep 207; *Steiglitz* v. *Egginton* (1815) Holt NP 141; *Marchant* v. *Morton, Down & Co* [1901] 2 KB 829). Express authority to execute a deed must be given by deed (*Steiglitz* v. *Egginton* (1815) Holt NP 141; *Berkeley* v. *Hardy* (1826) 5 B & C 355; PAA 1971 ss.1(1), 7(1)). Accordingly, such authority cannot be conferred by a partnership agreement which is under hand.

The issue whether one partner can bind the firm (if she has the express authority of the other partners) in a deed depends on the form of the deed.

---

5 *Gardiner* v. *Childs* (1837) 8 C & P 345.
6 *Marchant* v. *Morton Down & Co* [1901] 2 KB 829.
7 *Drake* v. *Beckham* (1843) 11 M & W 315.
8 *Niemann* v. *Niemann* (1889) 43 Ch D 198.
9 *Ex p Hodgkinson* (1815) 19 Ves 291.
10 *Simpson's Claim* (1887) 36 Ch D 532.
11 *Powell* v. *Brodhurst* [1901] 2 Ch 160.
12 *Mann* v. *D'Arcy* [1968] 2 All ER 172, 1 WLR 893.
13 *Central Motors (Birmingham) Ltd* v. *PA & SNP Wadsworth* [1983] CLY 80, [1983] 133 NLJ 555, CA.
14 *Marsh* v. *Joseph* [1897] 1 Ch 213, CA.
15 *Re Bourne, Bourne* v. *Bourne* [1906] 2 Ch 427, CA.
16 *Hatton* v. *Royle* (1858) 3 H & N 500.
17 *Ex p. Bonbonus* (1803) 8 Ves 540.
18 *Ex p. Bonbonus* (1803) 8 Ves 540; *Re Langmead's Trusts* (1855) 20 Beav 20.

The deed and the covenants it contains should be expressed to be made by the firm and not the partner as agent for the firm and the deed should be executed by the firm through its agent (the partner signing the deed) – i.e., as 'A [*the firm*] by its agent B [*the partner*]'.[19] If the deed is expressed to be executed in the name of a partner, only she will be bound (i.e., only she can sue and be sued), even though the deed may state that she is acting for the other partners (*Appleton* v. *Binks* (1804) 5 East 148; *Pickering's Case* (1871) LR 6 Ch App 525).

The above two statements, however, need to be considered in the light of case law which indicates the law more fully in this area:

- a deed executed by one partner, although it may not bind the firm or the other partners, will usually bind the partner who has executed it;[20]
- one partner can bind the firm if she executes a deed of release (*Hawkshaw* v. *Parkins* (1819) 2 Swan 539);
- one partner can bind the firm if she executes an assent to a debtor's deed of arrangement (*Dudgeon* v. *O'Connell* (1849) 12 I Iq R 566 (Ir));
- if a partner executes a document as a deed, the underlying transaction may still be binding on the firm if the transaction only needs to be executed under hand, and if the partner had authority (express or implied) to execute such a document under hand (even though the partner does not, as such, have authority to execute a document as a deed). For example, in a leading case in this area which concerned the assignment of a debt, the document containing the assignment of the debt could be executed under hand, but was executed as a deed. As a deed, one partner could not bind the partnership, but under hand the assignment was held binding on the firm (*Marchant* v. *Morton Down & Co* [1901] 2 KB 829);
- a partnership may be able to enforce the provisions of a deed which is executed by a partner as a trustee for the firm. The firm would need to sue in the name of the partner who executed the deed (*Harmer* v. *Armstrong* [1934] 1 Ch 65);

---

19 See *Lindley & Banks on Partnership*, 18th edn, Sweet & Maxwell, 2002, paras. 12–178, 12–179. The editor of *Lindley & Banks* suggests that this rule is preserved in PA 1890, s.6, which provides that a partnership (the firm and all the partners) will be bound by an act or instrument which relates to the business of the partnership if the act is done or the instrument is executed in the firm-name or in any other manner showing an intention to bind the firm, by any person authorised, whether a partner or not, but this proposition does not affect any general rule of law relating to the execution of deeds or negotiable instruments.

20 *Elliot* v. *Davis* (1800) 2 Bos & P 338; *Bowker* v. *Burdekin* (1843) 11 M & W 128; *Cumberlege* v. *Lawson* (1857) 1 CBNS 709; *Latch* v. *Wedlake* (1840) 11 Ad & El 959; *Lascaridi* v. *Gurney* (1862) 9 Jur NS 302.

- a deed can be executed on behalf of all the other partners if a partner signs for each of the partners where she is directed by, and is in the presence of, each of the partners (LP(MP)A 1989, s.1(3)(a)(ii)).[21]

Practical effects

The effect of the above appears to be that if:

- a partner has *explicit* authority, itself granted by deed, to execute a deed on behalf of the firm; and
- the deed is worded in the correct way; and
- executed in the correct way, then

that partner can bind the firm on her execution of a deed.

For a person who is a covenantee under a deed, it is not a formula which recommends itself with certainty: she must rely on whether a deed is correctly worded and the vagaries of case law. Although the deed may be enforceable against the partner who has executed it, she may not have sufficient resources to meet any claim.[22]

20.4   EXECUTION FORMALITIES

As a partnership does not have a separate identity from that of its partners, the formalities for execution will be governed by the status of the partner:

- *if a partner is an individual*: she would sign the deed in the presence of a witness. Each partner would need to sign the deed in the presence of a witness;[23] and
- *if the partner is a corporation*: a corporate partner would sign (through its officers) in accordance with the formalities required by the type of corporation it is.[24]

---

21 By signing (and having such signature attested by two witnesses), against each of the names of the partners. The practical effect of this seems unclear, as if all the partners are present when execution takes place in this way, it would be simpler for each of the partners to sign. There would also be no need to have two witnesses present; one would suffice.

22 See *Lindley & Banks on Partnership*, 18th edn, Sweet & Maxwell, 2002, para. 12–181, where it is indicated that lessors of property insist that all partners are made parties to a lease so that the covenants made in the lease can be enforced against each partner. See also *Encyclopaedia of Forms and Precedents*, vol. 12(2), 'Deeds', para. 41.

23 In compliance with LP(MP)A 1989, s.1(3). A partner who is an individual can also have the deed executed on their behalf, but the partner would need to authorise the person so executing. However, based on the discussion above, this is not likely to be a method which recommends itself to persons relying on a deed signed by a person on behalf of a partner.

24 For example, if a company is formed under or regulated by CA 2006, concerning the execution of documents, see s.44.

CHAPTER 21

Statutory declarations

21.1 INTRODUCTION

A statutory declaration is a statement contained in a document stating that the contents of the document are true. It is a means of giving evidence, proving facts or stating that certain things have been done or exist, and is used in non-litigation matters. It was considered as the non-litigation equivalent of an affidavit when affidavits were the main method of introducing written evidence in litigation.

The introduction in the nineteenth century of a procedure allowing a person to take a declaration was intended as a substitution for the use of oaths (such as in affidavits and affirmations) for specific non-litigation situations. This was done partly because of the formalities at that time necessary to swear an oath.

The legislation which introduced statutory declarations (Statutory Declarations Act 1835 (SDA 1835)) has been heavily amended, and the phraseology used in that legislation does not reflect the realities of a modern legal system. Also, unlike deeds and affidavits, there is no concise or up-to-date statement on the layout and requirements for the execution of a statutory declaration.

Many uses of statutory declarations are specified by government departments and agencies, often using specified pre-printed forms, such as a number of forms used for certain dealings with companies under CA 1985 (see below).

21.2 WHEN MUST A STATUTORY DECLARATION BE USED?

SDA 1835 itself provides a number of situations when a statutory declaration should be used. Subsequent legislation has specified further situations when statutory declarations are to be used.

Various government agencies require the use of statutory declarations. In addition, there are a number of situations when a statutory declaration is commonly used (although there is no legislative requirement to do so). Some examples of each type follow.

Situations under SDA 1835 when a statutory declaration is to be used

SDA 1835 provides for a declaration to be substituted for an oath in the following cases:

- where an attesting witness wishes to prove the execution of a will, codicil, deed or instrument in writing (s.16);
- where a competent person wishes to prove the signing, sealing, publication or delivery of a will, codicil, deed or instrument in writing (s.16);
- where the Bank of England wishes to (s.14):
  - prove the death of a proprietor of any transferable stocks or funds; or
  - identify the person of any such proprietor; or
  - remove any other impediment to the transfer of any such stocks or funds; or
  - otherwise deal with the loss or mutilation of any bank note;
- where a body corporate has the authority to administer or receive (by law, statute or by usage) an oath, affidavit or solemn affirmation, it can substitute a statutory declaration for such oaths, affirmations and affidavits (s.8);[1]
- where the Treasury uses an oath relating to customs or excise revenues, the office of stamps and taxes, etc. (s.2).

Legislative requirements for the use of a statutory declaration

The following are some common situations when a statutory declaration is required.

Under CA 1985[2]

Common examples under CA 1985:

- a solicitor engaged in the formation of a company or a person named as a director or secretary of the company is required to make a statutory declaration in the prescribed form to indicate that the requirements of CA 1985 in respect of the registration have been complied with (s.12);[3]
- a solicitor engaged in the formation of a company or a person named as a director or secretary of the company named in Form 10 is required to make a statutory declaration to confirm that a company is exempt from

---

1 '[I]t shall be lawful for the universities of Oxford and Cambridge, and for all other bodies corporate and politic'.
2 The forms mentioned in this section are forms in English. There are Welsh equivalents, which have the same numbers as the English forms, but with the words 'CYM' at the end.
3 Form 12 is the prescribed form.

the requirement to use 'limited' (or 'cyfyngedig') as part of its name (s.30);[4]

- a director or a secretary is required to make a statutory declaration confirming that a special resolution has been passed dealing with matters prescribed for the re-registration of a private company as a public company and that there has not been a change in the company's financial position (s.43);[5]
- the directors are required to make a statutory declaration that the whole membership of the company is agreeing to the re-registration of the company as unlimited and that if any of the members of the company have not agreed to the re-registration that the directors have taken all reasonable steps to satisfy themselves that the members who have agreed to the re-registration were lawfully empowered to do so (s.49);[6]
- a director or the secretary of a public company is required to make a statutory declaration that the public company has, among other things, the authorised minimum allotted share capital if it is to carry on any business or exercise any borrowing powers (s.117);[7]
- the directors of a company are required to make a statutory declaration where they wish to give financial assistance to a person who wishes to acquire shares in the company (ss.155–156);[8]
- the directors of a private company are required to make a statutory declaration containing several particulars (e.g., making enquiry into the state of affairs of the company) where the company is proposing to make a payment of capital for the redemption or purchase of its own shares (ss.173–174).[9]

Land Registry

Common examples under Land Registration Rules 2003:

- application for registration of a person in adverse possession (Form ADV1) requires a statutory declaration to be filed with it. The statutory declaration is not part of Form ADV1, and its precise form is not specified (r.188);[10]
- application to be registered as a person to be notified of an application for adverse possession (Form ADV2);

---

4 Form 30(5)(a) is the prescribed form. There are also Forms 30(5)(b) and 30(5)(c), which deal with the types of companies mentioned in CA 1985, s.680, and companies already formed but wishing to be exempt from the need to use 'Limited'.
5 Form 43(3)(e) is the prescribed form.
6 Form 49(8)(b) is the prescribed form.
7 Form 117 is the prescribed form.
8 Form 155(6)(a) and Form 155(6)(b) are the prescribed forms.
9 Form 173 is the prescribed form.
10 The statutory declaration requires certain matters to be set out as detailed in that rule. See also *Wontner's Guide to Land Registry Practice*, 20th edn, Sweet & Maxwell, 2003.

- caution against first registration (Form CT1);
- application to enter a unilateral notice (Form UN1);
- application to withdraw a caution (Form WCT);
- evidence of non-revocation of a power of attorney more than 12 months old and evidence in support of a power delegating trustees' functions to a beneficiary (rr.62 and 63).[11]

Criminal offences, etc.

Common examples include:

- where a summons has been issued under Magistrates' Courts Act 1980, s.1 and a magistrates' court has begun to try the information to which the summons relates, a defendant can make a statutory declaration at any time during the trial or thereafter that she did not know of the summons or the proceedings (Magistrates' Courts Act 1980, s.14);
- when contesting a penalty charge imposed regarding a vehicle (CPR 75).

When a statutory declaration is commonly used

Common situations include:

- on change of a person's name;[12]
- on change of a baby's or an infant's name;
- as evidence of incidental matters arising in proof of title to real property.[13]

21.3   FORM OF A STATUTORY DECLARATION

The form of a statutory declaration is specified by SDA 1835, ss.18, 20 and Schedule:

> I A.B. do solemnly and sincerely declare, that . . . and I make this solemn declaration conscientiously believing the same to be true, and by virtue of the provisions of (an Act made and passed in the . . . year of the reign of his present Majesty, intituled 'An Act' (here insert the title of this Act)).

Points to note

1. SDA 1835 does not provide any other information or guidance as to the layout or execution of a statutory declaration.

---

11 The wording is set out in Sched. 3.
12 For example, *Encyclopaedia of Forms and Precedents*, vol. 29, 'Name, Change of', Form 13 [423].
13 For example, *Perham v. Kempster* [1907] 1 Ch 373 at 381; *Rogers v. Phillips* (1966) 198 Estates Gazette 481 at 483.

2. 'I A.B.' is taken to mean by convention the name and address of the Declarant.
3. The requirements for execution and signature of a statutory declaration are to be found in other legislation.[14]
4. The words 'provisions of (an Act made and passed in the . . . year of the reign of his present Majesty, intituled 'An Act' (here insert the title of this Act))' are now replaced by 'Statutory Declarations Act 1835'.[15]

An example of the layout of a statutory declaration is set out at **section 21.5**.

21.4   REQUIREMENT TO SIGN A STATUTORY DECLARATION

SDA 1835 does not specifically state that a statutory declaration has to be signed by the Declarant or the Commissioner. The requirement to sign a statutory declaration can be derived from a number of other sources:

- an affidavit requires a jurat;[16]
- the jurat must be signed by all Deponents, be completed and signed by the person before whom the affidavit was sworn whose name and qualification must be printed beneath his signature, and contain the full address of the person before whom the affidavit was sworn;
- an 'affidavit' is taken to include a declaration and 'sworn' (i.e. 'swear') is taken to mean declare;
- Commissioners for Oaths and solicitors are required to state the place and date where an affidavit or oath is taken or made.

Irrespective of statutory requirements, by convention the *signature block/ jurat* used for affidavits has been utilised for statutory declarations replacing the word 'sworn' by 'declared'.

---

14 Solicitors Act 1974, s.81(3); COA 1889, s.5; Courts and Legal Services Act 1990, s.113(6). These Acts refer to 'oath or affidavit' which includes a statutory declaration: IA 1978, Sched. 1.
15 Such amendment being formerly made by the Short Titles Act 1896, s.1, Sched. 1. But this Act has been repealed by Statute Law (Repeals) Act 1995.
16 Which authenticates the affidavit: CPR PD 32.5.1; IA 1978, Sched. 1.

21.5   EXAMPLE STRUCTURE OF A STATUTORY DECLARATION[18]

Statutory Declaration

I [*full name*], of [*address*], do solemnly and sincerely declare that:

1.   I absolutely and entirely renounce, relinquish and abandon the use of my said former surname of [*former surname*] and assume, adopt and determine to take and use from the date hereof the surname of [*new surname*] in substitution for my former surname of [*former surname*].
2.   I shall at all times hereafter in all records, deeds and other writings and in all actions and proceedings, and in all dealings and transactions and on all occasions whatsoever, use and subscribe the said name of [*new surname*] as my surname in substitution for my former surname of [*former surname*] so relinquished as aforesaid to the intent that I may hereafter be called, known or distinguished not by the former surname of [*former surname*] but by [*new surname*] only.
3.   I authorise and require all persons at all times to designate, describe and address me by the adopted surname of [*new surname*].

AND I make this solemn declaration conscientiously believing the same to be true and by virtue of the Statutory Declarations Act 1835.

DECLARED at [*place where the Commissioner is taking the declaration of the Declarant*] this [*date*] of [*month and year*] }   (signature of Declarant)
(signature of Commissioner)

Before me

a [Commissioner for Oaths] [solicitor empowered to administer oaths]

---

18 This is an example of a statutory declaration where a person wishes to change their name. Other examples can be found in *Encylcopaedia of Forms and Precedents*, LexisNexis Butterworths.

CHAPTER 22

Powers of attorney

22.1 INTRODUCTION[1]

A power of attorney is a special form of agency, created by deed, where one person (the 'donor') gives to another person (the 'attorney' or the 'donee') the power (i.e. authority) to act on her behalf and in her name (Law Commission Consultation Paper 143, para. 8.3; *Brooke's Notary*, 12th edn, Sweet & Maxwell, 2002, p. 133, para. 8–02). Such power can be general or limited to authority to act in a particular matter, for a specific period of time, etc.

An attorney can be an individual or a corporation (reading PAA 1971, s.7(1), (2) and LPA 1925, s.74(4) together, and common law provisions).

A power of attorney is always required where the attorney will be asked to execute a deed on behalf of the donor.

The creation of a power of attorney by a donor, and the execution of a deed by an attorney on behalf of the donor are governed by the formalities described for individuals and different types of corporations in the relevant chapters of this book. The creation of a power of attorney is always required to be by deed (PAA 1971, s.1(1)).

This chapter therefore concentrates on the following points:

- specific points relating to the creation of a power of attorney not dealt with in other chapters;
- specific points relating to the execution of a deed by an attorney on behalf of the donor;
- the ability of a corporation (and primarily a company formed under or regulated by CA 2006 and CA 1985) to grant a power of attorney under various Acts.

---

1 This chapter does not deal with lasting powers of attorney (under the Mental Capacity Act 2005) which have their own particular rules.

22.2 CREATING A POWER OF ATTORNEY

A power of attorney is created by a document executed as a deed by the donor of the power (PAA 1971, s.1(1)). A donee of a power of attorney is not restricted only to executing deeds. At common law the authority to execute a deed on behalf of another person had to be given by deed (*Steiglitz* v. *Egginton* (1815) Holt 141 at 171 ER 193; *Powell* v. *London & Provincial Bank* [1893] 2 Ch 555 at 563).

The granting of a power of attorney can be:

* expressed in a document whose only purpose is to grant it; or
* contained in a document whose primarily purpose concerns other matters.[2]

Structure of a power attorney

As a power of attorney is executed as a deed, the points made about the structure, layout and contents of a deed in other chapters apply equally here. PAA 1971 also provides a form of a general power of attorney. This is not mandatory, and a form which is to the like effect and is expressed to be made under PAA 1971 can also be used. If either of these forms are used then they will operate to confer on the attorney the authority to do on behalf of the donor anything which the donor can lawfully do by an attorney (PAA 1971, s.10, Sched. 1). The suggested form is:

> **THIS GENERAL POWER OF ATTORNEY** is made this _____ day of _____ 200[. . .] _____ by AB of _____ .
>
> I appoint CD of [CD of _____ and EF of _____ [jointly [jointly and severally]] to be my attorney(s) in accordance with section 10 of the Powers of Attorney Act 1971

22.3 ATTORNEY EXECUTING A DEED

An attorney under common law executing a deed on behalf of a donor would sign the donor's name and then her (the attorney's) name, because not to do so:

* would render the execution void; and
* perhaps more importantly, may make the attorney personally liable on the deed (*Appleton* v. *Binks* (1804) 5 East 148).[3]

---

2 For example, the assignment of a patent is not required (like other conveyances of property) to be made by deed but only in writing and to be signed by, or on behalf of, the assignor or mortager: Patents Act 1977, s.30(6), as amended by SI 2004/2357. It is fairly common to include a clause in such an assignment to appoint the assignee as attorney of the assignor of the patent, in case any document subsequently needs to be executed as a deed.
3 This extends even to when the attorney is described in the deed as acting for and on behalf of the donor.

However, PAA 1971 provides that an attorney (who is an individual) can sign any document with her own signature by the authority of the donor of the power (PAA 1971, s.7(1)).[4] A document signed in this manner will be considered as effective as if executed by the attorney with the signature or the name of the donor of the power (PAA 1971, s.7(1)).

Although it is clear that an attorney can sign in her own name (and not in the name of the donor) under PAA 1971, there is uncertainty regarding how this provision relates to the provisions of other Acts even after the amendments made by RR(EDD)O 2005. The safest course in most situations appears to be to sign in both names, except where there is accepted practice to sign only in the name of the attorney and taking into account the points below under the section 'Practice points'.

Practice points

The deed that the attorney executes on behalf of the donor should:

- properly and fully identify the donor in the deed (*Harmer* v. *Armstrong* [1934] Ch 65);[5]
- state that the attorney is executing the deed on behalf of the donor or as an attorney (*Re Whiteley Partners Ltd* (1886) 32 Ch 337 at 340); and
- state that the attorney does not need any specific authority from the donor for the attorney to use her own name (*Clauss* v. *Pir* [1988] Ch 267 at 272).

22.4 ABILITY OF A CORPORATION TO GRANT A POWER OF ATTORNEY

The ability to grant a power of attorney is dependent on the authority given to the corporation by the Act of Parliament, charter, constitution, articles, etc. which forms it or governs its operation, and the power cannot extend beyond the authority given to it (*Ashbury Railway Carriage & Iron Co. Ltd* v. *Riche* (1875) LR 7 HL 653; *Baroness Wenlock* v. *River Dee Co.* (1885) 10 App. Cas. 354; *London County Council* v. *Attorney General* [1902] AC 165). It is not clear whether such a power must be express.[6]

---

4 This section also allows the attorney to do any other thing in her own name, but is limited by the extent of the power granted by the donor: *Clauss* v. *Pir* [1988] Ch 267 at 272.

5 Not to do so would in effect abolish the rule that an undisclosed principal cannot intervene on a deed. This point, and the following two, are cited in Law Commission Consultation Paper 143 at para. 8.13, note 25.

6 Law Commission Consultation Paper 143, para. 85, note 8; the Law Commission cites *Ferguson* v. *Wilson* (1866) LR 2 Ch App 77 at 89, which held that a corporation, because it cannot act in its own person, has by implication a general power to appoint and act by agents, including an attorney.

The ability of a company formed or regulated under CA 1985 or CA 2006 to grant a power of attorney

CA 2006 (and CA 1985) after October 2009

CA 2006 will permit a company to empower a person as the company's attorney to execute deeds and other documents on behalf of the company (CA 2006, s.47(1)). The company must execute an instrument as a deed to empower the person. The power can be either general or in respect of specified matters. Where a person, under such a power, executes a deed or another type of document, it will have the effect as if had been executed by the company. The power will have effect both within and outside the United Kingdom.

The effect of this change will affect companies formed and regulated under CA 1985 and CA 2006.

This appears to overcome the issue discussed below about whether a company can directly appoint an attorney. CA 1985 only expressly permitted the appointment of an attorney for use abroad. The other authority is to be found in Table A, art. 71 (see below). However, as discussed below there is doubt whether Table A, art. 71 can override the provisions of CA 1985, s.36A (CA 2006, s.44 (from April 2008)).

Perhaps the only remaining area of doubt is that CA 2006, s.44 (which indicates how a company can sign documents) and CA 2006, s.47 are not directly referenced against each other. But one aim of RR(EDD)O 2005 was to clear up (as far as possible) inconsistencies between PAA 1971, CA 1985 and LP(MP)A 1989. From October 2009, CA 2006, s.46 (until October 2009, CA 1985, s.36AA) provides that a document is validly executed as a deed for the purposes of LP(MP)A 1989, s.1(2)(b) by a company if, and only if, it is duly executed by a company and then delivered as a deed. LP(MP)A 1989, s.1(2)(b) provides that a deed can be executed by a person making it or a person authorised to execute it in the name or on behalf of that person. As noted above, CA 2006, s.47(2) expressly indicates that the document signed by an attorney is to be considered as if the company had executed the document.

CA 1985 until October 2009

CA 1985 itself (which will continue to apply until the relevant sections of CA 2006 come into force in October 2009) does not provide authority for a company to grant a power of attorney, but the validity of any acts done by the company by or on its behalf would be hard to challenge as:

- the validity of an act done by a company shall not be called into question on the ground of lack of capacity by reason of anything in the company's memorandum (CA 1985, s.35(1));
- in favour of a person dealing with a company in good faith, the power of the board of the directors to bind the company, or authorise others to do so, shall be deemed to be free of any limitation under the company's constitution (CA 1985, s.35A(1));[8] and
- a party to a transaction with a company is not bound to enquire as to whether it is permitted by the company's memorandum or as to any limitation on the powers of the board of directors to bind the company or authorise others to do so (CA 1985, s.35B).

The power to appoint an attorney within the United Kingdom is governed by the extent to which the company's memorandum and articles of association allow for the appointment of agents to act on its behalf. Table A, the default articles of association for most companies formed under CA 1985, gives to the directors the power to manage the business of the company (Companies (Tables A–F) Regulations 1985, SI 1985/805, Table A, art. 70) and art. 71 authorises the directors to:

> by power of attorney or otherwise, appoint any person to be the agent of the company for such purposes and on such conditions as they determine, including authority for the agent to delegate all or any of its powers.

The power of an attorney to execute deeds on behalf of the company would be valid and effective (*Brooke's Notary*, 12th edn, Sweet & Maxwell, 2002, p. 140, para. 8–06). However, there is no direct authority that specifically allows for one attorney to sign on behalf of a company, 'overriding' the provisions of CA 1985, s.36A (from April 2008, CA 2006, s.44).

CA 1985 allows a company, in writing under its common seal, to appoint an attorney, generally or in respect of any specified matters, to execute deeds on behalf of the company outside the United Kingdom (CA 1985, s.38(1)). Companies are no longer required to have a seal, and a document signed by a director and the secretary (or by two directors) and expressed in whatever form of words to be executed by the company has the same effect as if executed under the common seal of the company (CA 1985, s.36A(3) (from April 2008, CA 2006, ss. 45(1)) and 44(4)). A deed executed by such an attorney on behalf of the company has the same effect as if it were executed under the company's common seal (CA 1985, s.38(2)).

---

8 A person 'deals with' a company if he is a party to a transaction or other act to which the company is a party; he is not regarded as acting in bad faith by reason only of his knowing that an act is beyond the powers of the directors under the company's constitution, and he is presumed to have acted in good faith (unless the contrary is proved): CA 1985, s.35A(2).

If the company does not have the explicit power to appoint an attorney in its articles it still may be able to appoint an attorney, but in order to do so the company in general meeting is required to authorise the appointment (*Buckley on the Companies Act*, 14th edn, 1981, pp. 98–99, quoted in Law Commission Consultation Paper 143).

Other than appointing an attorney to execute a deed outside the United Kingdom, CA 1985 allows the company, in writing under its common seal, to authorise any person in particular territories to affix an 'official seal' to a deed or other document to which the company is party in that territory (CA 1985, s.39(3)), subject to the following:

- the company has objects that require or comprise the transaction of business in foreign countries;
- the articles of association of the company authorise the use of an official seal in any territory, district or place outside the United Kingdom;
- the official seal is a facsimile of the common seal with some additional wording on its face to indicate the name of every territory, district or place where it is used (CA 1985, s.39(1)).

The use of such a seal when duly affixed to a document has the same effect as the company's common seal (CA 1985, s.39(2)). This provision does not require that the person be appointed as an attorney, and Table A does not contain, by default, an article authorising the use of an official seal.

Can an individual sign documents on behalf of a company under a power of attorney? RR(EDD)O 2005 amended PAA 1971, s.7 to expressly permit execution by an individual attorney on behalf of a corporate donor.

An instrument executed in the manner provided by PAA 1971, s.7(1) (see **section 22.3**) is to be effective as if executed by the donee in any manner which would constitute due execution of that instrument by the donor or, as the case may be, as if done by the donee in the name of the donor. Where the instrument is executed by the donee as a deed, the instrument is to be effective as if executed by the donee in a manner which would constitute due execution of it as a deed by the donor only if it is executed in accordance with LP(MP)A 1989, s.1(3)(a). This is a reference to a document being validly executed as a deed by an individual if, and only if, it is signed by the individual in the presence of a witness who attests the signature.

Other sources of power for an attorney to execute a deed on behalf of a corporation

Conveyance of property – by an attorney (as an individual)

An individual can be authorised under a power of attorney to convey any interest in property in the name of or on behalf of a corporation (aggregate or sole). She would execute a deed (the conveyance) by signing the name of the corporation in the presence of at least one witness. Such execution is to take effect and be valid as if the corporation had executed the conveyance (LPA 1925, s.74(3)).[9]

Conveyance of property – by an attorney (corporation aggregate)

A corporation aggregate (i.e. not sole) can be authorised under a power of attorney to convey any interest in property in the name of or on behalf of any other person (including another corporation). The corporation's governing body (through its board of directors, council, etc.) will appoint an officer by resolution or otherwise. The officer will execute the deed or other instrument in the name of the other person or corporation. Where the deed or instrument appears to be executed by the officer appointed by the governing body, in favour of a purchaser, the instrument shall be deemed to have been executed by an officer duly authorised (LPA 1925, s.74(4)).[10]

Both these provisions allow other methods of execution (LPA 1925, s.74(6)). A company regulated by CA 1985 which was acting as a corporate attorney could sign in accordance with its articles of association and/or with CA 1985 (CA 1985, s.36A, as to which see **Chapter 16**).

22.5 HOW DOES AN ATTORNEY EXECUTE A DEED?

The basic principle appears to be that the attorney executes a deed complying with the formalities applicable to her status:

- *an attorney who is an individual*: she would sign the deed in the presence of a witness;[11] and
- *an attorney who is a corporation*: a corporate attorney would sign (through its officers) in accordance with the formalities required by the type of corporation it is.[12]

---

9 Property 'includes any thing in action, and any interest in real or personal property': LPA 1925, s.205(1)(xx). Conveyance 'includes a mortgage, charge, lease, assent, vesting declaration, vesting instrument, disclaimer, release and every other assurance of property or of an interest therein by any instrument, except a will; "convey" has a corresponding meaning': LPA 1925, s.205(1)(ii).
10 See n.10 above for meaning of 'property' and 'convey'.
11 In compliance with LP(MP)A 1989, s.1(3).
12 For example, if a company formed under or regulated by CA 1985 or CA 2006, it would comply with the provisions of s.36A or s.44.

CHAPTER 23

Statements of truth

23.1 INTRODUCTION

Certain documents that are used in litigation must contain a 'statement of truth'. The statement of truth has replaced the affidavit (or affirmation) as the main means of verifying the contents of a document in litigation save in a few cases, which are detailed in **Chapter 24**.

Most of these documents must be signed either by a party to the litigation or by their legal representative on their behalf. If the party is a corporation, an officer or senior employee of the corporation, or the corporation's legal representative, must sign the statement of truth. One type of document which must always be signed by the person making it is a witness statement. This cannot be signed on behalf of the person making it. Similarly, disclosure statements must be signed by the person making the search for documents.

The general position is that such documents need to have a physical signature placed on the document. Where electronic communications are used for:

- commencing litigation electronically; or
- making applications and filing other types of documents electronically

the statement of truth is made by typing on a computer the name of the person who is required to sign the electronic document.

23.2 WHAT IS A 'STATEMENT OF TRUTH'?

It is a statement that the party putting forward a document (other than a witness statement) believes the facts stated in the document are true (CPR 22.1(4)). If the document is a witness statement, it is a statement that its maker believes that the facts stated within are true.

If a party is conducting proceedings with a litigation friend, the statement of truth is a statement that the litigation friend believes the facts stated in the document being verified are true (CPR 22.1(5)) but only in relation to a statement of case, response or an application notice.

23.3 WHEN MUST A STATEMENT OF TRUTH BE USED?

The following are the types of documents or situations when a statement of truth must be used.

Generally

- Where a rule or Practice Direction requires that a document be verified by a statement of truth (other than those listed below) (CPR 22.1(1)(g)).

General category of documents

These include:

- a statement of case (CPR 22.1(1)(a));[1]
- amendments to a statement of case (unless the court orders otherwise) (CPR 22.1(2));
- a witness statement (CPR 22.1(1)(c));[2]
- where an applicant wishes to rely on the matters set out in her application notice as evidence (CPR 22.1(3), CPR PD 22.1.2).

Specific situations

These include:

- a response complying with an order under CPR 18.1 to provide further information (CPR 22.1(1)(b));[3]
- an acknowledgement of service in a claim begun by way of the Part 8 procedure (CPR 22.1(1)(d));[4]
- an application notice for a third-party debt order (CPR PD 22.1.4(1)(a), CPR 72.3);
- an application notice for a hardship payment order (CPR PD 22.1.4(1)(b), CPR 72.7);

---

1 Note the special meaning a 'statement of case' has; see **section 23.14**.

2 There are format and content requirements which are considered at **section 23.10**.

3 CPR 18.1 concerns where a court orders a party to clarify any matter which is in dispute in the proceedings, or orders a party to give additional information in relation to any such matter.

4 A 'Part 8' claim normally involves the following types of cases: where a court's decision is required on a question which is unlikely to involve a substantial dispute of fact or where a rule or practice direction permits or requires the use of the Part 8 procedure (CPR 8.1). A Part 8 claim can be used where there is a claim by or against a child or patient which has been settled before the commencement of proceedings and the sole purpose of the claim is to obtain the approval of the court in the settlement or a claim for provisional damages which has been settled before the commencement of proceedings and the sole purpose of the claim is to obtain a consent judgment (CPR PD 8.3.1). There is also a number of situations where a Part 8 claim must be used: specifically, any claim or application in relation to which an Act, rule or practice direction provides that the claim

- an application notice for a charging order CPR PD 22.1.4(1)(c), CPR 73.3);
- a certificate stating the reasons for bringing a possession claim or landlord and tenant claim in the High Court in accordance with CPR 55.3(2) and CPR 56.2(2) (CPR 22.1(1)(e));
- a notice of objections to an account being taken by the court, unless verified by an affidavit or witness statement (CPR PD 22.1.4(2));
- a schedule or counter-schedule of expenses and losses in a personal injury claim, and any amendments to such a schedule or counter-schedule (whether or not they are contained in a statement of case) (CPR PD 22.1.4(3));
- an expert witness report (CPR PD 22.1.3, CPR 35);[5]
- a disclosure statement (CPR 31.10(5), (6) and (7));[6]
- a certificate of service (CPR 22.1(1)(f)).

23.4 WHO MAY SIGN THE STATEMENT OF TRUTH: INDIVIDUALS

For a statement of case, a response or an application to the court

For a statement of case, a response or an application to the court, the following must sign a statement of truth:

- a party to the litigation (CPR 22.1(6)(a)(i), CPR PD 22.3.1(1)); or
- a party's litigation friend (CPR 22.1(6)(a)(i), CPR PD 22.3.1(1)); or
- the legal representative on behalf of a party or a litigation friend.

Witness statements

Only the maker of the witness statement can sign (CPR 22.1(6)(b), CPR PD 22.3.2).

23.5 WHO MAY SIGN THE STATEMENT OF TRUTH: WHERE THE PARTY IS A COMPANY OR OTHER CORPORATION

The statement of truth has to be signed by a person on behalf of a company or other corporation. The general rule is that:

---

or application is brought by originating summons, originating motion or originating application (CPR PD 8.3.3) and generally where it falls within a list of claims, petitions and applications set out in CPR PD 8.3.9 (subject to any special requirements set out in CPR PD 8.3.10 to CPR PD 8.3.22).

5 There are layout and content requirements; these are considered at **section 23.10**.
6 Although a disclosure statement is technically not a statement of truth, the maker of the statement is verifying the truth of the actions she has carried out.

- the person must be a person holding a senior position in that company or other corporation (CPR PD 22.3.4); or
- where the company or other corporation is legally represented, the legal representative may sign on the company's or other corporation's behalf.

In addition to signing the statement of truth, she must also state her position or role in the company or corporation. The person who is actually signing the statement of truth must sign and print her own name (and not the name of company or corporation she is signing on behalf of) (CPR PD 22.3.9).

What is meant by a 'senior position'?

Registered company or corporation (CPR PD 22.3.5(1))[7]

The following would be considered to hold a senior position:

- a director;
- the treasurer;
- the secretary;
- the chief executive;
- a manager;[8]
- other officer.

Corporation which is not a registered company (CPR PD 22.3.5(2))

The following would be considered to hold a senior position:

- a director;
- the treasurer;
- the secretary;
- the chief executive;
- a manager or other officer;
- the mayor;
- the chairman;
- the president;
- the town clerk.

Who is a 'manager' for a company?

The word 'manager' needs to be considered with the phrase 'a person holding a senior position'. It is suggested (not required) by the court rules that, for

---

7 The expression 'registered company or corporation' is not further explained or defined. Perhaps the meaning of a 'registered company' has the same meaning as a company registered under CA 2006 (see ss.1(1)(a), (b), 1171, for example). The role of 'treasurer' is not an office named in CA 2006.
8 The meaning is discussed below under the heading 'Who is a "manager" for a company?'

a manager to be able to sign a statement of truth, the following points should be considered (by the court) (CPR PD 22.3.11):

- the size of the company; and
- the size and nature of the claim.

The manager signing the document should have personal knowledge of the content of the document or should manage the persons who have the knowledge of the content.[9] For a small company, there may not be a manager holding a senior position apart from the directors of the company. For a larger company, there will be many managers. A statement of truth signed by the manager of a specialist claims, insurance or legal department is acceptable, if that manager is responsible for handling that claim or is responsible for the staff handling it.

23.6 WHO MAY SIGN THE STATEMENT OF TRUTH: PARTNERSHIP

The statement of truth may be signed by (CPR PD 22.3.6):

- any of the partners;
- any person having the control or management of the partnership business.

23.7 WHO MAY SIGN THE STATEMENT OF TRUTH: INSURER OR MOTOR INSURERS' BUREAU

An insurer or the Motor Insurers' Bureau ('Insurer') can sign a statement of truth on behalf of a party where the Insurer has a financial interest in the result of the proceedings brought wholly or partially by or against that party (CPR PD 22.3.6A).

---

9 The importance of the person signing the statement of truth having personal knowledge of the contents of the document is highlighted by the case of *Birmingham City Council* v. *Hosey*, although a decision of the county court (2 October 2002, Birmingham County Court, *Legal Action*, December 2002). In this case the statement of truth was 'signed' by the application of a rubber stamp. The stamp contained the signature of an official of the city council's litigation department. It was applied by a more junior employee of the litigation department. The city official had never seen any of the papers in the case, checked any facts or read any of the original documents in the case. All the city official had done was to authorise the junior employee to apply the stamp. On appeal from a district judge to a circuit judge, the circuit judge stated that the requirement to verify a statement of case by a statement of truth (in CPR 22.1(1)(a)) was not a mere technicality or a mere matter of form. Courts needed to rely on statements bearing a statement of truth. In this case the statement of truth had not been signed. The circuit judge also went on, it appears, to indicate that a statement of truth signed with a rubber stamp was not in compliance with CPR 5.3, which allows a document to be signed by 'printing or other technical means'. A statement of truth was not a document but a statement within a document.

An insurer who is conducting proceedings on behalf of several claimants or defendants can sign a statement of truth in a statement of case. A senior person responsible for the case as the lead insurer is able to sign, subject to the following requirements:

- the person signing needs to state the capacity in which he signs;
- the statement of truth has to be a statement that the lead insurer believes the facts stated in the document are true; and
- the court can order one or more of the parties also to sign the statement of truth (CPR PD 22.3.6B).

23.8 CONSEQUENCES IF A DOCUMENT IS NOT VERIFIED BY A STATEMENT OF TRUTH

Statement of case

For a statement of case, it will remain effective (unless and until it is struck out by the court) if it is not verified by a statement of truth (CPR 22.2(1)(a), CPR PD 22.4.1). But any of the matters contained in the statement of case cannot be relied on as evidence by the party who failed to verify it with a statement of truth (CPR 22.2(1)(b), CPR PD 22.4.1). She will only be able to rely on it once it has been verified by a statement of truth (CPR PD 22.4.1).

The court can strike out a statement of case that is not verified by a statement of truth (CPR 22.2(2)). It is open to any party to apply for an order that unless within such period as the court may specify, the statement of case is verified by the service of a statement of truth, the statement of case should be struck out (CPR 22.2(3), CPR PD 22.4.2).

Witness statement

If the maker of a witness statement fails to verify the witness statement the court can, but does not have to, direct that it shall not be admissible as evidence (CPR 22.3).

23.9 PERSONS WHO ARE UNABLE TO READ OR SIGN DOCUMENTS WHERE THE DOCUMENT IS TO BE VERIFIED BY A STATEMENT OF TRUTH

If a document contains a statement of truth which is to be signed by a person who is unable to read or sign the document ('Signer'), then the document must contain a statement made by an authorised person (CPR PD 22.3A.1). An authorised person is a person who can administer oaths or take affidavits. An authorised person does not need to be independent of the parties or the parties' representatives (CPR PD 22.3A.2).

The authorised person must certify that:

- she has read the document to the Signer;
- the Signer appears to understand the document;
- the Signer has approved the contents of the document;
- the declaration of truth has been read to the Signer;
- the Signer appears to understand the declaration and the consequences of making a false declaration; and
- the Signer signed or made her mark in the presence of the authorised person.

The approved form of the certificate to be used (CPR PD 22.3A.4, CPR PD 22 Annex) is:

> I certify that I [*name and address of authorised person*] have read over the contents of this document and the declaration of truth to the person signing the document [*if there are exhibits, add* and explained the nature and effect of the exhibits referred to in it] who appeared to understand (a) the document and approved its content as accurate and (b) the declaration of truth and the consequences of making a false declaration, and made his mark in my presence.

23.10 PARTICULAR TYPES OF DOCUMENTS

Witness statements, expert reports and disclosure statements, besides being verified by a statement of truth, are also required to be formatted in particular ways and must cover certain matters.

Witness statements

A witness statement must be in a certain form (CPR 32.8 and CPR PD 32.17–25) and must have a particular format for the statement of truth (CPR 22.1, CPR PD 32.20). A witness statement is now the principal method of giving evidence at trials and other hearings (CPR 32.2, CPR 32.4, CPR 32.5 and CPR 32.6, CPR PD 32.1.2). An example of the suggested layout of a witness statement is provided at **section 23.13**.

Format

The required format for a witness statement and its content is as follows (CPR PD 32.17–19, CPR PD 32.23). It should:

- be headed with the name and number of the proceedings, the court or Division in which the proceedings are allocated;
- include at the top right hand corner of the first page the following information:

- the name of the party on whose behalf the witness statement is made;
- the initials and surname of the witness;
- the number of the statement made by the witness (e.g. the third witness statement);
- the identifying initials and number of each exhibit referred to;
- the date the witness statement was made;

- set out in the heading (if the proceedings are between parties) the names of the parties as follows:

AB (and others)	Claimants/Applicants
CD	Defendants/Respondents

- be produced on durable quality A4 (210 mm 297 mm) paper;
- have a 35 mm margin on each side;
- normally be typed on one side of the paper only;
- be fully legible;
- be bound securely, but not so as to hamper filing;
- show the case number and initials of the witness on each page;
- have each page numbered consecutively;
- be divided into numbered paragraphs;
- express numbers and dates in figures;
- include any references to other document(s) in the margin of the witness statement or in bold text in the body of the witness statement;
- use a chronological sequence for events or matters dealt with in the witness statement;
- ensure that each paragraph is confined to a distinct portion of the subject;
- be expressed in the witness's own words (where practicable);
- be expressed in the first person;
- state the full name of the witness;
- state the witness's place of residence or, if they are making the statement in a professional, business or other occupational capacity, the address at which they work, plus the position they hold and the name of the firm or employer;
- give the witness's occupation, and if they do not have one a description of their role in the proceedings (e.g. in a possession action, the tenant);
- state whether the witness is a party to the proceedings, or whether they are employed by a party to the proceedings;
- indicate which of the statements are made from the witness's own knowledge and which statements are matters of information or belief and state the source for any matters of information or belief (and not include matters of opinion or mere conjecture).

The following requirements should also be met:

- exhibits used with a witness statement must be verified and identified by the witness. Exhibits are to be kept separately from the witness statement. If the witness makes more than one witness statement, the numbering of exhibits should be consecutive and not restart with each witness statement;
- where a witness refers to an exhibit they should state 'I refer to [*description of exhibit*] marked . . .';
- if the witness statement is required to be filed, it must be filed in the court where the action in which it was or is to be used, is proceeding or will proceed (or Division, or Office or Registry of the court or Division).

Wording to commence a witness statement

Unlike for affidavits, there is no rule which specifies an exact wording to be used to commence a witness statement. The following is a suggestion for the commencement of a witness statement:

> I, [*state full name*] . . .

Statement of truth requirements

The witness statement must include a statement by the intended witness that they believe the facts stated in it are true (**CPR PD 32.20.1**) in the following form (**CPR PD 32.20.2**):

> I believe that the facts stated in this witness statement are true.

Alterations to witness statements

Alterations need to be initialled by the person making the witness statement (or an authorised person, where the person making the witness statement is unable to read or sign the document) (**CPR PD 32.22.1**). If it is not initialled then the witness statement can only be used in evidence with the permission of the court (**CPR PD 32.22.2**).

Statements of case

A statement of case can be used as evidence in an interim application provided it is verified by a statement of truth (**CPR PD 32.26.1**) in the following form (**CPR PD 32.26.2**):

> [I believe] [the [party on whose behalf the statement of case is being signed] believes] that the facts stated in the statement of case are true

Expert witnesses

Expert witnesses are required to provide their expert evidence in a report (CPR 35.5), and comply with certain requirements (CPR 35.10). One of these is to make a statement of truth which indicates that the expert understands her duty to the court and that she has complied with that duty (CPR 35.10(2)). The statement of truth signed by an expert witness differs substantially from that found in other documents.

Form and content of the report

An expert's report must (CPR 35.10, CPR PD 35.2):[10]

1. maintain professional objectivity and impartiality at all times;
2. in addressing questions of fact and opinion, keep the two separate and discrete;
3. where facts are in dispute, not express a view in favour of one or other disputed set of facts as being improbable or less probable (unless their learning and experience indicates that one set of facts is improbable or less probable, when the expert will be allowed to express a view and the reasons for that view);
4. where facts are in dispute, express separate opinions on each set of facts;
5. be addressed to the court (and not to the parties);
6. give details of the expert's qualifications; give details of any literature or other material which the expert has relied on in making the report;
7. contain a statement setting out the substance of all facts and instructions given to the expert (whether given in writing or orally) which are material to the opinions expressed in the report or upon which those opinions are based;
8. provide a chronology of the relevant events;
9. make clear which of the facts stated in the report are within the expert's own knowledge;
10. say who carried out any examination, measurement, test or experiment which the expert has used for the report, give the qualifications of that person, and say whether or not the test or experiment has been carried out under the expert's supervision;
11. where there is a range of opinion on the matters dealt with in the report:

    (a) summarise the range of opinion;
    (b) give reasons for the expert's own opinion;

12. contain a summary of the conclusions reached;

---

10 See *Protocol for the Instruction of Experts to Give Evidence in Civil Claims*, para. 13 (can be found at the end of CDR PD 35). Sample experts reports are available from the Academy of Experts or the Expert Witness Institute.

13. if the expert is not able to give their opinion without qualification, state the qualification;
14. if the opinion was not formed independently, state clearly the source of the opinion; and
15. state that the expert understands their duty to the court and has complied and will continue to comply with that duty.

Form of statement of truth

An expert's report must be verified by a statement of truth as follows (CPR PD 35.2.4):

> I confirm that insofar as the facts stated in my report are within my own knowledge I have made clear which they are and I believe them to be true, and that the opinions I have expressed represent my true and complete professional opinion.

Disclosure statement

A disclosure statement is a statement (usually in a list of documents) made by the party disclosing the documents which:

- sets out the extent of the search that has been made to locate documents which she is required to disclose;
- certifies that she understands the duty to disclose documents; and
- certifies that to the best of her knowledge she has carried out that duty (CPR 31.10(6)).

Where the party is an organisation,[11] the disclosure statement must:

- identify the person making the list; and
- explain why she is considered an appropriate person to make the statement (CPR 31.10(7)).

Every list of documents must include a disclosure statement (CPR 31.10(5), CPR PD 31.4.1).[12]

The form of the disclosure statement is:

> I, the above named claimant [or defendant] [*if party making disclosure is a company, firm or other organisation identify here who the person making the disclosure statement is and why he is the appropriate person to make it*] state that I have carried out a reasonable and proportionate search to locate all the documents which I am required to disclose under the order made by the court on _____ day of _____. I did not search:
>
> (1) for documents predating _____
> (2) for documents located elsewhere than _____
> (3) for documents in categories other than _____

---

11 That is, a company, firm, association or other organisation.
12 Normally Form N265 is used.

I certify that I understand the duty of disclosure and to the best of my knowledge I have carried out that duty. I certify that the list above is a complete list of all documents which are or have been in my control and which I am obliged under the said order to disclose.[13]

23.11   MAKING CLAIMS ONLINE (CPR 7.12)

It is possible to start a claim through electronic means, as long as only a specified sum of money (currently, less than £100,000 in sterling, excluding any interests or costs) is being claimed (CPR PD 7E.4(1), (2)).[14] A claimant must not be a child or protected party or funded by the Legal Services Commission (CPR PD 7E.4(3)). A claim must be made against a single defendant only, or two defendants if the claim is made for a single amount against each of them (CPR PD 7E.4(4)). But a defendant cannot be the Crown or a person known to be a child or a protected party (CPR PD 7E.4(5)). The defendant must have an address for service in England and Wales (CPR PD 7E.4(6)).

A claim can also be defended online, including filing an acknowledgement of service, making admissions and filing a defence or a counterclaim (CPR PD 7E.6.1)

The requirement for the statement of truth applies equally to online claims and defences and who can sign them (CPR PD 7E.11.1). But the signature is made by the claimant (or defendant as the case may be) typing her name on an online form (CPR PD 7E.12).[15]

The statement of truth for an online statement of case must be in the form of (CPR PD 7E.11.2):

[I believe/The claimant believes] that the facts stated in this claim form are true

or

[I believe/The defendant believes] that the facts stated in this defence are true.

Submitting certain court documents and applications electronically

The courts will now accept through email certain court documents and applications electronically.[16]

---

13 CPR PD 31.4.1 and Annex. Normally the form of the disclosure statement is that on Form N265.

14 The scheme for making money claims online is set out in CPR PD 7E. Claims (and defences to claims) can be commenced from here: **www.hmcourts-service.gov.uk/ onlineservices/mcol/index.htm**.

15 There appears to be no requirement for the use of digital signatures (using private/ public keys).

16 CPR 5.5. There are detailed rules (as to such matters as the format of emails, layout, content, method of dealing with attachments, rules as to when an email is considered received, etc.) for such electronic communications. See CPR PD 5b.

A party wishing to file a document electronically should print out that document and sign the statement of truth in the normal way and file it. The party should file with the court a version of the document satisfying one of the following requirements:

- the name of the person who has signed the statement of truth is typed underneath the statement;
- the person who has signed the statement of truth has applied a facsimile of their signature to the statement in the document by mechanical means; or
- the document that is filed is a scanned version of the document containing the original signature to the statement of truth.[17]

23.12 SPECIFIC RULES AND ISSUES CONCERNING A LEGAL REPRESENTATIVE

1. A legal representative can sign any document required to be verified by a statement of truth on behalf of their client except for a witness statement (CPR 22.1(6), CPR PD 22.3.7) or disclosure statement (see point 7 below).
2. The belief that the legal representative is verifying by signing the statement of truth is that of the client, not the belief of the legal representative (CPR PD 22.3.7).
3. When signing, the legal representative must state the capacity (e.g., as a solicitor) in which he signs, and the name of his firm (if relevant) (CPR PD 22.3.7).
4. When a legal representative has signed a statement of truth, the legal representative's signature will be taken by a court as a statement that:

    (a) the client on whose behalf she has signed the statement of truth has authorised the legal representative to do so;
    (b) before the legal representative signed, she explained to the client that in signing the statement of truth she would be confirming the client's belief that the facts stated in the document were true; and
    (c) before the legal representative signed, she had informed the client of the possible consequences to the client if it should subsequently appear that the client did not have an honest belief in the truth of those facts (CPR PD 22.3.8).[18]

5. A legal representative must sign the statement of truth in her name and not that of her firm or employer (CPR PD 22.3.10).

---

17 CPR PD 5B.9.
18 For more specific guidance on continuing obligations as to whether the statement remains true, consult specialist litigation material.

6. An in-house legal representative employed by a party can sign a statement of truth, but only if they are a solicitor, barrister or other authorised litigator (but not an employee of the party who reports to the solicitor, barrister or other authorised litigator working as an in-house legal representative) (CPR PD 22.3.11).[19]

7. Disclosure statements: CPR 31 and CPR PD 31 Annex clearly envisage that disclosure statements will be signed by the parties to litigation and not their solicitors. In practice, however, clients usually send case documents which they identify as relevant to their solicitor. The solicitor will then prepare a list of documents and, especially in cases where disclosure is pursuant to a case management timetable and time is of the essence, she may then be asked to sign the statement.

This practice, in the authors' experience, can create practical difficulties. Another party can raise a technical objection to a disclosure statement which is not signed by a party but signed by his solicitor on his behalf. Even if the client is willing to sign and has asked the solicitor to sign simply to meet a deadline the practice can still create the appearance that the client 'has something to hide'. Furthermore, if a solicitor is signing on behalf of the client, this will involve departing from the pro forma in CPR PD 31 Annex.

Given the extended definition of document (in CPR 31.4) and draconian sanctions for making a false disclosure statement (see CPR 31.23) the authors recommend that any solicitor who, in exceptional circumstances, is willing to sign a disclosure statement in a list of documents on behalf of her client should give prior written notification to any other party of her intention to do so and only do so if all other parties agree to waive any objection. The statement should then make it clear that the solicitor is signing on behalf of her client so as not to mislead the court.

23.13 EXAMPLE STRUCTURE OF A WITNESS STATEMENT

Filed on behalf of:
Initials and surname of witness:
Statement Number of witness:
Identifying initials and number of each exhibit:
Date signed:

---

19 This is distinguished from the situation where a solicitor in private practice has an employee. In this situation, the employee would be able to sign the statement of truth, as he would come within the definition of 'legal representative'.

IN THE [*name of court*   Case number: [*case number*]
e.g. HIGH COURT OF
JUSTICE CHANCERY
DIVISION/CENTRAL
LONDON COUNTY COURT]

                  [*full name of the*   [Claimant]
                  claimant/applicant]   [Applicant]

                  and

                  [*full name of the*   [Defendant]
                  defendant/respondent]   [Respondent]

WITNESS STATEMENT OF [*name of witness*]

1.   My full name is [*state full name*] of [*address of witness (witness's work address if witness giving evidence in professional, business or other occupational capacity)*]

Or

1.   My full name is [*state full name*]. I am employed as the [*state occupation*] of the [*list company worked for and whether a party to the action – e.g. defendant or claimant*] at [*address where based*].
2.   I am the [*claimant/defendant – if individual*] in this action and make this witness statement in [. . .] *or* e.g.
3.   I am the [*position held by witness*] for the [*responsible for what*] for the [*claimant/defendant*] etc.
4.   I believe that the facts stated in this witness statement are true.

Signed   _____

Full name   _____

Date   _____

23.14 MEANING OF CERTAIN TERMS

The meaning of certain terms used in this chapter may not be clear to the non-lawyer and are explained briefly here:

1.   A 'statement of case' includes:

    (a)   a court document to begin litigation (such as Form N1 (the claim form, to start most types of action), Form N8 (probate claims), or Form 208 (so-called 'Part 8' claims);

    (b)   a document known as the 'particulars of claim'. Often it is possible to set out the facts on the court form. If not they will be set out in the particulars of claim;

(c)   the statement of facts or responses ('defence') put forward by the person against whom a claim is made.

2.   A 'litigation friend' means a person who acts on behalf of a child (a person under 18) or a patient (a person, suffering from a mental disorder, who is not capable of handling their own affairs) during litigation.

3.   A 'legal representative' includes a solicitor and the employee of a solicitor or barrister who has been instructed to act for a party.

CHAPTER 24

Affidavits

24.1 INTRODUCTION

An affidavit is a document containing a statement of evidence to be used for litigation purposes which is verified by the oath or solemn affirmation of the maker.[1] The oath or affirmation has to be taken before a person authorised to administer oaths for the relevant purpose. It is distinguished from most other documents used in litigation by the fact that it needs to be sworn by an oath or affirmed. An affidavit is defined as 'a written sworn statement of evidence' in the glossary to the Civil Procedure Rules (CPR).

The mandatory use of affidavits is now very limited. In a few specified circumstances, an affidavit can be used as an alternative to a witness statement.

For most litigation purposes a document verified by a statement of truth is the appropriate form in which evidence or facts are adduced (whether or not in the form of a witness statement), whether at trial or in statements of case or in applications to the court (CPR 32.2 and 32.5; see also **Chapter 23**). However, there is nothing to stop a person using an affidavit if they so wish (although there may be certain cost implications if they do) (CPR 32.15, CPR PD 32.1.2).

The above statements do not apply to non-contentious probate matters, where the use of affidavits is still extensive.

24.2 WHEN MUST AN AFFIDAVIT BE USED?

An affidavit must be used in the following circumstances.

---

1 However, there are a few, limited, circumstances when an affidavit has to be used for a non-litigation purpose; see further below.

Generally

Affidavits must be used:

- where sworn evidence is required by any enactment, rule, order or Practice Direction (CPR PD 32.1.4, e.g. Protection from Harassment Act 1997, s.3(5));
- where a court gives a direction that evidence shall be given by affidavit instead of or in addition to a witness statement or statement of case either on the court's own initiative or after a party has applied to the court for such a direction (CPR 32.15, CPR PD 32.1.6).

Some specific situations

These include:

- an application for a freezing injunction (CPR PD 32.1.4(2), CPR 25.1(f), (g) and CPR PD 25.3.1);
- an application for a search order (CPR PD 32.1.4(2), CPR 25.1(f), (g) and CPR PD 25.3.1);
- an order requiring an occupier to permit another to enter his land (CPR PD 32.1.4(2));
- an application for the issue of an arrest warrant for a defendant who has breached an injunction restraining that defendant from pursuing any conduct which amounts to harassment (Protection from Harassment Act 1997, s.3(5), CPR 65.29);
- an application by a judgment creditor applying for an order requiring a judgment debtor to attend court to provide information about the judgment debtor's means or any other matter about which information is needed to enforce a judgment or order (CPR 71.5);
- an application for an order against anyone for alleged contempt of court (CPR PD 32.1.4(3));
- committal proceedings (RSC Order 52, CCR Order 29);
- an application for summary judgment against a state;
- a divorce or judicial separation petition (Family Proceedings Rules 1991 (FPR 1991), r.2.24(3));
- an application for failure to provide reasonable maintenance (FPR 1991, r.3.1(2));
- an application under the Married Women's Property Act 1881 (FPR 1991, r.3.6(1));

- an application to make a minor a ward of court (FPR 1991, r.5.1(1));
- certain statements and documents relating to insolvency proceedings can only be made by affidavit (Insolvency Rules 1986 (IR 1986), r.7.57):[2]

  - various applications (e.g. for conversion, for administration) (IR 1986, rr.1.32, 2.2, 2.11);
  - statements of affairs (Insolvency Act 1986 (IA 1986), ss.47, 66, 98, 99, 131; IR 1986, rr.3.4, 4.33, 6.60);
  - further disclosure (IR 1986, rr.4.42, 6.66, 6.72);
  - accounts (IR 1986, rr.4.39, 4.40, 6.65, 6.70);
  - claims (IR 1986, rr.4.73, 4.77, 6.96, 6.99);
  - examinations (IR 1986, rr.9.3, 9.4);
  - certain other documents or statements which can be verified by affidavit or witness statement (IR 1986, r.7.57(5));

- an application by a solicitor to, among other things, seek restoration to the roll of solicitors kept by the Law Society or have her period of suspension terminated (Solicitors (Disciplinary Proceedings) Rules 1994, r.4(1)(c), (d));
- an application for an injunction to prevent environmental harm under Town and Country Planning Act 1990, ss.187B, 214A or Planning (Listed Buildings and Conservation Areas) Act 1990, s.44A or Planning (Hazardous Substances) Act 1990, s.26AA (RSC Order 110); this can also be made in the form of a witness statement;
- an application for a confiscation order under Drug Trafficking Act 1994 (RSC Order 115); this can also be made in the form of a witness statement.

Non-litigation situations

Affidavits are used for the purposes of the Bills of Sale Act 1878 (s.11, Sched. A).

Non-contentious probate matters

Note that:

- every application for a grant is to be supported by an oath by the applicant in the form applicable to the circumstances of the case (Non-Contentious Probate Rules 1987 (NCPR 1987, r.8);

---

2 Where an affidavit is specified in IR 1986 other than in the rules that follow in the list, a witness statement can be used instead. IR 1986, r.57(3) permits a creditor's affidavit of debt to be sworn before the creditor's own solicitor.

- unless a district judge or registrar otherwise directs, every oath or affidavit required on a personal application must be sworn or executed by all the Deponents before an authorised officer (NCPR 1987, r.5(7));[3]
- if:
  - there is no attestation clause; or
  - it is insufficient; or
  - a district judge has doubt about the due execution of a will,

  before admitting it to proof, the district judge can require an affidavit as to due execution from one or more of the attesting witnesses. If there are no attesting witnesses conveniently available, an affidavit may be required from any other person who was present when the will was executed (NCPR 1987, r.12(1)).[4]

The use of affidavits in non-contentious probate matters is still extensive, although in only one circumstance is there a specified form (NCPR 1987, Sched. 1, Form 1). It appears that the majority have been developed by custom and acceptance by the courts.[5]

The CPR do not extend to non-contentious probate proceedings (CPR 2.1), which means, among other things, that:

- the rules and the form of an affidavit that are specified below do not apply to non-contentious probate proceedings; and
- evidence is not given in a witness statement verified by statement of truth.

The former rules relating to civil litigation prior to the introduction of the Civil Procedure Rules still apply (NCPR 1987, r.3).[6]

24.3 WHO CAN MAKE AN AFFIDAVIT?

By implication, rather than direct rule, an affidavit can only be made by an individual.[7] The person making the affidavit is known as 'the Deponent'

---

3 'Authorised officer' means any officer of a registry who is for the time being authorised by the President of the Probate Division to administer any oath or to take any affidavit required for any purpose connected with his duties.
4 A district judge or registrar has discretion as to this evidence if the distribution of the estate will not be affected (NCPR 1987, r.12(3)). A statutory declaration may also be used as to the execution of a will (SDA 1835, s.16).
5 There is an extensive set of precedents in Appendix VI to *Tristram and Coote's Probate Practice*, 30th edn, LexisNexis Butterworths, 2006.
6 RSC Order 41 continues to apply. Although the requirements are similar to those under the CPR, there are differences. Because of the specialised nature of the topic, readers should consult *Tristram and Coote's Probate Practice*, 30th edn, LexisNexis Butterworths, 2006, ch. 22, and more generally, *Guide to Oaths and Affirmations*, 2nd edn, Law Society, ch. 2.
7 Such as CPR PD 32.4.1 stating that the affidavit should be expressed in the first person, in the maker's own words.

(CPR PD 32.2). More than one person can make the same affidavit (CPR PD 32.5.2).

24.4 REQUIREMENTS FOR AN AFFIDAVIT

An affidavit must be in a certain form (CPR 32.16 and CPR PD at paras. 2–16) and be signed and witnessed in a particular way (CPR PD 32.5.1, 32.5.2) for most civil litigation. These requirements are all now specified in a particular Civil Procedure Rule and the Practice Direction to that Rule.[8] An example of the suggested layout of, and the back-sheet to, an affidavit is provided at the end of this chapter.

Format

The required format and content for an affidavit are as follows. It should (CPR PD 32.6.1, 32.6.2):

- be produced on durable quality A4 (210 mm × 297 mm) paper;
- have a 35 mm margin on each side;
- normally be typed on one side of the paper only;
- be fully legible;
- where possible, be bound securely (but not so as to hamper filing) or otherwise each page should have the case number and initials of the Deponent and the person before whom the affidavit was sworn;
- have each page numbered consecutively;
- be divided into numbered paragraphs;
- express all numbers and dates in figures;
- include any references to other document(s) in the margin of the affidavit or in bold text in the body of the affidavit;
- use a chronological sequence for events or matters dealt with in the affidavit;
- ensure that, where possible, each paragraph is confined to a distinct portion of the subject;
- be expressed in the Deponent's own words (where practicable);[9]
- be expressed in the first person;
- commence with the words 'I [*full name of Deponent*] of [*address of Deponent*] [state on oath] [do solemnly and sincerely affirm]', unless the

---

8 What follows is an outline of the CPR requirements for an affidavit. The practicalities of, and issues involved in, the drafting and using of affidavits is outside the remit of this book. For example, the CPR have more detailed provisions regarding the handling and marking of exhibits (CPR PD 32.12–15).
9 An affidavit is not to be used as a vehicle for complex legal argument and an affidavit is to be used for the purpose of the Deponent's saying in their own words what their relevant evidence was: *Alex Lawrie Factors Ltd* v. *Morgan*, *The Times*,18 August 1999, CA.

Deponent is giving evidence in his professional, business or other occupational capacity, in which case he should give his business address, the position he holds and the name of his employer;

- give the Deponent's occupation, and if he does not have one a description of his role in the proceedings (e.g. in a possession action, the tenant);[10]
- state whether the Deponent is a party to the proceedings, or whether he is employed by a party to the proceedings;
- indicate which of the statements are made from the Deponent's own knowledge and which statements are matters of information or belief and state the source for any matters of information or belief;
- in the body of the affidavit, when referring to an exhibit, state 'there is now shown to me marked . . . the [*description of exhibit*]' (and if making more than one affidavit in the same proceedings, the numbering of the exhibits should run consecutively throughout and not start again with each affidavit).

If the affidavit is required to be filed, it must be filed in the court where the action in which it was or is to be used is proceeding or will proceed.[11]

Wording to commence an affidavit

Oaths

The wording to commence an affidavit to be sworn by oath (CPR PD 32.4.1(1) is:

I, [*full name*], of [*address*] state on oath

Affirmation

The wording to commence an affidavit to be affirmed is (CPR PD 32.16, OA 1978, s.6(2)):

I, [*full name*], of [*address*] do solemnly and sincerely affirm

Signature and witnessing requirements

The *signature block* is known as the 'jurat' (CPR PD 32.5.1).[12] The purpose of the jurat is to authenticate the affidavit (CPR PD 32.5.1). It must (CPR PD 32.5.2):

---

10 If an official receiver or the responsible insolvency practitioner is the Deponent, then the Deponent is to state the capacity in which she makes it, the position which she holds and the address at which she works: IR 1986, r.7.57(2).
11 Or Division, or Office or Registry of the court or Division.
12 The word 'jurat', technically, refers only to affidavits which are sworn by an oath, but will be used here for an affidavit either sworn by oath or made by an affirmation.

- be signed by the Deponent (or if more than one, all the Deponents);
- be signed by the Commissioner;
- state the name and qualification of the Commissioner (in print type);
- contain the full address of the Commissioner.

A Commissioner for Oaths is required to state in the jurat at which place and on what date the oath was administered or the affirmation was taken (Courts and Legal Services Act 1990 (CLSA 1990), s.113(6) and Solicitors Act 1974 (SA 1974), s.81(3)). The jurat should follow on immediately from the body of the affidavit and should not be put on a separate page from the body of the affidavit (CPR PD 32.5.2(4)). There appears to be no specified wording to be used for the jurat when an oath is sworn except as specified above. This is not the case for an affirmation where the specified words to be used instead of a jurat are: 'Affirmed at this day of [*month and year*], before me' (Oaths Act 1978 (OA 1978), s.6(2)).[13]

24.5   SWORN OR AFFIRMED

It is possible either to swear an oath (give 'evidence by affidavit') or make an affirmation (CPR PD 32.1.7, 2 and 16). An affirmation has the same force and effect as an oath (OA 1978, s.5(4)).

Oaths

The CPR do not set out the oath that is to be sworn or the affirmation to be made. This is set out in OA 1978. The default position is that the Deponent shall take a prescribed oath (OA 1978, s.1(1)):

> The person taking the oath shall hold the New Testament, or, in the case of a Jew, the Old Testament, in his uplifted hand, and shall say or repeat after the officer administering the oath the words 'I swear by Almighty God that . . .,' followed by the words of the oath prescribed by law.

There appear to be no 'words of the oath prescribed by law'. The customary words used are:

> I swear by Almighty God that this is my name and handwriting and that the contents of this my affidavit are true [and that these are the exhibits referred to therein].

The default position is that the Commissioner shall administer the oath in the form specified above, unless the Deponent voluntarily objects or is physically incapable of taking an oath (OA 1978, s.1(2)).

---

13 The suggested *signature block* in **Chapter 12** gives one possible layout for both oaths and affirmations.

If the person is neither a Christian nor a Jew, the oath can be administered in any lawful manner (OA 1978, s.1(3)).

The fact that a Deponent has no religious belief shall not affect the validity of the oath that she or he takes (OA 1978, s.4(2)).

Although an oath may have been administered in a form and manner other than prescribed by law to the Deponent, the Deponent will be bound by the oath as if it had been administered in such form and with such ceremonies as the Deponent may have declared binding (OA 1978, s.4(1)).

Affirmations

A Deponent is permitted to make an affirmation rather than an oath, whether under the CPR or under OA 1978.

The default position, as stated above, is that a Commissioner shall administer an oath. However, a Deponent may make an affirmation instead of an oath in certain situations. For example, where the Deponent objects to swearing an oath (OA 1978, s.5(1)), or where it is not reasonably practicable (without inconvenience or delay) to administer an oath in the manner appropriate to the Deponent's religious belief (OA 1978, s.5(2)).

The form of affirmation required (OA 1978, s.6(1)) is:

> I, _____ do solemnly, sincerely and truly declare and affirm,

and then proceed with the words of the oath prescribed by law, omitting any words of imprecation or calling to witness.

As for oaths, there appear to be no 'words of the oath prescribed by law'. The customary words used are:

> I [name of Deponent], do solemnly, sincerely and truly declare and affirm that this is my name and handwriting and that the contents of this my affirmation are true [and that these are the exhibits referred to therein].

Persons authorised to administer an oath or take an affirmation

The following are the persons who are authorised to administer an oath or take an affirmation in relation to an affidavit:[14]

- Commissioners for Oaths, comprising:

  - solicitors (holding a current practising certificate);
  - barristers;
  - notaries public (but not ecclesiastical notaries);
  - licensed conveyancers;

---

14 The more technical aspects of the persons fulfilling these roles are considered in **Chapters 26** and **27**.

- Fellows of the Institute of Legal Executives (if they pay a full subscription to the Institute; but not retired Fellows);[15]
- certain officials of the Supreme Court (COA 1889, s.2);
- circuit judges or district judges (County Courts Act 1984 (CCA 1984), s.58);
- justices of the peace (CCA 1984, s.58);
- certain officials of any county court appointed by the judge of that court for the purpose (CCA 1984, s.58);
- official receivers or deputy official receivers (IR 1986, r.7.57(4)).

Affidavits must be sworn before a person who must be independent of the parties or their representatives

The above persons cannot administer an oath or take an affidavit unless they are independent of the parties or any of the parties' representatives (CPR PD 32.9.2).

There are similar rules for Commissioners for Oaths, who may not administer an oath or take an affirmation in proceedings in which they are interested (COA 1889, s.1(3); SA 1974, s.81(2) and CLSA 1990, s.113(5)). There is one exception to this principle, that a creditor can make an affidavit of debt before her own solicitor (IR 1986, r.7.57(3)).

24.6 ALTERATIONS TO AFFIDAVITS

Any alteration to an affidavit must be initialled both by the Deponent and by the person before whom the affidavit is sworn or affirmed (CPR PD 32.8.1). If the affidavit has not been initialled it can only be used in evidence with the permission of the court.

24.7 EXAMPLE STRUCTURE OF AN AFFIDAVIT

Filed on behalf of:
Initials and surname of deponent:
Affidavit Number of deponent:
Identifying initials and number of each exhibit:
Date sworn:

IN THE [*name of court*   Case number: [*case number*]
e.g. HIGH COURT OF JUSTICE CHANCERY DIVISION/CENTRAL LONDON COUNTY COURT]

15 See further **Chapters 12** and **26** and COA 1889 and 1891.

[*full name of the*   [Claimant]
claimant/applicant]   [Applicant]

and

[*full name of the*   [Defendant]
defendant/respondent]   [Respondent]

AFFIDAVIT OF [*name of deponent*]

I, [*name of Deponent*], of [*address of Deponent* (*Deponent's work address if Deponent giving evidence in professional, business or other occupational capacity*)], [state on oath] [do solemnly and sincerely affirm]:

1. I am the [claimant/defendant – *if individual*] in this action and make this affidavit in [*e.g.*, in support of my application for. . .]

or, e.g.

1. I am the [*position held by Deponent*] for the [*responsible for what*] for the [*claimant/defendant*] etc.
2. I make this affidavit from facts that are [within my own knowledge] [based on information provided to me by [. . .]] [based on my belief]. [The facts and matters set out in this affidavit are, save where the contrary appears, within my own knowledge and are true. Where such facts and matters are not within my own personal knowledge they are true to the best of my information and belief, and derive from the source stated.]
3. [. . .]

[SWORN] [AFFIRMED] at [*address*
where the affidavit is sworn] the   }   (signature of deponent)
[*day*] of [*month*] [*year*]

Before me   (signature of person before whom affidavit is sworn)
                   (*name of person before whom affidavit is sworn*)
                   (*qualification of person before whom affidavit is*
                   sworn – e.g. Solicitor/Commissioner for Oaths etc.)
                   (*address of person before whom affidavit is sworn*)

Backsheet

Filed on behalf of
Initials and surname of deponent
Affidavit Number of deponent
Identifying initials and number of each exhibit
Date sworn

IN THE [*name of court*   Case number: [*case number*]
e.g. HIGH COURT OF
JUSTICE CHANCERY
DIVISION/CENTRAL
LONDON COUNTY COURT]

[*full name of the*   [Claimant]
claimant/applicant]   [Applicant]

and

[*full name of the*   [Defendant]
defendant/respondent]   [Respondent]

AFFIDAVIT OF [*name of Deponent*]

PART III

Specific issues

CHAPTER 25

Electronic signatures

25.1 INTRODUCTION

UK legislation expressly permits the recognition of electronic communications and electronic and digital signatures, based on EU Directives.[1] Much activity takes place through the use of electronic communications, including email, exchange of electronic documents and electronic commerce . However, only in the sphere of electronic commerce is the use of electronically and digitally signed communications commonplace.[2] Although it might be fair to write that the infrastructure is in place to obtain and use a digital signature, it is unlikely that many commercial contracts are concluded or emails are sent using digital signatures.[3] This chapter provides an outline of the law concerning:

- electronic signatures at present; and
- electronic conveyancing, because of its importance to the legal profession.[4]

---

1 Electronic Signatures Directive (1999/93/EC) and Electronic Commerce Directive (2000/31/EC).
2 Perhaps because the setting up of a secure communication is handled automatically as far as the user is concerned, having done no more than register (and then use) a user name and password, whereas obtaining a digital signature requires additional steps, such as contacting (and subscribing to and paying) a third party to obtain the digital signature, possibly using a hardware device to enable its use (such as a smartcard), and ensuring its use in every communication (as well installing/enabling its use in the software a user uses). See also *Report on the Operation of Directive 1999/93/EC on a Community Framework for Electronic Signatures*, COM(2006) 120 final, 15 March 2006 and press release IP/06/325, 17 March 2006, concerning the uptake of digital signatures.
3 For example, a full electronic conveyancing system, including the use of digital signatures, is at least two years away and may not be fully implemented until 2010, but it is possible for certain persons to file certain documents electronically with the Land Registry (but a digital signature is not involved in so doing). Also certain services from the government (see **www.gateway.gov.uk**) are available if the person using the service has a digital signature (filing a VAT return online, applying for child benefit, applying for an export licence), but these are unlikely to impact greatly on the day-to-day activities of executing a document.
4 It is hoped that in a future edition of this book a more detailed section on electronic signatures will be provided when there is further implementation of the use of digital signatures affecting a wider range of contracts, events and transactions. For users of this book, there are several sources of information to learn more about electronic and digital

25.2 IMPLEMENTING LEGISLATION

The basis of the United Kingdom's law in relation to electronic communications and electronic signatures is the Electronic Signatures Directive ('the Directive').[5] Electronic Communications Act 2000 (ECA 2000)[6] and Electronic Signatures Regulations 2002, SI 2002/318 (ESR 2002)[7] are the main implementing measures in the United Kingdom.

In summary:

1. ECA 2000:

    (a) makes electronic signatures admissible in evidence in legal proceedings; and

    (b) enables ministers:

        (i) to amend legislation to permit the usage of electronic communications; and

        (ii) to allow documents to be signed or executed in ways other than in writing and by signing (ECA 2000, s.8).[8]

2. ESR 2002 make provisions relating to:

    (a) the supervision of digital signature service providers;

    (b) their liability in certain circumstances;

    (c) certain data protection requirements on them.

25.3 WHAT IS AN 'ELECTRONIC SIGNATURE'?

An electronic signature can perform essentially the same role as a manuscript signature:

(a) a person's or body corporate's method of identifying themselves as the author or creator of the electronic data to which the electronic signature is attached; and/or

---

signatures. Perhaps the most comprehensive and up to date, at the date material for this book was prepared, is Mason, *Electronic Signatures in Law*, Butterworths, 2003, which will also give readers some understanding of the technical issues involved, and particularly the complex evidential problems involved if an electronic or digital signature is challenged.

5 Directive 1999/93 of the European Parliament and the Council of 13 December 1999 on a Community framework for electronic signatures.

6 Relevant sections of ECA 2000 came into force on 25 July 2000: SI 2000/1798, art. 2.

7 Came into force on 8 March 2002, ESR 2002, reg. 1.

8 This is an additional method, not a replacement for using the traditional method of writing, signing, etc. For example, Land Registration Act 2002 (LRA 2002), s.91, permits in addition to current methods of disposition of a registered estate by deed, disposition to take place through the use of an electronic document and electronic signatures. The specific requirements are set out later on in this chapter.

(b)   authenticating the electronic data to which the electronic signature is attached; and/or

(c)   agreeing or approving the contents of the electronic data to which the electronic signature is attached.

The term 'electronic signature' normally means a generic, technology-neutral, description of a variety of electronic methods for 'signing' some other data. A digital signature is differentiated from other forms of electronic signature primarily by the use of certain technical means (encryption and a password (or 'key')). Its authenticity is guaranteed by a third party, with the third party having validated the signatory and issued to the signatory a form of electronic certificate. In short, a digital signature should be thought of as a more secure form of electronic signature.

Legislation in the United Kingdom (and elsewhere) has tended to focus on authenticating the identity of the individual or organisation and not the electronic document to which the electronic signature is attached.

Examples of electronic signatures

The following are examples of electronic signatures:

- typing the name of a person at the bottom of an email, word-processing document, or on a web page;
- a manuscript signature that is scanned and becomes a graphic image that is inserted into a document;
- the clicking of an 'I accept' button or icon on a web page, where the intention is to enter into a legal obligation, usually a contract to purchase some goods or services;
- the use of a digital signature.

25.4   STATUTORY DEFINITION OF AN ELECTRONIC SIGNATURE

An electronic signature is (ECA 2000, s.7(2)):

so much of anything in electronic form as:

(a)   is incorporated into or otherwise logically associated with any electronic communication or electronic data; and

(b)   purports to be so incorporated or associated for the purpose of being used in establishing the authenticity of the communication or data, the integrity of the communication or data, or both.

Meaning of 'electronic communication'

An electronic communication means a communication (ECA 2000, s.15(1)):

transmitted (whether from one person to another, from one device to another or from a person to a device or vice versa) –

(a) by means of a telecommunication system (within the meaning of the Telecommunications Act 1984); or

(b) by other means but while in an electronic form; . . .

Meaning of 'authenticity of any communication or data'

The meaning of 'authenticity of any communication or data' in ECA 2000, s.15(2)(a), when considering the meaning of, and the admissibility in evidence in civil litigation of, an electronic signature relates primarily to whether the communication or data comes from a particular person:

references to the authenticity of any communication or data are references to any one or more of the following –

(i) whether the communication or data comes from a particular person or other source;

(ii) whether it is accurately timed and dated;

(iii) whether it is intended to have legal effect; . . .

Meaning of 'integrity of any communication or data'

A reference to integrity of any communication or data is a reference 'to whether there has been any tampering with or other modification of the communication or data' (ECA 2000, s.15(2)(b)).

Points to note

The following points should be noted in relation to the meaning given to an electronic signature in the above definition:

- it does not deal with the issue of what constitutes a genuine electronic signature;
- it does not deal with whether or when an electronic signature will have the necessary (authenticating) purpose;
- the evidential weight of an electronic signature is left to a court;
- it does not specify whether an electronic signature can satisfy signature requirements found in statute;[9]
- the burden of showing that a document is signed or not signed electronically may shift from the person who receives the signed document to the signatory.[10]

9 *Electronic Commerce: Formal Requirements in Commercial Transactions, Advice from the Law Commission*, December 2001, para. 3.27: ECA 2000, s.7: 'does not, therefore, assist in determining to what extent existing statutory signature requirements are capable of being satisfied electronically'.

10 See e.g., Mason, *Electronic Signatures in Law*, Butterworths, 2003, ch. 8, for examples of the implications of this proposition, and in particular his discussion of this point in relation to one order made under ECA 2000, s.8, Social Security (Electronic Communications) (Child Benefit) Order 2002, SI 2002/1789, at paras. 8.79–8.85.

25.5   STATUTORY DEFINITION OF A 'DIGITAL SIGNATURE'

The Directive, ECA 2000 and ESR 2002 do not use the words 'digital signature'.[11] They use the following terminology:

- an advanced electronic signature based on
- a qualified certificate, and which is created by
- a certification service provider;
- a secure signature-creation device with the qualified certificate being provided.

Meaning of 'advanced electronic signature'

An advanced electronic signature means an electronic signature (ESR 2002, reg. 2):

- which is uniquely linked to the signatory;
- which is capable of identifying the signatory;
- which is created using means that the signatory can maintain under his sole control; and
- which is linked to the data to which it relates, so that any subsequent change of the data is detectable.

Meaning of a 'qualified certificate'

A qualified certificate is provided by a certification-service-provider and the certificate must contain (ESR 2002, Sched. 1):

- an indication that the certificate is issued as a qualified certificate;
- the identification of the certification service provider and the state in which it is established;
- the name of the signatory or a pseudonym, which shall be identified as such;
- provision for a specific attribute of the signatory to be included if relevant, depending on the purpose for which the certificate is intended;
- signature-verification data which correspond to signature-creation data under the control of the signatory;
- an indication of the beginning and end of the period of validity of the certificate;
- the identity code of the certificate;
- the advanced electronic signature of the certification service provider issuing it;
- limitations on the scope of use of the certificate, if applicable; and

---

11 'Digital signature' is used in this chapter for the sake of convenience.

- limits on the value of transactions for which the certificate can be used, if applicable.

Meaning of a 'certification service provider'

A certification service provider means a person who issues certificates or provides other services related to electronic signatures and such persons must meet set standards for the quality of the service they provide, the staff they employ, the security of their systems, etc. (ESR 2002, reg. 2, Sched. 1).

Meaning of a 'signature-creation device'

A signature-creation device means configured software or hardware used to implement the signature-creation data (ESR 2002, reg. 2). Signature-creation data is data (including, but not limited to, codes or private cryptographic keys) which are used by the signatory to create an electronic signature.

25.6 ELECTRONIC SIGNATURES TO BE EFFECTIVE AS MANUSCRIPT SIGNATURES

The Directive provides that Member States are to ensure that:

- a digital signature is to satisfy the legal requirements of a signature in relation to data in electronic form in the same manner as a handwritten signature satisfies those requirements in relation to paper-based data (Directive, Art. 5(1));[12] and
- an electronic signature is not to be denied legal effectiveness solely on the grounds that is in electronic form or is not a digital signature (Directive, Art. 5(2)).

Points to note

1. The legal recognition of digital signatures and the legal effectiveness of electronic signatures provisions found in the Directive have not been translated into ECA 2000 or ESR 2002. It is assumed that they were already recognised in law.
2. The wording of the Directive appears to accord a higher status to digital signatures than to electronic signatures, but ECA 2000 does not draw a distinction between the two as far as admissibility in evidence is concerned (see below).

---

12 A digital signature being expressed in the following terms: 'advanced electronic signatures which are based on a qualified certificate and which are created by a secure-signature-creation device'. These terms are defined above.

3.   The Directive indicates that a digital signature is to be legally effective as a handwritten signature, but does not consider the legal effectiveness of a handwritten signature. ECA 2000 also does not deal with the legal effectiveness of a handwritten signature.

Admissibility of electronic signatures in evidence in legal proceedings

In legal proceedings an electronic signature is admissible in evidence where the electronic signature is incorporated into or logically associated with a particular electronic communication or particular electronic data. The electronic signature so incorporated or logically associated will be admissible in relation to any question as to the authenticity of the communication or data or as to the integrity of the communication or data. The certification by any person of such a signature is also admissible.[13]

25.7   ABILITY OF GOVERNMENT MINISTERS TO AMEND LEGISLATION TO PERMIT ELECTRONIC COMMUNICATIONS

Ministers are given powers to make orders to modify the provisions of any Act or statutory instrument[14] to authorise or facilitate the use of electronic communications for certain purposes (ECA 2000, s.8(1)).[15] These purposes are (ECA 2000, s.8(2)(a)–(g)):

- the doing of anything that under any such provisions is required to be or may be done or evidenced in writing or otherwise using a document, notice or instrument;
- the doing of anything which under any such provisions is required to be or may be done by post or other specified means of delivery;
- the doing of anything that under any such provisions is required to be or may be authorised by a person's signature or seal, or is required to be delivered as a deed or witnessed;

---

13 'Certification' means that a person has made a statement confirming that: the signature, a means of producing, communicating or verifying the signature, or a procedure applied to the signature is (either alone or in combination with other factors) a valid means of establishing the authenticity of the communication or data, the integrity of the communication or data, or both: ECA 2000, s.7(3). ECA 2000 does not deal further with digital signatures. The definition of, and the framework for regulation of, digital signatures is dealt with in the Regulations.
14 And any scheme, licence, authorisation or approval issued, granted or made by or under any such legislation.
15 A minister cannot make an order under this section unless he considers that the authorisation is such that the extent to which records of things done for that purpose will be available will be no less satisfactory in cases where use is made of electronic communications is limited: ECA 2000, s.8(3).

- the making of any statement or declaration which under any such provisions is required to be made under oath or to be contained in a statutory declaration;
- the keeping, maintenance or preservation, for the purposes or in pursuance of any such provisions, of any account, record, notice, instrument or other document;
- the provision, production or publication under any such provisions of any information or other matter;
- the making of any payment that is required to be or may be made under any such provisions.

Ministers can determine several issues to include in a statutory instrument including:

- the power to specify the electronic form to be taken by any electronic communications (ECA 2000, s.8(4)(a));
- determining criminal and other liabilities (ECA 2000, s.8(4)(i));
- provision, in relation to cases in which the use of electronic communications or electronic storage is so authorised, for the determination of any of the matters mentioned in ECA 2000, s.8(5), or as to the manner in which they may be proved in legal proceedings (ECA 2000, s.8(4)(g)).

The matters set out in ECA 2000, s.8(5)(a)–(e) are:

- whether a thing has been done using an electronic communication or electronic storage;
- the time at which, or date on which, a thing done using any such communication or storage was done;
- the place where a thing done using such communication or storage was done;
- the person by whom such a thing was done; and
- the contents, authenticity or integrity of any electronic data.

Orders made

Orders have been made under ECA 2000. Most of the orders give general powers for the use of electronic communications to ministers, but do not specify in detail how such powers will be used. Not all of them specify the use of electronic signatures. More than 60 orders have been made since the implementation of ECA 2000.[16]

---

16 For an outline of the details of some of the orders made, see the authors' section 'Electronic Communications and Electronic Signatures' in *Encyclopaedia of Forms and Precedents*, vol. 12(2), 'Deeds', paras. 3301–3659.

25.8   USE OF ELECTRONIC COMMUNICATIONS AND TAX LEGISLATION

There are separate powers under Finance Act 1999 (FA 1999) which also permit the use of electronic communications concerning:

- the delivery of information where it is required to be provided to the tax authorities by or under any legislation relating to a taxation matter;
- the making of payments under any such legislation.[17]

FA 1999 allows regulations to be made on the implementation of the powers to permit electronic communications, much in the same way as under ECA 2000, except that the powers permitted under FA 1999 are generally wider and include power to make regulations dealing with the following:

- authorising the use of electronic communications for the delivery of information and the making of payments to and from the tax authorities;
- the form in which information is to be provided electronically to the tax authorities;
- requiring a person to prepare and keep records of information which are to be supplied to the tax authorities by electronic means (as well as requiring the individual to provide those records);
- determining at what time information is delivered or a payment is made;
- specifying the conditions that need to be fulfilled for information to be delivered or a payment to be made;
- determining who is deemed to be delivering information or making a payment.

The powers provided under FA 1999 'shall also include power to make such provision as the persons exercising the power think fit (including provision for the application of conclusive or other presumptions) as to the manner of proving for any purpose' whether the use of electronic communications is taken to have resulted in the delivery of information or making of payment, the timing of delivery of information contained in an electronic communication, etc.[18] A number of orders have been made under FA 1999, covering matters relating to income tax, child benefit, Stamp Duty Land Tax and lottery duty.[19]

---

17 FA 1999, s.132(1).
18 FA 1999, s.132(4).
19 For details on the principal orders made under FA 1999, consult 'Electronic Communications and Electronic Signatures' in *Encyclopaedia of Forms and Precedents*, vol. 12(2), 'Deeds', para. 1340.

Electronic conveyancing

Currently much of the process of conveying land and interests in land remains paper-based.[20] The government has enacted legislation to enable the conveyancing process to be done electronically, which would, *inter alia*, involve disapplying existing provisions (LP(MP)A 1989, s.2 and LPA 1925, s.52(1)) that require contracts for the sale of land to be in writing and signed and for transfers and legal charges to be executed on paper as deeds.

The legislative framework for the use of electronic communications and facilitating of electronic conveyancing is found in ECA 2000, Land Registration Act 2002 (LRA 2002) and Land Registration Rules 2003.

The aim of LRA 2002 is to permit all steps in the conveyancing process to be carried out electronically, from carrying out searches, investigation of title, the drafting, amending and signing of contracts of sale and exchange of contracts, to the making of payments from buyer to seller (and involving the mortgagee as well).

There are intended to be three key elements:

- The Land Registry will be at the centre of the electronic conveyancing project. It will be in control of and run a secure communications system.
- Solicitors and others involved in the conveyancing process will have access to this information system (subject to meeting conditions of access).
- Funds will be transferred electronically among all the members of the electronic communications system.

At the time of material for this book was prepared, much of the more advanced parts of the Land Registry proposals remained to be completed, with a full system not due to be implemented until 2010. At present, electronic access to Land Registry records (obtaining official copies, making searches), providing documents to the Land Registry (such as notification of change of address, application to cancel a caution, etc.) and notifications of discharge (which mortgagees can do) are available. However, much of the work involved in implementing the necessary changes is still to be done, including making changes to applicable primary legislation such as LP(MP)A 1989.[21]

---

20 For example, contracts for sale or other disposition in land can only be made in writing and signed by all the parties (LP(MP)A 1989, s.2) and conveyances of land need to be by deed (LPA 1925, s.52(1)).

21 For further details, see **www.landregistry.gov.uk**. It appears that the original implementation plans have been delayed and, according to the Land Registry, in 2008 they will be focusing on delivery of electronic charges and electronic discharges, and preparing for electronic transfers in 2009. Two key areas of difficulty are the type of technology to be used to enable secure communications between the Land Registry, solicitors and others, and providing a system for the movement of electronic funds between all the organisations and persons involved in the conveyancing process. At the time material for this book was prepared, neither of these issues had reached a definitive solution.

Part 8 of LRA 2002 sets out the framework to allow dispositions to be done in an electronic format. An order under ECA 2000 would also need to be made to allow contracts for the sale or other disposition of land under LP(MP)A 1989, s.2 to be done in an electronic format.[22]

LRA 2002, s.91,[23] provides that a document in electronic form can be used where it concerns a disposition:

- of a registered estate or charge;
- of an interest that is the subject of a notice in the register; or
- that triggers the requirement of registration (LRA 2002, s.91(2)(a)–(c))

subject to certain conditions being met, that:

- the document makes provision for the time and date when it takes effect;
- the document has the electronic signature of each person by whom it purports to be authenticated;
- each electronic signature is certified; and
- such other conditions as rules may provide are met (LRA 2002, s.91(3)(a)–(d)).[24]

A document to which LRA 2002, s.91 applies is regarded:

- as being in writing and signed by each individual and sealed by each corporation, whose electronic signature it has (LRA 2002, s.91(4)); or
- for the purposes of any enactment as a deed (LRA 2002, s.91(5)).

A document in electronic form authenticated by an agent is assumed to be authenticated by her under the written authority of her principal (LRA 2002, s.91(6)).[25] If a notice of an assignment made by a document to which s.91 applies is given in electronic form according to the Land Registry rules, it is to be regarded for the purposes of any enactment as given in writing (LRA 2002, s.91(7)). Where a document is signed in electronic form by a director and a secretary or by two directors under CA 1985, s.36A(4) and (6) (presumption

---

22 In 2001, a consultation paper was issued by the (then) Lord Chancellor's Department, which contained a draft order to amend LP(MP)A 1989 by adding s.2A. The proposed order would have amended the then in force LRA 1925. LRA 2002 contains provisions (in s.91) similar to the proposed changes in LRA 1925.

23 For some the issues and criticisms of this provision of LRA 2002, see Mason, *Electronic Signatures in Law*, Butterworths, 2003.

24 References to an electronic signature and to certification are to be read in accordance with ECA 2000, s.7(2) and (3).

25 If a solicitor uses an electronic signature in an electronic conveyancing transaction on behalf of a client, then she will need to ensure she has adequate and detailed instructions from her client, to minimise negligence claims.

of due execution) it has effect with the substitution of 'authenticated' for 'signed' (LRA 2002, s.91(a)).

25.9   SUPERVISION OF 'CERTIFICATION SERVICE PROVIDERS'

Regulation 3 of ESR 2002 requires the Secretary of State to:

- keep under review the carrying on of activities of certification service providers who are established in the United Kingdom and who issue qualified certificates to the public and the persons by whom they are carried on with a view to her becoming aware of the identity of those persons and the circumstances relating to the carrying on of those activities;
- establish and maintain a register of certification service providers who are established in the United Kingdom and who issue qualified certificates to the public;
- record in the register the names and addresses of those certification service providers of whom she is aware who are established in the United Kingdom and who issue qualified certificates to the public;
- publish the register in such manner as she considers appropriate.

ESR 2002 do not require the Secretary of State to accredit, license or supervise certification service providers. For example, if there is evidence concerning the conduct of a certification service provider established in the United Kingdom which is detrimental to the interests of persons relying on its certificates, she can only make that evidence available to others (such as the public) (ESR 2002, reg. 3(5)).

25.10   LIABILITY OF CERTIFICATION SERVICE PROVIDERS

Where a certification service provider either (a) issues a certificate as a qualified certificate to the public, or (b) guarantees a qualified certificate to the public, and:

- a person reasonably relies on that certificate for any one of certain matters (see below); and
- that person suffers loss because of such reliance; and
- the certification service provider would be liable in damages in respect of any extent of the loss (had a duty of care existed between him and the person referred to immediately above, and had the certification service provider been negligent)

then the certification service provider shall be so liable to the same extent notwithstanding that there is no proof that the certification service provider was negligent unless the certification service provider proves that he was not negligent (ESR 2002, reg. 4(1)).[26] A duty of care is imposed between the certification service provider and the person who reasonably relies on the certificate (ESR 2002, reg. 4(2)).

Meaning of 'certain matters' on which a person reasonably relies

The certain matters on which a person may rely are:

- the accuracy of any of the information contained in the qualified certificate at the time of issue;
- the inclusion in the qualified certificate of all the details required to be included in a qualified certificate (see list at **section 25.5**);
- the holding by the signatory identified in the qualified certificate at the time of its issue of the signature-creation data corresponding to the signature-verification data given or identified in the certificate; or
- the ability of the signature-creation data and the signature-verification data to be used in a complementary manner in cases where the certification service provider generates them both (ESR 2002, reg. 4(1)(b)(i)–(iv)).

25.11 TYPES OF LIABILITY OF CERTIFICATION SERVICE PROVIDERS

A certification service provider may have the following types of relationship (and exposure to liability) when it issues a qualified certificate:

- **With a signatory**: there will normally be a contractual relationship. The signatory will need to enter into a contract with a certification service provider to obtain a key to encode the signatory's electronic communications.
- **With a recipient**: a recipient of an electronic communication signed with a digital signature will wish to rely on that qualified certificate to indicate that the signatory is the sender of the electronic communication and that the signatory is who she says she is. The relationship between the certification-service-provider and the recipient will normally be based not on contract, but on tort. ESR 2002 indicate that, unlike other relationships founded in tort, a certification service provider does not have to have a duty of care, it is imposed whether it, in fact, exists or not (ESR 2002, reg. 4(2)).
- **With regulatory bodies**: there is currently no regulatory scheme concerning certification service providers. There is a voluntary scheme in the

---

26 This provision reverses the usual standard of proof: normally it is for the person who has suffered loss or damage to show that the person who has caused that loss or damage has been negligent. A similar obligation (and duty of care) is placed on the certification-service-provider where a person reasonably relies on a certificate which should have been revoked.

United Kingdom.[27] As indicated above, for a certification service provider who does not meet the criteria of this voluntary scheme or fails to provide an adequate service, the only sanction would be the making public of such failure by the Secretary of State. The certification service provider would not be stopped from providing its service.

---

27 Further details on this scheme can be found at **www.tscheme.org**.

CHAPTER 26

Commissioners for Oaths

26.1   INTRODUCTION

This chapter concerns the persons authorised:

- to administer oaths and take affirmations for an affidavit; and
- to take statutory declarations

(all of which are referred to as 'oaths' in this chapter).

This chapter lists the persons generally authorised to take oaths, and provides a summary of the law in this area. There are other persons who can administer oaths, more usually confined to specific situations; these are dealt with in **Chapter 27**.

26.2   WHO IS ENTITLED TO ADMINISTER AN OATH?

The following are entitled to administer an oath ('the Commissioners'):

- solicitors (holding a current practising certificate);
- barristers;
- notaries public (but not ecclesiastical notaries);
- licensed conveyancers;
- Fellows of the Institute of Legal Executives (if they pay a full subscription to the Institute; but not retired Fellows).

26.3   TITLE OF 'COMMISSIONER FOR OATHS'

All the Commissioners have the right to use the title 'Commissioners for Oaths' (CLSA 1990, s.113(10)).

26.4   WHAT POWERS DOES A COMMISSIONER HAVE IN REGARD TO OATHS?

The law is contained in three Acts ('the Oath Acts'):

- Commissioners for Oaths Act 1889 (COA 1889);
- Commissioners for Oaths Act 1891 (COA 1891); and
- Stamp Duties Management Act 1891 (SDMA 1891).

The provisions of the three Acts are outlined below.

Commissioners for Oaths Act 1889

A Commissioner can administer any oath or take any affidavit for the purposes of any court or matter in England (COA 1889, s.1(2)).
  The words 'oath' and 'affidavit' are defined in COA 1889, s.11:

- 'oath' is defined as including an affirmation and a declaration;
- 'affidavit' is defined as including an affirmation, statutory or other declaration, acknowledgement, examination, and attestation or protestation of honour.

Commissioners for Oaths Act 1891

Where Merchant Shipping Act 1995 or Customs Consolidation Act 1876 require an oath or affidavit to be taken or made before any particular person or officer, and whether at any particular place, or within any specified limits or otherwise, such oath or affidavit may be taken or made before a Commissioner at any place (COA 1891, s.1).

Stamp Duties Management Act 1891

A statutory declaration required to be made in pursuance of, or for the purposes of, that or any other Act for the time being in force relating to stamp duties may be made before a Commissioner or a justice of the peace in any part of the United Kingdom (SDMA 1891, s.24).

Point to note

The formal title for the person to administer an oath is a 'Commissioner for Oaths'. Such a person was appointed under COA 1889, s.1(1). Although this section has been repealed (CLSA 1990, s.113(2)) the power of a Commissioner for Oaths continues (as described below).

26.5   POWER TO APPOINT COMMISSIONERS

The power to appoint Commissioners is principally contained in Solicitors Act 1974 (SA 1974) and CLSA 1990. The following can exercise the powers of a Commissioner for Oaths.

Authorised person

An authorised person has the powers conferred on a Commissioner for Oaths under the Oaths Acts (CLSA 1990, s.113(3)). Any reference to such a Commissioner for Oaths in any enactment or instrument made after the commencement of the CLSA 1990 will include a reference to an authorised person (unless the context otherwise provides).

Who is an 'authorised person'?

An authorised person is any:

- authorised advocate or authorised litigator (other than one who is a solicitor) (CLSA 1990, s.113(1)(a)):

  - an 'authorised advocate' is any person (including a barrister or a solicitor) who has the right of audience granted by an authorised body in accordance with CLSA 1990 (CLSA 1990, s.119);[1]
  - an 'authorised litigator' is any person (including a solicitor) who has a right to conduct litigation granted by an authorised body in accordance with CLSA 1990 (CLSA 1990, s.119); or

- person who is a member of a professional or other body prescribed by the Lord Chancellor (CLSA 1990, s.113(1)(b)).[2] The Lord Chancellor has made two orders to designate the Council for Licensed Conveyancers[3] and the Institute of Legal Executives[4] as prescribed bodies.

---

1 An authorised body means (in relation to rights of audience only) the General Council of the Bar, and (in relation to rights of audience and rights to conduct litigation) the Law Society and any professional or other body so designated by Order in Council (CLSA 1990, ss.27(9) and 28(5)).

2 The power given to the Lord Chancellor has to be for the purposes of this section.

3 Commissioners for Oaths (Prescribed Bodies) Regulations 1994, SI 1994/1380, reg. 3: the Council for Licensed Conveyancers shall be a prescribed body, and every licensed conveyancer shall have the powers conferred on a Commissioner for Oaths by the Oaths Acts.

4 Commissioners for Oaths (Prescribed Bodies) Regulations 1995, SI 1995/1676, reg. 2: the Institute of Legal Executives shall be a prescribed body for the purposes of CLSA 1990, s.113. The bye-laws of the Institute provide that Fellows of the Institute who pay a full subscription to the Institute shall be 'authorised persons' under s.113(1).

A general notary

A general notary is a public notary (CLSA 1990, s.113(1)).[5]

A general notary has the powers conferred on a Commissioner for Oaths under COA 1889 and COA 1891 (CLSA 1990, s.113(4)).[6] Any reference to such a Commissioner for Oaths in any enactment or instrument made after the commencement of CLSA 1990 will include a reference to a general notary (unless the context otherwise provides).

Solicitors

A solicitor who holds a practising certificate which is in force, has the powers conferred on a Commissioner for Oaths by the Oaths Acts (SA 1974, s.81(1)). Any reference to such a Commissioner for Oaths in any enactment or instrument made after the commencement of SA 1974 will include a reference to such a solicitor (unless the context otherwise provides).

Other sources of power

In addition to the powers described above, a notary can:

- take a statutory declaration under Statutory Declarations Act 1835 (SDA 1835), ss.15, 16 and 18;
- administer oaths relating to stamp and other duties (SDMA 1891, s.24).

These are specific powers. CLSA 1990 provides notaries with a wider power to administer oaths.

26.6 REQUIREMENT FOR A COMMISSIONER TO STATE AT WHAT PLACE AND ON WHAT DATE AN OATH IS TAKEN

A Commissioner is required to state in the *signature block* (formally known as the jurat or attestation clause) the place where, and the date on which, the oath is administered (COA 1889, s.5; SA 1974, s.81(3); CLSA 1990, s.113(6)).

26.7 ADMITTANCE INTO EVIDENCE

A document which contains a statement as specified under the previous heading and purporting to be sealed or signed by a Commissioner shall be admitted into evidence:

---

5 That is, a notary other than an ecclesiastical notary.
6 SDMA 1891 already conferred on notaries the same powers as those of Commissioners for Oaths under that Act.

- without proof of the seal or signature; and
- without proof that the Commissioner is a barrister, licensed conveyancer, Fellow of the Institute of Legal Executives, public notary or solicitor (or that the solicitor holds a practising certificate which is in force) (SA 1974, s.81(4); CLSA 1990, s.113(7)).

26.8   WHEN A COMMISSIONER CANNOT ADMINISTER AN OATH

Below are the specific provisions as to when a Commissioner or other person must not administer an oath. In addition, the Solicitors' Code of Conduct 2007 imposes on solicitors particular obligations when they wish to administer an oath (set out in **Appendix 3**). Although these obligations only apply to solicitors, other persons who can administer oaths may regard them as an indication of good practice.

Overriding rule concerning some affidavits

The Civil Procedure Rules state that an affidavit must be sworn before a person independent of the parties or their representatives (CPR PD 32.9.2). This rule covers not only Commissioners but also other persons permitted to administer an oath.

The following are the specific provisions relating to Commissioners.

Barrister, Fellow of the Institute of Legal Executives, licensed conveyancer and public notary

A Commissioner who is a barrister, Fellow of the Institute of Legal Executives, licensed conveyancer or public notary cannot administer oaths in any proceedings in which she is interested (CLSA 1990, s.113(5)). Proceedings mean proceedings in any court (CLSA 1990, s.119).[7] This would appear to mean that in a matter which did not involve a proceeding in any court one of these types of Commissioner could administer an oath in a proceeding in which they were interested. This would seem a strange conclusion. Most affidavits (in the few circumstances where they are still used) are used in connection with proceedings in a court, so there is perhaps no problem with these types of documents. Statutory declarations are rarely, if ever, used in proceedings in a court (CPR 75 being an exception).

---

7 Before the introduction of the CPR, the meaning of 'proceedings' was not confined to litigious proceedings (RSC Order 41, r.8).

Solicitor

A solicitor is not to administer oaths:

- in a proceeding in which she is solicitor to any of the parties; or
- in a proceeding in which she is interested (SA 1974, s.81(2); COA 1889, s.1(3)).

Solicitors' Code of Conduct 2007, rule 10.03, states:

> You must not [administer an oath] where you or your firm is acting for any party in the matter.

This is taken to mean that a solicitor is not to administer oaths for either litigation or non-litigation matters where she or her firm is acting for any of the parties.[8]

Type of barristers who can act as Commissioners

The Professional Conduct Committee of the Bar Council has decided that:

- acting as a Commissioner is not a legal service;
- barristers in independent practice can act as a Commissioner to administer an oath, on payment of the prescribed fee and where they are not instructed in a case, without the intervention of a solicitor;
- an employed barrister can act as a Commissioner to administer an oath, but not where her employers are interested;
- a clerk to justices (who qualifies as an employed barrister under the Code of Conduct of the Bar) can act as a Commissioner, but not where her employers are interested;[9]
- non-practising barristers (who are not employed barristers), do not enjoy a right of audience, and therefore are not entitled to act as Commissioners.

---

8 The full text of rule 10.03 and the guidance to it is set out in **Appendix 3**.
9 Employers of clerks to justices are not deemed to be interested in matters where the justices' only involvement is in the exercise of their judicial function.

CHAPTER 27

Other persons authorised to administer oaths

27.1 INTRODUCTION

This chapter provides details about persons other than Commissioners who are entitled to administer oaths. 'Commissioners' and 'oaths' have the meaning given at **section 26.1**. The persons listed in this chapter who have the power to administer oaths (whether generally or in specific situations) are in addition to Commissioners.

27.2 COURT RULES AS TO WHO CAN ADMINISTER OATHS AND TAKE AFFIDAVITS

The Civil Procedure Rules state that only the following can administer oaths and take affidavits:

- Commissioners for Oaths, practising solicitors and other persons authorised by statute (CPR PD 32.9.1(1), (2) and (3));[1]
- certain officials of the Supreme Court (with a reference to COA 1889, s.2) (CPR PD 32.9.1(4));
- a circuit judge or district judge (with a reference to CCA 1984, s.58) (CPR PD 32.9.1(5));
- any justice of the peace (with a reference to CCA 1984, s.58) (CPR PD 32.9.1(6));
- certain officials of any county court appointed by the judge of that court for that purpose (with a reference to CCA 1984, s.58) (CPR PD 32.9.1(7)).

An affidavit must be sworn before a person independent of the parties or their representatives (CPR PD 32.9.2).

The specific provisions mentioned above are described further below, together with situations which are not specifically mentioned above.

---

1 Refers to the various provisions giving power to Commissioners. Note 8 to CPR PD 32 refers to the Administration of Justice Act 1985, s.65, which has been repealed by the Access to Justice Act 1999, s.106, Sched. 15, Part II, from 1 January 2000 (see SI 1999/3344, art. 2(d)). Commissioners, solicitors and others authorised by statute are covered in **Chapter 26**.

27.3 GENERAL POWER TO ADMINISTER AN OATH BY CERTAIN COURT OFFICIALS

Every person who, being an officer of or performing duties in relation to any court, is for the time being so authorised by a judge of the court, or by or in pursuance of any rules or orders regulating the procedure of the court, and every person directed to take an examination in any cause or matter in the Senior Courts,[2] shall have authority to administer any oath or take any affidavit required for any purpose connected with his duties (COA 1889, s.2). Based on the wording, this power is not restricted to affidavits but would include statutory declarations as the words 'oath' and 'affidavit' include a declaration and a statutory declaration for the purposes of the Act.

This is thought to be restricted to the power to administer an oath for use in the Supreme Court.[3]

27.4 POWER TO ADMINISTER AN AFFIDAVIT FOR USE IN THE COUNTY COURTS

An affidavit can be sworn or affirmed for use in the county court before any of the following (CCA 1984, s.58):

- the judge or district judge of any court;
- any justice of the peace;
- any officer[4] of any court appointed by the judge of that court for the purpose.

Such a power is only given in relation to affidavits (none of the above can take a statutory declaration).

---

2 Formerly the Supreme Court of England and Wales, renamed by Constitutional Reform Act 2005, s.59.

3 Under former rules governing court procedure (RSC Order 32, r.8 (now repealed)) the specific officials were specified: holders of any of the offices listed in the Supreme Court Act 1981, column 1 of Part II and Part III of Sched. 2 (including deputies of such an official and temporary additional officials): Official Solicitor; Master, Queen's Bench Division; Queen's Coroner and Attorney and Master of the Crown Office and Registrar of Criminal Appeals; Admiralty Registrar; Master, Chancery Division; Registrar in Bankruptcy of the High Court; Taxing Master of the Supreme Court; District Judge of the Principal Registry of the Family Division; Master of the Court of Protection.

4 An 'officer' means 'in relation to a court . . . any district judge or deputy district judge assigned to that court, and any clerk, bailiff, usher or messenger in the service of that court': CCA 1984, s.147.

27.5   DIVORCE COUNTY COURT

In relation to family proceedings pending or treated as pending in a divorce county court (which for some purposes includes the principal registry) (Matrimonial and Family Proceedings Act 1984 (MFPA 1984), s.42), in addition to the persons mentioned above, an affidavit can also be sworn or affirmed for use in a designated county court before any of the following (FPR 1991, as amended by SI 2005/2922, r.10.13):

- a district judge of the principal registry; or
- any officer of the principal registry of the Family Division of the High Court authorised by the president (COA 1889, s.2); or
- any clerk of the Central Office of the Royal Courts of Justice authorised to take affidavits for the purposes of proceedings in the Supreme Court.

27.6   BANKRUPTCY AND WINDING UP PROCEEDINGS

An affidavit required for the purposes of IA 1986, Part IV, can be sworn in the United Kingdom before 'any court, judge or person lawfully authorised to take and receive affidavits' (s.200(1)),[5] which would cover the persons mentioned above.

Rules relating to insolvency proceedings further specify as follows.

1. The practice and procedure of the High Court is to be used with regard to affidavits, their form and contents for insolvency proceedings (Insolvency Rules 1986 (IR 1986), r.7.57(1)).[6]
2. The official receiver, or the deputy official receiver, or any officer duly authorised in that behalf can take affidavits and declarations (IR 1986, r.7.57(4)).[7]
3. In an affidavit made by the official receiver or the responsible insolvency practitioner ('Deponent') for the purpose of insolvency proceedings, the Deponent shall state:

    (a)   the capacity in which he makes the affidavit;
    (b)   the position he holds; and
    (c)   the address at which he works (IR 1986, r.7.57(2)).

---

5 All courts, judges, justices, commissioners or persons acting judicially are to take judicial notice of the seal, stamp or signature (as the case may be) of any such court, judge or person, attached appended or subscribed to any such affidavit, or to any other document to be used for the purposes of Part IV: IA 1986, s.200(2).
6 There is no longer a separate High Court provision for affidavits. The rules are now covered by CPR 32 and the Practice Direction to it.
7 It is not clear whether this power is restricted to insolvency proceedings.

4. An affidavit of debt made by a creditor can be sworn before her own solicitor (IR 1986, r.7.57(3)). This appears to be an exception for this particular case as, for solicitors, there is an express provision that they cannot administer an oath or take an affirmation of any of the parties to proceedings (SA 1974, s.81).

5. Certain statements and documents relating to insolvency proceedings can only be made by affidavit (IR 1986, r.7.57):

   (a) statements of affairs (IR 1986, rr.3.4, 4.33 and 6.60);
   (b) further disclosure (IR 1986, rr.4.42, 6.66 and 6.72);
   (c) accounts (IR 1986, rr.4.39, 4.40, 6.65 and 6.70);
   (d) claims (IR 1986, rr.4.73, 4.77, 6.96 and 6.99);
   (e) examinations (IR 1986, rr.9.3 and 9.4).

6. Certain other documents or statements can be verified by affidavit or witness statement (IR 1986, r.7.57(5)).

27.7 JUSTICES OF THE PEACE

In addition to their powers given for the use of affidavits in the county court, justices of the peace also have the following powers.

1. A justice of the peace may administer any oath or take any affidavit which is required for the purpose of an application for a grant of probate or letters of administration made in any non-contentious or common form probate proceedings (CLSA 1990, s.56(1)):

   (a) a justice before whom any oath or affidavit is taken or made for the above purposes shall state in the *signature block* at what place and on what date the oath or affidavit is taken or made;
   (b) no justice shall exercise the powers conferred by this section in any proceedings in which he is interested;
   (c) a document purporting to be signed by a justice administering an oath or taking an affidavit shall be admitted in evidence without proof of the signature and without proof that he is a justice.

2. A justice of the peace may administer a statutory declaration (SDA 1835, s.18).

27.8   BILLS OF SALE

An affidavit required by or for the purposes of the Bills of Sale Act 1878 can be sworn before a Master of any division of the High Court of Justice or before any Commissioner empowered to take affidavits in the Supreme Court of Judicature (Bills of Sale Act 1878, s.17).

CHAPTER 28

Notaries public

28.1   INTRODUCTION

The role (and even the existence) of notaries is unfamiliar to many people in England and Wales (including a large number of English lawyers and other professionals). The reality is that a notary is likely only to be encountered when a person is involved in a transaction or event taking place in another country and she is told that she needs to use a notary public.[1]

This chapter provides an introduction to the work of notaries[2] and deals with some of the common practical issues or questions that arise when a notary is used or documents need to be executed for use abroad and the involvement of a notary is required.[3] The chapter concludes with a few common examples of the type of documents that a notary is likely to generate.

A distinguishing feature of the work of notaries compared to other English lawyers, leaving aside what they actually do is the level of formality that is involved in the work they do. This often comes as a (great) surprise to other lawyers, and even more so to non-lawyers.

Common assumptions are that when a notary is required:

- the notary does not need to pay attention to the contents of the document;
- the notary does not need to enquire as to whether the person who is to sign the document is willing to be bound by it, etc.; and

---

1 A notary's proper title is a 'notary public' (or in some legislation 'public notary').
2 The history of and routes to qualification can be found in N. P. Ready, *Brooke's Notary*, 12th edn, Sweet & Maxwell, 2002, or at **www.thenotariessociety.org.uk/** or **www.facultyoffice.org.uk/Notaries1.html**.
3 The information set out in this chapter deals only with matters from the point of view of notaries qualified and practising in England and Wales. At present it appears that such notaries cannot work as English notaries in other countries, in particular other European countries. It is not entirely clear whether notaries from other countries can work as notaries in England and Wales.

- the role of the notary is limited to no more than putting her signature and seal on a document,

much in the same way that an English lawyer is generally not interested in the contents of a statutory declaration which they are to take or the intention of the person making it.[4] These assumptions are incorrect.

Notaries are (almost) uniquely among English lawyers concerned not only:

- with the formal and often self-probative aspects of creating a legally binding document (who signs, where they sign, number of witnesses, how the document is to be formatted and bound); but also
- with other aspects such as the status, capacity, authority and identity of a person who is to sign a document, as well as the person's understanding of the contents of a document and the person's willingness to be bound by it.

28.2   WHAT IS COVERED IN THIS CHAPTER

This chapter will deal with the following topics:

- professional matters;
- how to determine when a notary is needed;
- common types of documents a notary deals with;
- the role of a notary;
- what a notary will not be doing;
- dealing with documents which are not in English;
- copying of documents;
- client confidentiality;
- record keeping;
- use of electronic communications;
- identifying and dealing with companies;
- which legal system(s) a document must comply with;
- legalisation.

At the end of the chapter there are number of examples of the types of document that a notary will produce when dealing with such matters as a power of attorney or a copy of a passport.

---

4 Except to the limited extent that they are concerned under e.g. Solicitors' Code of Conduct 2007, see pp.86–8 for an outline of the issues a solicitor should consider when taking a statutory declaration.

28.3 PROFESSIONAL MATTERS

Qualification

In England and Wales, a person wishing to become a notary is required to:

- study to the same academic level as if she wished to qualify as a solicitor or a barrister;[5]
- undertake and pass a two-year part-time diploma (covering subjects such as notarial practice, and usually also roman/civil law and international law);
- be admitted as a notary;[6] and
- during the first two years of practice, work under the supervision of a more experienced notary.

Practice

On being admitted as a notary, the notary will need a seal,[7] which she will use in virtually all documents she notarises.

Notaries, like other English lawyers, are required to obtain an annual practising certificate, maintain professional indemnity insurance[8] and undertake a certain amount of continuing education each year. They are governed by formal rules as to how they practise, and as to what they can and cannot do.[9]

Although notaries are a separate and distinct form of lawyer, most notaries are also solicitors.[10] Some are qualified as lawyers in other jurisdictions.

Although a notary (as a solicitor) may be employed by, or be a partner in, a firm of solicitors, the rules that govern the work of a notary[11] require the notary to keep her notarial practice identifiably separate from that of her firm.[12]

---

5 Having a law degree or a postgraduate diploma in law. This is not required if the person is already a solicitor or barrister.

6 This includes making an oral declaration, including swearing allegiance to the Crown, to an official of the body which is the front line regulator for notaries, the Faculty Office of the Archbishop of Canterbury, or a Church of England priest sent delegated authority for the purpose. In return, the newly qualified notary receives a handwritten scroll (called a 'Faculty').

7 Similar to the type used by companies to seal documents or shares (if the company has one).

8 If a notary works for a firm of solicitors, she usually has the benefit of the firm's professional indemnity policy.

9 Notaries Practice Rules 2001. See **www.facultyoffice.org.uk/Notaries1.html**.

10 Notaries predate the other two forms of lawyers, with the first distinctly English notaries active in the thirteenth century.

11 Notarial Practice Rules 2001.

12 This will mean, e.g., a notary working also as a solicitor in a firm of solicitors must issue invoices in her own name and not in the name of the firm of solicitors, keep her notarial files separate from that of the firm of solicitors and restrict access to them to herself and only to other persons who are identified as providing administrative or clerical assistance in her notarial work. The fees the notary receives have to be kept in a separate account from that of the firm of solicitors.

The front-line regulator for notaries is the Faculty Office of the Archbishop of Canterbury.[13] The representative body for notaries is the Notaries Society,[14] which plays a similar representative role on behalf of notaries as do the Law Society or the Bar Council for solicitors or barristers respectively. The society does not have any disciplinary or formal complaints powers (these are both handled by the Faculty Office), but does have an informal complaints procedure.

There are about 900 practising notaries in England and Wales.[15]

Some terminology

Notarial act

Not all the matters that a notary is asked to deal with have to be dealt with by a notary, or will not be valid, effective or enforceable if dealt with by someone other than a notary.[16] Where the involvement of a notary is essential for any action, event or transaction to be valid, effective or legally enforceable, such involvement is called a 'notarial act'. A definition provided by the Notaries Practice Rules 2001 defines 'notarial act' as 'any act that has validity by virtue only of its preparation, performance, authentication or attestation or verification by a notary'.

For example, if a person wishes to make a statement in the form of a statutory declaration (for use in England and Wales and certain other jurisdictions) the person can choose to do so before any solicitor or other Commissioner for Oaths, including a notary (acting as a Commissioner for Oaths). The fact that the declaration is not made before a notary will not affect its validity. However, if the declaration is made for use in another country, and in that country it is valid only if the declaration is made before a notary, then the validity of the declaration will be subject to its being done before a notary. In this latter example there will be a notarial act.

What constitutes a notarial act and the 'notarial certificate'

Every notarial act must contain certain statements when a notary is involved in a matter, event or transaction. Without these statements there can be no notarial act. The elements are as follows:

---

13 For an understanding of why notaries are regulated by a department of the Church of England (and other historical points), refer to the standard work on notaries, *Brooke's Notary*, n. 2 above.
14 See **www.thenotariessociety.org.uk/**.
15 A notary can be found by conducting a search at **www.thenotariessociety.org.uk/**.
16 Examples of when a notary is usually required are dealt within **section 28.4** and **section 28.5**.

- the date of the notarial act;
- the name and place of practice of the notary;
- the place where the notarial act took place;
- the name(s) of the client and any witnesses;
- whether the client appeared before the notary;
- that the client has been properly identified (and often how they were identified);
- a description of the document or transaction which is the subject of the notarial act;
- the nature of the notarial act;
- the signature(s) of the client and any witnesses (if a document needs to be signed by them);
- (after all that is needed is carried out) the signature and seal of the notary.

A 'notarial certificate' is the wording which encompasses all the above information. In some cases it is spread throughout a document (such as in Example 1 below), or the information may be set out in a separate document prepared by the notary and attached to another document which a client has signed (such as in Example 2 below).

Documents in 'public form' or 'private form'

Some documents that a notary creates are in a particular form, the so-called 'public form'[17] (those documents not in public form being in 'private form'). The method of distinguishing such documents and their importance is a subject which is perhaps of most interest or relevance to notaries. However, the issue retains some general relevance because of the 'status' of such a document in other countries (particularly in civil law countries) and the role which it fulfils. The notary is considered the 'author' of a document in public form (irrespective of whether the document has been supplied by someone else).

In practice, a document in public form must usually be laid out in a certain way and normally does not have a notarial certificate attached to it, but is in itself the 'notarial certificate' (as in Example 2 below).

For documents in private form, the information for a notarial act may be included in a separate notarial certificate attached to the document.

Recognition of notarial acts in England and Wales

Until recently, a notarial act of an English notary did not, generally, enjoy recognition as being either probative or directly enforceable in the English courts.[18]

---

17 Sometimes also called 'authentic form'.
18 The have been a number of cases (some of which are conflicting) over several centuries which have dealt with this issue. These are set out in *Brooke's Notary*, n. 2 above.

This has changed with the amendment of the Civil Procedure Rules, which now provide that:

> A notarial act or instrument may be received in evidence without further proof as duly authenticated in accordance with the requirements of law unless the contrary is proved.[19]

One consequence of this change is that it would appear that an act of an English notary is put on the same footing as that of a foreign notary (which has always enjoyed such recognition).

28.4 WHEN IS A NOTARY NEEDED?

Notaries are usually only needed when a person (whether an individual or a company) is involved in some matter which is taking place in another country. The following examples are common situations which require the involvement of a notary:[20]

- where a person is providing authority or permission to another person to carry out certain activities on their behalf in another country (e.g. a power of attorney or agency agreement);
- where a person is carrying out or is involved in a transaction in another country;
- where a person is providing some information or making a statement about themselves or their civil or other status for use in another country (e.g. on marrying abroad);
- where a person is providing information, making statements or agreeing to some procedural or other step which is to be used in court or other official proceedings or matters for registration in another country;
- where a person requires some fact about herself or her status or a given state of affairs to be verified by a notary which is to be used in another country;
- where a person needs a copy of a document made and certified as a true copy for use in another country.

In the first four instances, these situations normally involve the client signing a document, almost invariably before a notary (and sometimes in front of additional witnesses).

In the fifth instance, the notary often carries out some fact checking or the obtaining of some information from third parties and then makes a statement in relation to those facts or that information (the client requesting verification often does not need to sign anything).

---

19 CPR 32.20, inserted by SI 2005/2292, from 1 October 2005.
20 Examples of the documents a notary deals with are listed at **section 28.7**.

In the sixth instance, a photocopy or a duplicate of an original document is supplied by a client and the copy is authenticated by the notary,[21] with the notary sometimes checking with the issuer of the document to confirm that the document has been issued to the client. If the original document cannot be or is not checked with the issuer, the notary will sometimes require the client to confirm that the document that is to be copied is genuine (by the client's making a statutory or non-statutory declaration). Again, the client usually does not have to sign anything (other than any declaration).

Except in a few very minor instances, English notaries do not have any role within England and Wales.[22]

28.5   HOW TO DETERMINE WHEN A NOTARY IS NEEDED

There is no infallible way for a person to know when a notary is needed. The section above lists the areas where a notary is often required, and **section 28.7** gives some practical examples.

In practice, a person will usually only be aware that a notary is needed when they are involved in some event, matter or transaction in another country and they are told they need to use a notary. For example, if a person is buying a property abroad, and they have instructed a local lawyer, the local lawyer may require the client to sign a power of attorney authorising the local lawyer to act for the client. The power of attorney will be sent to the client with an instruction that it should be signed before a notary.

28.6   MUST AN ENGLISH NOTARY BE USED WHEN A NOTARY IS REQUIRED?

The need to use an English notary often arises because the client cannot easily go to the country where the event, matter or transaction they are involved with is taking place. If they were able to, they could sign the document in the country concerned before a local notary.

28.7   COMMON TYPES OF DOCUMENTS DEALT WITH BY A NOTARY

A notary can deal with potentially any type of document. In practice, notaries see the same types of documents repeatedly. The following list pro-

---

21 By stating it is a true copy of the original provided by the client. See also **section 28.11**.
22 Two specific instances are where a foreign bill of exchange is dishonoured when presented for payment or where a ship comes to a British port and the captain needs to make a report to a notary (called a 'ship protest'). These situations rarely occur, with many notaries never undertaking these tasks. These topics are covered in *Brooke's Notary*, n. 2 above.

vides the common situations or documents which need the involvement of a notary:

Powers of attorney

This is perhaps the most common document that a notary is required to deal with.

Documents often required by individuals

Documents as to the status of individuals

These include documents evidencing:

- freedom to marry;
- that a couple are cohabiting;
- that a person is divorced;
- change of name;
- consent by parent for minor child to marry;
- declaration as to parentage;
- consent by one or both parents for a child to travel abroad;
- evidence of marriage, civil partnership, death or birth in England and Wales;[23]
- evidence and/or declaration of marriage, death or birth abroad;
- evidence as to qualifications held by an individual;
- evidence that no criminal convictions are held.[24]

Foreign adoption

For foreign adoptions, it is necessary for a large number of documents to be notarised, including copies and originals of many official documents issued by various government departments and agencies, local authorities, plus medical reports, social worker's reports, letters of supports from friends and family, employers, etc.[25]

---

23 Requests for these are usually obtained either from the local authority in which such events occur or directly from **www.gro.gov.uk**.
24 Although this is normally done by obtaining a certificate in the first instance from the Criminal Records Bureau.
25 In practice, the information that needs to be gathered, and the way it is to be presented, is set out in guidance issued by the Department of Health.

Immigration and emigration

These include:

- sponsorship undertakings and declarations;
- declaration as to maintenance;
- acknowledgement of responsibility for an immigrant;
- declarations as to certain facts for emigration to another country.

Companies

- Certificate of due execution by a company (or on behalf of a company) of a document. This will often be a statement by a notary in a notarial certificate stating that a deed or contract, for example, has been signed by the duly authorised representatives of a company and is binding on the company.
- Verification of information about the status, constitution and structure of a company, such as:

  - that a company is incorporated in England and Wales;
  - that it has limited liability;
  - what its shareholding is;
  - what the company does;
  - how it is constituted and what its constitutional documents are;
  - whether it requires a licence to carry out some or all of its activities;
  - who the officers (directors and secretary) of the company are;
  - who carries out the management of the company;
  - whether there are any limitations (such as in constitutional documents or in resolutions of the shareholders/directors) on the powers of the managers to carry out their functions;
  - whether the company is in good standing and in existence.

- Authenticating copies of:

  - certificate of incorporation;
  - certificate on change of name;
  - memorandum and articles of association;
  - minutes of shareholders' or directors' meeting which indicate that:

    - a company wishes to enter into a transaction;
    - the company is willing to undertake a matter (such as opening a branch in another country);
    - a particular person is authorised to act for the company.

- Authenticating copies of accounting and auditing records, etc. This type of notarised documentation is often required in the following types of situation:

  - where a company is starting a business or opening a subsidiary or branch in another country;

- where a company is dealing with aspects of corporate administration, such as opening a bank account;
- where a company is filing and prosecuting applications for certain intellectual property rights, such as patents and trade marks (particularly in non-Patent Cooperation Treaty countries);
- where a company is arranging work (and residence) permits for its employees;
- where a company is involved in shipping;
- where a company is required to comply with certain foreign or ownership investment formalities.

Contracts or agreements which are intended for use abroad (where e.g. one of the parties is located in another country or the contract is to be performed wholly or partially in another country) usually do not need to be signed before a notary.[26] However, this may not apply for certain types of contract, particularly those involving real property. In some civil law countries, such contracts or some forms of transaction must be dealt with by, and signed in the presence of, a notary.

28.8 WHAT IS THE ROLE OF A NOTARY?

A notary is required to do some or all of the following tasks:

- enquiring as to identity and checking that the client is who they say they are (as far as it is possible to do so);
- checking that the client has the authority, and the capacity, to sign the document they wish to sign (and if the client is an organisation, also checking that the person who is signing has the authority to do so on behalf of the organisation); this involves checking any relevant or available documentation (sometimes by making independent searches) and by asking appropriate questions of the client;[27]
- in appropriate cases, verifying some or all of the facts stated in a document;
- checking whether the client understands the contents, meaning and effect of the document (especially if it is not in English);[28]

---

26 The authors have experience of many clients entering into commercial contracts of all different types and values and importance, with parties based in many countries in the world, but cannot recall an occasion when a written contract has needed to be notarised.
27 For example, if the client is an individual and is under a particular age then they may not have the capacity to enter into a transaction or deal with an event.
28 In appropriate cases this might mean reading the whole document to the client and checking their understanding of each of the points contained in the document. However, although this duty (and other related duties) may appear to suggest that the role of the notary is to go through a document line-by-line and have extensive discussions with the client about the document and the underlying transaction, this is not always the case.

- checking whether the client understands the consequences of signing the document they have brought to be notarised;
- dealing with the formalities to make the document legally effective (as far as it possible to do so) for use in the country of destination. This can involve formatting the document, ensuring that appropriate wording concerning the client, her status and identity are present, that the document is signed in the way required by the destination country, etc.;
- if the client is signing a document, seeing the client sign the document;
- if witnesses are needed, ensuring that the witnesses are present and that they see the client sign, and seeing the witnesses themselves sign;
- checking that all of the required elements of a notarial act are present in the document itself or in a separate document (or adding the required information);[29]
- if the document is longer than one page (or if the notarial certificate is on a separate sheet of paper), securely binding all the pages together. This is most often achieved by the use of rivets and ribbon[30] (with the ends of the tape being placed under the seal).

28.9   WHAT A NOTARY WILL NOT BE DOING

A notary's role will generally not extend to advising, or discussing with, the client:

- the full legal or other effects of the document(s);
- the full underlying transaction or event to which the document relates;
- the full legal or any other issues concerning the transaction or any other matter or event.

There are a number of reasons for this: first, the notary is usually not qualified to provide legal advice in the country in which the document concerned is to be used. Secondly, the client will often have a lawyer to assist with legal issues concerning the transaction or event they are involved in. Thirdly, the client may not wish to discuss such matters with the notary (whether or not the client is being assisted by another lawyer).

28.10   DEALING WITH DOCUMENTS WHICH ARE NOT IN ENGLISH

As indicated above, part of the role of a notary is to check that the client understands the content, nature and effect of the document she will be

---

29 See discussion of what constitutes a notarial act and the 'notarial certificate' above, pp. 285–6, as to what information is needed.
30 Staples or other methods of binding documents are not used. The aim is to ensure, as far as possible, that pages cannot be removed or added, etc., and that where any removal or addition is made, this can be easily detected.

signing. If the document that the client is to sign is in another language and the client (and/or the notary) does not understand the language, then the notary cannot fulfil a vital part of her role. There are a number of possible permutations here, including:

- the client does not understand the language but the notary does (and to a sufficient degree to understand fully the legal and technical wording used); or
- the client does understand the language but the notary does not; or
- where both the client and the notary understand the language of the document.

In such situations, there is usually no problem as one can explain the content of the document to the other. However, although a client may indicate that they understand the language of the document, the notary will not be relieved of the responsibility to ensure that the client has understanding of the document, especially if the document is expressed in technical and legal language.

Documents drafted by foreign lawyers will often contain such wording, the meaning of which or the consequences of it under a foreign law (just as with some documents drafted by English lawyers) may not be easily understood by a client.

Where the document cannot be understood by the notary (either directly by her understanding the document's language or by the client's satisfactorily explaining the document to the notary), then a notary should have the document either interpreted or translated. The interpreter and translator should be professionally qualified.[31]

A common situation is that a document is provided to a client which is accompanied by an English translation. For example, a power of attorney intended for use in Spain may be supplied in a two-column format, with one column being in Spanish and the second column in English. A notary should not accept the translation at face value. The same considerations as indicated above equally apply. Unless the notary has sufficient understanding of the Spanish (legal) language then the notary will not usually be able to satisfy herself as to the accuracy of the English version. There are a number of ways of dealing with such situations:

- to obtain confirmation from the person who prepared the translation; e.g., if the document has been provided by a Spanish lawyer, then the notary may ask the Spanish lawyer to state (preferably in writing) that the translation is accurate. Notaries should not rely on any assurance as to the accuracy of a translation by someone who is not professionally qualified;

---

31 For example, by being a member of the Institute of Linguists or the Institute of Translation and Interpreting. It would not, e.g., be acceptable to rely on a document translated by a member of the client's family.

- to obtain an opinion from a person in England qualified to render an opinion on the translation;
- to obtain a further, proper translation made by a professionally qualified translator.

Obtaining translations or the interpretation of a document adds to the expense of getting a document notarised. One way to minimise expense is to use a notary whose knowledge of a particular language is sufficient to properly understand the document. But whatever method is chosen, a client will still need to understand the document. Having a document explained to them will in itself add to the cost (whoever does it).

28.11   COPYING OF DOCUMENTS

Background

Notaries are often asked to notarise copies of a document and state that the copy is a true, fair and complete copy of the original.

There are a number of issues when a notary is asked to do this. The main issue relates to what the notary is considered to be doing when she makes a copy of a document. For most notaries in England, when a notary states that a copy of a document is a true copy of the original, the notary is in fact stating (and/or a third party is assuming or relying on the fact) that the original document is valid or genuine and what is recorded on it is accurate and true. This is called authenticating the document.

For example: a client is applying to an overseas university to study for a postgraduate qualification. As part of the application process, the client needs to submit a notarised copy of her first degree certificate and the client comes to the notary with the degree certificate. In effect, what the overseas university is asking the notary to state is that:

- the copy of the degree certificate is a true, fair and complete copy of the degree certificate provided by the client; and
- the original document records correctly that the client did study at the university stated on the document and was awarded the stated degree and class of degree, etc. as recorded on the degree certificate provided by the client.

The position is different for a solicitor or other lawyer who is certifying that a copy of a document is a true copy of a document (where the copy of the document is intended for use in England and Wales). A lawyer who so certifies a copy of another document is taken as doing nothing more than stating that fact. The lawyer is not authenticating the copy (or the information contained in it).

Best practice among notaries is to do the following when asked to provide a notarised copy of a document:

- the notary should check with the issuer of the original document that the document is valid, genuine or authentic and has been issued to the person named in it or to whom it relates and that the facts contained in the document are accurate; or
- if the client does not wish the notary to carry out such checks, then the notary should:
  - qualify the notarial certificate by stating that the original has not been verified with the issuer of the original document; and/or
  - incorporate in the notarial certificate a statutory declaration made by the client, where (only) the client is stating that the original of the copied document is genuine; and
  - inform the client that the reduced 'value' of this limited notarial certificate may make the notarised copy of the document unacceptable to the person or organisation who is to receive it.

Many clients, when they ask a notary to notarise a copy of an 'original' document, assume that the duty of a notary is to do no more than when a solicitor or other lawyer certifies a copy of an 'original' document; i.e. stating that one piece of paper is a true copy of another piece of paper. Clients will often expect that a notary needs to do no more than photocopy the document, add a phrase that the copy is a true copy of the original and sign and affix their notarial seal. Clients may be unhappy with the thought that they have to pay for the additional time taken to verify the validity of a document, or even that a notarial certificate needs to be prepared which requires to be bound, etc. onto the copy of the document.

Documents which should not normally be copied

Many official documents should not normally be copied by a notary (let alone anyone else).

First, there is the position regarding Crown copyright.[32] Works created by officers or servants of the Crown in the course of their duties will be protected by Crown copyright.[33] These will include the documents which are most often required for use in other countries, such as copies of passports, birth, marriage, civil partnership and death certificates, and certificates issued by the Registrar of Companies.

Secondly, there is guidance from the Office for Public Sector Information (OPSI) which deals with when and how a large range of public documents can be used or copied:[34]

---

32 For information on Crown copyright, see *Copinger and Skone James on Copyright*, 15th edn, Sweet and Maxwell, 2005, ch. 10, in particular paras. 10.37–10.38 on copying of birth, marriage and death certificates, and para. 10.50 on passports.

33 Copyright, Designs and Patents Act 1988, s.163.

34 All the guidance can be found at **www.opsi.gov.uk/advice/crown-copyright/copyright-guidance/index.htm**.

For passports and birth, marriage, civil partnership and death certificates, the following is the guidance issued by OPSI:

- **Passports:**

  8. Page 31 (the 'bio page') of the British Passport contains the personal details of the passport holder. The Identity and Passport Service suggests that passport holders record the information on this page and keep it in a safe place separate to the passport. This will help the Identity and Passport Service process an application for a replacement passport if the current passport is lost or is stolen.

  Passport holders' identity and personal information are valuable. Criminals can find out an individual's personal details and use them to open bank accounts and get credit cards, loans, state benefits and documents such as passports and driving licences. If an identity is stolen, the individual may have difficulty getting loans, credit cards or a mortgage until the matter is sorted out. The Identity and Passport Service advises passport holders to only agree to the reproduction of the personal details page in the passport if they are satisfied that the person or organisation they are giving this to will protect it from unauthorised disclosure.

  The Identity and Passport Service advises organisations who wish to retain a reproduction of the personal details in the passport that they should obtain the consent of the individual to do so. They also advise organisations to retain a record of the consent and to store the passport details securely.

  For most purposes, notaries will only need to copy the 'bio' page and usually only do so in black and white.[35]

- **Birth, marriage, civil partnership and death certificates:**

  The guidance states that the copying of these certificates is permitted:

  (b) by individuals or organisations for their own record keeping purposes, provided that the copies are not passed to others as evidence of birth, death or marriage;
  (c) within the context of judicial proceedings.

  This guidance is unlikely to cover the situation where a person needs to provide a copy of e.g. a marriage certificate. In such situations, it is possible to obtain duplicate certificates signed by the registrar (or authorised official) of births, marriages, civil partnerships and deaths from the local authority in which these events occurred within a few days of requesting a duplicate.[36]

Thirdly, the position regarding relevant legislation concerning money laundering and criminal activities applies equally to notaries and other types of English and Welsh lawyers.

---

35 Guidance regarding passports changes over time. Previous guidance indicated that passports should not be copied except for record-keeping purposes and copies should not be made in colour. Occasionally, notaries are asked to notarise colour copies of passports and will generally do so if satisfied that there is a proper requirement.
36 At a cost of £7 at the time material for this book was prepared.

How notaries deal with copies

Notarised copies of documents are valuable, and with the heightened concern regarding money laundering and the facilitating of other criminal activity, the way in which many notaries now deal with copies (particularly of passports and other certificates) has changed over recent years. Many notaries (in addition to their other duties referred to above, such as checking the identity of a client, etc.) will now:

- require the client to state why he needs the copy of the original document and, in appropriate cases, ask for evidence showing why the copy is needed;
- prepare a notarial certificate which indicates:
  - how the client was identified;
  - what has been copied;
  - how many pages have been copied;
  - that what has been copied is an extract (if not the whole document);
  - what pages or what extract has been copied (e.g. page 32 and the photograph page of a British passport);
  - the reason the client has given for the use of the copied document;
  - in which country the copied document will be used;
  - the date when the original of the copied document was provided to the notary; and
- securely bind the certificate to the copied document.

Some notaries still write in hand on a copied document some of the details indicated above. This method is no longer considered best practice among many English notaries.

28.12   CLIENT CONFIDENTIALITY

The duty a notary has to a client is different from that of other English lawyers. The principal duty of the notary is not to the person the notary directly deals with but to the matter, transaction or event that the person is involved in.[37] The notary is required to be impartial and independent. In

---

37 The requirement that the principal duty of the notary is to the matter, transaction or event and not to the client derives from the oath that the notary takes on admittance as a notary: '[I] will faithfully exercise the Office of a Public Notary. I will faithfully make Contracts or Instruments for or between any Party or Parties requiring the same and I will not add or diminish anything without the Knowledge and Consent of such Party or Parties that may alter the substance of the Fact. I will not make or attest any Act Contract or Instrument in which I shall know there is Violence or Fraud and in all things I will act uprightly and justly in the Business of a Public Notary according to the best of my Skill and Ability'.

consequence, the duties of maintaining confidentiality and legal privilege are more limited where a client instructs a notary compared with such duties as between an English lawyer and her client.

One consequence of these duties can mean that interested third parties can require a notary to provide to them details about the client, state what was done for the client or provide copies of documents provided to the notary by the client or provided by the notary to the client.

For example, a client may wish to purchase a property in another country and signs a power of attorney to enable a local lawyer to deal with all aspects of the purchase, completion and post-completion formalities. If the client fails to complete, the local lawyer, the purchaser and regulatory or government authorities in the other country could all claim to be interested or involved in the transaction and consequently demand access to the notary's files. Documents and information provided by the client could be disclosed.

In reality, it is unlikely that, if a notary was thus approached, she would simply hand over documents and information to a person or organisation claiming an interest in them without taking sensible and prudent steps, such as:

- informing and consulting with her front-line regulator, the Faculty Office; and
- making appropriate checks as to the identity, status, etc. of the person requesting access.

28.13   RECORD KEEPING

Notaries are subject to rules as to the records they keep, the length of time that they must keep them, and their appropriate retention for posterity.

Documents created in public form[38] must be kept permanently (or a complete photocopy needs to be kept). Other documents which a notary creates or notarises need to be kept for a minimum of 12 years.

In practice, most notaries will keep all documents without limit of time, and increasingly such documentation is held in electronic form. Also, notaries are subject to the requirements of Data Protection Act 1998.

Notaries are also required to keep a register which lists all the work they do (with certain details being included). This requirement to keep a register is a professional requirement and is part of the notarial task that a notary is required to carry out for each client she sees.[39]

---

38 See the discussion as to documents in 'public form' or 'private form' above, p.266.
39 This needs to record the date of the notarial act, the person for whom the notarial work was undertaken, an address allowing the person to be identified, the nature of the notarial act, the fee charged, etc.

When a notary ceases practice, her records will be passed on to another notary or be deposited in county archives or with the Faculty Office.

28.14 USE OF ELECTRONIC COMMUNICATIONS

Notaries in England and Wales work almost exclusively with paper records. Although they will create their notarial documents with the use of computers, communicate with clients and third parties via email and can store virtually all their records electronically, the only valid way they can carry out their work is with writing (whether through the use of a computer printer or by handwriting) and the use of their handwritten signature and their seal impressed onto a document.

A way of simplifying (and certainly speeding up) matters would be for a notary, when she has completed her work, simply to send the notarised document in an electronic format to the intended recipient, rather than the paper document being sent in the post or by courier, as at present.

The main difficulty with this would be as to how the recipient in another country would recognise that a document provided to them electronically has originated from the notary and that the notary has in fact notarised the document. There is also the issue of how the electronic document would be legalised (verification of the notary's seal and signature).

An issue within England and Wales is that English notaries have little need to communicate with each other or send notarised documents to each other. Their role, as indicated above, is to carry out notarial acts for use in other countries. This is different from the position in many other (particularly civil law) countries, where notaries frequently need to send notarised documents to other notaries.

In some countries, systems have been developed to permit the electronic exchange of documents.[40]

The central issue is to ensure that the electronic document which is sent by the notary in England and Wales has not been altered, added to, etc. before or after it reaches its destination. There are, of course, different technical methods of securing documents. One method which has been actively developed in England and Wales is the use of digital signatures through a public key system. Notaries would register with an organisation, who would hold and administer a notary's public key digital signature. Notaries would receive on registration a USB key which would hold their key, and with this they would sign their documents. The notary would create her document in the normal way, scan the document into her computer, create a PDF file and apply her digital signature.

---

40 For example, in Austria and some states in the United States.

Whatever the technical method which is chosen, it must in practice be recognised by the Foreign and Commonwealth Office (FCO) and by the professionals and others who will be receiving the document. This is still some way off. At the time material for this book was prepared, discussions as to the method to be used by notaries and the FCO and other interested parties were still at an early stage.

Consequently, for some years yet notarisation will continue to mean the use of paper which has to be physically sent to the destination country.

28.15   IDENTIFYING AND DEALING WITH COMPANIES[41]

Where a notary deals with a company she will need:

- to identify the company itself;
- to check whether the company has the authority, capacity and intention to enter into a transaction or deal with an event; and
- to identify the individual(s) signing on behalf of the company and whether they have the authority and capacity to do so.

Identification steps

- Identify the company with the Registrar of Companies. This will normally involve ensuring that the company is formed or regulated under CA 1985 or CA 2006 and that the main details provided by the client company match the information held by the Registrar.
- Obtain information from the Registrar of Companies concerning the identity of the company's officers, the company's composition and standing. At a minimum, this will normally mean obtaining the current appointment record (which will identify who the current directors are, the company secretary, if the company has one, its filing history, etc.) and also obtaining other essential information (e.g. memorandum and articles of association, recent annual returns, etc.).[42] A check may also be made as to whether there are any matters recorded with the Registrar, e.g. late filing of returns.[43]
- Obtain a 'certificate of good standing' from the Registrar of Companies.[44]

---

41 Companies incorporated under CA 2006 or its predecessors.
42 This information is available at a modest cost from the Registrar of Companies' website if the documents are delivered electronically to the notary.
43 Such issues may need to be noted in the notarial certificate.
44 This can only be obtained (at the time material for this book was prepared) by telephone, and not online from the website of the Registrar of Companies (or the subscription service offered by the Registrar, Companies House Direct).

These certificates are often obtained the first time a notary deals with a company, and they also need to be provided when a company is carrying out particular activities (such as opening a bank account, or opening a local branch).

Authority and capacity

- Check the company's memorandum and articles of association to establish whether the event or transaction is within the powers of the company and/or whether there are special procedures laid down as to how the company is to deal with such activities (i.e. whether particular types of meeting need to be called, notices issued, issues be reserved to particular directors, and the extent to which the 'default' articles of association have been incorporated or excluded).
- Check the client company's minute book(s) as to whether there are any decisions of the directors or shareholders which restrict the company and/or the individual who is to sign documents on behalf of the company, e.g. a company may require a particular shareholder to give her consent in particular circumstances, or only certain directors may be permitted to sign particular documents.

Authority and capacity of individuals who are to sign documents

- Personally identify the individuals who are to sign any documents (i.e. through their passports and evidence of their residential address to the satisfaction of the notary).
- Ensure that individuals who are to sign are of the correct status to sign the document in question; e.g. if the document is a deed, ensure that it is signed in the ways permitted by CA 2006, s.44, or if the person or organisation receiving the document requires the document to be signed by a particular individual, then ensure that the individual signs the document as authorised by the company by deed and where appropriate in compliance with Powers of Attorney Act 1971.
- Ensure that the individuals who are to sign a document are authorised to do so, normally by requiring a board resolution to be passed to that effect. Sometimes reference is made to the relevant provision of CA 2006 (s.44).

Authorising an individual to sign for or on behalf of a company

Directors of companies formed under CA 1985 (and also, from October 2009, CA 2006) have wide powers to run and manage the affairs of the company. However, they are still only the agents of the company and a notary will wish to ensure that the company is willing to be bound by the documents signed by the directors (or others). One way is simply to ask the representatives of the company (with the persons who are to sign the document) to prove the chain of authority. Another way is to obtain specific authority via a board resolution itself signed and authenticated.

In practice, most notaries when dealing with a company will normally require to see a board resolution authorising the person who is to sign the document in question ('the Signatory'). There are a number of practical and legal reasons for this:

- to ensure that the Signatory has the authority to bind the company. As noted above, directors of companies, for example, have wide powers to run and manage the affairs of the company under English law.[45] The position may be different in other countries, where it can be a requirement that persons who are to sign for or on behalf of a company need first to obtain specific authority to do so;
- to provide protection to persons who rely on contracts and other documents (such as powers of attorney signed by a Signatory). Under CA 2006, s.44(5), there is a presumption that documents executed as specified by s.44 are deemed to be validly executed by the company.[46] This presumption can only be relied upon by a purchaser acting in good faith for valuable consideration. This limited presumption excludes a whole range of transactions and persons from relying on it. For example:
  - commercial/contractual transactions: persons other than a purchaser may need to rely on the fact that the Signatory is authorised to bind the company, e.g. a transaction might need registration with a foreign regulatory authority and that authority may rely on the fact that the person(s) who signed for the company were authorised to do so;
  - where the Signatory is required to confirm some fact, such as whether an employee is in fact an employee, this confirmation may be required by a foreign organisation or regulatory authority of the employee in that country;
  - statements about the company's organisational or constitutional status, events that have taken place, etc.: a Signatory may e.g. be asked to confirm that a copy of minutes of a board meeting are genuine or indicate that the company/board of directors have taken a certain decision; if the company is opening a subsidiary or a bank account in another country, then various regulatory and banking authorities may need to see such a statement;
- to protect the notary: a notary will never be in the class of persons who can rely on the presumption in CA 2006, s.44(5). If the person who signs for a company is not in fact authorised, a person who relies on a docu-

---

45 Subject always to any restrictions found in the articles of association, resolutions of the shareholders, shareholders' agreements, etc.
46 See **Chapters 4** and **16**.

ment purportedly executed by a company could potentially sue the notary if the company later disclaims the document (or the transaction or event set out in the document is invalid).

When to use board resolutions

Because of the above issues, many notaries, for the more important type of documents signed by or on behalf of a company, will:

- require the company to hold a board meeting and pass a board resolution to the effect that the event or transaction in question be entered into or take place, and to authorise the person(s) who are to sign any documents for or on behalf of the company (more often than not, the draft document(s) will be tabled and mentioned in the resolution itself); or
- require sight of a previously passed board resolution to like effect and which is worded so that it clearly covers the event or transaction in question and specifically authorises the persons who are to sign.

For more routine documents a notary will often not require a board resolution. This begs the question of what is a 'routine' document. There cannot be a definitive list, but documents which do no more than record or note some existing fact about a company or any of its assets or employees are less likely to need a board resolution.[47] But documents such as powers of attorney, contracts, documents agreeing to enter into any kind of financial arrangement or facility, or agreeing to a charge, etc. will (virtually) always require a board resolution.[48]

28.16   WHICH LEGAL SYSTEM MUST A DOCUMENT COMPLY WITH?

One of the roles of the notary is to create a document which will be legally binding and effective in the country where the document is intended to be used.

This role will include, in appropriate cases, ensuring that the document:

- is laid out in the right manner ('form');
- contains the right wording at its commencement and its end;
- is certified or authenticated as to the information within it ('content');

---

47 For example, a director indicating in a document that a person is an employee of a company, or a director stating that a copy of a document attesting to the statement of the director is a true copy and record of a board meeting held on a certain date.

48 This will extend even to requiring a one-member company (where the member is also the sole director) to pass a board resolution authorising that same member/director to sign the document.

- is signed by a client in the way required by the receiving country (such as ensuring the client signs in the right places, before the correct number of witnesses, and in some cases using the right coloured ink, etc.); and
- contains the correct information about, and the signature and seal of, the notary.

One particular area of difficulty is whether documents should be executed in a way that also makes them legally binding and effective in England and Wales. Although among notaries there is no definitive view on this matter, many notaries believe that any document they deal with should also be legally binding in England and Wales, at least as to the manner of its execution.

In practice, the need to create a document which is legally binding both in England and Wales and abroad does not normally create particular problems, except in one area, the creation of deeds. A deed is a form unknown in civil jurisdictions. For a document such as a power of attorney to be binding in England and Wales, it has to be executed as a deed; no other method of execution is permissible to create a validly binding power, but some lesser documents such as agency agreements may not need to be by deed.

28.17   LEGALISATION

What is legalisation?

Legalisation is the process whereby a notary's seal and signature are verified as being genuine. Some official documents (whether or not they are notarised) can also be legalised: the signature of the official (and seal, if the official has one) can also be verified as being genuine.[49]

Who carries out legalisation in England and Wales?

The FCO and/or a country's consulate/embassy.[50]

---

49 Documents such as birth, marriage, civil partnership and death certificates or certificates of good standing issued by the Registrar of Companies are sometimes legalised without a notary being involved (since they are signed by public officials). However, in some countries, such documents will not be acceptable unless a notary has certified or authenticated them.

50 There are a small number of countries where legalisation takes place in those countries' embassies or consulates situated outside England and Wales; e.g. Cape Verde (done in that country's consulate in The Hague) or the Central African Republic (done in that country's consulate in Paris).

What legalisation is not

Legalisation does not mean that the contents or legal effectiveness of a document have been checked, authorised or approved by the United Kingdom or any other government or authority which is carrying out the legalisation.[51]

When legalisation is required

Legalisation is required for most documents which are to be used in many countries. Those which do not require legalisation are mainly Commonwealth countries (but not all of them) and most states in the United States.

There are also categories of documents going to countries which normally do not require legalisation, regardless of the country of origin concerned.

How is it determined whether legalisation is required and who carries it out?

There are essentially three categories:

- **Only by the FCO**. Many countries have implemented an international convention (the Hague Convention).[52] For these countries, legalisation is carried out only by the FCO. This is also often called 'obtaining an apostille'. Most European countries and a number of Latin-American countries have implemented the Hague Convention.[53]
- There are a few countries which have implemented the Hague Convention but still require, in addition to legalisation by the FCO, legalisation by their consulate/embassy. India is the most noticeable example of this requirement.[54]
- **Legalisation is not required**. Most Commonwealth countries and many states in the United States do not require legalisation at all. Although some Commonwealth countries have implemented the Hague Convention, they still do not require any form of legalisation.

---

51 The apostille placed on a document by the FCO concludes with the following words: 'An apostille or legalisation certificate only confirms that the signature, seal or stamp on the document is genuine. It does not mean that the contents of the document are correct or that the Foreign and Commonwealth Office approves of its contents'.

52 Hague Convention of 5 October 1961 Abolishing the Requirement of Legalisation for Foreign Public Documents. Technically, the affixing of an apostille is a replacement for the need for legalisation (which needed to take place before 1961). In reality, obtaining an apostille is a simplified form of legalisation. For the sake of simplicity of presentation, 'legalisation' is used to describe the process of certifying the seal and signature of a notary, whether or not the Hague Convention applies.

53 A list of principal countries which are members of the Hague Convention is given below, p.307.

54 But in practice in India, the requirements as to which documents need to be legalised and which do not vary according to the state or area the document is destined for. In some cases the 'amount' of legalisation varies as well (i.e. whether just by the Indian High Commission, or just by the FCO, or both).

- **By the country's embassy/consulate**. Countries which are not in the above two categories generally require legalisation at their embassy or consulate. The procedure is that legalisation is first carried out at the FCO and then also at the embassy/consulate of the country involved.

However, there are many variations. For example, for several Arab countries, a particular chamber of commerce also needs to stamp the document.

Who can obtain legalisation

Legalisation does not need to be done by the notary who notarises a document; it can be carried out by anyone who has possession of the document, such as the notary's client or even a third party who has the document.

What does legalisation involve

The FCO maintains an electronic database of notaries' signatures and seals and it will compare the signature and seal on a document with that database. For documents signed by government officials, the FCO may check directly with the issuing department, office or agency to establish whether the document has in fact been signed by the government official.

Consulates or embassies will often require the notary to send a sample seal and signature. However, where legalisation is required by a consulate, the document often needs to be legalised first by the FCO. In such cases, the consulate or embassy will often be stating that the signature of the FCO official and the FCO seal are genuine, rather than that of the notary.

How to recognise when a document is legalised

The FCO attaches a piece of paper (called an 'apostille') often on the reverse page of the notarised document where the signature and seal of the notary are placed. The apostille certifies the authenticity of the notary's signature, the capacity in which the notary acted (i.e. as notary) and the authenticity of the notary's seal or stamp placed on the documents. In addition, the seal of the FCO is also impressed on the document.

Legalisation by embassies or consulates usually consists of placing some form of stamp on the document, often close to or on the apostille.

Countries where the Hague Convention applies (and legalisation is only carried out by the FCO)

Albania	Denmark	Luxembourg	Saint Vincent and
Andorra	Dominica	Macedonia	the Grenadines
Antigua and	Ecuador	(Former	Samoa*
Barbuda*	El Salvador	Yugoslav	San Marino
Argentina	Estonia	Republic of)	Serbia
Armenia	Fiji	Malawi	Seychelles*
Australia*	Finland	Malta	Slovakia
Austria	France	Marshall Islands	Slovenia
Azerbaijan	Georgia	Mauritius	South Africa*
Bahamas*	Germany	Mexico	Spain
Barbados*	Greece	Moldova,	Suriname
Belarus	Grenada*	Republic of	Swaziland*
Belgium	Honduras	Monaco	Sweden
Belize	Hungary	Montenegro	Switzerland
Bosnia and	Iceland	Namibia*	Tonga*
Herzegovina	India**	Netherlands	Trinidad and
Botswana*	Ireland	New Zealand*	Tobago*
Brunei	Israel	Niue	Turkey**
Darussalam*	Italy	Norway	Ukraine
Bulgaria	Japan	Panama	United Kingdom
China, People's	Kazakhstan	Poland	of Great
Republic of,	Korea,	Portugal	Britain and
Hong Kong	Republic of	Romania	Northern
Colombia	Latvia	Russian	Ireland
Cook Islands	Lesotho*	Federation	United States of
Croatia	Liberia	Saint Kitts and	America**
Cyprus	Liechtenstein	Nevis*	Venezuela
Czech Republic	Lithuania	Saint Lucia*	

Notes:

*   Do not require legalisation of documents notarised by an English notary.

** **India:** although legalisation by the FCO is required, it appears that at least in some parts of India a document will not be accepted unless the document has a stamp (legalisation) from the Indian High Commission (IHC) from London or Birmingham. the current practice of the IHC is no longer to stamp documents (at the time material for the book was finalised). However, notaries find that the IHC will sometimes stamp a document (depending on the official receiving the document). The contradictions and problems have not been resolved yet.

United States: only a few states normally require an apostille (or it is advisable to obtain one): California, District of Columbia, Iowa, Kansas, Maryland, New Jersey, New York, Pennsylvania, Rhode Island, Washington, West Virginia, Wisconsin

Turkey: for some mercantile and shipping documents, the documents need to go first to the Turkey-British Chamber of Commerce and then to the Turkish Consulate.

Other countries

For many countries other than those in the above list, a notarised document will need first to go to the FCO and then to the country's embassy or consulate.[55] For some countries (particularly some Arab countries) the document may also first need to go to a local or other chamber of commerce.

Countries where legalisation is not normally required

Anguilla
Antigua and
   Barbuda
Australia
Bahamas
Barbados
Bermuda
Botswana
Canada
Cayman Islands
Channel Islands
Dominica
Falkland Islands
Fiji
Ghana (except for
   some mercantile
   documents)

Gibraltar
Grenada
Guyana
Ireland
Jamaica
Kenya
Lesotho
Madagascar
Malawi
Man, Isle of
Montserrat
Namibia
New Zealand
Nigeria
Papua New
   Guinea

Pitcairn Island
Saint Helena
Saint Kitts and
   Nevis
Saint Lucia
Saint Vincent
   and the
   Grenadines
Samoa
Seychelles
Sierra Leone
Singapore (except
   for some
   mercantile
   documents)
Solomon Islands

South Africa
Sri Lanka
Swaziland
Tanzania
The Gambia
Tonga
Trinidad and
   Tobago
Turks and Caicos
   Islands
Tuvalu
Uganda
Vanatu
Zambia
Zimbabwe

How long obtaining legalisation may take

In the case of the FCO, for persons willing to visit the FCO office and wait, it will usually take two to three hours for a document to be legalised there and then.[56] By post, the FCO will normally return a legalised document within one to two weeks. Where in addition to or instead of legalisation by the FCO, legalisation needs to take place at a country's embassy or consulate, between two to five working days may need to be allowed.[57] Use of a notarial agent may speed this up, but at an extra cost.

---

55 The fees charged vary widely. Some countries charge several hundred pounds for each document.

56 The legalisation department of the FCO is currently in central London, but is due to move to central Milton Keynes in summer 2008, with a 'premium' service available in central London (at a cost of £67 per a document, with documents being processed within a few hours, but only available to 'business' customers). See **www.fco.gov.uk** for details.

57 There are many variations as to these procedures, including some consulates or embassies not allowing documents to be sent or returned by post (hand delivery is only permissible), or only allowing payment by particular means (e.g. postal orders), etc.

28.18 EXAMPLES

The following provides a few examples of how a notary might deal with common routine notary tasks, the creation of a power of attorney for an individual or a company (registered under or regulated by CA 1985 or CA 2006).

Individual signing a power of attorney

1. Meet the client.
2. Examine their identification (such as passport and utility bill or bank statement).
3. Ask them verbally to confirm their identity and address (e.g. 'Is your name Rachael Isabella Simona Kennedy?' or 'Could you tell me your name?' or 'Do you live at this address?').[58]
4. Ask the client to fill out a form which records their name, address and other contact details, and in which the client will also provide a specimen signature.[59]
5. Read the power of attorney that the client wishes to sign.
6. Read any instructions provided with the power of attorney.[60]
7. Check whether the details of identification match those in the power of attorney and amend it accordingly or obtain further explanation or instructions.[61]
8. Check whether the document is in the public or private form.
9. If in the public form, check whether all the details required to create a notarial act are present in the power of attorney.[62]

---

58 This may seem a odd thing to do, and would not be something that a English solicitor would do when carrying out their money laundering check on a client. However, because of the value of notarised documents, notaries need to be particularly careful that they do not facilitate criminal activity. For example, in some countries the value of a notarised copy of a passport is the same as the original passport. A forged British passport obtained in England of which a copy is notarised could be used in criminal activity in other countries, with the notarised copy being relied on by others (such as regulatory authorities, banks or lawyers) assuming that the original passport was genuine. Some notaries, who have been the target of criminals, have reported instances of a person appearing before them with a passport requesting a notarised copy, but being unable when asked to spell their own name or state their own address, etc.

59 This is retained by, and for use only by, the notary.

60 If the power of attorney has been provided by a lawyer or notary of the destination country, the lawyer/notary may have particular requirements as to how the document should be dealt with (how and where it should be signed, witnesses, etc.).

61 For example, where a woman on marriage has taken her husband's surname, her identification documentation also only shows her married surname, but the power of attorney gives the surname the woman used before her marriage. In such a case the notary may require sight of the client's marriage certificate in addition to other identification documentation.

62 A simplified example of a document in public form is set out at Example 1 below. See the discussion of what constitutes a notarial act and the 'notarial certificate' above, pp. 285–6, for details of the contents of a notarial act.

10. Discuss with the client, at a minimum, the following:

    (a) whether they have read the power of attorney;

    (b) whether any factual matters are correctly set out;[63]

    (c) the client's explanation of the purpose of the power of attorney;

    (d) whether the client agrees to grant the power of attorney to the person(s) named in the document and whether they know who they are;

    (e) point out any matters which need the client's attention, such as:

        (i) the extent of some of the powers;[64]

        (ii) the consequences of some of the powers;

        (iii) whether there is any wording in the power of attorney providing for a time limit on its operation;

        (iv) whether there is any wording in the power of attorney permitting the attorney(s) to represent both sides in a transaction, to act where there is a conflict of interest, or whether they can enter into a transaction as a contracting party.

11. Where required, read the text of the power of attorney to the client.[65]

12. If witnesses are required to be present, ensure their presence and note down their details (full names, address and other contact details).

13. Confirm with the client that the client is willing to be bound by the power of attorney.

14. If there are any handwritten amendments, ask the client to initial the changes and the notary will initial them.[66]

15. Ask the client to initial each page except the signature page, and to sign on the signature page, doing these things only in the presence of the witnesses (if any) and the notary.

---

63 For example, in some French powers of attorney permitting a French notary to purchase property on behalf of a client, the details of the property to be purchased are set out in great detail (such as details as to the precise size of the property to be bought).

64 For example, some Spanish powers of attorney are expressed in very general terms, and are worded so that the attorney can buy any property, borrow any sums of money, etc. There are also sometimes provisions included allowing the attorney to act where there is a conflict of interest or to become a contracting party (neither of which would be acceptable for an English lawyer instructed to deal with the conveyance of a property). There is often no mention of the specific transaction that the client is to enter into. The argument put forward by Spanish lawyers/notaries for this is that details about what is to be bought cannot be specified at the time the power of attorney is granted and that the attorney should not normally be handicapped by too restrictive a power of attorney. When the actual transaction is to take place, the argument goes, the attorney will seek further instructions or permission from the client before committing the client.

65 In some countries, the notary is required to read out documents such as a power of attorney to the client. This type of instruction is sometimes requested from English notaries.

66 For some countries, handwritten amendments are not permitted.

16. The notary will also initial each page and add her signature on the signature page.
17. If witnesses are present, they will also add their initials to every page except the signature page and sign on the signature page.
18. If the document is not in public form, prepare a separate document (notarial certificate) which records the required information for a notarial act (see Example 2 below).
19. On completion, bind the power of attorney securely together (with any separate notarial certificate, if there is one). Binding usually takes place using rivets and then using tape to bind the document together. The notarial seal is usually impressed onto a self-adhesive red sticker placed over the ends of the tape (see Example 3 below). The ends of the tape and the red sticker will appear next to where the notary signs.[67] If the notary is preparing a separate certificate, the ends of the tape and the sticker are placed on the certificate. If the document is in public form then the ends of the tape and the sticker are placed next to where the notary signs (i.e. the signature page). The notary then impresses her seal on the sticker.
20. If the power of attorney is in private form, the notary will normally make a copy, or if it is in public form, she may create two or more originals, one of which will be retained by the notary, with the second original being provided to the client.
21. The notarised power of attorney will then be handed to the client or it will be sent away to be legalised (if required).

Company signing a power of attorney

1. Obtain the full name of the company.[68]
2. Obtain the current appointments record and basic constitutional documents[69] available from the Registrar of Companies.
3. Consider the documents obtained, in particular as to whether the company has the powers to enter into the transaction or event envisaged or whether it can execute the power of attorney.
4. Obtain a certificate of good standing from the Registrar of Companies.[70]

---

67 If the seal and the signature of the notary are not together on the same page, legalisation may be refused. For example, the FCO generally rejects documents where the notary's seal and signature are not together.
68 For example, there might be several companies within a group, some with similar names.
69 Such as the memorandum and articles of association, certificate of incorporation, annual return, etc.
70 This is only available by telephone and not from the Registrar of Companies' website. Certificates take different formats as to the information they contain (whether any registered charges are included, details of shareholders, etc.). It is also necessary to request that the certificate be signed (otherwise it is, by default, provided unsigned).

5. Visit the client company.
6. Inspect the client company's books, in particular the minutes for board meetings and shareholders, to see whether there are any restrictions as to what the company can do or as to who can sign documents such as powers of attorney.
7. Identify the director(s)/company secretary who are to sign the power of attorney in the same way as for an individual.
8. Examine any board resolution authorising:

   (a) the company to execute the power of attorney;
   (b) the particular method of execution (if specified); and
   (c) the director(s)/company who are to sign.

   The board resolution may be specific to the power of attorney and transaction or event underlying it or may be more general and authorise the intended signors to sign such documents which relate to a specified transaction or event.

9. Read the draft power of attorney that the client company has supplied.
10. Read any instructions provided with the power of attorney.
11. Check whether the details of the company are correctly set out in the power of attorney and amend it accordingly if necessary.
12. Check whether the document is in the public or private form.
13. If in the public form, check whether all the details required to create a notarial act are present.
14. Discuss with the contact person of the client company, at a minimum, the following:

    (a) whether they have read the power of attorney;
    (b) whether any factual matters in the power of attorney are correctly set out;
    (c) the client contact's explanation of the purpose of the power of attorney;
    (d) whether the client contact agrees to grant the power of attorney to the person(s) named in the document and whether they know who they are;
    (e) point out any matters which need the client company's particular attention, such as:

        (i) the extent of some of the powers;
        (ii) the consequences of some of the powers;
        (iii) whether there is any wording in the power of attorney providing for a time limit on its operation;
        (iv) whether there is any wording in the power of attorney permitting the attorney(s) to represent both sides in a transaction, to act where there is a conflict of interest, or whether they can enter into a transaction as a contracting party.

15. Confirm with the client contact that the client company is willing to be bound by the power of attorney.

16. If the authorised signatories who are to sign are different from the client contact person, confirm with them that they understand the type of document they are signing, what it is for and whether they are willing to sign for the company.

17. The notary should see the director(s)/company secretary initial each page except for the signature page, see them sign on the signature page, and if only one director is signing ensure that a witness is present who can attest the director's signature.

18. If there are any handwritten amendments, ask the director(s)/secretary to initial the changes and the notary will initial them.

19. The notary will also initial each page and add her signature on the signature page.

20. If witnesses are present, they will also add their initials to every page except the signature page and sign on the signature page.

21. If the document is not in public form, prepare a document (notarial certificate) which records the required information for a notarial act (see Example 4 below).

22. On completion, bind the power of attorney securely together (and any notarial certificate, if there is one). Binding usually takes place using rivets and then using tape to bind the document together. The notarial seal is usually impressed onto a self-adhesive red sticker placed over the ends of the tape (see Example 3 below). The ends of the tape and the red sticker will appear next to where the notary signs.[71] If the notary is preparing a certificate, the ends of the tape and the sticker are placed on the certificate. If the document is in public form, then the ends of the tape and the sticker are placed next to where the notary signs (i.e. the signature page). The notary then impresses her seal on the sticker.

23. If the power of attorney is in private form, the notary will normally make a copy, or if it is in public form, she may create two or more originals, one of which will be retained by the notary, with the second original being provided to the client.

24. The notarised power of attorney will then be handed to the client company, or the document will be sent away to be legalised (if required).

---

71 If the seal and the signature of the notary are not together on the same page, legalisation may be refused. For example, the FCO generally rejects documents where the notary's seal and signature are not together.

Example 1: simplified French power of attorney in public form[72]

PROCURATION

L'AN DEUX MILLE [HUIT]

Le [5 février]

Pardevant Maître Victor Julian Warner, notaire public, à 49 Moor Mead Road, St Margarets, TW1 1JS, Angleterre, dûment admise et assermentée, soussigné, en la présence réelle du témoin instrumentaire ci-après nommé,

A COMPARU

Monsieur Charles Allan BAUDELAIRE, poète, demeurant à 1 St James Square, London, EX11 4PW

Né à Whitehall, Londres (Grande Bretagne) le 12, décembre 1963

Titulaire du passeport britannique numéro 06666666, délivré le 21 septembre 1999 et valable jusqu'au 21 septembre 2009

Époux de Madame Jane Charlotte AUSTIN, ensemble marié sous le régime équivalent au régime français de la séparation de biens et ce à défaut de contrat préalable à leur union cél

Et Madame, son épouse, demeurant ensemble à 1 St James Square, London, EX11 4PW.

Et né à Bath (Grande Bretagne), le 01 juillet 1961.

Titulaire du passeport britannique numéro 0999999, délivré le 29 juin 1999 et valable jusqu'au 29 juin 2009

Mariés sans contrat à Bristol (Grande Bretagne), le 02 novembre 1990.

«Non résidents» au sens de la réglementation fiscale.

La ou les personnes désignées ci-dessus seront dénommées dans le corps du présent acte "Le MANDANT" terme qui inclura tant le singulier que le pluriel que le genre masculin et féminin)

Le MANDANT par ces présentes, constitue pour son mandataire spécial :

Joseph Kosma, demeurant à 1 rue de la poète, Paris, XX11, France dénommé(s) sous le vocable "le Mandataire"

auquel il donne pouvoir de, pour lui et en son nom:

[list of powers to be given to the attorney(s)]

---

72 The wording is drawn from various examples provided by notaries at a number of seminars run by the Notaries Society. It is only to give an idea of *some* of the content of a power of attorney in public form. It should never be used in a real transaction.

DONT ACTE

en [*number of pages of power of attorney*] [sur modèle émanant de l'étude de Maître Joseph Kosma, notaire à 1 rue de la poète, Paris, XX11, France. Fait et passé à St. Margarets en présence de Adolphe Appolleniare , témoin instrumentaire requis.

AUX EFFETS ci-dessus, passer et signer tous actes et procès-verbaux, élire domicile, substituer et généralement faire le nécessaire.

LE PRESENT ACTE rédigé sur [ ] pages,
A été signé par les parties, après lecture,
Aux lieu et date indiqués en tête des présentes.

(signature of donors)

(signature of notary and seal of notary)

Example 2: notarial certificate attached to a power of attorney (not in public form) signed by individuals

I, Victor Julian Warner of 49 Moor Mead Road, St Margarets, TW1 1JS, England, Notary Public, duly admitted and authorised to practise in England and Wales, CERTIFY as follows:

that at 49 Moor Mead Road, St Margarets, TW1 1JS, England on 5 February 2008 appeared

CHARLES ALLAN BAUDELAIRE, date of birth 12 December 1963, residing at 1 St James Square, London, EX11 4PW, England, British citizen

Identified by his own statement and production of current British passport, passport number 066666666, expiring on 21 September 2009

and

JANE CHARLOTTE AUSTIN, date of birth 1 July 1961, resident at 1 St James Square, London, EX11 4PW, England, British citizen

Identified by her own statement and production of current British passport, passport number 09999999, expiring on 29 June 2009

and each of **CHARLES ALLAN BAUDELAIRE** and **JANE CHARLOTTE AUSTIN** signed the annexed power of attorney (comprising 4 A4 sheets of paper) in my presence, with the document being for use in France (and in connection with their purchase of a property)

Signed and sealed by me on 5 February 2008 at 49 Moor Mead Road, St Margarets, TW1 1JS, England

---

Victor Julian Warner, Notary Public

England and Wales

Protocol Number: 2008/001

Example 3: notarial certificate attached to a power of attorney (not in public form) signed by directors for a company

I, Victor Julian Warner of 49 Moor Mead Road, St Margarets, TW1 1JS, England, Notary Public, duly admitted and authorised to practise in England and Wales, CERTIFY as follows:

that the annexed Power of Attorney (comprising 1 A4 sheet of paper and the document being for use in France)

was signed for and on behalf of **INTELLECTUAL PROPERTY LIMITED**, a company registered in England and Wales with registered number 99999999, and having its registered office and principal place of business at Work House, 1 St James Square, London, XX11 1ED by

CHARLES ALLAN BAUDELAIRE, date of birth 12 December 1963, residing at 1 St James Square, London, EX11 4PW, England, British citizen

Identified by his own statement and production of current British passport, passport number 066666666, expiring on 21 September 2009

and

JANE CHARLOTTE AUSTIN, date of birth 1 July 1961, resident at 1 St James Square, London, EX11 4PW, England, British citizen

Identified by her own statement and production of current British passport, passport number 09999999, expiring on 29 June 2009

and each of **CHARLES ALLAN BAUDELAIRE** and **JANE CHARLOTTE AUSTIN** signed in their capacity as a director of **INTELLECTUAL PROPERTY LIMITED** duly authorised pursuant to a resolution of the board of directors of **INTELLECTUAL PROPERTY LIMITED** dated 4 February 2008

in my presence at Work House, 1 St James Square, London, XX11 1ED on 5 February 2008

Signed and sealed by me on 5 February 2008 at 49 Moor Mead Road, St Margarets, TW1 1JS, England

---

Victor Julian Warner, Notary Public

England and Wales

Protocol Number: 2008/002

Example 4: Notarial certificate attached to a copy of a British passport

I, Victor Julian Warner of 49 Moor Mead Road, St Margarets, TW1 1JS, England, Notary Public, duly admitted and authorised to practise in England and Wales, CERTIFY as follows:

that the paper writing annexed hereto is a true copy of an extract (page 32 and the photograph page) from the United Kingdom of Great Britain and Northern Ireland passport of **JANE CHARLOTTE AUSTIN**, date of birth 1 July 1961, passport number 9999999999, expiring on 29 June 2009 (and comprising 1 A4 sheet of paper)

with **JANE CHARLOTTE AUSTIN**, residing at 1 St James Square, London, EX11 4PW, England, British citizen

and the copy of these pages from the passport is made for the purpose as stated by JANE CHARLOTTE AUSTIN of being used in connection with **JANE CHARLOTTE AUSTIN'S** application to obtain a national insurance number in Spain

and the passport was produced by **JANE CHARLOTTE AUSTIN** to me on 3 February 2008

Signed and sealed by me on 3 February 2008 at 49 Moor Mead Road, St Margarets, TW1 1JS, England

---

Victor Julian Warner, Notary Public

England and Wales

Protocol Number: 2008/004

Example 4: example of bound document

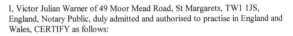

I, Victor Julian Warner of 49 Moor Mead Road, St Margarets, TW1 1JS, England, Notary Public, duly admitted and authorised to practise in England and Wales, CERTIFY as follows:

that at 49 Moor Mead Road, St Margarets, TW1 1JS, England on the 5 February 2008 appeared

CHARLES ALLAN BAUDELAIRE, date of birth 12 December 1963, residing at 1 St James Square, London, EX11 4PW,, England, British citizen

Identified by his own statement and production of current British passport, passport number 066666666, expiring on 21 September 2009

and

JANE CHARLOTTE AUSTIN, date of birth 1 July 1961, resident at 1 St James Square, London, EX11 4PW, England, British citizen

Identified by her own statement and production of current British passport, passport number 09999999, expiring on 29 June 2009

and each of **CHARLES ALLAN BAUDELAIRE** and **JANE CHARLOTTE AUSTIN** signed the annexed power of attorney (comprising 4 A4 sheets of paper) in my presence, with the document being for use in France (and in connection with their purchase of a property)

Signed and sealed by me on 5 February 2008 at 49 Moor Mead Road, St Margarets, TW1 1JS, England

Victor Julian Warner, Notary Public
England and Wales

Protocol Number: 2008/001

Victor Julian Warner
Notary Public
49 Moor Mead Road, St Margarets, TW1 1JS

Tel: 020 8892 0092
Fax: 020 8892 0092
Email: vwarner@andnotary.eu

Member of the Notaries Society

Not registered (as a notary) for VAT

CHAPTER 29

Welsh language

29.1 INTRODUCTION

Legislation concerning the use of the Welsh language appears to be confined to its use in the court system and a few instances which touch on some of the matters raised in this book (concerning delivery of forms to the Registrar of Companies, powers of attorney and delivery of forms to the Land Registry). There appears to be no specific legislation (whether primary or secondary) covering the general use of Welsh in statutory declarations, deeds or contracts.

29.2 USE OF WELSH IN LEGAL PROCEEDINGS UNDER WELSH LANGUAGE ACT 1993

Use of the Welsh language in legal proceedings in courts situated in Wales

A party in legal proceedings in Wales can speak in the Welsh language subject to:

- prior notice being given as may be required by the rules of court; and
- any necessary provision for interpretation being made accordingly (Welsh Language Act 1993, s.22).

Use of Welsh in documents in proceedings in or having a connection with Wales

Court rules can be made to allow the use of Welsh in documents in proceedings in or having a connection with Wales (Welsh Language Act 1993, s.22(2)).

Practice Directions

It appears no court rules under the Welsh Language Act 1993 have specifically been made, but a Practice Direction to CPR 39 has been made relating to the use of the Welsh language.[1] These Practice Directions deal with more specific points relating to the use of Welsh in court proceedings, and are outside the remit of this book, except for one point. This deals with where a party is required to complete an allocation questionnaire. He must include details of:

- any person who is to give oral evidence in Welsh; and
- any documents in Welsh (including witness statements and documents to be disclosed under CPR 31) in the allocation questionnaire (CPR PD 39 WEL, Rule 2.1).

Court forms and other documents used in court proceedings and the statement of truth

There are no court rules or Practice Directions concerning the use of court forms, or the wording to be used for the statement of truth. However, the Court Service has adopted a policy of making court forms bilingual or in some cases just in Welsh. The forms and other documents in Welsh can be found at: **www.hmcourts-service.gov.uk/cms/wales.htm**. Such forms contain the Welsh language equivalent of the statement of truth. However, there appears to be no version of the statement of truth in Welsh to replace those found in the CPR and CPR PDs (for example, for the statement of truth for a witness statement, CPR PD 32.26). But practically, no doubt, those found in the forms prepared by the Court Service can be adapted for use in witness statements, etc.

The Court Service has also produced a guide to the use of Welsh in the administration of justice,[2] which gives more detailed day-to-day guidance than that found in the Practice Directions.

29.3   USE OF OATHS

There is also available a power to enable the Lord Chancellor to make rules prescribing a Welsh form of any oath or affirmation to be administered and taken or made by any person in any court (Welsh Language Act 1993, s.23). Such Welsh forms are to have the like effect as if the oath/affirmation had been administered and taken or made in the English language.

---

1 CPR PD 39 WEL (Practice Direction relating to the use of the Welsh Language in Cases in the Civil Courts in Wales).
2 Welsh Language Scheme, prepared under the Welsh Language Act 1993, available at **www.hmcourts-service.gov.uk/cms/miscellaneous.htm**. Readers should consult Part 4 in particular about corresponding with courts in Wales, use of forms, etc.

It appears that the Lord Chancellor has not made any rules under this provision, and that the versions made in 1943 continue to apply.[3]

29.4   USE OF WELSH IN TRANSACTIONS WITH THE LAND REGISTRY

The Registrar has a general power to publish forms and directions he considers necessary or desirable for facilitating the conduct of the business of registrations under LRA 2002 (s.100(4)).

To this effect the prescribed forms[4] if published in a Welsh language version by the Registrar are to be regarded as having the same effect as the English versions.[5] Similarly, if Welsh language versions of the specified *signature block* are approved by the Registrar, they are to be regarded as having the same effect as the English versions (Land Registration Rules 2003, r.208(2)).

29.5   USE OF WELSH IN STATUTORY FORM OF POWERS OF ATTORNEY

The form of power of attorney found in PAA 1971, Sched. 1[6] also has a Welsh equivalent:

Gwneir y PWER ATWRNAI CYFFREDINOL hwn ar y   dydd o   20   gan AB o

Rwyf yn penodi CD o

[*neu* CD o   a

EF o   ar y cyd *neu*

ar y cyd ac yn unigol] i fod yn atwrnai (atwrneiod) ar fy rhan yn unol ag adran 10 Deddf Pwerau Atwrnai 1971.

TYSTIWYD CAN[7]

---

3 Welsh Courts (Oaths and Interpreters) Rules 1943, SI 1943/683. These are not set out in this book as they relate to making oaths and affirmations only in court.
4 Such as those set out in the several chapters of this book concerning deeds.
5 Land Registration Rules 2003, r.208(1). There are Welsh equivalents to the forms printed in this book in Part I; see also **www.cofrestrfatir.gov.uk/publications/default.asp?fl=1& pubtype=1**.
6 See **section 22.2** for the English equivalent.
7 Powers of Attorney (Welsh Language Forms) Order 2000, SI 2000/215, Sched., Part II.

CHAPTER 30

Criminal offences

30.1 INTRODUCTION

This chapter deals with criminal offences that:

- arise from statements made in; or
- concern the execution of the various types of

documents dealt with in this book.

30.2 STATUTORY DECLARATIONS

A person commits an offence if she knowingly and wilfully makes (otherwise than on oath) a statement false in a material particular, and the statement is made in a statutory declaration (Perjury Act 1911 (PA 1911), s.5). The Court of Appeal has held[1] that:

- the words 'knowingly and wilfully' import an intention to do the particular act proscribed with knowledge of the material circumstances which render it an offence; but
- such words do not include or import, as an additional requirement, some further or ulterior intention on the part of the defendant, where such further or ulterior intention would narrow the ambit of the offence and

---

1 *R* v. *Sood* [1998] 2 Cr App Rep 355, CA. The case concerned a GP signing a 'medical certificate of cause of death' concerning the death of one of his patients. He stated falsely that he had seen the patient when he had not. Another GP in the same practice had seen the patient. It is a statutory requirement that, in signing such a certificate, a GP must state either that he has seen the deceased patient within 14 days prior to death, or during the patient's illness at some point, and specify the cause of death. The judge at first instance ruled that, since it was admitted that the GP had deliberately completed the medical certificate knowing that the details which it contained were false, (i) the offence under s.5 was complete and (ii) the defendant had no defence that he honestly believed he was entitled to do as he did. The GP was fined £100 (with £1,600 costs). From the decision of the Court of Appeal, it appears that disciplinary proceedings were also pending. The GP's argument that what he did was common practice among GPs was rejected by the court.

enable a defendant to avoid liability by reference to such additional elements; and

- there is no necessity to prove an intention to deceive:

> We consider that the general 'mischief' at which offences contained in the Perjury Act are aimed is the intentional making of false statements by persons who are at the time under oath, or who make some declaration in performance of a public duty or function, or in various specific circumstances make a statement in a situation in which veracity is demanded in the interests of public administration. If that is correct, the motive with which the statement is made, and whether or not there is an active intention to deceive, is essentially irrelevant. The vice is the abuse of the occasion and the likely perpetuation of falsehood in relation to matters of public record.[2]

A convicted person can face up to two years' imprisonment or a fine, or both (PA 1911, s.5).

30.3 STATEMENTS MADE IN DOCUMENTS OTHER THAN STATUTORY DECLARATIONS

The offence set out above applies equally to statements made by a person in other types of documents, where the person is authorised or required to make, attest or verify that statement by a public general Act. PA 1911, s.5(b) gives a comprehensive list of documents that are covered: an abstract, account, balance sheet, book, certificate, declaration, entry, estimate, inventory, notice, report, return, or other document.

30.4 FALSE STATEMENT MADE IN A DOCUMENT VERIFIED BY A STATEMENT OF TRUTH

The party or person verifying a statement of case needs to have an honest belief in the truth of the statement made in it. To verify a statement of case that contains a false statement without an honest belief in its truth could lead to proceedings for contempt of court.[3]

Following *Malgar Ltd* v. *R. E. Leach (Engineering) Ltd* [2000] FSR 393 the tests that are likely to be applied in any proceedings for comtempt are:

- that the individual who made the false statement knew that what he was saying was false; and

---

2 From the judgment in *R* v. *Sood* [1998] 2 Cr App Rep 355, CA.
3 CPR PD 22.5, CPR 32.14. CPR PD 32.28 sets out the procedure where it is believed that a false statement has been made. It should be noted that CPR PD 22.5 only concerns statements of case, while CPR 32.14 refers to 'a document verified by a statement' which would encompass all documents required to be verified by a statement of truth. It is not clear why the restriction in CPR PD 22.5 is applied only to statements of case.

- that the false statement was likely to interfere with the course of justice.

Such proceedings can only be brought by the Attorney General or by any other person with the permission of the court (CPR 32.14).

A party alleging that a statement of truth or a disclosure statement is false shall refer the allegation to the court dealing with the claim (CPR PD 32.28.1). According to CPR PD 32.28.2 the court may:

- exercise any of its powers under the rules;
- consider whether there has been a contempt of court, and if there is to punish the contempt;
- direct the party alleging the contempt to refer the matter to the Attorney General for his consideration.

Applications to the Attorney General should be in writing, with a copy of the order from the judge referring the matter to the Attorney General. The information to be provided to the Attorney General should include the statement which is alleged to be false, an indication of why it is false, why the maker knew it was false at the time she made it, and an explanation why contempt of court proceedings are appropriate (in light of the overriding objective in CPR 1). The Attorney General prefers applications to come only after the judge has considered the allegation.

If a party wishes itself to commence proceedings for contempt of court, when it applies for permission, the party needs to provide the information described in the previous paragraph, and the result of an application to the Attorney General (CPR PD 32.28.3).

The law of contempt is not changed. A new form of contempt is not introduced (CPR PD 32.28.4). A consideration of the laws of contempt is outside the remit of this book; readers should consult the standard texts.

30.5 AFFIDAVITS

Affidavits used in judicial proceedings

Offence committed

Any person lawfully sworn as a witness or as an interpreter in judicial proceedings who wilfully makes a statement material in those proceedings, which:

- she knows to be false; or
- she does not believe to be true

shall be guilty of perjury, and shall on conviction on indictment be liable to imprisonment for a term not exceeding seven years or to a fine, or both (PA 1911, s.1(1)).[4]

Meaning of judicial proceedings

The meaning of judicial proceedings includes any (PA 1911, s.1(2)):

- court;
- tribunal; or
- person having by law power to hear, receive, and examine evidence on oath.

The meaning of a court includes the European Court (or any court attached to it) (European Communities Act 1972, s.11(1)).[5]

Affidavits sworn outside of a court

The above relates generally to statements made on oath in a court. Affidavits are generally made outside of court before a person authorised to administer an oath.[6] PA 1911 expressly covers statements made on oath but outside of a court and for use in judicial proceedings, which would cover an affidavit at s.1(3):

> Where a statement made for the purposes of a judicial proceeding is not made before the tribunal itself, but is made on oath before a person authorised by law to administer an oath to the person who makes the statement, and to record or authenticate the statement, it shall, for the purposes of this section, be treated as having been made in a judicial proceeding.

Form of oath

For the purposes of PA 1911, the form and ceremonies used in administering an oath are immaterial, if the court or person before whom the oath is taken has power to administer an oath for the purpose of verifying the statement in question, and if the oath has been administered in a form and with ceremonies

---

4 'Wilfully' means making a statement deliberately and not inadvertently or by mistake: *R* v. *Millward* [1985] QB 519, 80 Cr App Rep 280; making a statement not knowing at the time it was made whether it was true or false can be perjury: *R* v. *Mawbey* (1796) 6 Term Rep 619 at 637; or where a person does not believe a statement to be true when in fact it is true: *R* v. *Rider* (1986) 83 Cr App Rep 207, CA. A statement made by a person lawfully sworn in England for the purposes of judicial proceedings outside England will be treated as a statement in a judicial proceeding in England: PA 1911, s.1(4).
5 European Court means the Court of Justice of the European Communities: European Communities Act 1972, s.1(2), Sched. 1, Pt II.
6 See the list of persons so authorised at p. 271.

which the person taking the oath has accepted without objection, or has declared to be binding on him (PA 1911, s.15(1)).

An oath includes 'affirmation' and 'declaration' and the expression 'swear' includes 'affirm' and 'declare' (PA 1911, s.15(2)).

Overlap with other offences

If a person makes a false statement, and it is a corrupt practice under another Act of Parliament, or subjects the offender to any other penalty, the offender's liability under PA 1911 is in addition to his liability under the other Act of Parliament (PA 1911, s.16(1)). Where making a false statement is by any other Act of Parliament made punishable on summary conviction, proceedings may be taken under either Act of Parliament (PA 1911, s.16(3)).[7]

Affidavits not used in judicial proceedings

Any person who:

- being required or authorised by law to make any statement on oath for any purpose, and being lawfully sworn (otherwise than in a judicial proceeding) wilfully makes a statement which is material for that purpose and which he knows to be false or does not believe to be true; or
- wilfully uses any false affidavit for the purposes of the Bills of Sale Act 1878,

shall be liable to imprisonment for a term not exceeding seven years or to a fine, or both (PA 1911, s.2).[8]

30.6 CONTRACTS AND DEEDS

It is not usual for contracts or deeds to be the subject of criminal sanctions.[9] In certain circumstances, for example if:

- a document described as or required to be a deed is stated to be made as a deed, when it was not so made; or

---

7 But if such an offence in an Act passed before the commencement of PA 1911, as originally enacted, is made punishable only on summary conviction, it will remain only so punishable.

8 For the form of oath (i.e. sworn/affirmed) and meaning of judicial proceedings, see above.

9 For example, if a party to a contract gives as a warranty of fact that she has the power to enter into the contract, but in reality she knows that she cannot, the other party to the contract would normally have various remedies available to pursue in the civil courts, such as an action for breach of warranty, mistake, fraudulent misrepresentation, etc., depending on the circumstances.

- a deed or contract is executed by a person who claims the authority of another person to execute the deed, when in fact the first person did not have the necessary authority; or
- a deed or contract is stated to be executed on a stated date when it is executed on another date

this could, subject to the requirements of Forgery and Counterfeiting Act 1981 (FCA 1981), amount to forgery.

Offence of forgery

A person is guilty of forgery if he makes a false instrument, with the intention that he or another shall use it to induce somebody to accept it as genuine, and by reason of so accepting it to do or not to do some act to his own or any other person's prejudice (FCA 1981, s.1).[10]

Meaning of an 'instrument'

An instrument includes any document, whether of a formal or informal character (FCA 1981, s.8(1)(a)). This definition would cover contracts and deeds. An instrument also includes devices onto which information is electronically or otherwise recorded, such as a disk, tape, sound track or other form of device (FCA 1981, s.8(1)(d)).

Meaning of 'false instrument'

Under FCA 1981, s.9(1), an instrument is false if:

- it purports to have been made in the form in which it is made by a person who did not in fact make it in that form; or
- it purports to have been made in the form in which it is made on the authority of a person who did not in fact authorise its making in that form; or
- it purports to have been made in the terms in which it is made by a person who did not in fact make it in those terms; or
- it purports to have been made in the terms in which it is made on the authority of a person who did not in fact authorise its making in those terms; or
- it purports to have been altered in any respect by a person who did not in fact alter it in that respect; or
- it purports to have been altered in any respect on the authority of a person who did not in fact authorise the alteration in that respect; or

---

10 The intention to have the instrument accepted as genuine is not sufficient. There must also be an intention to induce the recipient to act or omit to act to his own or another person's prejudice: *R* v. *Tobierre* [1986] 1 All ER 346, 82 Cr App Rep 212, CA.

- it purports to have been made or altered on a date on which, or at a place at which, or otherwise in circumstances in which, it was not in fact made or altered; or
- it purports to have been made or altered by an existing person but he did not in fact exist.[11]

Meaning of 'make' or 'made'

A person is treated for the above purposes as making a false instrument if he alters an instrument so as to make it false in any respect (whether or not it is false in some other respect apart from that alteration) (FCA 1981, s.9(2)).

Meaning of 'prejudice' and 'induce'

An act or omission intended to be induced is to a person's prejudice, if, and only if, it is one which if it occurs (FCA 1981, s.10(1)):

- will result:
  - in his temporary or permanent loss of property; or
  - in his being deprived of an opportunity to earn remuneration or greater remuneration; or
  - in his being deprived of an opportunity to gain a financial advantage otherwise than by way of remuneration; or
- will result in somebody being given an opportunity:
  - to earn remuneration or greater remuneration from him; or
  - to gain a financial advantage from him otherwise than by way of remuneration; or
- will be the result of his having accepted a false instrument as genuine, or a copy of a false instrument as a copy of a genuine one, in connection with his performance of any duty.[12]

---

11 'Purports' for the purposes of this section means that the instrument, in order to be false, must tell a lie about itself: *R* v. *More* [1987] 3 All ER 825 at 830, [1987] 1 WLR 1578 at 1585, HL.
12 'Loss' includes not getting what one might get as well as parting with what one has: PA 1911, s.10(5).

CHAPTER 31

Fees and value added tax

31.1 POWER TO SET FEES FOR COMMISSIONERS FOR OATHS AND AMOUNT CHARGEABLE

Two Acts give power to the Secretary of State to set the fees that Commissioners for Oaths can charge for the taking of an oath or declaration, Solicitors Act 1974 (SA 1974) and CLSA 1990. Statutory instruments have been made setting the level of fees. These have remained unchanged since 1993.

Under Solicitors Act 1974

SA 1974, s.81A provides that:

(1) The Secretary of State may, with the concurrence of the Lord Chief Justice and the Master of the Rolls, by order prescribe the fees to be charged by –

    (a) commissioners for oaths; and
    (b) solicitors exercising the powers of commissioners for oaths by virtue of section 81,

in respect of the administration of an oath or the taking of an affidavit.

(2) Any order under this section shall be made by statutory instrument, which shall be laid before Parliament after being made.

(3) In this section 'affidavit' has the same meaning as in the Commissioners for Oaths Act 1889.

Under Courts and Legal Services Act 1990

CLSA 1990, s.113(8) provides that the Secretary of State may, with the concurrence of the Lord Chief Justice and the Master of the Rolls, by order prescribe the fees to be charged by authorised persons exercising the powers of Commissioners for Oaths by virtue of that section in respect of the administration of an oath or the taking of an affidavit. By s.120(1), that power is exercisable by statutory instrument, and s.120(6) provides that any such statutory instrument shall be subject to annulment in pursuance of a resolution of either House of Parliament.

Statutory instruments specifying the fees chargeable

The orders currently in force are:

- Commissioners for Oaths (Fees) Order 1993, SI 1993/2297 (made under SA 1974, s.81A); and
- Commissioners for Oaths (Authorised Persons) (Fees) Order 1993, SI 1993/2298 (made under CLSA 1990, s.113(8)).

Fees chargeable

- Both the orders provide that the fee to be charged by Commissioners for Oaths for taking an affidavit, declaration or affirmation shall be, for each person making the same, £5.00, and in addition for each exhibit or schedule required to be marked, £2.00.

31.2   VAT ISSUES

If the Commissioner is liable to value added tax (VAT) the fees prescribed by the 1993 Order are inclusive of VAT. If the Deponent is also a taxable person, and asks for a tax invoice, the invoice can be of the less detailed kind described in HM Revenue and Customs Notice 700 (*The VAT Guide*, revised April 2002), para. 16.6. At the end of each accounting period the Commissioner should account to HM Revenue and Customs for the appropriate fraction of the total fees received. At the current standard rate of VAT of 17.5 per cent, the fraction is 7/47ths.

By agreement between the Law Society and HM Revenue and Customs (see *Law Society's Gazette*, 8 June 1994) oath fees retained personally by associate or assistant solicitors are not subject to VAT unless the associate or assistant solictor:

- is registered or liable to register for VAT as a result of the aggregate of taxable supplies made to their own account; or
- is required to account to their firm for oath fees received, in which case the fees should be dealt with as part of the firm's taxable turnover.

Presumably the same principles apply to other employed Commissioners.

Oath fees earned by sole practitioners or partners remain part of the turnover of the 'taxable person' and liable to VAT.

31.3 AUTHORITY UNDER STATUTORY DECLARATIONS ACT 1835 PERMITTING A FEE TO BE CHARGED

Statutory Declarations Act 1835, s.19, provides that when a declaration is made under that Act such fees as would have been payable on making an affidavit shall be payable upon making the declaration.

The Council of the Law Society has expressed the opinion that it is improper for a Commissioner to share any part of his fee, e.g. by allowing to a solicitor's clerk for whom papers are being sworn some part of the fee as a gratuity. In *The Guide to the Professional Conduct of Solicitors 1999* (now superseded), point 4 of the commentary to principle 17.06 states that it is improper for a solicitor to share any part of his fees with any person, since the administration of oaths is the discharge of a public office.

It is not improper for an employed Commissioner to account to his employer for fees received. This is a matter for agreement between the Commissioner and the employer.

31.4 FEES CHARGEABLE IN THE COURTS

County court

An affidavit to be used in a county court may be sworn before a judge, district judge of any court or justice of the peace (or an officer of a county court appointed by the judge for that purpose) without the payment of any fee (County Courts Act 1984, s.58(2)).

High Court and Court of Appeal

The fee payable in the High Court or the Court of Appeal on taking an affidavit or an affirmation or attestation upon honour in lieu of an affidavit or a declaration except for the purpose of receipt of dividends from the Accountant General and for a declaration by a shorthand writer appointed in insolvency proceedings, for each person making the same, is £10.00, and for each exhibit therein referred to and required to be marked, £2.00 (Courts Act 2003, s.92; Civil Proceedings Fees Order 2008, SI 2005/1053, art. 2, Sched. 1).

Magistrates' court

A fee of £25 is to be paid for every oath, affirmation or solemn declaration not otherwise charged (no fee is payable for the swearing in of witnesses in civil proceedings or in any case where an Act directs that no fee shall be taken) (Courts Act 2003, s.92; Magistrates' Courts Fees Order 2008, SI 2008/1052, art. 2, Sched. 1).

APPENDIX 1

Selected statutory materials (as amended)

Contents

STATUTORY DECLARATIONS ACT 1835

2 Treasury may substitute a declaration in lieu of an oath, etc, in certain cases

In any case where by any Act or Acts made or to be made relating to the revenues of custom or excise, the office of stamps and taxes, the war office, the army pay office, the office of the treasurer of the navy, or the ordnance, his Majesty's Treasury, Chelsea Hospital, Greenwich Hospital, the Board of Trade, or any of the offices of his Majesty's principal secretaries of state, the India board, the office for auditing the public accounts, the national debt office, or any office under the control, direction, or superintendence of the Treasury, or by any official regulation in any department, any oath, solemn affirmation, or affidavit might, but for the passing of this Act, be required to be taken or made by any person on the doing of any act, matter, or thing, or for the purpose of verifying any book, entry, or return or for any other purpose whatsoever, it shall be lawful for the Treasury, if they shall so think fit, by writing under their hands and seals, to substitute a declaration to the same effect as the oath, solemn affirmation, or affidavit, which might but for the passing of this Act be required to be taken or made; and the person who might under the Act or Acts imposing the same be required to take or make such oath, solemn affirmation, or affidavit, shall, in presence of the commissioners, collector, other officer or person empowered by such Act or Acts to administer such oath, solemn affirmation, or affidavit, make and subscribe such declaration; and every such commissioner, collector, other officer or person, is hereby empowered and required to administer the same accordingly.

3 Copy of instrument substituting declaration shall be published in the gazette; and after 21 days from the date thereof the provisions of this Act shall apply

When the lords commissioners of his Majesty's Treasury shall, in any such case as herein-before mentioned, have substituted in writing under their hands and seals a declaration in lieu of an oath, solemn affirmation, or affidavit, such lords commissioners shall, as soon as conveniently may be, cause a copy of the instrument substituting such declaration to be inserted and published in the London Gazette; and from and after the expiration of twenty-one days next following the day of the date of the gazette, wherein the copy of such instrument shall have been published, the provisions of this Act shall extend and apply to each and every case specified in such instrument, as well and in the same manner as if the same were specified and named in this Act.

4 And no oath shall be administered for which such declaration has been substituted

After the expiration of the said twenty-one days it shall not be lawful for any commissioner, collector, officer, or other person to administer or cause to be administered, or receive or cause to be received, any oath, solemn affirmation, or affidavit, in the lieu of which such declaration as aforesaid shall have been directed by the Treasury to be substituted.

7 Oaths in courts of justice, etc, still to be taken

Provided also, that nothing in this Act contained shall extend or apply to any oath, solemn affirmation, or affidavit, which now is or hereafter may be made or taken, or be required to be made or taken, in any judicial proceeding in any court of justice, or in any proceeding for or by way of summary conviction before any justice or justices of the peace; but all such oaths, affirmations, and affidavits shall continue to be required, and to be administered, taken, and made, as well and in the same manner as if this Act had not been passed.

8 Universities of Oxford and Cambridge and other bodies may substitute declarations for oaths

It shall be lawful for the universities of Oxford and Cambridge, and for all other bodies corporate and politic, and for all bodies now by law or statute or by any valid usage authorized to administer or receive any oath, solemn affirmation, or affidavit, to make statutes, byelaws, or orders authorizing and directing the substitution of a declaration in lieu of any oath, solemn affirmation, or affidavit now required to be taken or made: Provided always, that such statutes, byelaws, or orders be otherwise duly made and passed according to the charter, laws, or regulations of the particular university, other body corporate and politic, or other body so authorized as aforesaid.

13 Justices, etc, not to administer oaths, etc, touching matters whereof they have no jurisdiction by statute—Proviso as to certain oaths

It shall not be lawful for any justice of the peace or other person to administer or cause to allow to be administered, or to receive or cause or allow to be received, any oath, affidavit, or solemn affirmation touching any matter or thing whereof such justice or other person hath not jurisdiction or cognizance by some statute in force at the time being: Provided always, that nothing herein contained shall be construed to extend to any oath, affidavit, or solemn affirmation before any justice in any matter or thing touching the preservation of the peace, or the prosecution, trial, or punishment of offences, or touching any proceedings before either of the Houses of Parliament or any committee thereof respectively, nor to any oath, affidavit, or affirmation which may be required by the laws of any foreign country to give validity to instruments in writing designed to be used in such foreign countries respectively.

14 Declarations substituted for oaths and affidavits required by Bank of England on the transfer of stock

In any case in which it has been the usual practice of the Bank of England to receive affidavits on oath to prove the death of any proprietor of any stocks or funds transferable there, or to identify the person of any such proprietor, or to remove any other impediment to the transfer of any such stocks or funds, or relating to the loss, mutilation, or defacement of any bank note, no such oath or affidavit shall in future be required to be taken or made, but in lieu thereof the person who might have been required to take or make such oath or affidavit shall make and subscribe a declaration to the same effect as such oath or affidavit.

15 Declarations substituted for oaths and affidavits required by 5 Geo 2 c 7, and 54 Geo 3 c 15

In any action or suit brought or intended to be brought in any court of law or equity within any of the territories, plantations, colonies, or dependencies abroad, being within and part of his Majesty's dominions, for or relating to any debt or account, wherein any person residing in Great Britain and Ireland shall be a party, or for or relating to any lands, tenements, or hereditaments or other property situate, lying, and being in the said places respectively, it shall and may be lawful to and for the plaintiff or defendant, and also to and for any witness to be examined or made use of in such action or suit, to verify or prove any matter or thing relating thereto by solemn declaration or declarations in writing in the form in the schedule hereunto annexed, made before any justice of the peace, notary public, or other officer now by law authorized to administer an oath, and certified and transmitted under the signature and seal of any such justice, notary public duly admitted and practising, or other officer; which declaration, and every declaration relative to such matter or thing as aforesaid, in any foreign kingdom or state, or to the voyage of any ship or vessel, every such justice of the peace, notary public, or other officer shall be and he is hereby authorized and empowered to administer or receive; and every declaration so made, certified, and transmitted, shall in all such actions and suits be allowed to be of the same force and effect, as if the person or persons making the same had appeared and sworn or affirmed the matters contained in such declaration viva voce in open court, or upon a commission issued for the examination of witnesses or of any party in such action or suit respectively; provided that in every such declaration there shall be expressed the addition of the party making such declaration and the particular place of his or her abode.

16 Declaration in writing sufficient to prove execution of any will, codicil, etc

It shall and may be lawful to and for any attesting witness to the execution of any will or codicil, deed or instrument in writing, and to and for any other competent person, to verify and prove the signing, sealing, publication, or delivery of any such will, codicil, deed, or instrument in writing, by such declaration in writing made as aforesaid; and every such justice, notary, or other officer shall be and is hereby authorized and empowered to administer or receive such declaration.

17 Crown debts in suits on behalf of his Majesty to be proved by declaration

In all suits now depending or hereafter to be brought in any court of law or equity by or in behalf of his Majesty, in any of his said Majesty's territories, plantations, colonies, possessions, or dependencies, for or relating to any debt or account, his Majesty shall and may prove his debts and accounts and examine his witness or witnesses by declaration, in like manner as any subject or subjects is or are empowered or may do by this present Act.

18 Voluntary declaration in the form in the schedule may be taken—Making false declaration a misdemeanor

It shall and may be lawful for any justice of the peace, notary public, or other officer now by law authorized to administer an oath, to take and receive the declaration of any person voluntarily making the same before him in the form in the schedule to this Act annexed.

19 Fees payable on oath shall be paid on declarations substituted in lieu thereof

Whenever any declaration shall be made and subscribed by any person or persons under or in pursuance of the provisions of this Act or any of them, all and every such fees or fee as would have been due and payable on the taking or making any legal oath, solemn affirmation, or affidavit shall be in like manner due and payable upon making and subscribing such declaration.

20   Declarations to be in the form prescribed in schedule

In all cases where a declaration in lieu of an oath shall have been substituted by this Act, or by virtue of any power or authority hereby given, or where a declaration is directed or authorized to be made and subscribed under the authority of this Act, or of any power hereby given, although the same be not substituted in lieu of an oath heretofore legally taken, such declaration, unless otherwise directed under the powers hereby given, shall be in the form prescribed in the schedule hereunto annexed.

SCHEDULE

I A.B. do solemnly and sincerely declare, that . . . and I make this solemn declaration conscientiously believing the same to be true, and by virtue of the provisions of (an Act made and passed in the . . . year of the reign of his present Majesty, intituled 'An Act' (*here insert the title of this Act*)).

COMMISSIONERS FOR OATHS ACT 1889

1 Appointment and powers of commissioners for oaths

(1) ...

(2) A commissioner for oaths may in England or elsewhere administer any oath or take any affidavit for the purposes of any court or matter in England including any of the ecclesiastical courts or jurisdictions, matters ecclesiastical, matters relating to applications for notarial faculties, and matters relating to the registration of any instrument whether under an Act of Parliament or otherwise and take any bail or recognizance in or for the purpose of any civil proceeding in the Supreme Court.

(3) Provided that a commissioner for oaths shall not exercise any of the powers given by this section in any proceeding in which he is solicitor to any of the parties to the proceeding, or clerk to any such solicitor or in which he is interested.

2 Powers of certain officers of court, etc., to administer oaths

Every person who being an officer of or performing duties in relation to any court is for the time being so authorised by a judge of the court, or by or in pursuance of any rules or orders regulating the procedure of the court, and every person directed to take an examination in any cause or matter in the Supreme Court, shall have authority to administer any oath or take any affidavit required for any purpose connected with his duties.

3 Taking of oaths out of England

(1) Any oath or affidavit required for the purpose of any court or matter in England, or for the purpose of the registration of any instrument in any part of the United Kingdom, may be taken or made in any place out of England before any person having authority to administer an oath in that place.

(2) In the case of a person having such authority otherwise than by the law of a foreign country, judicial and official notice shall be taken of his seal or signature affixed, impressed, or subscribed to or on any such oath or affidavit.

4 Appointment of persons to administer oaths for prize proceedings

The Lord Chancellor may, whenever it appears to him necessary to do so, authorise any person to administer oaths and take affidavits for any purpose relating to prize proceedings in the Supreme Court, whilst that person is on the high seas or out of Her Majesty's dominions, and it shall not be necessary to affix any stamp to the document by which he is so authorised.

5 Jurat to state where and when oath is taken

Every commissioner before whom any oath or affidavit is taken or made under this Act shall state truly in the jurat or attestation at what place and on what date the oath or affidavit is taken or made.

6 Powers as to oaths and notarial acts abroad

(1) Every British ambassador, envoy, minister, chargé d'affaires and secretary of embassy or legation exercising his functions in any foreign country and every British consul-general, consul, vice-consul, acting consul, pro-consul, and consular agent, acting consul general, acting vice-consul, and acting consular agent exercising his functions in any foreign place may, in that country or place, administer any oath and take any affidavit, and also do any notarial act which any notary public can do within the United Kingdom; and every oath, affidavit and notarial act administered, sworn, or done by or before any such person shall be as effectual as if duly administered, sworn, or done by or before any lawful authority in any part of the United Kingdom.

(2) Any document purporting to have affixed, impressed, or subscribed thereon or thereto the seal and signature of any person authorised by this section to administer an oath in testimony of any oath, affidavit, or act being administered, taken, or done by or before him, shall be admitted in evidence without proof of the seal or signature being the seal or signature of that person, or of the official character of that person.

11 Definitions

In this Act unless the context otherwise requires:

'Oath' includes affirmation and declaration;

'Affidavit' includes affirmation, statutory or other declaration, acknowledgment, examination, and attestation or protestation of honour;

'Swear' includes affirm, declare, and protest;

'Supreme Court' means the Supreme Court of Judicature in England.

15 Short title

This Act may be cited as the Commissioners for Oaths Act 1889.

LAW OF PROPERTY ACT 1925

57 Description of deeds

Any deed, whether or not being an indenture, may be described (at the commencement thereof or otherwise) as a deed simply, or as a conveyance, deed of exchange, vesting deed, trust instrument, settlement, mortgage, charge, transfer of mortgage, appointment, lease or otherwise according to the nature of the transaction intended to be effected.

74 Execution of instruments by or on behalf of corporations

(1) In favour of a purchaser an instrument shall be deemed to have been duly executed by a corporation aggregate if a seal purporting to be the corporation's seal purports to be affixed to the instrument in the presence of and attested by –

    (a) two members of the board of directors, council or other governing body of the corporation, or

    (b) one such member and the clerk, secretary or other permanent officer of the corporation or his deputy.

(1A) Subsection (1) of this section applies in the case of an instrument purporting to have been executed by a corporation aggregate in the name or on behalf of another person whether or not that person is also a corporation aggregate.

(1B) For the purposes of subsection (1) of this section, a seal purports to be affixed in the presence of and attested by an officer of the corporation, in the case of an officer which is not an individual, if it is affixed in the presence of and attested by an individual authorised by the officer to attest on its behalf.

(2) The board of directors, council or other governing body of a corporation aggregate may, by resolution or otherwise, appoint an agent either generally or in any particular case, to execute on behalf of the corporation any agreement or other instrument which is not a deed in relation to any matter within the powers of the corporation.

(3) Where a person is authorised under a power of attorney or under any statutory or other power to convey any interest in property in the name or on behalf of a corporation sole or aggregate, he may as attorney execute the conveyance by signing the name of the corporation in the presence of at least one witness who attests the signature, and such execution shall take effect and be valid in like manner as if the corporation had executed the conveyance.

(4) Where a corporation aggregate is authorised under a power of attorney or under any statutory or other power to convey any interest in property in the name or on behalf of any other person (including another corporation), an officer appointed for that purpose by the board of directors, council or other governing body of the corporation by resolution or otherwise, may execute the instrument by signing it in the name of such other person or, if the instrument is to be a deed, by so signing it in the presence of a witness who attests the signature; and where an instrument appears to be executed by an

officer so appointed, then in favour of a purchaser the instrument shall be deemed to have been executed by an officer duly authorised.

(5) The foregoing provisions of this section apply to transactions wherever effected, but only to deeds and instruments executed after the commencement of this Act, except that, in the case of powers or appointments of an agent or officer, they apply whether the power was conferred or the appointment was made before or after the commencement of this Act or by this Act.

(6) Notwithstanding anything contained in this section, any mode of execution or attestation authorised by law or by practice or by the statute, charter, memorandum or articles, deed of settlement or other instrument constituting the corporation or regulating the affairs thereof, shall (in addition to the modes authorised by this section) be as effectual as if this section had not been passed.

74A   Execution of instrument as a deed

(1) An instrument is validly executed by a corporation aggregate as a deed for the purposes of section 1(2)(b) of the Law of Property (Miscellaneous Provisions) Act 1989, if and only if –

(a)   it is duly executed by the corporation, and

(b)   it is delivered as a deed.

(2) An instrument shall be presumed to be delivered for the purposes of subsection (1)(b) of this section upon its being executed, unless a contrary intention is proved.

CORPORATE BODIES' CONTRACTS ACT 1960

1 Cases where contracts need not be under seal

(1) Contracts may be made on behalf of any body corporate, wherever incorporated, as follows –

(a) a contract which if made between private persons would be by law required to be in writing, signed by the parties to be charged therewith, may be made on behalf of the body corporate in writing signed by any person acting under its authority, express or implied, and

(b) a contract which if made between private persons would by law be valid although made by parol only, and not reduced into writing, may be made by parol on behalf of the body corporate by any person acting under its authority, express or implied.

(2) A contract made according to this section shall be effectual in law, and shall bind the body corporate and its successors and all other parties thereto.

(3) A contract made according to this section may be varied or discharged in the same manner in which it is authorised by this section to be made.

(4) Nothing in this section shall be taken as preventing a contract under seal from being made by or on behalf of a body corporate.

(5) This section shall not apply to the making, variation or discharge of a contract before the commencement of this Act but shall apply whether the body corporate gave its authority before or after the commencement of this Act.

2 Exclusion of companies under Companies Acts

This Act shall not apply to any company formed and registered under the Companies Act 1985 or an existing company as defined in that Act or to a limited liability partnership.

POWERS OF ATTORNEY ACT 1971

1 Execution of powers of attorney

(1) An instrument creating a power of attorney shall be executed as a deed by the donor of the power.

(2) ...

(3) This section is without prejudice to any requirement in, or having effect under, any other Act as to the witnessing of instruments creating powers of attorney and does not affect the rules relating to the execution of instruments by bodies corporate.

3 Proof of instruments creating powers of attorney

(1) The contents of an instrument creating a power of attorney may be proved by means of a copy which –

  (a) is a reproduction of the original made with a photographic or other device for reproducing documents in facsimile; and

  (b) contains the following certificate or certificates signed by the donor of the power or by a solicitor duly certificated notary public or stockbroker, that is to say –

   (i) a certificate at the end to the effect that the copy is a true and complete copy of the original; and

   (ii) if the original consists of two or more pages, a certificate at the end of each page of the copy to the effect that it is a true and complete copy of the corresponding page of the original.

(2) Where a copy of an instrument creating a power of attorney has been made which complies with subsection (1) of this section, the contents of the instrument may also be proved by means of a copy of that copy if the further copy itself complies with that subsection, taking references in it to the original as references to the copy from which the further copy is made.

(3) In this section 'duly certificated notary public' has the same meaning as it has in the Solicitors Act 1974 by virtue of section 87(1) of that Act and 'stockbroker' means a member of any stock exchange within the meaning of the Stock Transfer Act 1963 or the Stock Transfer Act (Northern Ireland) 1963.

(4) This section is without prejudice to section 4 of the Evidence and Powers of Attorney Act 1940 (proof of deposited instruments by office copy) and to any other method of proof authorised by law.

(5) For the avoidance of doubt, in relation to an instrument made in Scotland the references to a power of attorney in this section and in section 4 of the Evidence and Powers of Attorney Act 1940 include references to a factory and commission.

4 Powers of attorney given as security

(1) Where a power of attorney is expressed to be irrevocable and is given to secure –

(a)   a proprietary interest of the donee of the power; or

(b)   the performance of an obligation owed to the donee,

then, so long as the donee has that interest or the obligation remains undischarged, the power shall not be revoked –

(i)   by the donor without the consent of the donee; or

(ii) by the death, incapacity or bankruptcy of the donor or, if the donor is a body corporate, by its winding up or dissolution.

(2)   A power of attorney given to secure a proprietary interest may be given to the person entitled to the interest and persons deriving title under him to that interest, and those persons shall be duly constituted donees of the power for all purposes of the power but without prejudice to any right to appoint substitutes given by the power.

(3)   This section applies to powers of attorney whenever created.

5   Protection of donee and third persons where power of attorney is revoked

(1)   A donee of a power of attorney who acts in pursuance of the power at a time when it has been revoked shall not, by reason of the revocation, incur any liability (either to the donor or to any other person) if at that time he did not know that the power had been revoked.

(2)   Where a power of attorney has been revoked and a person, without knowledge of the revocation, deals with the donee of the power, the transaction between them shall, in favour of that person, be as valid as if the power had then been in existence.

(3)   Where the power is expressed in the instrument creating it to be irrevocable and to be given by way of security then, unless the person dealing with the donee knows that it was not in fact given by way of security, he shall be entitled to assume that the power is incapable of revocation except by the donor acting with the consent of the donee and shall accordingly be treated for the purposes of subsection (2) of this section as having knowledge of the revocation only if he knows that it has been revoked in that manner.

(4)   Where the interest of a purchaser depends on whether a transaction between the donee of a power of attorney and another person was valid by virtue of subsection (2) of this section, it shall be conclusively presumed in favour of the purchaser that that person did not at the material time know of the revocation of the power if –

(a)   the transaction between that person and the donee was completed within twelve months of the date on which the power came into operation; or

(b)   that person makes a statutory declaration, before or within three months after the completion of the purchase, that he did not at the material time know of the revocation of the power.

(5)   Without prejudice to subsection (3) of this section, for the purposes of this section knowledge of the revocation of a power of attorney includes knowledge of the occurrence of any event (such as the death of the donor) which has the effect of revoking the power.

(6) In this section 'purchaser' and 'purchase' have the meanings specified in section 205(1) of the Law of Property Act 1925.

(7) This section applies whenever the power of attorney was created but only to acts and transactions after the commencement of this Act.

6 Additional protection for transferees under stock exchange transactions

(1) Without prejudice to section 5 of this Act, where –

(a) the donee of a power of attorney executes, as transferor, an instrument transferring registered securities; and

(b) the instrument is executed for the purposes of a stock exchange transaction,

it shall be conclusively presumed in favour of the transferee that the power had not been revoked at the date of the instrument if a statutory declaration to that effect is made by the donee of the power on or within three months after that date.

(2) In this section 'registered securities' and 'stock exchange transaction' have the same meanings as in the Stock Transfer Act 1963.

7 Execution of instruments, etc. by donee of power of attorney

(1) If the donee of a power of attorney is an individual, he may, if he thinks fit –

(a) execute any instrument with his own signature, and

(b) do any other thing in his own name,

by the authority of the donor of the power; and any [instrument executed or thing done in that manner shall, subject to subsection (1A) of this section, be as effective as if executed by the donee in any manner which would constitute due execution of that instrument by the donor or, as the case may be, as if done by the donee in the name of the donor].

[(1A) Where an instrument is executed by the donee as a deed, it shall be as effective as if executed by the donee in a manner which would constitute due execution of it as a deed by the donor only if it is executed in accordance with section 1(3)(a) of the Law of Property (Miscellanous Provisions) Act 1989.]

(2) For the avoidance of doubt it is hereby declared that an instrument to which subsection (3) of section 74 of the Law of Property Act 1925 applies may be executed either as provided in that subsection or as provided in this section.

(3) . . .

(4) This section applies whenever the power of attorney was created.

[**NOTE**: Words in brackets apply to instruments executed since 15 September 2005.]

10 Effect of general power of attorney in specified form

(1) Subject to subsection (2) of this section, a general power of attorney in the form set out in Schedule 1 to this Act, or in a form to the like effect but expressed to be made under this Act, shall operate to confer –

    (a)   on the donee of the power; or

    (b)   if there is more than one donee, on the donees acting jointly or acting jointly or severally, as the case may be,

authority to do on behalf of the donor anything which he can lawfully do by an attorney.

(2)   Subject to section 1 of the Trustee Delegation Act 1999, this section does not apply to functions which the donor has as a trustee or personal representative or as a tenant for life or statutory owner within the meaning of the Settled Land Act 1925.

11   Short title, repeals, consequential amendments, commencement and extent

(1)   This Act may be cited as the Powers of Attorney Act 1971.

(2)   The enactments specified in Schedule 2 to this Act are hereby repealed to the extent specified in the third column of that Schedule.

(3)   ...

(4)   ...

(5)   Section 3 of this Act extends to Scotland and Northern Ireland but, save as aforesaid, this Act extends to England and Wales only.

SCHEDULE 1   Form of General Power of Attorney for Purposes of Section 10

This General Power of Attorney is made this [. . .] day of [. . .] 19[. . .] by AB of [. . .]

I appoint CD of [. . .] (*or* CD of [. . .] and EF of [. . .] jointly *or* jointly and severally) to be my attorney(s) in accordance with section 10 of the Powers of Attorney Act 1971.

In Witness etc.,

SOLICITORS ACT 1974

81 Administration of oaths and taking of affidavits

(1) Subject to the provisions of this section, every solicitor who holds a practising certificate which is in force shall have the powers conferred on a commissioner for oaths by the Commissioners for Oaths Acts 1889 and 1891 and section 24 of the Stamp Duties Management Act 1891; and any reference to such a commissioner in an enactment or instrument (including an enactment passed or instrument made after the commencement of this Act) shall include a reference to such a solicitor unless the context otherwise requires.

(2) A solicitor shall not exercise the powers conferred by this section in a proceeding in which he is solicitor to any of the parties or in which he is interested.

(3) A solicitor before whom any oath or affidavit is taken or made shall state in the jurat or attestation at which place and on what date the oath or affidavit is taken or made.

(4) A document containing such a statement and purporting to be sealed or signed by a solicitor shall be admitted in evidence without proof of the seal or signature, and without proof that he is a solicitor or that he holds a practising certificate which is in force.

[**NOTE**: The Interpretation Act 1978, Sched.1 defines an 'oath' or 'affidavit' to include a declaration. Section 81 would cover a solicitor taking a statutory declaration.]

81A Fees for administering oaths and taking affidavits

(1) The Secretary of State may, with the concurrence of the Lord Chief Justice and the Master of the Rolls, by order prescribe the fees to be charged by –

(a) commissioners for oaths; and

(b) solicitors exercising the powers of commissioners for oaths by virtue of section 81,

in respect of the administration of an oath or the taking of an affidavit.

(2) Any order under this section shall be made by statutory instrument, which shall be laid before Parliament after being made.

(3) In this section 'affidavit' has the same meaning as in the Commissioners for Oaths Act 1889.

INTERPRETATION ACT 1978

5 Definitions

In any Act, unless the contrary intention appears, words and expressions listed in Schedule 1 to this Act are to be construed according to that Schedule.

SCHEDULE 1
WORDS AND EXPRESSIONS DEFINED

[. . .]

'Oath' and 'affidavit' include affirmation and declaration, and 'swear' includes affirm and declare.

[. . .]

'Statutory declaration' means a declaration made by virtue of the Statutory Declarations Act 1835.

OATHS ACT 1978

[**NOTE**: This Act repealed and replaced the Oaths Acts of 1838, 1888, 1909 and 1961 and ss.8 and 32(2) of the Administration of Justice Act 1977.]

PART I
ENGLAND, WALES AND NORTHERN IRELAND

1   Manner of administration of oaths

(1)   Any oath may be administered and taken in England, Wales or Northern Ireland in the following form and manner –

> The person taking the oath shall hold the New Testament, or, in the case of a Jew, the Old Testament, in his uplifted hand, and shall say or repeat after the officer administering the oath the words 'I swear by Almighty God that . . .', followed by the words of the oath prescribed by law.

(2)   The officer shall (unless the person about to take the oath voluntarily objects thereto, or is physically incapable of so taking the oath) administer the oath in the form and manner aforesaid without question.

(3)   In the case of a person who is neither a Christian nor a Jew, the oath shall be administered in any lawful manner.

(4)   In this section 'officer' means any person duly authorised to administer oaths.

PART II
UNITED KINGDOM

Oaths

3   Swearing with uplifted hand

If any person to whom an oath is administered desires to swear with uplifted hand, in the form and manner in which an oath is usually administered in Scotland, he shall be permitted so to do, and the oath shall be administered to him in such form and manner without further question.

4   Validity of oaths

(1)   In any case in which an oath may lawfully be and has been administered to any person, if it has been administered in a form and manner other than that prescribed by law, he is bound by it if it has been administered in such form and with such ceremonies as he may have declared to be binding.

(2)   Where an oath has been duly administered and taken, the fact that the person to whom it was administered had, at the time of taking it, no religious belief, shall not for any purpose affect the validity of the oath.

Solemn Affirmations

5   Making of solemn affirmations

(1)   Any person who objects to being sworn shall be permitted to make his solemn affirmation instead of taking an oath.

(2) Subsection (1) above shall apply in relation to a person to whom it is not reasonably practicable without inconvenience or delay to administer an oath in the manner appropriate to his religious belief as it applies in relation to a person objecting to be sworn.

(3) A person who may be permitted under subsection (2) above to make his solemn affirmation may also be required to do so.

(4) A solemn affirmation shall be of the same force and effect as an oath.

6 Form of affirmation

(1) Subject to subsection (2) below, every affirmation shall be as follows –

'I, [. . .] do solemnly, sincerely and truly declare and affirm,'

and then proceed with the words of the oath prescribed by law, omitting any words of imprecation or calling to witness.

(2) Every affirmation in writing shall commence –

'I, [. . .] of [. . .], do solemnly and sincerely affirm,'

and the form in lieu of jurat shall be 'Affirmed at [. . .] this [. . .] day of [. . .] 19[. . .], Before me.'

COMPANIES ACT 1985

35 A company's capacity not limited by its memorandum

(1) The validity of an act done by a company shall not be called into question on the ground of lack of capacity by reason of anything in the company's memorandum.

(2) A member of a company may bring proceedings to restrain the doing of an act which but for subsection (1) would be beyond the company's capacity; but no such proceedings shall lie in respect of an act to be done in fulfilment of a legal obligation arising from a previous act of the company.

(3) It remains the duty of the directors to observe any limitations on their powers flowing from the company's memorandum; and action by the directors which but for subsection (1) would be beyond the company's capacity may only be ratified by the company by special resolution. A resolution ratifying such action shall not affect any liability incurred by the directors or any other person; relief from any such liability must be agreed to separately by special resolution.

(4) The operation of this section is restricted by section 65(1) of the Charities Act 1993 and section 112(3) of the Companies Act 1989 in relation to companies which are charities; and section 322A below (invalidity of certain transactions to which directors or their associates are parties) has effect notwithstanding this section.

35B No duty to enquire as to capacity of company or authority of directors

A party to a transaction with a company is not bound to enquire as to whether it is permitted by the company's memorandum or as to any limitation on the powers of the board of directors to bind the company or authorise others to do so.

36 Company contracts: England and Wales

Under the law of England and Wales a contract may be made –

(a) by a company, by writing under its common seal, or

(b) on behalf of a company, by any person acting under its authority, express or implied;

and any formalities required by law in the case of a contract made by an individual also apply, unless a contrary intention appears, to a contract made by or on behalf of a company.

36A Execution of documents: England and Wales

(1) Under the law of England and Wales the following provisions have effect with respect to the execution of documents by a company.

(2) A document is executed by a company by the affixing of its common seal.

(3) A company need not have a common seal, however, and the following subsections apply whether it does or not.

(4) A document signed by a director and the secretary of a company, or by two directors of a company, and expressed (in whatever form of words) to be

executed by the company has the same effect as if executed under the common seal of the company.

[(4A) Where a document is to be signed by a person as a director or the secretary of more than one company, it shall not be taken to be duly signed by that person for the purposes of subsection (4) unless the person signs it separately in each capacity.]

[(5) ...]

(6) In favour of a purchaser a document shall be deemed to have been duly executed by a company if it purports to be signed by a director and the secretary of the company, or by two directors of the company [. . .].

A 'purchaser' means a purchaser in good faith for valuable consideration and includes a lessee, mortgagee or other person who for valuable consideration acquires an interest in property.

[36AA Execution of deeds: England and Wales

(1) A document is validly executed by a company as a deed for the purposes of section 1(2)(b) of the Law of Property (Miscellaneous Provisions) Act 1989, if and only if –

(a) it is duly executed by the company, and

(b) it is delivered as a deed.

(2) A document shall be presumed to be delivered for the purposes of subsection (1)(b) upon its being executed, unless a contrary intention is proved.]

[**NOTE**: Words in brackets apply to instruments executed since 15 September 2005.]

LAW OF PROPERTY (MISCELLANEOUS PROVISIONS) ACT 1989

1   Deeds and their execution

(1)   Any rule of law which –

(a)   restricts the substances on which a deed may be written;

(b)   requires a seal for the valid execution of an instrument as a deed by an individual; or

(c)   requires authority by one person to another to deliver an instrument as a deed on his behalf to be given by deed,

is abolished.

(2)   An instrument shall not be a deed unless –

(a)   it makes it clear on its face that it is intended to be a deed by the person making it or, as the case may be, by the parties to it (whether by describing itself as a deed or expressing itself to be executed or signed as a deed or otherwise); and

(b)   it is validly executed as a deed [–]

[(i)   by that person or a person authorised to execute it in the name or on behalf of that person, or

(ii)   by one or more of those parties or a person authorised to execute it in the name or on behalf of one or more of those parties].

[(2A)For the purposes of subsection (2)(a) above, an instrument shall not be taken to make it clear on its face that it is intended to be a deed merely because it is executed under seal.]

(3)   An instrument is validly executed as a deed by an individual if, and only if –

(a)   it is signed –

(i)   by him in the presence of a witness who attests the signature; or

(ii)   at his direction and in his presence and the presence of two witnesses who each attest the signature; and

(b)   it is delivered as a deed [. . .].

(4)   In subsections (2) and (3) above 'sign', in relation to an instrument, includes [–]

[(a)   an individual signing the name of the person or party on whose behalf he executes the instrument; and

(b)]   making one's mark on the instrument

and 'signature' is to be construed accordingly.

[(4A) Subsection (3) above applies in the case of an instrument executed by an individual in the name or on behalf of another person whether or not that person is also an individual.]

(5)   Where a solicitor, duly certificated notary public or licensed conveyancer, or an agent or employee of a solicitor, duly certificated notary public] or licensed conveyancer, in the course of or in connection with a transaction [. . .], purports to deliver an instrument as a deed on behalf of a party to the instrument, it shall be conclusively presumed in favour of a purchaser that he is authorised so to deliver the instrument.

(6) In subsection (5) above –

['purchaser' has the same meaning] as in the Law of Property Act 1925;

'duly certificated notary public' has the same meaning as it has in the Solicitors Act 1974 by virtue of section 87 of that Act [. . .]

[. . .]

(7) Where an instrument under seal that constitutes a deed is required for the purposes of an Act passed before this section comes into force, this section shall have effect as to signing, sealing or delivery of an instrument by an individual in place of any provision of that Act as to signing, sealing or delivery.

(8) The enactments mentioned in Schedule 1 to this Act (which in consequence of this section require amendments other than those provided by subsection (7) above) shall have effect with the amendments specified in that Schedule.

(9) Nothing in subsection (1)(b), (2), (3), (7) or (8) above applies in relation to deeds required or authorised to be made under –

(a) the seal of the county palatine of Lancaster;
(b) the seal of the Duchy of Lancaster; or
(c) the seal of the Duchy of Cornwall.

(10) The references in this section to the execution of a deed by an individual do not include execution by a corporation sole and the reference in subsection (7) above to signing, sealing or delivery by an individual does not include signing, sealing or delivery by such a corporation.

(11) Nothing in this section applies in relation to instruments delivered as deeds before this section comes into force. [31 July 1990, SI, 1990/1775, art. 2(2).]

2 Contracts for sale etc. of land to be made by signed writing

(1) A contract for the sale or other disposition of an interest in land can only be made in writing and only by incorporating all the terms which the parties have expressly agreed in one document or, where contracts are exchanged, in each.

(2) The terms may be incorporated in a document either by being set out in it or by reference to some other document.

(3) The document incorporating the terms or, where contracts are exchanged, one of the documents incorporating them (but not necessarily the same one) must be signed by or on behalf of each party to the contract.

(4) Where a contract for the sale or other disposition of an interest in land satisfies the conditions of this section by reason only of the rectification of one or more documents in pursuance of an order of a court, the contract shall come into being, or be deemed to have come into being, at such time as may be specified in the order.

(5) This section does not apply in relation to –

(a) a contract to grant such a lease as is mentioned in section 54(2) of the Law Property Act 1925 (short leases);
(b) a contract made in the course of a public auction; or

(c) a contract regulated under the Financial Services and Markets Act 2000, other than a regulated mortgage contract, a regulated home reversion plan or a regulated home purchase plan;

and nothing in this section affects the creation or operation of resulting, implied or constructive trusts.

(6) In this section –

'disposition' has the same meaning as in the Law of Property Act 1925;

'interest in land' means any estate, interest or charge in or over land . . .

'regulated mortgage contract', 'regulated home reversion plan' and 'regulated home purchase plan' must be read with –

(a) section 22 of the Financial Services and Markets Act 2000,
(b) any relevant order under that section, and
(c) Schedule 22 to that Act.

(7) Nothing in this section shall apply in relation to contracts made before this section comes into force.

[**NOTE**: Words in brackets apply to instruments executed since 15 September 2005.]

COURTS AND LEGAL SERVICES ACT 1990

113 Administration of oaths and taking of affidavits

(1) In this section –

'authorised person' means –

(a) any authorised advocate or authorised litigator, other than one who is a solicitor (in relation to whom provision similar to that made by this section is made by section 81 of the Solicitors Act 1974); or

(b) any person who is a member of a professional or other body pre-scribed by the Secretary of State for the purposes of this section; and

'general notary' means any public notary other than –

(a) an ecclesiastical notary;

(3) Subject to the provisions of this section, every authorised person shall have the powers conferred on a commissioner for oaths by the Commissioners for Oaths Acts 1889 and 1891 and section 24 of the Stamp Duties Management Act 1891; and any reference to such a commissioner in an enactment or instrument (including an enactment passed or instrument made after the commencement of this Act) shall include a reference to an authorised person unless the context otherwise requires.

(4) Subject to the provisions of this section, every general notary shall have the powers conferred on a commissioner for oaths by the Commissioners for Oaths Acts 1889 and 1891; and any reference to such a commissioner in an enactment or instrument (including an enactment passed or instrument made after the commencement of this Act) shall include a reference to a general notary unless the context otherwise requires.

(5) No person shall exercise the powers conferred by this section in any proceedings in which he is interested.

(6) A person exercising such powers and before whom any oath or affidavit is taken or made shall state in the jurat or attestation at which place and on what date the oath or affidavit is taken or made.

(7) A document containing such a statement and purporting to be sealed or signed by an authorised person or general notary shall be admitted in evi-dence without proof of the seal or signature, and without proof that he is an authorised person or general notary.

(8) The Secretary of State may, with the concurrence of the Lord Chief Justice and the Master of the Rolls, by order prescribe the fees to be charged by authorised persons exercising the powers of commissioners for oaths by virtue of this section in respect of the administration of an oath or the taking of an affidavit.

(9) In this section 'affidavit' has the same meaning as in the Commissioners for Oaths Act 1889.

(10) Every –

(a)   solicitor who holds a practising certificate which is in force;
(b)   authorised person;
(c)   general notary;

shall have the right to use the title 'Commissioner for Oaths'.

COMPANIES ACT 2006

43 Company contracts

(1) Under the law of England and Wales or Northern Ireland a contract may be made –

 (a) by a company, by writing under its common seal, or

 (b) on behalf of a company, by a person acting under its authority, express or implied.

(2) Any formalities required by law in the case of a contract made by an individual also apply, unless a contrary intention appears, to a contract made by or on behalf of a company.

44 Execution of documents

(1) Under the law of England and Wales or Northern Ireland a document is executed by a company –

 (a) by the affixing of its common seal, or

 (b) by signature in accordance with the following provisions.

(2) A document is validly executed by a company if it is signed on behalf of the company –

 (a) by two authorised signatories, or

 (b) by a director of the company in the presence of a witness who attests the signature.

(3) The following are 'authorised signatories' for the purposes of subsection (2) –

 (a) every director of the company, and

 (b) in the case of a private company with a secretary or a public company, the secretary (or any joint secretary) of the company.

(4) A document signed in accordance with subsection (2) and expressed, in whatever words, to be executed by the company has the same effect as if executed under the common seal of the company.

(5) In favour of a purchaser a document is deemed to have been duly executed by a company if it purports to be signed in accordance with subsection (2).

 A 'purchaser' means a purchaser in good faith for valuable consideration and includes a lessee, mortgagee or other person who for valuable consideration acquires an interest in property.

(6) Where a document is to be signed by a person on behalf of more than one company, it is not duly signed by that person for the purposes of this section unless he signs it separately in each capacity.

(7) References in this section to a document being (or purporting to be) signed by a director or secretary are to be read, in a case where that office is held by a firm, as references to its being (or purporting to be) signed by an individual authorised by the firm to sign on its behalf.

(8)   This section applies to a document that is (or purports to be) executed by a company in the name of or on behalf of another person whether or not that person is also a company.

45   Common seal

(1)   A company may have a common seal, but need not have one.

(2)   A company which has a common seal shall have its name engraved in legible characters on the seal.

(3)   If a company fails to comply with subsection (2) an offence is committed by –

(a)   the company, and

(b)   every officer of the company who is in default.

(4)   An officer of a company, or a person acting on behalf of a company, commits an offence if he uses, or authorises the use of, a seal purporting to be a seal of the company on which its name is not engraved as required by subsection (2).

(5)   A person guilty of an offence under this section is liable on summary conviction to a fine not exceeding level 3 on the standard scale.

(6)   This section does not form part of the law of Scotland.

46   Execution of deeds

(1)   A document is validly executed by a company as a deed for the purposes of section 1(2)(b) of the Law of Property (Miscellaneous Provisions) Act 1989 (c. 34) and for the purposes of the law of Northern Ireland if, and only if –

(a)   it is duly executed by the company, and

(b)   it is delivered as a deed.

(2)   For the purposes of subsection (1)(b) a document is presumed to be delivered upon its being executed, unless a contrary intention is proved.

47   Execution of deeds or other documents by attorney

(1)   Under the law of England and Wales or Northern Ireland a company may, by instrument executed as a deed, empower a person, either generally or in respect of specified matters, as its attorney to execute deeds or other documents on its behalf.

(2)   A deed or other document so executed, whether in the United Kingdom or elsewhere, has effect as if executed by the company.

Formalities of doing business under the law of Scotland

48   Execution of documents by companies

(1)   The following provisions form part of the law of Scotland only.

(2)   Notwithstanding the provisions of any enactment, a company need not have a company seal.

(3)   For the purposes of any enactment –

    (a)   providing for a document to be executed by a company by affixing its common seal, or

    (b)   referring (in whatever terms) to a document so executed,

a document signed or subscribed by or on behalf of the company in accordance with the provisions of the Requirements of Writing (Scotland) Act 1995 (c. 7) has effect as if so executed.

Other matters

49   Official seal for use abroad

(1)   A company that has a common seal may have an official seal for use outside the United Kingdom.

(2)   The official seal must be a facsimile of the company's common seal, with the addition on its face of the place or places where it is to be used.

(3)   The official seal when duly affixed to a document has the same effect as the company's common seal.

This subsection does not extend to Scotland.

(4)   A company having an official seal for use outside the United Kingdom may –

    (a)   by writing under its common seal, or

    (b)   as respects Scotland, by writing subscribed in accordance with the Requirements of Writing (Scotland) Act 1995,

authorise any person appointed for the purpose to affix the official seal to any deed or other document to which the company is party.

(5)   As between the company and a person dealing with such an agent, the agent's authority continues –

    (a)   during the period mentioned in the instrument conferring the authority, or

    (b)   if no period is mentioned, until notice of the revocation or termination of the agent's authority has been given to the person dealing with him.

(6)   The person affixing the official seal must certify in writing on the deed or other document to which the seal is affixed the date on which, and place at which, it is affixed.

50   Official seal for share certificates etc

(1)   A company that has a common seal may have an official seal for use –

    (a)   for sealing securities issued by the company, or

    (b)   for sealing documents creating or evidencing securities so issued.

(2)   The official seal –

    (a)   must be a facsimile of the company's common seal, with the addition on its face of the word 'Securities', and

    (b)   when duly affixed to the document has the same effect as the company's common seal.

51   Pre-incorporation contracts, deeds and obligations

(1)   A contract that purports to be made by or on behalf of a company at a time when the company has not been formed has effect, subject to any agreement to the contrary, as one made with the person purporting to act for the company or as agent for it, and he is personally liable on the contract accordingly.

(2)   Subsection (1) applies –

    (a)   to the making of a deed under the law of England and Wales or Northern Ireland, and

    (b)   to the undertaking of an obligation under the law of Scotland,

as it applies to the making of a contract.

52   Bills of exchange and promissory notes

A bill of exchange or promissory note is deemed to have been made, accepted or endorsed on behalf of a company if made, accepted or endorsed in the name of, or by or on behalf or on account of, the company by a person acting under its authority.

FOREIGN COMPANIES (EXECUTION OF DOCUMENTS) REGULATIONS 1994, SI 1994/950)

Citation and commencement

1   These Regulations may be cited as the Foreign Companies (Execution of Documents) Regulations 1994 and shall come into force on 16th May 1994.

Application of sections 36 to 36C Companies Act 1985

2   Sections 36, 36A, 36B and 36C of the Companies Act 1985 shall apply to companies incorporated outside Great Britain with the adaptations and modifications set out in regulations 3 to 5 below.

3   References in the said sections 36, 36A, 36B and 36C to a company shall be construed as references to a company incorporated outside Great Britain.

Adaptation of section 36

4   (1)   Section 36 shall apply as if –

   (a)   after the words 'common seal,' in paragraph (a) there were inserted 'or in any manner permitted by the laws of the territory in which the company is incorporated for the execution of documents by such a company,', and

   (b)   for paragraph (b) there were substituted –

      '(b)   on behalf of a company, by any person who, in accordance with the laws of the territory in which the company is incorporated, is acting under the authority (express or implied) of that company;'.

Adaptation of section 36A

5   Section 36A shall apply as if –

   (a)   at the end of subsection (2) there were inserted –

      ', or if it is executed in any manner permitted by the laws of the territory in which the company is incorporated for the execution of documents by such a company.',

   (b)   for subsection (4) there were substituted –

      '(4)   A document which –

      (a)   is signed by a person or persons who, in accordance with the laws of the territory in which the company is incorporated, is or are acting under the authority (express or implied) of that company, and

      (b)   is expressed (in whatever form of words) to be executed by the company,

      has the same effect in relation to that company as it would have in relation to a company incorporated in England and Wales if executed under the common seal of a company so incorporated.', and

(c)   in subsection (6) for the words from 'a director' to 'directors of the company' there were substituted 'a person or persons who, in accordance with the laws of the territory in which the company is incorporated, is or are acting under the authority (express or implied) of that company'.

REGULATORY REFORM (EXECUTION OF DEEDS AND DOCUMENTS) ORDER 2005, SI 2005/1906

1 Citation, commencement, application and extent

(1) This Order may be cited as the Regulatory Reform (Execution of Deeds and Documents) Order 2005 and shall come into force at the end of the period of 12 weeks beginning with the day on which it is made.

(2) The provisions of this Order shall not apply in relation to any instrument executed before the date on which this Order comes into force.

(3) This Order extends to England and Wales only.

2 Interpretation

In this Order –

> 'the 1925 Act' means the Law of Property Act 1925;
>
> 'the 1985 Act' means the Companies Act 1985;
>
> 'the 1989 Act' means the Law of Property (Miscellaneous Provisions) Act 1989.

3 Execution by corporations

For section 74(1) of the 1925 Act substitute –

> '(1) In favour of a purchaser an instrument shall be deemed to have been duly executed by a corporation aggregate if a seal purporting to be the corporation's seal purports to be affixed to the instrument in the presence of and attested by –
>
> (a) two members of the board of directors, council or other governing body of the corporation, or
>
> (b) one such member and the clerk, secretary or other permanent officer of the corporation or his deputy.'.

4 Execution of deeds by corporations

After section 74 of the 1925 Act insert –

> **'74A Execution of instrument as a deed**
>
> (1) An instrument is validly executed by a corporation aggregate as a deed for the purposes of section 1(2)(b) of the Law of Property (Miscellaneous Provisions) Act 1989, if and only if –
>
> (a) it is duly executed by the corporation, and
>
> (b) it is delivered as a deed.
>
> (2) An instrument shall be presumed to be delivered for the purposes of subsection (1)(b) of this section upon its being executed, unless a contrary intention is proved.'.

5   Repeal of irrebuttable presumption of delivery

In section 36A(6) of the 1985 Act (which makes provision to deem documents to be duly executed by companies) omit the words from 'and, where' to 'executed'.

6   Execution of deeds by companies

After section 36A of the 1985 Act insert –

'36AA   Execution of deeds: England and Wales

(1)   A document is validly executed by a company as a deed for the purposes of section 1(2)(b) of the Law of Property (Miscellaneous Provisions) Act 1989, if and only if –

(a)   it is duly executed by the company, and

(b)   it is delivered as a deed.

(2)   A document shall be presumed to be delivered for the purposes of subsection (1)(b) upon its being executed, unless a contrary intention is proved.'.

7   Execution on behalf of another person

(1)   After section 74(1) of the 1925 Act insert –

'(1A)   Subsection (1) of this section applies in the case of an instrument purporting to have been executed by a corporation aggregate in the name or on behalf of another person whether or not that person is also a corporation aggregate.'.

(2)   After section 36A(6) of the 1985 Act insert –

'(7)   This section applies in the case of a document which is (or purports to be) executed by a company in the name or on behalf of another person whether or not that person is also a company.'.

(3)   In section 1(2)(b) of the 1989 Act (requirements for valid execution as a deed), for the words from 'by' to the end substitute –

'(i)   by that person or a person authorised to execute it in the name or on behalf of that person, or

(ii)   by one or more of those parties or a person authorised to execute it in the name or on behalf of one or more of those parties.'.

(4)   After section 1(4) of the 1989 Act insert –

'(4A)   Subsection (3) above applies in the case of an instrument executed by an individual in the name or on behalf of another person whether or not that person is also an individual.'.

365

8 Execution under seal not evidence of intention to create a deed

After section 1(2) of the 1989 Act insert –

> '(2A) For the purposes of subsection (2)(a) above, an instrument shall not be taken to make it clear on its face that it is intended to be a deed merely because it is executed under seal.'.

9 Extension of presumption of authority to deliver

In section 1(5) of the 1989 Act (presumption of authority to deliver an instrument on behalf of another) omit the words 'involving the disposition or creation of an interest in land'.

10 Minor and consequential amendments and repeals

(1) Schedule 1 has effect.
(2) The enactments specified in Schedule 2 are repealed to the extent specified in the third column of that Schedule.

SCHEDULE 1
MINOR AND CONSEQUENTIAL AMENDMENTS

Article 10(1)

Law of Property Act 1925

1 Section 74 of the 1925 Act (execution by or on behalf of corporations) shall be amended in accordance with paragraphs 2 to 4.
2 After subsection (1A), inserted by article 7(1) above, insert –

> '(1B) For the purposes of subsection (1) of this section, a seal purports to be affixed in the presence of and attested by an officer of the corporation, in the case of an officer which is not an individual, if it is affixed in the presence of and attested by an individual authorised by the officer to attest on its behalf.'.

3 In subsection (3) (execution of conveyance by individual in the name or on behalf of a corporation), after 'witness' insert 'who attests the signature'.
4 In subsection (4) (execution by corporation as attorney) –

(a) for 'deed or other instrument' substitute 'instrument by signing it', and
(b) after 'such other person' insert 'or, if the instrument is to be a deed, by so signing it in the presence of a witness who attests the signature'.

Powers of Attorney Act 1971

5 Section 7 of the Powers of Attorney Act 1971 (execution of instrument by donee of power of attorney) shall be amended in accordance with paragraphs 6 to 8.
6 Subsection (1) (effect of execution by donee), for the words from 'document' to the end substitute 'instrument executed or thing done in that manner shall, subject to subsection (1A) of this section, be as effective as if executed by the donee

in any manner which would constitute due execution of that instrument by the donor or, as the case may be, as if done by the donee in the name of the donor'.

7   After subsection (1) insert –

> '(1A)   Where an instrument is executed by the donee as a deed, it shall be as effective as if executed by the donee in a manner which would constitute due execution of it as a deed by the donor only if it is executed in accordance with section 1(3)(a) of the Law of Property (Miscellaneous Provisions) Act 1989.'.

8   Omit subsection (3).

Companies Act 1985

9   Section 36A of the 1985 Act (execution of documents: England and Wales) shall be amended in accordance with paragraphs 10 to 12.

10   After subsection (4) insert –

> '(4A)   Where a document is to be signed by a person as a director or the secretary of more than one company, it shall not be taken to be duly signed by that person for the purposes of subsection (4) unless the person signs it separately in each capacity.'.

11   After subsection (7), inserted by article 7(2) above, insert –

> '(8)   For the purposes of this section, a document is (or purports to be) signed, in the case of a director or the secretary of a company which is not an individual, if it is (or purports to be) signed by an individual authorised by the director or secretary to sign on its behalf.'.

12   In Schedule 22 to the 1985 Act (application of provisions of that Act to unregistered companies), in the entries relating to Part 1 –

(a)   in the first column, after '36A' insert ', 36AA', and
(b)   in the second column, after 'documents' insert 'and deeds'.

Law of Property (Miscellaneous Provisions) Act 1989

13   Section 1 of the 1989 Act (deeds and their execution) shall be amended in accordance with paragraphs 14 and 15.

14   In subsection (4) (interpretation of references to signing an instrument), for the words from 'making' to the end substitute –

> '(a)   an individual signing the name of the person or party on whose behalf he executes the instrument; and
> (b)   making one's mark on the instrument,
>
> and "signature" is to be construed accordingly.'.

15   In subsection (6) (interpretation) in the definitions of 'disposition' and 'purchaser', for '"disposition" and "purchaser" have the same meanings' substitute '"purchaser" has the same meaning'.

Companies Act 1989

16 In section 130(6) of the Companies Act 1989 (power to make regulations applying provisions of the 1985 Act to foreign companies), after 'documents;' insert 'execution of deeds;'.

Land Registration Act 2002

17 At the end of section 91(9) of the Land Registration Act 2002 (application of section 36A of the Companies Act 1985 in relation to electronic conveyancing), insert '(and subsection (8) of that section, in so far as it relates to the document, shall be read accordingly)'.

SCHEDULE 2
REPEALS

Article 10(2)

Chapter	Short title	Extent of repeal
1971 c 27.	The Powers of Attorney Act 1971.	Section 7(3).
1985 c 6.	The Companies Act 1985.	In section 36A – (a) subsection (5); and (b) in subsection (6), the words from 'and, where' to 'executed'.
1989 c 34.	The Law of Property (Miscellaneous Provisions) Act 1989.	In section 1 – (a) in subsection (3)(b), the words from 'by him' to the end; (b) in subsection (5), the words 'involving the disposition or creation of an interest in land'; and (c) in subsection (6), the definition of 'interest in land' and the word 'and' preceding it.

DRAFT OVERSEAS COMPANIES REGULATIONS 2008 (DECEMBER 2007 – NOT YET FINAL)

Please note that this is not yet final. For the latest revised or final version of this draft statutory instrument, please see **www.berr.gov.uk/bbf/co-act-2006**.

Company contracts and execution of documents by overseas companies

77.–(1) Sections 43 (company contracts), 44 (execution of documents), 45 (common seal), 46 (execution of deeds), 47 (execution of deeds or other documents by attorney), 48 (execution of documents by companies), 51 (pre-incorporation contracts) and 52 (bills of exchange and promissory notes) apply to overseas companies with the adaptations and modifications set out in paragraphs (2) to (4).

(2) References to a company in the sections specified in paragraph (1) shall be read as references to an overseas company.

(3) Section 43 shall apply as if –

   (a) in subsection (1)(a), after the words 'common seal', there were inserted 'or in any manner permitted by the laws of the territory in which the company is incorporated for the execution of documents by such a company,', and

   (b) for subsection (1)(b) there were substituted –

      '(b) on behalf of a company, by any person who, in accordance with the laws of the territory in which the company is incorporated, is acting under the authority (express or implied) of that company.'.

(4) Section 44 shall apply as if –

   (a) for subsection (1)(b) there were substituted –

      '(b) if it is executed in any manner permitted by the laws of the territory in which the company is incorporated for the execution of documents by such a company.',

   (b) for subsections (2), (3) and (4) there were substituted –

      '(2) A document which –

         (a) is signed by a person who, in accordance with the laws of the territory in which the company is incorporated, is acting under the authority (express or implied) of that company, and

         (b) is expressed (in whatever form of words) to be executed by the company,

      has the same effect in relation to that company as it would have in relation to a company incorporated in England and Wales or Northern Ireland if executed under the common seal of a company so incorporated.',

    (c)   in subsection (7) for the words –

        (i)   'a director or secretary' there were substituted 'a person who, in accordance with the laws of the territory in which the company is incorporated, is acting under the authority (express or implied) of that company', and

        (ii)   'that office' there were substituted 'that person'.

        (iii) delete the words 'held by'.

APPENDIX 2

Selected Civil Procedure Rules and Practice Directions

PART 22
STATEMENT OF TRUTH

Documents to be verified by a statement of truth

22.1(1) The following documents must be verified by a statement of truth –

    (a)   a statement of case;

    (b)   a response complying with an order under rule 18.1 to provide further information;

    (c)   a witness statement;

    (d)   an acknowledgement of service in a claim begun by way of the Part 8 procedure;

    (e)   a certificate stating the reasons for bringing a possession claim or a landlord and tenant claim in the High Court in accordance with rules 55.3(2) and 56.2(2);

    (f)   a certificate of service; and

    (g)   any other document where a rule or practice direction requires.

  (2) Where a statement of case is amended, the amendments must be verified by a statement of truth unless the court orders otherwise.

(Part 17 provides for amendments to statements of case)

  (3) If an applicant wishes to rely on matters set out in his application notice as evidence, the application notice must be verified by a statement of truth.

  (4) Subject to paragraph (5), a statement of truth is a statement that –

    (a)   the party putting forward the document;

    (b)   in the case of a witness statement, the maker of the witness statement; or

    (c)   in the case of a certificate of service, the person who signs the certificate,

believes the facts stated in the document are true.

  (5) If a party is conducting proceedings with a litigation friend, the statement of truth in –

    (a)   a statement of case;

    (b)   a response; or

    (c)   an application notice,

is a statement that the litigation friend believes the facts stated in the document being verified are true.

(6)   The statement of truth must be signed by –

(a)   in the case of a statement of case, a response or an application –

(i)   the party or litigation friend; or
(ii) the legal representative on behalf of the party or litigation friend; and

(b)   in the case of a witness statement, the maker of the statement.

(7)   A statement of truth which is not contained in the document which it verifies, must clearly identify that document.

(8)   A statement of truth in a statement of case may be made by –

(a)   a person who is not a party; or
(b)   by two parties jointly,

where this is permitted by a relevant practice direction.

Failure to verify a statement of case

22.2(1)   If a party fails to verify his statement of case by a statement of truth –

(a)   the statement of case shall remain effective unless struck out; but
(b)   the party may not rely on the statement of case as evidence of any of the matters set out in it.

(2)   The court may strike out a statement of case which is not verified by a statement of truth.

(3)   Any party may apply for an order under paragraph (2).

Failure to verify a witness statement

22.3   If the maker of a witness statement fails to verify the witness statement by a statement of truth the court may direct that it shall not be admissible as evidence.

Power of the court to require a document to be verified

22.4(1)   The court may order a person who has failed to verify a document in accordance with rule 22.1 to verify the document.

(2)   Any party may apply for an order under paragraph (1).

PRACTICE DIRECTION – STATEMENTS OF TRUTH

THIS PRACTICE DIRECTION SUPPLEMENTS CPR PART 22

Documents to be verified by a statement of truth

1.1   Rule 22.1(1) sets out the documents which must be verified by a statement of truth. The documents include:

(1)   a statement of case,
(2)   a response complying with an order under rule 18.1 to provide further information,

(3) a witness statement,

(4) an acknowledgment of service in a claim begun by the Part 8 procedure,

(5) a certificate stating the reasons for bringing a possession claim or a landlord and tenant claim in the High Court in accordance with rules 55.3(2) and 56.2(2),

(6) a certificate of service.

1.2 If an applicant wishes to rely on matters set out in his application notice as evidence, the application notice must be verified by a statement of truth.[1]

1.3 An expert's report should also be verified by a statement of truth. For the form of the statement of truth verifying an expert's report (which differs from that set out below) see the practice direction which supplements Part 35.

1.4 In addition, the following documents must be verified by a statement of truth:

(1) an application notice for –

(a) a third party debt order (rule 72.3),

(b) a hardship payment order (rule 72.7), or

(c) a charging order (rule 73.3);

(2) a notice of objections to an account being taken by the court, unless verified by an affidavit or witness statement;

(3) a schedule or counter-schedule of expenses and losses in a personal injury claim, and any amendments to such a schedule or counter-schedule, whether or not they are contained in a statement of case.

1.5 The statement of truth may be contained in the document it verifies or it may be in a separate document served subsequently, in which case it must identify the document to which it relates.

1.6 Where the form to be used includes a jurat for the content to be verified by an affidavit then a statement of truth is not required in addition.

Form of the statement of truth

2.1 The form of the statement of truth verifying a statement of case, a response, an application notice or a notice of objections should be as follows:

'[I believe] [the (*claimant or as may be*) believes] that the facts stated in this [*name document being verified*] are true.'

2.2 The form of the statement of truth verifying a witness statement should be as follows:

'I believe that the facts stated in this witness statement are true.'

2.3 Where the statement of truth is contained in a separate document, the document containing the statement of truth must be headed with the title of the proceedings and the claim number. The document being verified should be identified in the statement of truth as follows:

---

1 See rule 22.1(3).

(1) claim form: 'the claim form issued on [*date*]',

(2) particulars of claim: 'the particulars of claim issued on [*date*]',

(3) statement of case: 'the [*defence or as may be*] served on the [*name of party*] on [date]',

(4) application notice: 'the application notice issued on [*date*] for [*set out the remedy sought*]',

(5) witness statement: 'the witness statement filed on [*date*] or served on [*party*] on [*date*]'.

Who may sign the statement of truth

3.1   In a statement of case, a response or an application notice, the statement of truth must be signed by:

(1) the party or his litigation friend,[2] or

(2) the legal representative[3] of the party or litigation friend.

3.2   A statement of truth verifying a witness statement must be signed by the witness.

3.3   A statement of truth verifying a notice of objections to an account must be signed by the objecting party or his legal representative.

3.4   Where a document is to be verified on behalf of a company or other corporation, subject to paragraph 3.7 below, the statement of truth must be signed by a person holding a senior position[4] in the company or corporation. That person must state the office or position he holds.

3.5   Each of the following persons is a person holding a senior position:

(1) in respect of a registered company or corporation, a director, the treasurer, secretary, chief executive, manager or other officer of the company or corporation, and

(2) in respect of a corporation which is not a registered company, in addition to those persons set out in (1), the mayor, chairman, president or town clerk or other similar officer of the corporation.

3.6   Where the document is to be verified on behalf of a partnership, those who may sign the statement of truth are:

(1) any of the partners, or

(2) a person having the control or management of the partnership business.

3.6A   An insurer or the Motor Insurers' Bureau may sign a statement of truth in a statement of case on behalf of a party where the insurer or the Motor Insurers' Bureau has a financial interest in the result of proceedings brought wholly or partially by or against that party.

3.6B   If insurers are conducting proceedings on behalf of many claimants or defendants a statement of truth in a statement of case may be signed by a senior person responsible for the case at a lead insurer, but –

---

2 See Part 21 (Children and Protected Parties).
3 See rule 2.3 for the definition of legal representative.
4 See rule 6.4(4).

(1) the person signing must specify the capacity in which he signs;

(2) the statement of truth must be a statement that the lead insurer believes that the facts stated in the document are true; and

(3) the court may order that a statement of truth also be signed by one or more of the parties.

3.7 Where a party is legally represented, the legal representative may sign the statement of truth on his behalf. The statement signed by the legal representative will refer to the client's belief, not his own. In signing he must state the capacity in which he signs and the name of his firm where appropriate.

3.8 Where a legal representative has signed a statement of truth, his signature will be taken by the court as his statement:

(1) that the client on whose behalf he has signed had authorised him to do so,

(2) that before signing he had explained to the client that in signing the statement of truth he would be confirming the client's belief that the facts stated in the document were true, and

(3) that before signing he had informed the client of the possible consequences to the client if it should subsequently appear that the client did not have an honest belief in the truth of those facts (see rule 32.14).

3.9 The individual who signs a statement of truth must print his full name clearly beneath his signature.

3.10 A legal representative who signs a statement of truth must sign in his own name and not that of his firm or employer.

3.11 The following are examples of the possible application of this practice direction describing who may sign a statement of truth verifying statements in documents other than a witness statement. These are only examples and not an indication of how a court might apply the practice direction to a specific situation.

Managing Agent An agent who manages property or investments for the party cannot sign a statement of truth. It must be signed by the party or by the legal representative of the party.

Trusts Where some or all of the trustees comprise a single party one, some or all of the trustees comprising the party may sign a statement of truth. The legal representative of the trustees may sign it.

Insurers and the Motor Insurers' Bureau If an insurer has a financial interest in a claim involving involving its insured then, if the insured is the party, the insurer may sign a statement of truth in a statement of case for the insured party. Paragraphs 3.4 and 3.5 apply to the insurer if it is a company. The claims manager employed by the insurer responsible for handling the insurance claim or managing the staff handling the claim may sign the statement of truth for the insurer (see next example). The position for the Motor Insurers' Bureau is similar.

Companies Paragraphs 3.4 and 3.5 apply. The word manager will be construed in the context of the phrase 'a person holding a senior position' which it is used to define. The court will consider the size of the company and the size and nature of the claim. It would expect the manager signing the statement of truth to have personal knowledge of the content of the document or to be responsible for managing those who have that knowledge of the content. A small company may not have a manager, apart from the directors, who holds a senior position. A large company will have many such managers. In a larger company with specialist claims, insurance or legal departments the statement may be signed by the manager of such a department if he or she is responsible for handling the claim or managing the staff handling it.

In-house legal representatives
Legal representative is defined in rule 2.3(1). A legal representative employed by a party may sign a statement of truth. However a person who is not a solicitor, barrister or other authorised litigator, but who is employed by the company and is managed by such a person, is not employed by that person and so cannot sign a statement of truth. (This is unlike the employee of a solicitor in private practice who would come within the definition of legal representative.) However such a person may be a manager and able to sign the statement on behalf of the company in that capacity.

Inability to persons to read or sign documents to be verified by a statement of truth

3A.1   Where a document containing a statement of truth is to be signed by a person who is unable to read or sign the document, it must contain a certificate made by an authorised person.

3A.2   An authorised person is a person able to administer oaths and take affidavits but need not be independent of the parties or their representatives.

3A.3   The authorised person must certify:

(1)   that the document has been read to the person signing it;

(2)   that that person appeared to understand it and approved its content as accurate;

(3)   that the declaration of truth has been read to that person;

(4)   that that person appeared to understand the declaration and the consequences of making a false declaration; and

(5)   that that person signed or made his mark in the presence of the authorised person.

3A.4   The form of the certificate is set out at Annex 1 to this Practice Direction.

Consequences of failure to verify

4.1   If a statement of case is not verified by a statement of truth, the statement of case will remain effective unless it is struck out,[5] but a party may not rely on the contents of a statement of case as evidence until it has been verified by a statement of truth.

4.2   Any party may apply to the court for an order that unless within such period as the court may specify the statement of case is verified by the service of a statement of truth, the statement of case will be struck out.

4.3   The usual order for the costs of an application referred to in paragraph 4.2 will be that the costs be paid by the party who had failed to verify in any event and forthwith.

Penalty

5   Attention is drawn to rule 32.14 which sets out the consequences of verifying a statement of case containing a false statement without an honest belief in its truth, and to the procedures set out in paragraph 28 of the practice direction supplementing Part 32.

ANNEX

Certificate to be used where a person is unable to read or sign a document to be verified by a statement of truth

I certify that I [*name and address of authorised person*] have read over the contents of this document and the declaration of truth to the person signing the document [*if there are exhibits, add* 'and explained the nature and effect of the exhibits referred to in it'] who appeared to understand (a) the document and approved its content as accurate and (b) the declaration of truth and the consequences of making a false declaration, and made his mark in my presence.

PART 32
EVIDENCE

Power of court to control evidence

32.1(1)   The court may control the evidence by giving directions as to –

    (a)   the issues on which it requires evidence;

    (b)   the nature of the evidence which it requires to decide those issues; and

    (c)   the way in which the evidence is to be placed before the court.

  (2)   The court may use its power under this rule to exclude evidence that would otherwise be admissible.

  (3)   The court may limit cross-examination.

---

5 See rule 22.2(1).

Evidence of witnesses – general rule

32.2(1) The general rule is that any fact which needs to be proved by the evidence of witnesses is to be proved –

(a) at trial, by their oral evidence given in public; and

(b) at any other hearing, by their evidence in writing.

(2) This is subject –

(a) to any provision to the contrary contained in these Rules or elsewhere; or

(b) to any order of the court.

Evidence by video link or other means

32.3 The court may allow a witness to give evidence through a video link or by other means.

Requirement to serve witness statements for use at trial

32.4(1) A witness statement is a written statement signed by a person which contains the evidence which that person would be allowed to give orally.

(2) The court will order a party to serve on the other parties any witness statement of the oral evidence which the party serving the statement intends to rely on in relation to any issues of fact to be decided at the trial.

(3) The court may give directions as to –

(a) the order in which witness statements are to be served; and

(b) whether or not the witness statements are to be filed.

Use at trial of witness statements which have been served

32.5(1) If –

(a) a party has served a witness statement; and

(b) he wishes to rely at trial on the evidence of the witness who made the statement,

he must call the witness to give oral evidence unless the court orders otherwise or he puts the statement in as hearsay evidence.

(Part 33 contains provisions about hearsay evidence)

(2) Where a witness is called to give oral evidence under paragraph (1), his witness statement shall stand as his evidence in chief unless the court orders otherwise.

(3) A witness giving oral evidence at trial may with the permission of the court –

(a) amplify his witness statement; and

(b) give evidence in relation to new matters which have arisen since the witness statement was served on the other parties.

(4) The court will give permission under paragraph (3) only if it considers that there is good reason not to confine the evidence of the witness to the contents of his witness statement.

(5) If a party who has served a witness statement does not –

    (a) call the witness to give evidence at trial; or

    (b) put the witness statement in as hearsay evidence, any other party may put the witness statement in as hearsay evidence.

Evidence in proceedings other than at trial

32.6(1) Subject to paragraph (2), the general rule is that evidence at hearings other than the trial is to be by witness statement unless the court, a practice direction or any other enactment requires otherwise.

(2) At hearings other than the trial, a party may, rely on the matters set out in –

    (a) his statement of case; or

    (b) his application notice, if the statement of case or application notice is verified by a statement of truth.

Order for cross-examination

32.7(1) Where, at a hearing other than the trial, evidence is given in writing, any party may apply to the court for permission to cross-examine the person giving the evidence.

(2) If the court gives permission under paragraph (1) but the person in question does not attend as required by the order, his evidence may not be used unless the court gives permission.

Form of witness statement

32.8 A witness statement must comply with the requirements set out in the relevant practice direction.

(Part 22 requires a witness statement to be verified by a statement of truth)

Witness summaries

32.9(1) A party who –

    (a) is required to serve a witness statement for use at trial; but

    (b) is unable to obtain one, may apply, without notice, for permission to serve a witness summary instead.

(2) A witness summary is a summary of –

    (a) the evidence, if known, which would otherwise be included in a witness statement; or

    (b) if the evidence is not known, the matters about which the party serving the witness summary proposes to question the witness.

(3) Unless the court orders otherwise, a witness summary must include the name and address of the intended witness.

(4)   Unless the court orders otherwise, a witness summary must be served within the period in which a witness statement would have had to be served.

(5)   Where a party serves a witness summary, so far as practicable rules 32.4 (requirement to serve witness statements for use at trial), 32.5(3) (amplifying witness statements), and 32.8 (form of witness statement) shall apply to the summary.

Consequence of failure to serve witness statement or summary

32.10   If a witness statement or a witness summary for use at trial is not served in respect of an intended witness within the time specified by the court, then the witness may not be called to give oral evidence unless the court gives permission.

Cross-examination on a witness statement

32.11   Where a witness is called to give evidence at trial, he may be cross-examined on his witness statement whether or not the statement or any part of it was referred to during the witness's evidence in chief.

Use of witness statements for other purposes

32.12(1) Except as provided by this rule, a witness statement may be used only for the purpose of the proceedings in which it is served.

(2) Paragraph (1) does not apply if and to the extent that –

(a)   the witness gives consent in writing to some other use of it;

(b)   the court gives permission for some other use; or

(c)   the witness statement has been put in evidence at a hearing held in public.

Availability of witness statements for inspection

32.13(1) A witness statement which stands as evidence in chief is open to inspection during the course of the trial unless the court otherwise directs.

(2) Any person may ask for a direction that a witness statement is not open to inspection.

(3) The court will not make a direction under paragraph (2) unless it is satisfied that a witness statement should not be open to inspection because of –

(a)   the interests of justice;

(b)   the public interest;

(c)   the nature of any expert medical evidence in the statement;

(d)   the nature of any confidential information (including information relating to personal financial matters) in the statement; or

(e)   the need to protect the interests of any child or protected party.

(4)   The court may exclude from inspection words or passages in the statement.

False statements

32.14(1) Proceedings for contempt of court may be brought against a person if he makes, or causes to be made, a false statement in a document verified by a statement of truth without an honest belief in its truth.

(Part 22 makes provision for a statement of truth)

(2) Proceedings under this rule may be brought only –

(a) by the Attorney General; or

(b) with the permission of the court.

Affidavit evidence

32.15(1) Evidence must be given by affidavit instead of or in addition to a witness statement if this is required by the court, a provision contained in any other rule, a practice direction or any other enactment.

(2) Nothing in these Rules prevents a witness giving evidence by affidavit at a hearing other than the trial if he chooses to do so in a case where paragraph (1) does not apply, but the party putting forward the affidavit may not recover the additional cost of making it from any other party unless the court orders otherwise.

Form of affidavit

32.16 An affidavit must comply with the requirements set out in the relevant practice direction.

Affidavit made outside the jurisdiction

32.17 A person may make an affidavit outside the jurisdiction in accordance with –

(a) this Part; or

(b) the law of the place where he makes the affidavit.

Notice to admit facts

32.18(1) A party may serve notice on another party requiring him to admit the facts, or the part of the case of the serving party, specified in the notice.

(2) A notice to admit facts must be served no later than 21 days before the trial.

(3) Where the other party makes any admission in response to the notice, the admission may be used against him only –

(a) in the proceedings in which the notice to admit is served; and

(b) by the party who served the notice.

(4) The court may allow a party to amend or withdraw any admission made by him on such terms as it thinks just.

Notice to admit or produce documents

32.19(1) A party shall be deemed to admit the authenticity of a document disclosed to him under Part 31 (disclosure and inspection of documents) unless he serves notice that he wishes the document to be proved at trial.

(2) A notice to prove a document must be served –

(a) by the latest date for serving witness statements; or
(b) within 7 days of disclosure of the document, whichever is later.

Notarial acts and instruments

32.20 A notarial act or instrument may be received in evidence without further proof as duly authenticated in accordance with the requirements of law unless the contrary is proved.

PRACTICE DIRECTION – EVIDENCE

THIS PRACTICE DIRECTION SUPPLEMENTS CPR PART 32

Evidence in general

1.1 Rule 32.2 sets out how evidence is to be given and facts are to be proved.
1.2 Evidence at a hearing other than the trial should normally be given by witness statement[1] (see paragraph 17 onwards). However a witness may give evidence by affidavit if he wishes to do so[2] (and see paragraph 1.4 below).
1.3 Statements of case (see paragraph 26 onwards) and application notices[3] may also be used as evidence provided that their contents have been verified by a statement of truth.[4]

(For information regarding evidence by deposition see Part 34 and the practice direction which supplements it.)

1.4 Affidavits must be used as evidence in the following instances:

(1) where sworn evidence is required by an enactment,[5] rule, order or practice direction,
(2) in any application for a search order, a freezing injunction, or an order requiring an occupier to permit another to enter his land, and
(3) in any application for an order against anyone for alleged contempt of court.

1.5 If a party believes that sworn evidence is required by a court in another jurisdiction for any purpose connected with the proceedings, he may apply to the court for a direction that evidence shall be given only by affidavit on any pre-trial applications.
1.6 The court may give a direction under rule 32.15 that evidence shall be given by affidavit instead of or in addition to a witness statement or statement of case:

---

1 See rule 32.6(1).
2 See rule 32.15(2).
3 See Part 23 for information about making an application.
4 Rule 32.6(2) and see Part 22 for information about the statement of truth.
5 See, e.g., s.3(5)(a) of the Protection from Harassment Act 1997.

(1)   on its own initiative, or

(2)   after any party has applied to the court for such a direction.

1.7   An affidavit, where referred to in the Civil Procedure Rules or a practice direction, also means an affirmation unless the context requires otherwise.

Affidavits

Deponent

2   A deponent is a person who gives evidence by affidavit or affirmation.

Heading

3.1   The affidavit should be headed with the title of the proceedings (see paragraph 4 of the practice direction supplementing Part 7 and paragraph 7 of the practice direction supplementing Part 20); where the proceedings are between several parties with the same status it is sufficient to identify the parties as follows:

Number:

A.B. (and others)	Claimants/Applicants
C.D. (and others)	Defendants/Respondents (as appropriate)

3.2   At the top right hand corner of the first page (and on the back-sheet) there should be clearly written:

(1)   the party on whose behalf it is made,

(2)   the initials and surname of the deponent,

(3)   the number of the affidavit in relation to that deponent,

(4)   the identifying initials and number of each exhibit referred to, and

(5)   the date sworn.

Body of affidavit

4.1   The affidavit must, if practicable, be in the deponent's own words, the affidavit should be expressed in the first person and the deponent should:

(1)   commence 'I (*full name*) of (*address*) state on oath . . .',

(2)   if giving evidence in his professional, business or other occupational capacity, give the address at which he works in (1) above, the position he holds and the name of his firm or employer,

(3)   give his occupation or, if he has none, his description, and

(4)   state if he is a party to the proceedings or employed by a party to the proceedings, if it be the case.

4.2   An affidavit must indicate:

(1)   which of the statements in it are made from the deponent's own knowledge and which are matters of information or belief, and

(2)   the source for any matters of information or belief.

4.3   Where a deponent:

(1)   refers to an exhibit or exhibits, he should state 'there is now shown to me marked '. . .' the (*description of exhibit*)', and
(2)   makes more than one affidavit (to which there are exhibits) in the same proceedings, the numbering of the exhibits should run consecutively throughout and not start again with each affidavit.

Jurat

5.1   The jurat of an affidavit is a statement set out at the end of the document which authenticates the affidavit.
5.2   It must:

(1)   be signed by all deponents,
(2)   be completed and signed by the person before whom the affidavit was sworn whose name and qualification must be printed beneath his signature,
(3)   contain the full address of the person before whom the affidavit was sworn, and
(4)   follow immediately on from the text and not be put on a separate page.

Format of affidavits

6.1   An affidavit should:

(1)   be produced on durable quality A4 paper with a 3.5cm margin,
(2)   be fully legible and should normally be typed on one side of the paper only,
(3)   where possible, be bound securely in a manner which would not hamper filing, or otherwise each page should be endorsed with the case number and should bear the initials of the deponent and of the person before whom it was sworn,
(4)   have the pages numbered consecutively as a separate document (or as one of several documents contained in a file),
(5)   be divided into numbered paragraphs,
(6)   have all numbers, including dates, expressed in figures, and
(7)   give the reference to any document or documents mentioned either in the margin or in bold text in the body of the affidavit.

6.2   It is usually convenient for an affidavit to follow the chronological sequence of events or matters dealt with; each paragraph of an affidavit should as far as possible be confined to a distinct portion of the subject.

Inability of deponent to read or sign affidavit

7.1   Where an affidavit is sworn by a person who is unable to read or sign it, the person before whom the affidavit is sworn must certify in the jurat that:

(1)   he read the affidavit to the deponent,
(2)   the deponent appeared to understand it, and
(3)   the deponent signed or made his mark, in his presence.

7.2   If that certificate is not included in the jurat, the affidavit may not be used in evidence unless the court is satisfied that it was read to the deponent and that he appeared to understand it. Two versions of the form of jurat with the certificate are set out at Annex 1 to this practice direction.

Alterations to affidavits

8.1   Any alteration to an affidavit must be initialled by both the deponent and the person before whom the affidavit was sworn.

8.2   An affidavit which contains an alteration that has not been initialled may be filed or used in evidence only with the permission of the court.

Who may administer oaths and take affidavits

9.1   Only the following may administer oaths and take affidavits:

   (1)   Commissioners for oaths,[6]
   (2)   Practising solicitors,[7]
   (3)   other persons specified by statute,[8]
   (4)   certain officials of the Supreme Court,[9]
   (5)   a circuit judge or district judge,[10]
   (6)   any justice of the peace,[11] and
   (7)   certain officials of any county court appointed by the judge of that court for the purpose.[12]

9.2   An affidavit must be sworn before a person independent of the parties or their representatives.

Filing of affidavits

10.1   If the court directs that an affidavit is to be filed,[13] it must be filed in the court or Division, or Office or Registry of the court or Division where the action in which it was or is to be used, is proceeding or will proceed.

10.2   Where an affidavit is in a foreign language:

   (1)   the party wishing to rely on it –

      (a)   must have it translated, and
      (b)   must file the foreign language affidavit with the court, and

   (2)   the translator must make and file with the court an affidavit verifying the translation and exhibiting both the translation and a copy of the foreign language affidavit.

---

6 Commissioner for Oaths Act 1889 and 1891.
7 Section 81 of the Solicitors Act 1974.
8 Section 65 of the Administration of Justice Act 1985, s.113 of the Courts and Legal Services Act 1990 and the Commissioners for Oaths (Prescribed Bodies) Regulations 1994 and 1995.
9 Section 2 of the Commissioners for Oaths Act 1889.
10 Section 58 of the County Courts Act 1984.
11 Section 58 as above.
12 Section 58 as above.
13 Rules 32.1(3) and 32.4(3)(b).

Exhibits

Manner of exhibiting documents

11.1   A document used in conjunction with an affidavit should be:

(1) produced to and verified by the deponent, and remain separate from the affidavit, and

(2) identified by a declaration of the person before whom the affidavit was sworn.

11.2   The declaration should be headed with the name of the proceedings in the same way as the affidavit.

11.3   The first page of each exhibit should be marked:

(1) as in paragraph 3.2 above, and

(2) with the exhibit mark referred to in the affidavit.

Letters

12.1   Copies of individual letters should be collected together and exhibited in a bundle or bundles. They should be arranged in chronological order with the earliest at the top, and firmly secured.

12.2   When a bundle of correspondence is exhibited, the exhibit should have a front page attached stating that the bundle consists of original letters and copies. They should be arranged and secured as above and numbered consecutively.

Other documents

13.1   Photocopies instead of original documents may be exhibited provided the originals are made available for inspection by the other parties before the hearing and by the judge at the hearing.

13.2   Court documents must not be exhibited (official copies of such documents prove themselves).

13.3   Where an exhibit contains more than one document, a front page should be attached setting out a list of the documents contained in the exhibit; the list should contain the dates of the documents.

Exhibits other than documents

14.1   Items other than documents should be clearly marked with an exhibit number or letter in such a manner that the mark cannot become detached from the exhibit.

14.2   Small items may be placed in a container and the container appropriately marked.

General provisions

15.1   Where an exhibit contains more than one document:

(1) the bundle should not be stapled but should be securely fastened in a way that does not hinder the reading of the documents, and

(2)   the pages should be numbered consecutively at bottom centre.

15.2   Every page of an exhibit should be clearly legible; typed copies of illegible documents should be included, paginated with 'a' numbers.

15.3   Where affidavits and exhibits have become numerous, they should be put into separate bundles and the pages numbered consecutively throughout.

15.4   Where on account of their bulk the service of exhibits or copies of exhibits on the other parties would be difficult or impracticable, the directions of the court should be sought as to arrangements for bringing the exhibits to the attention of the other parties and as to their custody pending trial.

Affirmations

16   All provisions in this or any other practice direction relating to affidavits apply to affirmations with the following exceptions:

(1)   the deponent should commence 'I (*name*) of (*address*) do solemnly and sincerely affirm . . .', and

(2)   in the jurat the word 'sworn' is replaced by the word 'affirmed'.

Witness statements

Heading

17.1   The witness statement should be headed with the title of the proceedings (see paragraph 4 of the practice direction supplementing Part 7 and paragraph 7 of the practice direction supplementing Part 20); where the proceedings are between several parties with the same status it is sufficient to identify the parties as follows:

Number:

A.B. (and others)	Claimants/Applicants
C.D. (and others)	Defendants/Respondents (as appropriate)

17.2   At the top right hand corner of the first page there should be clearly written:

(1)   the party on whose behalf it is made,

(2)   the initials and surname of the witness,

(3)   the number of the statement in relation to that witness,

(4)   the identifying initials and number of each exhibit referred to, and

(5)   the date the statement was made.

Body of witness statement

18.1   The witness statement must, if practicable, be in the intended witness's own words, the statement should be expressed in the first person and should also state:

(1)   the full name of the witness,

(2)   his place of residence or, if he is making the statement in his professional, business or other occupational capacity, the address at which he works, the position he holds and the name of his firm or employer,

(3)   his occupation, or if he has none, his description, and

(4)   the fact that he is a party to the proceedings or is the employee of such a party if it be the case.

18.2   A witness statement must indicate:

(1)   which of the statements in it are made from the witness's own knowledge and which are matters of information or belief, and

(2)   the source for any matters of information or belief.

18.3   An exhibit used in conjunction with a witness statement should be verified and identified by the witness and remain separate from the witness statement.

18.4   Where a witness refers to an exhibit or exhibits, he should state 'I refer to the (*description of exhibit*) marked '. . .''.

18.5   The provisions of paragraphs 11.3 to 15.4 (exhibits) apply similarly to witness statements as they do to affidavits.

18.6   Where a witness makes more than one witness statement to which there are exhibits, in the same proceedings, the numbering of the exhibits should run consecutively throughout and not start again with each witness statement.

Format of witness statement

19.1   A witness statement should:

(1)   be produced on durable quality A4 paper with a 3.5cm margin,

(2)   be fully legible and should normally be typed on one side of the paper only,

(3)   where possible, be bound securely in a manner which would not hamper filing, or otherwise each page should be endorsed with the case number and should bear the initials of the witness,

(4)   have the pages numbered consecutively as a separate statement (or as one of several statements contained in a file),

(5)   be divided into numbered paragraphs,

(6)   have all numbers, including dates, expressed in figures, and

(7)   give the reference to any document or documents mentioned either in the margin or in bold text in the body of the statement.

19.2   It is usually convenient for a witness statement to follow the chronological sequence of the events or matters dealt with, each paragraph of a witness statement should as far as possible be confined to a distinct portion of the subject.

Statement of truth

20.1   A witness statement is the equivalent of the oral evidence which that witness would, if called, give in evidence; it must include a statement by the intended witness that he believes the facts in it are true.[14]

20.2   To verify a witness statement the statement of truth is as follows:

'I believe that the facts stated in this witness statement are true'.

---

14 See Part 22 for information about the statement of truth.

20.3   Attention is drawn to rule 32.14 which sets out the consequences of verifying a witness statement containing a false statement without an honest belief in its truth.

(Paragraph 3A of the practice direction to Part 22 sets out the procedure to be followed where the person who should sign a document which is verified by a statement of truth is unable to read or sign the document.)

21   Omitted

Alterations to witness statements

22.1   Any alteration to a witness statement must be initialled by the person making the statement or by the authorised person where appropriate (see paragraph 21).

22.2   A witness statement which contains an alteration that has not been initialled may be used in evidence only with the permission of the court.

Filing of witness statements

23.1   If the court directs that a witness statement is to be filed,[15] it must be filed in the court or Division, or Office or Registry of the court or Division where the action in which it was or is to be used, is proceeding or will proceed.

23.2   Where the court has directed that a witness statement in a foreign language is to be filed:

   (1) the party wishing to rely on it must –

       (a)   have it translated, and
       (b)   file the foreign language witness statement with the court, and

   (2) the translator must make and file with the court an affidavit verifying the translation and exhibiting both the translation and a copy of the foreign language witness statement.

Certificate of court officer

24.1   Where the court has ordered that a witness statement is not to be open to inspection by the public[16] or that words or passages in the statement are not to be open to inspection[17] the court officer will so certify on the statement and make any deletions directed by the court under rule 32.13(4).

Defects in affidavits, witness statements and exhibits

25.1   Where:

   (1) an affidavit,
   (2) a witness statement, or
   (3) an exhibit to either an affidavit or a witness statement,

---

15 Rule 32.4(3)(b).
16 Rule 32.13(2).
17 Rule 32.13(4).

does not comply with Part 32 or this practice direction in relation to its form, the court may refuse to admit it as evidence and may refuse to allow the costs arising from its preparation.

25.2   Permission to file a defective affidavit or witness statement or to use a defective exhibit may be obtained from a judge[18] in the court where the case is proceeding.

Statements of case

26.1   A statement of case may be used as evidence in an interim application provided it is verified by a statement of truth.[19]

26.2   To verify a statement of case the statement of truth should be set out as follows:

'[I believe] [the (*party on whose behalf the statement of case is being signed*) believes] that the facts stated in the statement of case are true'.

26.3   Attention is drawn to rule 32.14 which sets out the consequences of verifying a witness statement containing a false statement without an honest belief in its truth.

(For information regarding statements of truth see Part 22 and the practice direction which supplements it.)

(Practice directions supplementing Parts 7, 9 and 17 provide further information concerning statements of case.)

Agreed bundles for hearings

27.1   The court may give directions requiring the parties to use their best endeavours to agree a bundle or bundles of documents for use at any hearing.

27.2   All documents contained in bundles which have been agreed for use at a hearing shall be admissible at that hearing as evidence of their contents, unless –

(1)   the court orders otherwise; or
(2)   a party gives written notice of objection to the admissibility of particular documents.

Penalty

28.1(1)   Where a party alleges that a statement of truth or a disclosure statement is false the party shall refer that allegation to the court dealing with the claim in which the statement of truth or disclosure statement has been made.

(2)   the court may –

(a)   exercise any of its powers under the rules;
(b)   initiate steps to consider if there is a contempt of court and, where there is, to punish it;

---

18 Rule 2.3(1); definition of judge.
19 See rule 32.6(2)(a).

(The practice direction to RSC Order 52 (Schedule 1) and CCR Order 29 (Schedule 2) makes provision where committal to prison is a possibility if contempt is proved)

(c) direct the party making the allegation to refer the matter to the Attorney General with a request to him to consider whether he wishes to bring proceedings for contempt of court.

28.2(1) An application to the Attorney General should be made to his chambers at 9 Buckingham Gate London SW1E 6JP in writing. The Attorney General will initially require a copy of the order recording the direction of the judge referring the matter to him and information which –

(a) identifies the statement said to be false; and
(b) explains –

  (i) why it is false, and
  (ii) why the maker knew it to be false at the time he made it; and

(c) explains why contempt proceedings would be appropriate in the light of the overriding objective in Part 1 of the Civil Procedure Rules.

(2) The practice of the Attorney General is to prefer an application that comes from the court, and so has received preliminary consideration by a judge, to one made direct to him by a party to the claim in which the alleged contempt occurred without prior consideration by the court. An application to the Attorney General is not a way of appealing against, or reviewing, the decision of the judge.

28.3 Where a party makes an application to the court for permission for that party to commence proceedings for contempt of court, it must be supported by written evidence containing the information specified in paragraph 28.2(1) and the result of the application to the Attorney General made by the applicant.

28.4 The rules do not change the law of contempt or introduce new categories of contempt. A person applying to commence such proceedings should consider whether the incident complained of does amount to contempt of court and whether such proceedings would further the overriding objective in Part 1 of the Civil Procedure Rules.

Video conferencing

29.1 Guidance on the use of video conferencing in the civil courts is set out at Annex 3 to this practice direction.

A list of the sites which are available for video conferencing can be found on Her Majesty's Courts Service website at **www.hmcourts-service.gov.uk**.

ANNEX 1

Certificate to be used where a deponent to an affidavit is unable to read or sign it

Sworn at [. . .] this [. . .] day of [. . .]. Before me, I having first read over the contents of this affidavit to the deponent [*if there are exhibits, add* 'and explained the nature and effect of the exhibits referred to in it'] who appeared to understand it and approved its content as accurate, and made his mark on the affidavit in my presence.

Or; (after, *Before me*) the witness to the mark of the deponent having been first sworn that he had read over etc. (*as above*) and that he saw him make his mark on the affidavit. (*Witness must sign*).

Certificate to be used where a deponent to an affirmation is unable to read or sign it

Affirmed at [. . .] this [. . .] day of [. . .]. Before me, I having first read over the contents of this affirmation to the deponent [*if there are exhibits, add* 'and explained the nature and effect of the exhibits referred to in it'] who appeared to understand it and approved its content as accurate, and made his mark on the affirmation in my presence.

Or, (after, *Before me*) the witness to the mark of the deponent having been first sworn that he had read over etc. (*as above*) and that he saw him make his mark on the affirmation. (*Witness must sign*).

ANNEX 2

Omitted

ANNEX 3

[Video conferencing guidance]

APPENDIX 3

Extracts from the Solicitors' Code of Conduct 2007

RULE 10 – RELATIONS WITH THIRD PARTIES

INTRODUCTION

Rule 10 draws together a variety of obligations linked by the need to deal with third parties in a proper manner. The rule as it applies to your overseas practice is modified by 15.10.

RULE 10 – RELATIONS WITH THIRD PARTIES

10.01   Not taking unfair advantage

You must not use your position to take unfair advantage of anyone either for your own benefit or for another person's benefit.

10.02   Agreeing costs with another party

When negotiating the payment of your client's costs by another firm's client or a third party, you must give sufficient time and information for the amount of your costs to be agreed or assessed.

10.03   Administering oaths

You can administer oaths or affirmations or take declarations if you are a solicitor or an REL. You must not do so where you or your firm is acting for any party in the matter.

10.04   Contacting other party to a matter

You must not communicate with any other party who to your knowledge has retained a lawyer or licensed conveyancer to act in a matter, except:

(a)   to request the name and address of the other party's lawyer or licensed conveyancer;
(b)   where it would be reasonable to conclude that the other party's lawyer or licensed conveyancer has refused or failed for no adequate reason either to pass on messages to their client or to reply to correspondence, and has been warned of your intention to contact their client direct;
(c)   with that lawyer or licensed conveyancer's consent; or
(d)   in exceptional circumstances.

10.05 Undertakings

(1) You must fulfil an undertaking which is given in circumstances where:

    (a) you give the undertaking in the course of practice;

    (b) you are a principal in a firm, and any person within the firm gives the undertaking in the course of practice;

    (c) you give the undertaking outside the course of practice, but as a solicitor; or

    (d) you are an REL based at an office in England and Wales, and you give the undertaking within the UK, as a lawyer of an Establishment Directive state, but outside your practice as an REL.

(2) You must fulfil an undertaking within a reasonable time.

(3) If you give an undertaking which is dependent upon the happening of a future event, you must notify the recipient immediately if it becomes clear that the event will not occur.

(4) When you give an undertaking to pay another's costs, the undertaking will be discharged if the matter does not proceed unless there is an express agreement that the costs are payable in any event.

10.06 Dealing with more than one prospective buyer in a conveyancing transaction

(1) Each time a seller of land, other than in a sale by auction or tender, either:

    (a) instructs you to deal with more than one prospective buyer; or

    (b) to your knowledge:

        (i) deals directly with another prospective buyer (or their conveyancer); or

        (ii) instructs another conveyancer to deal with another prospective buyer;

    you must, with the client's consent, immediately inform the conveyancer of each prospective buyer, or the prospective buyer if acting in person.

(2) If the seller refuses to agree to such disclosure, you must immediately stop acting in the matter.

(3) You must not act for both the seller and any of the prospective buyers.

(4) You must not act for more than one of the prospective buyers.

10.07 Fees of lawyers of other jurisdictions

(1) If in the course of practice you instruct a lawyer of another jurisdiction you must, as a matter of professional conduct, pay the lawyer's proper fees unless the lawyer is practising as a solicitor or barrister of England and Wales; or

    (a) you have expressly disclaimed that responsibility at the outset, or at a later date you have expressly disclaimed responsibility for any fees incurred after that date;

    (b) the lawyer is an REL or is registered with the Bar of England and Wales under the Establishment Directive; or

    (c) the lawyer is an RFL based in England and Wales and practising in a firm.

(2) If in the course of practice you instruct a business carrying on the practice of a lawyer of another jurisdiction you must, as a matter of professional conduct, pay the proper fees for the work that lawyer does, unless:

(a) you have expressly disclaimed that responsibility at the outset, or at a later date you have expressly disclaimed responsibility for any fees incurred after that date; or

(b) the business is a firm.

GUIDANCE TO RULE 10 – RELATIONS WITH THIRD PARTIES
Not taking unfair advantage – 10.01

1. Subrule 10.01 does not only apply to your actions which arise out of acting for a client. For example, if you are personally involved in a road accident and use your position as a solicitor unfairly to harass or intimidate the other motorist, you would breach 10.01. If, on the other hand, you intimidated the other motorist without making reference to your position as a solicitor, you would not breach 10.01. However, you should have regard to 1.06 (Public confidence) in respect of your general behaviour outside practice.

2. Particular care should be taken when you are dealing with a person who does not have legal representation. You need to find a balance between fulfilling your obligations to your client and not taking unfair advantage of another person. To an extent, therefore, 10.01 limits your duty to act in the best interests of your client. For example, your duty may be limited where an unrepresented opponent provides badly drawn documentation. In the circumstances you should suggest the opponent finds legal representation. If the opponent does not do so, you need to ensure that a balance is maintained between doing your best for the client and not taking unfair advantage of the opponent's lack of legal knowledge and drafting skills.

3. You should take care, when dealing with an unrepresented third party, that any help given does not inadvertently create a contractual relationship with that party. For further information see Cordery on Solicitors. See also note 3 of the guidance to rule 2 (Client relations). You should also be careful, when dealing with unqualified persons, that you are not involved in possible breaches of the Solicitors Act 1974, in terms of the prohibitions relating to reserved work. For further details see 20.02 (Reserved work) and the guidance to that rule.

4. There may be situations where it is inappropriate for you to use the title 'solicitor' in advancing your personal interests. You should consider public confidence in the profession – see 1.06 (Public confidence).

5. It would be unfair to demand anything that is not recoverable through the proper legal process. This would include a letter of claim and any other communication with another party to the action. For instance, where you are instructed to collect a simple debt, you should not demand from the debtor the cost of the letter of claim, since it cannot be said at that stage that such a cost is legally recoverable.

6. The following are some further examples of how you should act in order to ensure you comply with 10.01 and core duty 1.02 (Integrity):

(a) If a person sends you documents or money subject to an express condition, you should return the documents or money if you are unwilling or unable to comply with the condition.

(b) If you are sent documents or money on condition that they are held to the sender's order, you should return the documents or money to the sender on demand.

(c) If you ask anyone to supply copies of documents, you should expect to pay a proper charge for them.

Agreeing costs with another party – 10.02

7. Subrule 10.02 applies to all types of work. Its application is clear in litigation matters but will also commonly be relevant to other matters, such as where a landlord's solicitor's costs for dealing with a request for a licence to assign a lease are to be paid by the tenant.
8. You should expect to supply information about the basis of charging (for example an hourly rate or an estimate of the total amount) together with an indication of the nature of the elements of the work done or to be done.

Administering oaths – 10.03

9. You may administer oaths if you are:

    (a) a solicitor with a current practising certificate – see section 81(1) of the Solicitors Act 1974; or
    (b) an REL, under the Establishment Directive.

10. When administering oaths or affirmations or taking declarations, you must ensure the giver:

    (a) is present;
    (b) signs the document in your presence or, if the document is already signed, confirms that the signature is their own and that any attachments are correct; and
    (c) appears to understand what they are doing and that the purpose is to confirm that the contents of the document and any attachments are true.

11. You are not responsible for the contents of the document, but if you have a good reason to believe that the contents may be false, you should not proceed.
12. Section 81(2) of the Solicitors Act 1974 and other related legislation prohibits you administering an oath where you are or your firm is acting for any party in the matter. The effect of this section would, for example, prevent a solicitor administering an oath for the solicitor's own spouse where it arises out of a personal matter.
13. When the document has already been signed, it is sufficient for you to accept the giver's word that it is their signature, unless there is clear evidence to the contrary.

Contacting other party to a matter – 10.04

14. Subrule 10.04 requires that you do not contact another party to a matter, subject to exceptions, if that party is represented by a lawyer or a licensed conveyancer. It is not intended to prevent you from dealing with other types of representative, if appropriate. If you are asked to deal with such a representative you should ensure that you are not involved in possible breaches of the Solicitors Act 1974 (see note 3 above) and that to do so is in your client's best interest. For example, where the other party is disabled and vulnerable you may well think it appropriate to deal with a representative from a specialist advice organisation or a disability charity. To do so, may mean that the matter is dealt with more efficiently

and that you derive some protection from an allegation that you are acting in breach of 10.01 (Not taking unfair advantage). On the other hand, you would be unlikely to want to deal with a person purporting to represent another party who clearly does not have the relevant knowledge or skill.

15. Where an enquiry agent has been instructed, the agent may serve documents where the other party's lawyer or licensed conveyancer has refused to accept service, but should not take a statement or in any other way communicate with the other party.

16. Care should be taken if you are instructed in a dual capacity. For example, if you are additionally instructed as an estate agent for the seller, you may contact the buyer, but solely about estate agency matters.

17. The other party's lawyer or licensed conveyancer may consent explicitly to your contacting their client, or this may be implied, such as when a protocol is being followed or where it has been agreed that certain documents be sent to all parties.

18. It is not always easy to establish why another lawyer or licensed conveyancer involved in a matter is not responding to correspondence. If you reasonably consider that the other lawyer or licensed conveyancer may be refusing or failing to take instructions from their client, or may be refusing or failing to communicate your requests or correspondence to their client, then a warning should give them the opportunity to object if an incorrect conclusion has been drawn. If there is no valid objection, then you should be able to advance the matter by directly contacting the other client.

19. It is recommended that any communications permitted by 10.04 between you and another lawyer or licensed conveyancer's client be in writing.

20. Subrule 10.04 extends to your contact with the in-house lawyers or licensed conveyancers of organisations. For example, if you are acting for a client in a matter concerning a local authority, and you have express or implied notice that the authority's solicitor has been instructed to act in the matter, you must not discuss that matter directly with the appropriate committee chair, any individual councillor or any political group on the authority. You can be involved in political lobbying of individual councillors or a political group on the local authority on behalf of a client, even if you know that the authority's solicitor has been instructed to deal with the legal issues.

21. Where the other party is an organisation, you will not breach 10.04 by contacting employees who are not responsible for the giving of instructions because they are not regarded as the client for the purpose of 10.04. However, you should have regard to any contractual obligations employees may have to their employer. It may be appropriate to notify the employer or its lawyer or licensed conveyancer of your intention to contact the employee. This would enable the employee to be advised as to the appropriate response.

22. Lawyers or licensed conveyancers employed by organisations such as the Solicitors Regulation Authority or the Land Registry may properly deal with represented clients when carrying out a statutory function.

23. There may be other situations where it becomes necessary to communicate directly with a represented client. Subrule 10.04(d) refers to these as 'exceptional circumstances'. Such circumstances would include where you are contacted by the client of another lawyer or licensed conveyancer. Care should be taken to avoid taking unfair advantage of this situation but it is acceptable for you to deal with

that client's request, if appropriate, and explain that in future they should contact you through their own lawyer or licensed conveyancer.

Undertakings – 10.05

24. An undertaking is any statement, made by you or your firm, that you or your firm will do something or cause something to be done, or refrain from doing something, given to someone who reasonably relies upon it (see rule 24 (Interpretation)). It can be given orally or in writing and need not include the word 'undertake'. However, it is recommended that oral undertakings be confirmed or recorded in writing for evidential purposes.
25. An agreement to pay a trading debt such as your electricity bill is not normally an undertaking. Once an undertaking is given and the recipient has relied upon it, it can only be withdrawn by agreement.
26. You are not obliged to give or accept undertakings.
27. In 10.05(1)(b) 'person within the firm' includes anyone held out by the firm as representing the firm, as well as locums, agents, consultants and other employees.
28. It is important that there be a time frame within which an undertaking should be fulfilled. In the event that no specific time is referred to when the undertaking is given, fulfilment 'within a reasonable time' will be expected. What amounts to a 'reasonable time' will depend on the circumstances but the onus is on the giver to ensure that the recipient is kept informed of the likely timescale and any delays to it.
29. Failure to fulfil an undertaking may result in disciplinary action.
30. If an undertaking requires the recipient to take certain steps and the recipient fails to do so, the giver may ask the Solicitors Regulation Authority to give notice to the recipient that unless these steps are taken within a period of time it will not then consider a complaint.
31. All undertakings given by solicitors and RELs can be enforced by the court. (See court rules for the appropriate procedure to be followed.) The Solicitors Regulation Authority will not investigate complaints of breaches of undertakings given to the court unless the court makes a complaint to the Authority.
32. Where you undertake to pay the costs of another party or a professional agent's costs, unless a specific amount is agreed, the term 'costs' will mean 'proper costs'. This allows you to request an assessment of the costs by the court.
33. If a complaint is made to the Solicitors Regulation Authority concerning an alleged breach of an undertaking and it is found that the undertaking was pro-cured by fraud, deceit or, in certain circumstances, innocent misrepresentation, the Authority is unlikely to take any action in respect of the alleged breach.
34. The Solicitors Regulation Authority will generally interpret an ambiguous undertaking in favour of the recipient.
35. If you give an undertaking 'on behalf' of a client it will usually fall within the def-inition of an undertaking (see rule 24 (Interpretation)) and its performance would, therefore, be your responsibility. If this is not what you intend, you should ensure that liability is disclaimed or it is made clear that you are simply informing the other party about your client's intentions.
36. A promise to give an undertaking is normally treated as an undertaking and will be binding.

37. Where an undertaking has been breached, the aggrieved party may seek compensation. Your firm's insurance as required by the Solicitors' Indemnity Insurance Rules should cover valid claims. If you are in in-house practice, you should consider whether your employer has appropriate insurance. You will remain personally liable in conduct, and may also be financially liable, regardless of whether you have adequate insurance.

38. An undertaking is binding even if it is to do something outside your control. For example, if you undertake to make a payment out of the proceeds of sale of an asset, unless you clearly state to the contrary, you will be expected to make the payment even if the fund (gross or net) is insufficient.

39. If you have received written instructions from your client that are expressed as irrevocable, they are nonetheless revocable, until you have acted on them in such a way as to change your personal position.

40. Certain areas of work, particularly conveyancing, involve the use of standard undertakings. Care should be taken when using standard undertakings to ensure that they suit the specific circumstances. For further details, please refer to a specialist publication.

41. Guidance on undertakings can be obtained from the Professional Ethics Guidance Team.

Seller's solicitor dealing with more than one prospective buyer – 10.06

42. When you are asked to 'deal' with more than one prospective buyer you must comply with 10.06. 'Deal' means any communication you have with any of the relevant parties intended to progress the matter – for example, the sending of a draft contract or a plan of the property. Communicating information of an estate agency nature, such as sending out particulars of sale or showing prospective buyers around a property, would not amount to 'dealing' for the purposes of 10.06. If you provide information for an estate agent or Home Information Pack provider only as part of the creation of a Home Information Pack, you will not have 'dealt' with prospective buyers for the purpose of 10.06. However, providing additional information to buyers, either direct or through the estate agent or Home Information Pack provider, will normally amount to 'dealing'.

43. This requirement is sometimes known as the 'contract races' rule. This has created the impression that when a transaction is proceeding under such terms, whichever party presents their contract ready for exchanging first is the 'winner'. In fact, the terms of the arrangement are entirely at the discretion of the parties and speed may or may not be a factor. You should be careful to agree the terms of the arrangement.

44. If you are required to inform another conveyancer of your intention to proceed with two or more prospective buyers, you should do so immediately by the most suitable means. If the information is given in person or on the telephone, there is no requirement that the details be confirmed in writing but this is advisable.

45. Special care should be taken when dealing with unqualified conveyancers or unrepresented buyers. See notes 2 and 3 above.

Fees of lawyers of other jurisdictions – 10.07

46. Subrule 10.07 does not apply when you merely introduce or refer a client to a lawyer of another jurisdiction. However, when you instruct such a lawyer, you will

be accepting the liability to pay the lawyer's proper fees unless one of the exceptions in 10.07 applies. For example, if you do not hold money on account and your client is declared bankrupt, you may have to pay the lawyer's proper fee out of your own funds.

47. The fees of a lawyer of another jurisdiction may be regulated by a scale approved by the relevant bar association or law society. You can contact the International Unit of the Law Society for advice.

48. In the event that a dispute arises concerning the payment of the fees of a lawyer of a CCBE state, 16.07 and note 12 of the guidance to rule 16 (European cross-border practice) should be consulted and the necessary action taken before starting any proceedings.

An opinion of the Council of the Notaries Society regarding the signing of documents not in the presence of a notary

CERTIFYING UNATTESTED SIGNATURES

A Notary may properly witness a signature only if it is signed in his presence. Similarly he may authenticate the due execution of a document only if it is executed in his physical presence. Occasionally a notary may be asked to verify that a signature is genuine, even though he was not present when the signing took place.

If he accepts such instructions then he must adhere to the following minimum standards:

1. On a prior occasion the Notary must have first seen the signatory affix his signature to a form which is retained in the protocol file of the Notary.
2. The Notary should check the continued existence of the signatory regularly.
3. If the signatory is a representative of an organisation or company his continued authority should be checked regularly.
4. The Notary should at the time of verifying the signature take such steps as are reasonable to ensure that the signatory has in fact signed the particular document.
5. The certificate must be unequivocal and must not state or imply that the signature has been affixed in the presence of the Notary or that the document is has been properly executed.

Notaries must be aware of the risks of issuing such certificates and should, if in any doubt at all, decline to act.

It is the opinion of the Council of the Notaries Society that there can be no professional objection to a Notary certifying the fact that the signature on a document is that of a signatory known to him provided that the Notary follows the foregoing procedure.

Dated this 23rd day of April 2002
Christopher J Vaughan
President
By authority of the Council

Index

Proxy signatures 13
Public notaries *see* Notaries

Recitals
  deeds 148
Record keeping
  notaries 298–9
Registered land
  deeds of transfer 17, 19–20, 25, 31, 32–3, 41–4, 71–2, 80
  power of attorney and 94–5
  statutory declarations and 216
Religion
  oaths and 108, 111–3, 114, 250
Royal Charter corporations *see* Corporations
Rubber stamp signature 134

Schedules
  contracts 12
  deeds 18, 31, 44, 53–4, 62–3, 70, 80, 149
  power of attorney 95–6
Scilly Isles 206
Scotland
  execution of deeds by Scottish companies 186
Seals
  deeds and
    companies 39–41, 61–2, 184, 185, 186, 189–91
    corporations 167, 170–3, 178–80
    local authorities 68–70, 203, 204
  notaries 284
  power of attorney and companies 94
Signature
  affidavits 248–9
  companies 301–3
  contracts 123–4
    land 131–3
  effect of 140
  electronic *see* Electronic signatures
  invalid 130–2
  meanings 124, 125
    court decisions 125–33
  power of attorney 89–90, 92–5, 97
  rubber stamp 134
  statements of truth 229–32
  statutory declarations 218
  valid 125–30
Signature block
  affidavits 108, 115, 248
  contracts 10–1, 12, 123

deeds
  executed by companies 38–44, 45
  executed by corporations 29–31, 32
  executed by foreign companies 60–2, 63
  executed by individuals 17, 18–24, 149–51
  executed by limited liability partnerships 51–3, 54
  executed by local authorities 68–70, 71
  executed by partnerships 78–80, 81
  statements of truth 99–102, 105
  statutory declarations 83
Solicitors 242
  as Commissioners for Oaths 274, 276
  remuneration agreement 136
  statements of truth and 239–40
Statements of case 232, 241–2, 325
Statements of truth 227
  amendments 103
  attachments/exhibits 103
  checklist 99
  consequences if document not verified by 232
  definition 227
  disclosure statements 237–8, 240
  expert witnesses 236–7
  false statement made in documents verified by 323–4
  fees charged 103
  legal representatives and 239–40
  meaning of terms 241–2
  online claims 238–9
  persons unable to read or sign documents 103–4, 232–3
  points to note for legal representatives 104–6
  professional persons present 103
  signature 229–32
  signature block 99–102, 105
  variations to procedure 103–4
  when must be used 228–9
  witness statements 232, 233–5, 240–1
Statutory declarations 86–8, 214
  affirmation/oath 83–4
  amendments 86
  attachments/exhibits 85
  checklist 82